UNDERSTANDING BUSINESS: MARKETS

This book – *Understanding Business: Markets* – is one of a series of four readers which constitute the main teaching texts of the Open University course *Understanding Business Behaviour* (B200). The other titles are: *Understanding Business: Environments* edited by Michael Lucas; *Understanding Business: Processes* edited by David Barnes; and *Understanding Business: Organisations* edited by Graeme Salaman.

This course is one of three core courses which are compulsory elements in the Open University's BA in Business Studies. In addition to the compulsory courses, students who are working toward this degree also study courses which include topics such as Economics, Organisational Change, Design and Innovation and Quantitative Methods.

The approach of *Understanding Business Behaviour* (B200) as an introductory course in Business Studies is innovative. The traditional approach employed by courses in this area is to offer introductions to the key social science disciplines: sociology, economics, law, etc. This course uses another approach: it focuses not on disciplines but on key elements of the business world: environments, markets, processes and organisations. This still allows for the discussion of relevant social science theory and research but organises this material not by the logic of academic structures and disciplines but by the logic of business applications and relevance.

As with all Open University courses, students are not only supplied with teaching texts; they also receive comprehensive guidance on how to study and work through these texts. In the case of B200, this guidance is contained in four Study Guides which are supplied to students separately. These guides explain the choice of readings, identify key points and guide the students' work and understanding. A core feature of the guides is an explicit focus on the identification, development, deployment and testing of a series of business graduate skills. These include study skills, cognitive skills of analysis and assessment, IT, and numeracy.

Each student is allocated a local tutor and is encouraged to participate in a strategically integrated set of tutorials which are held throughout the course.

Details of this and other Open University courses and qualifications may be obtained from the Student Registration and Enquiry Service, PO Box 197, Walton Hall, Milton Keynes, MK7 6BJ, United Kingdom; tel: +44 (0) 870 333 4340; e-mail: general-enquiries@open.ac.uk.

Alternatively, you may visit the Open University website at http://www.open.ac.uk where you can learn about the wide range of courses and packs offered at all levels by The Open University.

To purchase a selection of Open University course materials, contact Open University Worldwide, Michael Young Building, Walton Hall, Milton Keynes, MK7 6AA, United Kingdom: tel.+44 (0) 1908 858785; fax: +44 (0) 1908 858787; e-mail: ouwenq@open.ac.uk; website: http://www.ouw.co.uk.

SERIES INTRODUCTION

It is hardly necessary to justify the study of business, or to over-emphasise the importance of a knowledge and understanding of business organisations and their functions, or of the environments of business. The world of business is the world in which we live and work, every aspect of which may well be on the verge of fundamental change as a result of the Internet and converging communications technologies. It affects us as consumers, workers, voters, citizens, whether of nations, unions of nations or of the world. We have to understand it. We have to understand how organisations work and their core processes. This involves an understanding of their impact on employees and consumers; how markets work (and don't work); the role and nature of business environments and how these impact on business organisations (or vice versa).

This book is one in a series of four readers which bring together classic and seminal materials, many of them summaries and reviews, which are designed to achieve the teaching objectives of the Open University course *Understanding Business Behaviour* (B200) – a core course in the Open University's BA in Business Studies. The volumes are organised in an innovative way around four key areas of the world of business: environments, markets, processes and organisations.

The volumes have been designed to supply a selection of key introductory materials in each of these areas of business applications and, with the use of appropriate study guidance, to allow the identification, development, deployment and practice of a range of skills required from Business Studies courses in general. Therefore, while they constitute the core teaching resources of this Open University course, they would also make admirable selections for any course concerned with these areas. They are not intended to be cutting edge or fashionable. They are designed as a resource for anyone seeking an understanding of the nature and development of the world of business.

Each of these volumes has been edited by an individual member of the course team. But in a very real sense they are collective products of the course team as a whole. That is why all the members of the course team deserve recognition and acknowledgement for their contribution to the course and to these collections. The course team consisted of:

David Barnes, Hannah Brunt, Rob Clifton, Mike Conboy, Martin Dowling, Gill Gowans, Carol Howells, Jacky Holloway, Bob Kelly, Mike Lucas, Alison Macmillan, Chris Marshall, Jane Matthews, Konrad Mau, Terry Morris, John O'Dwyer, John Olney, Anthea Rogers, Judy Rumbelow, Graeme Salaman, Dawn Storer, Jane Sturges, Vivek Suneja, Tricia Tierney, Richard Whipp.

Two other members of the team deserve special mention for their enormous contribution to the course as a whole and to the work of managing the course team and the processes involved in assembling and organising these collections: Chris Bollom and Georgina Marsh. To them, many thanks.

UNDERSTANDING BUSINESS: MARKETS

A multidimensional approach to
the market economy

**Edited by
VIVEK SUNEJA
at The Open University**

Routledge
Taylor & Francis Group

LONDON AND NEW YORK

In association with

The Open University

First published 2000
by Routledge
2 Park Square, Milton Park, Abingdon OX14 4RN

Simultaneously published in the USA and Canada
by Routledge
270 Madison Ave, New York, NY 10016

Revised special edition printed 2006

Routledge is an imprint of the Taylor & Francis Group

Typeset in Plantin and Rockwell by
Keystroke, High Street, Tettenhall, Wolverhampton
Printed and bound in Great Britain by
Bell & Bain Ltd, Glasgow

British Library Cataloguing in Publication Data
A catalogue record for this book is available from the British Library

Library of Congress Cataloging in Publication Data
Understanding business: markets : a multidimensional approach to the market economy /
    edited by Vivek Suneja.
    p. cm.
    "One of a series of four readers which constitute the main teaching texts of the Open
    University course Understanding business behaviour (B200)"—Half t.p.
    Includes bibliographical references and index.
    1. Capitalism. 2. Markets. I. Title: Markets : a multidimensional approach to the
    market economy. II. Suneja, Vivek, 1963–
    HB501 .U564 2000
    380.1—dc21   00–035381

ISBN10: 0–415–40501–7 (pbk)
ISBN13: 978–0–415–40501–0

CONTENTS

FIGURES

TABLES

ACKNOWLEDGEMENTS

The authors and publishers would like to thank the following for granting permission to reproduce material in this work:

Jonathan Cape Ltd for excerpts from Will Hutton, *The State We're In*. Published by Jonathan Cape, 1995.

Elsevier Science for excerpts from Singh *et al.*, *Openness and Market Friendly Approach, in World Development*, 1994, Vol. 22, No. 12.

Granta Books, for excerpts from J. Gray, *False Dawn: The Delusions of Global Capitalism* (1998).

HarperCollins Publishers Inc, for excerpts from M.K. Bennett, *The World's Food*. Copyright © 1954 by Harper & Brothers, renewed © 1982 by Helen B. Lucine, Stephen W. Bennett and John F. Bennett.

Macmillan Press Ltd, for an excerpt from *Population Growth and Land Use*. © Colin Clark 1967, and for excerpts from *International Economics*, 3rd edition. Copyright © Bo Södersten 1970, Bo Södersten and Geoffrey Reed 1994.

Office for National Statistics, for excerpts from *United Kingdom National Accounts*, 1992; *Social Trends 22*, 1992. Office for National Statistics © Crown copyright; *Family Expenditure Survey, 1992*; *Great Britain Annual Abstract of Statistics, 1992*. Office for National Statistics © Crown copyright; *Business Monitor PA 1002: Report on the Census Production 1990*, Summary Volume.

The Orion Publishing Group Ltd, for excerpts from Eric Hobsbawm, *The Age of Revolution 1789-1848*, published by Weidenfeld and Nicholson and excerpts from Eric Hobsbawm, *The Age of Empire: 1875-1914*. In the US to Random House Inc for excerpts from Eric Hobsbawm, *The Age of Empire: 1875-1914*. Copyright © 1987 by E. J. Hobsbawm.

Oxford University Press, for excerpts from Richard G. Lipsey and K. Alec Chrystal, *Principles of Economics*, 9th edition (1999). © 1999 Richard G. Lipsey and K. Alec Chrystal.

Pearson Education Ltd, for excerpt from Brian Atkinson and Robin Miller, Business Economics © Addison Wesley Longman Ltd, 1998

University of California Press for an excerpt from Andre Gunder Frank, *ReOrient: Global Economy in the Asian Age* (1998).

Every effort has been made to contact copyright holders for their permission to reprint material in this book. The publishers would be grateful to hear from any copyright holder who is not here acknowledged and will undertake to rectify any errors or omissions in future editions of this book.

INTRODUCTION

Understanding Business: Markets is designed to provide the undergraduate and postgraduate students of business and economics, including those studying for the MBA, lucid insight into how market economies work (and don't work). In contrast to the limited neoclassical economics perspective offered by most titles on the subject, this book explores the nature of market economies through a distinctive, multidimensional approach. It deals comprehensively with various issues of the market economy through historical, socio-economic as well as global perspectives.

THE *SOCIAL* NATURE OF MARKETS AND MARKET ECONOMIES

Market economies are socially constructed institutions that facilitate the production, exchange and consumption of goods and services. They are of course just one of the several ways in which economic activity can be organised, such as through feudalism, slavery, caste systems and centrally planned economies. Like other economic institutions, markets are embedded in a variety of social institutions including property and power relations, legal systems and cultural and normative systems.

All the readings included in this book demonstrate sensitivity to the social dimension of economic behaviour. Wheelock (chapter 3), for example, explores consumption as a social process, and emphasises the significance of socio-cultural influences, such as inter-personal comparison, status and advertising on the consumption behaviour of households. Similarly, in his analysis of the role and behaviour of organisations, Costello (chapter 5) stresses the importance of social and cultural norms in both shaping the multiple objectives that different organisations may seek to pursue, as well as the means that firms may employ to achieve these diverse objectives. Firms, for example, can very substantially differ in the incentives and cultures that they employ to motivate their employees, and these differences can in part be accounted for by the values and the vision of the firm's 'leader', and the wider industrial and national culture in which the organisation operates. In addition to social influences, political institutions also very significantly impact upon the nature and workings of markets. Hobsbawm (chapter 11) shows us how social, economic and political forces in the national and international spheres *interacted* to produce the conditions that ignited and then sustained the British industrial revolution.

ECONOMICS IS MORE THAN NEOCLASSICAL ANALYSIS

The social science discipline of economics has many traditions of thought including neoclassical, Marxist, Austrian, Keynesian and institutional traditions. Most introductory economics texts these days, however, almost exclusively present a neoclassical treatment of the subject. Our book differs very substantially in this respect, and adopts a multiple perspective approach to economic theory and analysis. Brown (chapter 6), for example, in her analysis of how markets work, explores competing economic theories on the nature of competition and power in markets. Hutton (chapter 12) in his study on the diversity of capitalism and Singh (chapter 14) in his analysis of the East Asian 'miracle', demonstrate an application of the insights offered by competing traditions in economics to an analysis of economic phenomena and events. Similarly, the historical analysis of Frank (chapter 1), Hobsbawm (chapter 2) and Bairoch (chapter 9) is informed by a keen awareness of the diversity of traditions in economic theory.

THE DIVERSITY OF MARKET ECONOMIES

Frequently, studies of market economies by economists trained in the Anglo-American tradition of economics, proceed as if there is one uniform and universal kind of market economy in the world, and markets everywhere and at all times work in a similar fashion. However, in reality, the way in which markets and market economies work in different parts of the world displays systematic and quite profound variation. The labour market, for example, operates in a very different fashion in the hire and fire culture of the USA compared to the unionised environment of continental Europe or the large-scale sector of the Japanese economy characterised by life-time employment practices. Similarly, the way in which capital markets work in different parts of the world displays considerable variation. These differences in the workings of markets are often a consequence of a variety of influences, such as historical forces and social, cultural and political factors. Hutton (chapter 12) draws our attention to the global diversity in market institutions and practices by highlighting some of the distinctive features of American, British, Rhineland and Japanese capitalisms. He also offers some views about the possible advantages and disadvantages of these alternative market systems. Gray (chapter 13) inquires whether the current pattern of globalisation of capital and product markets threatens to eliminate this diversity.

A HISTORICAL PERSPECTIVE

An important feature of this book is the use of a historical perspective. This serves several purposes: it contextualises the conceptual discussion, illustrates some of the important theoretical arguments and directs our attention to the vital role of historical developments as influences on current patterns of economic activity. It also gives us a sense of perspective and proportion. As an example, consider the fact that large parts of the world that we today call 'developing' and 'newly industrialising', such as the populous regions of India and China, were the world's most industrialised and economically developed regions during long periods of world history including the early modern age (see chapter 1 by Frank). Similarly, the story of the British industrial revolution (see chapter 2 by Hobsbawm) vividly illustrates how important 'globalisation' was in creating and nurturing the British industrial revolution.

Bairoch (chapter 9), in his historical account of protectionism in Europe and America, points out that practically all of today's major industrialised Western nations protected their infant industrial sectors from international competition during the initial phases of industrialisation. An appreciation of this historical fact raises interesting questions in the context of the current policy debate on globalisation: should, for example, today's newly industrialising nations be permitted to protect their economies against unbridled international competition so that they can promote indigenous industrialisation in their economies? Similarly, what useful lessons can we learn from the nature of 'globalisation' that characterised the age of the empire? (see chapter 11 by Hobsbawm). If we accept, for example, that World War I was caused in part by economic rivalry between emerging industrial economies, how can we prevent the recurrence of such tensions as new industrial economies now emerge to challenge the economic supremacy of the G7 nations?

THE SIGNIFICANCE OF THE GLOBAL

The increasing integration of the world economy in recent times has meant that the 'international' now has very direct and significant impact on the 'national' and the 'local'. This book reflects the profound significance of this development. However, we question whether the degree and the *nature* of globalisation that we are now witnessing is inevitable, and whether it is desirable. The increased integration of the world economy in the last two decades has not been a simple matter of responding to opportunities offered by new technological developments. It has also been due to liberalisation of product and capital markets undertaken as a consequence of multilateral trade negotiations, or as in the case of many developing nations, as part of IMF and World Bank programmes. The 'mainstream' view has been that trade and capital liberalisation benefits all trading nations and aids economic development and poverty reduction in developing countries (see, for example, the discussion in chapter 8 by Lipsey and Chrystal). This proposition is however debatable on both theoretical and empirical grounds as the chapter by Singh demonstrates (chapter 14). Singh argues that two of the most successful stories of industrialisation and struc-tural transformation in the post-war era, namely those of Japan and South Korea, are characterised by extensive regulation of both international trade and foreign investment, and by the protection and promotion of infant industries. Gray (chapter 13) argues that the unregulated operation of global markets is harmful not just for developing nations but can also injure the developed world in several ways. Their analysis raises important questions about how best to influence the nature and degree of globalisation so that it serves the twin social goals of economic effectiveness and fairness for all the world's citizens.

THE BENEFITS AND LIMITS OF MARKETS

Our discussion on the benefits and costs of the unfettered operation of international markets leads us to the wider question of the benefits and limits of markets. Some kinds of market failure have been documented by economists for a long time, such as those associated with externalities and public goods (see chapter 7 by Lipsey and Chrystal). The influence of monopoly power on social welfare is a more contentious affair as is discussed by Brown (chapter 6): monopolies may at times be good for the economy if they utilise the super-normal profits to finance risky innovation projects. Similarly, the relative effectiveness of markets and non-market mechanisms in promoting economic development in developing countries is a matter of considerable debate. Singh (chapter 14) takes issue with the 'free trade' and 'market friendly' policies advocated by the IMF and World Bank for developing countries, and demonstrates the very significant part played by the state in promoting structural transformation in Japan and South Korea. Hutton (chapter 12) shows us how developed nations have sought to cope with market imperfections in distinctly diverse ways, and have come to employ a variety of practices, institutions and regulations for this purpose.

STRUCTURE OF THE BOOK

The reader begins with a historical account of the global economy in the AD 1400–1800 period and the British industrial revolution (*Section 1: The Evolution of the Modern World Economy*). In *Section 2: Economic Agents*, we explore the role and behaviour of households and organisations in a market economy. *Section 3: How Markets Work* presents competing models of how markets function, and discusses the nature of competition and power in markets. *Section 4: Market Failure* explores the various sources and dimensions of market failure and the circumstances under which government intervention may remedy some of these failures. *Section 5: The Global Market* investigates issues relating to international trade and investment in both theoretical and historical contexts. Finally, *Section 6: Markets: Good Servants, Bad Masters?* explores the limitations of markets and the diverse ways in which different nations have sought to govern markets.

SOME FINAL REMARKS

As this book is intended for both the specialist and non-specialist reader, we have kept the mathematics to a bare minimum: all that is assumed of the reader in this respect is the ability to interpret elementary graphs and the knowledge of ratios and percentages. This reader does not cover a range of issues relating to the market economy that are conventionally referred to as "macroeconomic" issues. These are taken up in the first of the four readers that comprise this series: *Understanding Business: Environments* by Michael Lucas.

We hope that you shall enjoy reading this book. This book does not aim to provide you with all the answers. Indeed we take the position that nobody has all the answers. The chief purpose of this book is to provoke you to think and to question. Hopefully, you will come up with some solutions of your own, and raise some new questions as well. *Bon Voyage!*

SECTION 1: THE EVOLUTION OF THE MODERN WORLD ECONOMY

INTRODUCTION

This section presents a brief historical account of some important aspects of the evolution of the global economy in the early modern age.

Chapter 1, *The global economy, AD 1400–1800* by Frank outlines some of the key features of the global economy in the early modern period. He demonstrates that prior to the events surrounding the British industrial revolution in the 1780s, Asia was the world's leading industrial centre, with India and China being the world's premier industrial nations. Asia was preponderant in the world economy not only in population and production, but also in productivity, competitiveness and international trade. The cotton weavers of Gujarat in western India alone exported three million pieces of cotton manufactures annually during the late seventeenth century. Frank challenges the 'eurocentric' myth that Asians were inferior to Europeans in technology and in their economic and financial institutions. European advances in science did not have any significant impact on Western technology before the 1870s – almost a century after the British industrial revolution. Frank also argues that the world economy was quite considerably 'global' throughout the 1400–1800 period, with different parts of the world linked to each other through the flow of goods, technology, ideas and people.

Chapter 2, *The British industrial revolution* by Hobsbawm is a fascinating account of the industrial revolution in Britain. Hobsbawm explores the economic, social and political forces that shaped the industrial revolution, and emphasises the vital role of international developments in bringing about Britain's rapid industrialisation. Britain began its emergence as a Newly Industrialising Economy through protectionism and other stimulation of its domestic cotton textile industry. The supply of raw cotton on highly favourable terms from settlements in the Caribbean and southern United States, and the captive colonial markets in India and elsewhere, played their part. The 'political revolution' that had taken place in Britain almost a century earlier, the sympathy and the willingness of the state to support private profit making activity and the Enclosure Acts that helped to raise agricultural productivity while providing an industrial workforce of the dispossessed, critical factors as well. Subsequently, the emergence of the railways, a by-product of the mines, played a big part in the creation of a capital goods industry. As industrialisation proceeded, the class of industrialists prospered, but the fate of the working classes initially grew worse. It was not until considerably later, after much protest and revolt, that the workers were able to have a share in the prosperity that industrialisation and growth brought. The industrialisation of Britain was, of course, to have a great impact on the economies of the British colonies, and on the rest of the world.

1

THE GLOBAL ECONOMY, AD 1400–1800: COMPARISONS AND RELATIONS*

Andre Gunder Frank

Although it is difficult to "measure" the economic output of early modern Asia . . . every scrap of information that comes to light confirms a far greater scale of enterprise and profit in the East than in the West. Thus Japan, in the second half of the sixteenth century, was the world's leading exporter of silver and copper, her 55,000 miners surpassing the output of Peru for the former and of Sweden for the latter. Though Western sources tend to stress the role of eight or so Dutch ships which docked in Japan each year, in fact the eighty or so junks from China were far more important. It was the same in south-east Asia: the Europeans . . . [and] their ships were outnumbered ten-to-one by Chinese vessels; and the Europeans' cargoes consisted in the main, not of Western wares but of Chinese porcelain and silk.

The outputs of both commodities was stunning. In Nanking alone, the ceramic factories produced a million pieces of fine glazed pottery every year, much of it specifically designed for export – those for Europe bore dynastic motifs, while those for Islamic countries displayed tasteful abstract patterns. . . . In India, the city of Kasimbazar in Bengal produced, just by itself, over 2 million pounds of raw silk annually during the 1680s, while cotton weavers of Gujarat in the west turned out almost 3 million pieces a year for export alone. By way of comparison, the annual export of silk from Messina . . . Europe's foremost silk producer . . . was a mere 250,000 pounds . . . while the largest textile enterprise in Europe, the Leiden "new drapery," produced less than 100,000 pieces of cloth per year. Asia, not Europe, was the centre of world industry throughout early modern times. It was likewise the home of the greatest states. The most powerful monarchs of their day were not Louis XIV or Peter the Great, but the Manchu emperor K'ang-hsi (1662–1772) and the "Great Moghul" Aurangzeb (1658–1707).

(*The Times Illustrated History of the World* [1995: 206])

QUANTITIES: POPULATION, PRODUCTION, PRODUCTIVITY, INCOME, AND TRADE

The so-called European hegemony in the modern world system was very late in developing and was quite incomplete and never unipolar. In reality, during the period 1400–1800, sometimes regarded as one of "European expansion" and "primitive accumulation" leading to full capitalism, the world economy was still very predominantly under Asian influences. The Chinese Ming/Qing, Turkish Ottoman, Indian Mughal, and Persian Safavid empires were economically and politically very powerful and only waned vis-à-vis the Europeans toward the end of this period and thereafter. Therefore, if anything, the modern world system was under Asian hegemony, not European. Likewise, much of the real dynamism of the world economy lay in Asia throughout this period, not in Europe. Asians were preponderant in the world economy and system not only in population and production, but also in productivity, competitiveness, trade, in a word, capital formation until 1750 or 1800. Moreover, contrary to latter-day European mythology, Asians had the technology and developed the economic and financial institutions to match. Thus, the "locus" of accumulation and power in the modern world system did not really change much during those centuries. China, Japan, and India in particular ranked first overall, with Southeast Asia and West Asia not far behind. The deficitary Europe was clearly of less significance than Asia in the world economy in all respects. Moreover, its economy was based on imports and not on exports, which were the sine qua non of industrial ascendance, then as now. It is also difficult to detect even any significant change in the relative position among the Asian powers, Europe included. Europe did not emerge as a Newly Industrializing Economy (NIE) challenging Asia until the late eighteenth and early nineteenth centuries. Only then and not before did the world economic center of gravity began to shift to Europe.

The preponderance of Asian economic agents in Asia and of Asia itself in the world economy has been masked not only by the attention devoted to "the rise of the West" in the world, but also by the undue focus on European economic and political penetration of Asia. This chapter will document and emphasize how very out of focus this perspective of European expansion is in real world terms. However, the argument is not and cannot remain confined to mere comparisons between Europe and Asia or its principal economies in China and India. The analytically necessary emphasis must be shifted to the worldwide economic *relations* in productivity, technology, and their enabling and supporting economic and financial institutions, which developed on a global scale – not just on a regional, let alone European, scale. Contrary to the Eurocentric perspective, the Europeans did not in any sense "create" the world economic system itself nor develop world "capitalism."

Population, production, and income

Data on world and regional population growth before the nineteenth century, or even the twentieth, are admittedly speculative. Examination of a sizable variety of sources and the relatively small variations in their estimates none the less affords a clear and very revealing picture of world and comparative regional population growth rates. Still used are the estimates for the seventeenth and eighteenth centuries by A. M. Carr-Saunders (1936) and his revisions of Walter Willcox (1931), who in turn also revised his own earlier estimates (see Willcox 1940). Carr-Saunders's work has been slightly modified in various publications of the Population Division of the United Nations (1953, 1954, and later). Colin Clark (1977) constructs estimates using the above plus nine other sources; his tabulation is summarized below in table 1.2. M. K. Bennett (1954) relies on many of the same sources as well as others to make his own estimates. His data are the most comprehensive and detailed and are the source for table 1.1. These estimates were compared and found to be very similar to a variety of others that are not specifically used here and whose sources are not cited, if only because they group their regions differently (for instance including all of Asiatic Russia in "Europe"). However, the estimates are checked for the key year 1750 by comparing them with John Durand's (1967, 1974) evaluations of many population series, as well as against those by Wolfgang Kollman (1965) reproduced in Rainer Mackensen and Heinze Wewer (1973).

All of these world and regional population growth estimates reveal essentially the same significant story, so that we will not err much by using the figures from Bennett (1954). World (as well as European) population declined in the fourteenth century and resumed its upward growth from 1400 onward. World population grew by about 20 percent in the fifteenth century and by about 10 per-cent in the sixteenth century (all figures cited here are rounded percentages of the totals listed in table 1.1). However, subtracting the precipitous post-Columbian population decline in the Americas (which these tables underestimate [. . .]), in the rest of the world population still grew by 16 percent in the sixteenth century. Then world population growth accelerated to 27 percent in the seventeenth century, or 29 percent outside of the Americas. The mid-seventeenth century seems to have been a period of inflection and even further acceleration, so that in the century from 1650 to 1750 world population growth increased to 45 percent. These significant increases in world population growth were supported by concomitant increases in production, which were fueled by increases in the world supply and distribution of money [. . .]

Table 1.1 World and regional population growth (in millions, rounded)

	Year										
Region	1000	1200	1300	1400	1500	1600	1650	1700	1750	1800	1850
Europe	42	62	73	45	69	89	100	115	140	188	266
All Asia	168	203	216	224	254	292	319	402	508	612	743
Asiatic Russia	3	7	8	9	11	13	14	15	16	17	19
Southwest Asia	32	34	33	27	29	30	30	31	32	33	34
India	48	51	50	46	54	68	80	100	130	157	190
China (major)	70	89	99	112	125	140	150	205	270	345	430
Japan	4	8	11	14	16	20	23	27	32	28	33
Southeast Asia	11	14	15	16	19	21	22	24	28	32	37
Africa	50	61	67	74	82	90	90	90	90	90	95
The Americas	13	23	28	30	41	15	9	10	11	29	59
World Total	275	348	384	373	446	486	518	617	749	919	1,163

Source: M. K. Bennett (1954: table 1)

The regional distribution and variation in this population growth is significant as well. In the fifteenth and sixteenth centuries, population growth was relatively fast in Europe at 53 and 28 percent respectively, so that Europe's share of world population rose from 12 percent in 1400 to 18 percent in 1600. After that however, the European share of world population remained almost stable at 19 percent until 1750, when it finally began to increase to 20 percent in 1800 and 23 percent by 1850. Yet at the same time from 1600 onward, population rose more and faster in Asia. Having been about 60 percent of world population in the fifteenth and sixteenth centuries, Asia's share of world population rose from 60 percent in 1600 to 65 percent in 1700, 66 percent in 1750, and 67 percent in 1800, according to Bennett's estimates. That is because population grew at about 0.6 percent a year in the previously already more densely populated Asia, while in Europe it grew at only 0.4 percent per year. According to the later figure of Livi-Bacci (1992: 68), the rate of population growth in Europe was only 0.3 percent. That is, in relative terms Europe population grew at only half or two-thirds of what it did in the much larger Asia, where absolute growth was of course much greater still. This faster growth of population in Asia is also confirmed by Clark (1977), whose estimates of the Asian shares of world population are about 54 percent in 1500, 60 percent in 1600, and 1650, and 66 percent for 1700, 1750, and 1800. Mackensen and Wewer (1973) and Durand (1967, 1974) also confirm the 66 percent estimate for the share of all of Asia for 1750.

Moreover, population growth was even faster in Asia's most important regions and economies: 45 percent from 1600 to 1700 and even 90 percent over the century and a half from 1600 to 1750 in China and Japan, and 47 and 89 percent in India during the same periods – compared with 38 and 74 percent respectively in all of Asia, and only 29 and 57 percent in Europe. Clark's estimates (see table 1.2) suggest an even greater gap in population growth rates: 100 percent in India from 1600 to 1750, and after its mid-century crisis [. . .] , also in China from 1650 to 1750, compared with only 56 and 44 percent during the same periods in Europe. Only in the rest of Asia, that is in Central Asia (partly represented by Asiatic Russia in table 1.1), and West and Southeast Asia, was population growth slower, at 9 and 19 percent. For Southeast-Asia, Bennett estimates 28 million in 1750 and 32 million in 1800, while Clark suggests 32 million and 40 million for the same dates but is apparently including Ceylon. Durand (1974) regards even this last estimate as too low. Thus for the 1600–1750 period, Southeast Asian population growth would have been 33 percent according to Bennett (table 1.1) and 100 percent according to Clark (table 1.2), that is the same as in China and India, which seems more reasonable from the evidence of their close economic relations [. . .] According to Durand's (1974) suggestion, population

Table 1.2 World Population (in millions, rounded)

Year	1200	1500	1600	1650	1700	1750	1800
World	348	427	498	516	641	731	890
Europe	51	68	83	90	106	130	173
Asia	248	231	303	311	420	484	590
China	123	100	150	100	150	207	315
Japan	12	16	18	22	26	26	26
India	75	79	100	150	200	200	190
Africa	61	85	95	100	100	100	100
Americas	23	41	15	13	13	15	25
Oceania	1	2	2	2	2	2	2

Source: Colin Clark (1977: table 3.1)

Note: Clark's table 3.1 also includes estimates for AD 14, 350, 600, 800, 1000, and 1340 as well as additional detail since 1500.

growth in Southeast Asia was higher still, and thus would also have been much higher than in Europe during this same 1600–1750/1800 period.

Thus, population grew more slowly only in West and perhaps in Central Asia, and in Africa; and it was of course negative in the Americas. Total African population remained stable at 90 million (other estimates, including table 1.2, suggest stability at 100 million) over the three centuries from 1500 to 1800 and therefore was a declining share of world totals. As a result of the Columbian "encounter" and "exchange" of course, in the Americas population declined absolutely by at least 75 percent (but by 90 percent according to [. . .] more careful estimates [. . .]). Therefore it declined relative to the growing world total between 1500 and 1650, and then grew only slowly till 1750.

In summary, and all variations and doubts about population estimates notwithstanding, during the period from 1400 until 1750 or even 1800 population grew much faster in Asia and especially in China and India, than in Europe. Alas, we lack estimates of total and regional production for this same period, but it stands to reason that this much faster population growth in Asia can have been possible only if its production also grew faster to support its population growth. The theoretical possibility that production or income per capita nonetheless remained stable in Asia and/or declined relative to those in Europe seems implausible [. . .] , and is empirically disconfirmed by the estimates below of world total and comparative regional production in GNP terms and per capita incomes.

Hard data on global production and income are of course also hard to come by for this period, both because they are difficult to find or construct and because few people have been interested to do so. However, a number of scholars have taken the trouble to construct estimates for part of the eighteenth century because they have wanted to use them as a base line to measure more recent Western and world economic growth, in which there is more interest. So much the better for us, since these estimates also offer some indication of world and regional production and income for at least the end of our period.

Braudel (1992) cites world and regional GNP estimates by Paul Bairoch for 1750. Total world GNP was US $155 billion (measured in 1960 US dollars), of which $120 billion or 77 percent was in "Asia" and $35 billion in all the "West," meaning Europe and the Americas, but also including Russia and Japan because of how Bairoch grouped his estimates (to highlight subsequent growth in the "West"). If we reallocate Japan and Siberian Russia to Asia, its share of world GNP was then surely over 80 percent. Out of $148 billion GNP in 1750, Bairoch himself allocates $112 billion or 76 percent to what is in the "Third" World today, including Latin America, and $35 billion or 24 percent to the countries that are today "developed," including Japan. For 1800, after the beginning of the industrial revolution in England, Bairoch's corresponding estimates are a total of $183 billion, of which $137 billion or 75 percent were in the part of the world that is today underdeveloped. Only $47 billion, or only 33 percent of world GNP, was in what are today's industrialized countries (Bairoch and Levy-Leboyer 1981: 5). More than another half-century later in 1860, total GNP had risen to $280 billion, and the respective amounts were $165 billion or almost 60 percent for today's "Third" World and $115 billion or still only just over 40 percent for the now developed countries (recalculated from Braudel 1992: 534).

Thus, in 1750 and in 1800 Asian production was much greater, and it was more productive and competitive than anything the Europeans and the Americas were able to muster, even with the help of the gold and silver they brought from the Americas and Africa. If Asia produced some 80 percent of world output at the end of our period in the eighteenth century, we can only speculate on what the proportions may have been at the beginning or in the middle of that four-hundred-year period. Were they the same, because over four hundred years production in Afro-Asia and Europe together with the Americas grew at the same rate? Or was the Western proportion lower and the Afro-Asian one even higher, because Europe grew faster and its American colonies threw their output into the balance?

The comparative population growth rates cited above must incline us against either of these hypotheses. Rather the reverse, the Asian share of the world total was lower in the fifteenth century and then grew because the Asian economies grew even faster in the following centuries than the Europeans did. The evidence on relative population growth rates above, as well as scattered evidence [elsewhere], and our argument [elsewhere] about higher inflation in Europe than in Asia, all support this last hypothesis: production also grew faster in Asia than in Europe! Moreover, if inflation and prices were higher in Europe than in Asia, perhaps they may also have introduced an upward bias into Bairoch's calculations of GNP in the West, relative to the East. In that case, the gap in real production and consumption between Asia and Europe and America may have been greater still than the 80:20 ratio cited above.

Particularly significant is the comparison of Asia's 66 percent share of population, confirmed by all above cited estimates for 1750, with its 80 percent share of production in the world at the same time. So, two-thirds of the world's people in Asia produced four-fifths of total world output, while the one-fifth of world population in Europe produced only part of the remaining one-fifth share of world production to which Africans and Americans also contributed. Therefore on average Asians *must* have been significantly more productive than Europeans in 1750! A fortiori, the most productive Asians in China and India, where population had also grown much faster, must have been that much more productive than the Europeans. In Japan between 1600 and 1800, population increased by only about 45 percent, but agricultural output doubled, so productivity must have increased substantially (Jones 1958: 155). By 1800, wages of cotton spinners, per capita income, life expectancy, and stature or height of people was similar in Japan and England, but by the early nineteenth century, average quality of life may have been higher in Japan than in Britain (Jones 1988: 160, 158).

Indeed Bairoch's estimate of per capita GNP for China in 1800 is (1960) US $228, which compares rather well with his estimates for various years in the eighteenth century for England and France, which range from $150 to $200. By 1850, China's GNP had declined to $170 per capita, and of course India's GNP also declined in the nineteenth century and probably had already declined in the last half of the eighteenth century (Braudel 1992: 534).

Indeed, all per capita income estimates also disconfirm the Eurocentric prejudices of those who might wish to argue that the greater production observed for Asia only reflects its higher population compared to that of little Europe. Bairoch (1993) reviews estimates of worldwide differentials in per capita income. As late as 1700 to 1750 he finds a maximum worldwide differential of 1 to 2.5. However he also cites a later estimate of 1 to 1.24 by Simon Kuznets, estimates of 1 to 2.2 and 2.6 by David Landes, and 1 to 1.6 or 1.3 or even 1.1 by Angus Maddison. Bairoch also reviews seven other estimates including contemporary eighteenth-century views, and himself arrives at an estimate of 1 to 1.1, or virtual parity of incomes or standards of living around the world.

Perhaps the most important standard of living "index" – the years of expectancy of life itself – was similar among the various regions of Eurasia (Pomeranz 1997: chap. 1, pp. 8–12). It was certainly not low in China if septuagenarians were common – and in 1726 nearly one percent of the population was over seventy years of age, including some more than one hundred years old (Ho Ping-ti 1959: 214).

According to estimates by Maddison (1991: 10), in 1400 per capita production or income were almost the same in China and Western Europe. For 1750 however, Bairoch found European standards of living *lower* than those in the rest of the world and especially in China, as he testifies against in Bairoch 1997 [. . .] . Indeed, for 1800 he estimates income in the "developed" world at $198 per capita, in all the "underdeveloped" world at $188, but in China at $210 (Bairoch and Levy-Leboyer 1981: 14). Ho Ping-ti's (1959: 269, 213) population studies have already suggested that in the eighteenth century the standard of living in China was rising and peasant income was no lower than in France and certainly higher than in Prussia or indeed in Japan. Gilbert Rozman (1981: 139) also makes "international comparisons" and concludes that the Chinese met household needs at least as well as any other people in premodern times. Interestingly, even the per capita consumption of sugar seems to have been higher in China, which had to use its own resources to produce it, than in Europe, which was able to import it cheaply from its slave plantation colonies (Pomeranz 1997: chap. 2, pp. 11–15). For India, Immanuel Wallerstein (1989: 157–8) cites evidence from Ifran Habib, Percival Spear, and Ashok V. Desai, all to the effect that in the seventeenth century per capita agricultural output and standards of consumption were certainly not lower and probably higher than contemporary ones in Europe and certainly higher than Indian ones in the early and mid-twentieth century. Ken Pomeranz (1997) however suggests that European standards of consumption were higher than Asian ones.

That is, all available estimates of world and regional population, production, and income, as well as the discussion above on world trade, confirm that Asia and various of its regional economies were far more productive and competitive and had far and away more weight and influence in the global economy than any or all of the "West" put together until at least 1800. If this was not due only to Asia's greater population, as its ratios of population to production and its per capita income figures show indirectly and inferentially, how was this possible? Part of the answer lies in ample direct evidence on Asia's greater productivity and competitiveness in the world economy, to which we turn below. Moreover, Asia's preeminence was also rendered possible by technology and economic institutions [. . .] .

Productivity and competitiveness

We have some direct evidence on Asia's absolute and relative productiveness and competitiveness, especially in industrial production and world trade. K.N. Chaudhuri (1978) rightly observes that

> the demand for industrial products, even in a pre-machine age, measures the extent of specialisation and the division of labour reached by a society. There is no question that from this point of view the Indian subcontinent and China possessed the most advanced and varied economies in Asia in the period from 1500 to 1750.
>
> (Chaudhuri 1978: 204–5)

Not only in Asia, however, but in the world!

> It is clear that Asia's absorption of silver, and to a lesser extent gold for a limited period in the seventeenth century, was primarily the result of a relative difference in international production cost and prices. It was not until the large-scale application of machinery in the nineteenth century radically altered the structure of production costs that Europe was able to bridge the effect of the price differentials.
>
> (Chaudhuri 1978: 456)

Yet it has also been argued that Indian competitiveness in textiles was not so much due to more advanced or sophisticated mechanical productive equipment. Kanakalatha Mukund (1992) argues that the Indians' advantage lay in the highly developed skills of their (handicrafts) workers. That in turn was due in part to the also high degree of specialization in and subdivision among the various productive processes. Moreover, Indian competitiveness was also based on an organizational structure that permitted rapid flexible adaptation to shifting market demands for types and styles of textiles that were produced and exported. Additionally, India was preeminent in the growth and quality of its long-staple cotton and in the chemical technology and industry to dye it. Finally, costs of production were low because wages were low, because wage-good foodstuffs for the producers were cheap; and in turn that is because Indian agriculture produced them efficiently at low cost.

Chaudhuri summarizes some of the industrial production in Asia:

> The three great crafts of Asian civilisations were of course textiles, cotton and silk, metal goods including jewellery, [and] ceramics and glassware. There were in addition a whole range of subsidiary craft manufactures which shared all the attributes of industrial technology and organization: paper, gunpowder, fireworks, bricks, musical instruments, furniture, cosmetics, perfumery; all these items were indispensable parts of daily life in most parts of Asia . . . The surviving historical material, whether relating to the process of manufacturing or the system of distribution, shows quite clearly that most Asian craft industries involved intermediate stages, and the separation of functions was social as well as technical. In the textile industry before a single peace of chintz or muslim reached the hands of the public, it needed the services of farmers growing raw cotton, harvesters, those who ginned the cotton fibre, carders, spinners, weavers, bleachers, printers, painters, glazers, and repairers. . . . A list of historical objects fashioned from metal itself would be a long one. Agricultural tools and implements, metal fastenings, doors and locks in buildings, cooking utensils, heavy and fine armaments, religious artifacts, coins, and jewellery. . . . An active and varied trade developed in all parts of Asia in coarse cloth, earthenware pottery, iron implements, and brass utensils. Ordinary people as well as the well-off bought these simple goods of everyday use. . . .
>
> (Chaudhuri 1990: 302, 319, 323, 305)

As a joke has it, a puzzled customs officer wondered about the guy who kept crossing the border with wheelbarrows that appeared empty. It took quite a while until the customs officer got wise to what the guy was doing: he was smuggling wheelbarrows! Well, it was no joke but serious business that the preponderant majority of shipping, albeit with goods of whatever origin and engaged in legal as well as contraband trade among Asian ports, was on Asian ships built with Asian materials and labor of West, South, East, and Southeast Asian origin and financed by Asian capital. Thus, shipping, naval and port construction, and their maintenance and finance were in and of themselves already a major, continuing, and growing "invisible" industry all around Asia, which dwarfed all European interlopers probably until the nineteenth-century advent of the steamship.

An analogous "invisible industry" was coinage – minting and re-minting – for local, regional, and national use, and also very much so for export. The production, assaying, and exchange of gold, silver, copper, tin, iron, and other metal coins, specie in bar and other bullion form, and of cowrie shell, badam, and other currencies (including textiles) was big business for state and private interests, to which Frank Perlin (1993) and others have devoted extensive studies. In principle, coins could be accepted at face or weight value, although not entirely so in case they may have been debased; bullion had to be assayed for weight and purity, which implied a business cost but also provided still another state or private business opportunity.

In world economic terms China, not India, was the front-runner, exporting huge quantities of valuable commodities and importing vast quantities of silver. India, however, does not seem to have been far behind China in this regard, being the seat of very significant industrial centers, particularly in cotton textiles, and importing huge quantities of bullion, particularly gold (for which India was a "sink"). [It is a] Eurocentric myth that the Asians just hoarded the money they received. On the contrary, Asians *earned* this money first because they were *more* industrious and more productive to begin with; the additional money then generated still more Asian demand and production.

West Asia too seems to have continued to prosper both from its own industrial base, in cotton and silk textiles for instance, and from transshipments of commodities between Europe and the rest of Asia. Both Southeast Asia and Central Asia appear to have prospered, largely on the transshipments of bullion and goods between regions, but in the case of Southeast Asia, also in terms of its locally produced silk, exported especially to Japan.

Europeans were able to sell very few manufactures to the East, and instead profited primarily from inserting themselves into the "country trade" within the Asian economy itself. Europe's source of profits was overwhelmingly derived from the carrying trade and from parleying multiple transactions in bullion, money, and commodities in multiple markets, and most importantly, *across the entire world economy*. Previously, no one power or its merchants had been able to operate in *all* markets simultaneously or systematically to integrate its activities between all of them in such a coherent logic of profit maximization. The main key for the European ability to do so was their control over huge supplies of bullion. Their naval capabilities were a much smaller and long indecisive factor; and their imperial or private company forms of commercial organization were not so different from those of their competitors, as we will note below. Europeans did arbitrage the differentials in exchange rates between gold and silver across all the countries of Asia, and placed themselves in a middleman role in some trade circuits, particularly between China and Japan in the sixteenth and early seventeenth centuries. Nonetheless in world economic terms, for at least three centuries from 1500 to 1800 the most important, and indeed almost only, commodity that Europe was able to produce and export was money – and for that it relied on its colonies in the Americas.

One thing is very clear: Europe was not a major industrial center in terms of exports to the rest of the world economy. [We demonstrated elsewhere] that in fact Europe's inability to export commodities other than money generated a chronic balance of payments deficit and a constant drain of bullion from Europe to Asia. Only Europe's colonial sphere in the Americas explains its viability in the world economy, without which it could not have made good its huge deficits in the commodities trade with Asia. Even so it never had enough money to do so as the poor Europeans wished, for as a Dutch trader reported home in 1632, "we have not failed to find goods . . . but we have failed to produce the money to pay for them" (Braudel 1979: 221). This problem was not overcome until the end of the eighteenth century and especially the nineteenth century, when the flow of money was finally reversed, to go from East to West.

World trade 1400–1800

In view of the above documentation about Asian population, production, productivity, competitiveness, domestic and regional trade, and their continued growth, it should come as no surprise that international trade was also predominantly Asian. Yet the mythology has grown up that world trade was created by and dominated by Europeans, even in Asia. We confront below the several reasons for this myth.

The Portuguese, and after them Europeans generally, have "bewitched" historians into devoting attention to themselves all out of proportion to their importance in Asian trade. Giving credit where credit is due, this enthrallment with the Portuguese, the Dutch, and the British is due in part to the fact that it is they who left the most records of Asian trade. Of course, these records also reflect their own participation and interests, more than those of their Asian partners and competitors.

The Eurocentric position about European participation in Asian trade has however become subject to increasing revision. W. H. Moreland's (1936: 201) now classic *A Short History of India* argued that "the immediate effects produced by the Portuguese in India were not great." The next major salvo came from a former Dutch official in Indonesia, J. C. van Leur (1955), who challenged the then still dominant Eurocentric view in a series of comments:

> the general course of Asian international trade remained essentially unchanged. . . . The Portuguese colonial regime, then, did not introduce a single new economic element into the commerce of southern Asia. . . . In quantity Portuguese trade was exceeded many times by the trade carried on by Chinese, Japanese, Siamese, Javanese, Indians . . . and Arabs. . . . Trade continued inviolate everywhere. . . . The great intra-Asian trade route retained its full significance. . . . Any talk of a European Asia in the eighteenth century [a fortiori earlier!] is out of the question.
>
> (Van Leur 1955: 193, 118, 165, 164, 165, 274)

Indeed, asserts van Leur (1955: 75), "the Portuguese Empire in the Far East was actually more idea than fact," and even that had to give way to reality, as M. A. P. Meilink-Roelofsz (1962) repeatedly observes, despite her defense of the Europeanist position. She in turn challenges the van Leur thesis in her carefully researched text on the European influence on Asian trade, which she explicitly claims was greater and earlier than van Leur allows. Yet her own evidence, and her repeated disallowance of the real impact of the Portuguese, seem to end even more support to "van Leur's thesis that it was only about 1800 that Europe began to outstrip the East" (Meilink-Roelofsz 1962: 10). Her own research concentrates especially on insular Southeast Asia, which experienced the greatest European impact in Asia; and yet even there she shows that indigenous and Chinese trade successfully resisted the Dutch.

Now, more and more scholarship – for example, Chaudhuri (1978), Ashin Das Gupta and M. N. Pearson (1987), Sinnappah Arasaratnam (1986), and Tapan Raychaudhuri and Irfan Habib (1982) – has confirmed van Leur's message that Asian trade was a flourishing and ongoing enterprise into which the Europeans only entered as an added and relatively minor player.

Asian pepper production more than doubled in the sixteenth century alone, and much of that was consumed in China (Pearson 1989: 40). Of the relatively small share, certainly less than a third, that was exported to Europe, sixteen times more spices were transported overland by Asians through West Asia than went around the Cape on Portuguese ships in 1503, and even by 1585 almost four times as much went by the Red Sea route as the Cape route (Das Gupta 1979: 257). Even though shipping was their forte, the Portuguese never carried more than 15 percent of the Moluccan cloves to Europe, and the vast bulk of Southeast Asian pepper and other spices was exported to China. Moreover, some ships flying Portuguese flags were really owned and run by Asians, who used that "flag of convenience" to benefit from the lower customs duties accorded Portugal in some ports (Barendse 1997: chap. 1). Yet with all their military and political strong-arm attempts to "monopolize" trade and to charge tribute tolls to others, Portugal's nonetheless very small share of inter-Asian trade provided 80 percent of their profits, and only 20 percent came from their trade around the Cape of Good Hope, which they had pioneered (Das Gupta and Pearson 1987: 71, 78, 84, 90; Subrahmanyam 1990: 361). This is illustrated by the itemized documentation in a Portuguese book published in 1580, which records in Portuguese cruzados just how profitable particular routes and voyages were. For the relatively short Macao–Siam, Macao–Patane, and Macao–Timor trips, the profits were 1,000 cruzados each; for Macao–Sunda, 6,000 to 7,000 cruzados; and for Goa–Malacca–Macao–Japan, 35,000 cruzados. By comparison, for the entire Lisbon–Goa voyage via the Cape of Good Hope the owner received 10,000 to 12,000 cruzados and the ship's captain 4,000 cruzados (cited in Lourido 1996: 18–19).

Though so important for the Portuguese, their share of the exports of silver from Japan was never more than 10 percent of the Japanese total between 1600 and 1620 and only briefly rose to a maximum of 37 percent in the 1630s (Das Gupta and Pearson 1987: 76). In India also, even at the height of their sixteenth-century "penetration" of Asia, the Portuguese handled only some 5 percent of Gujarati trade. Despite their base at Goa, Portuguese procurement was less than 10 percent of south-western Indian pepper production. The maintenance of Portugal's "*Estado da India*" cost its taxpayers and the state more than its direct earnings from India, although its private merchants did benefit from it, as other European "servants" did from their companies (Barendse 1997: chap. 1).

The small Portuguese trade in East and Southeast Asia was replaced by the Dutch. Yet despite all their efforts to monopolize trade at least in parts of Southeast Asia, the Dutch never succeeded in doing so [. . .] . Indeed, even the inroads that the Dutch made primarily at the expense of the Portuguese were again replaced by the Chinese and other East Asians, whose domination of their seas – not to mention their lands – was never seriously challenged. From the late seventeenth century onward, "European penetration was actually reversed" (Das Gupta and Pearson 1987: 67). Europeans were outcompeted by the Chinese, whose shipping between 1680 and 1720 increased threefold to Nagasaki and reached its maximum at Batavia, when the 1740 massacre of Chinese took place (Das Gupta and Pearson 1987: 87). For instance, in the four years after shipping was legally reopened again in 1684, Nagasaki received an average of nearly 100 Chinese ships a year, or two a week; over the longer period to 1757, the average was still over 40 a year. In 1700, Chinese ships brought over 20 thousand tons of goods to South China, while European ones carried away 500 tons in the same year. In 1737 it was 6 thousand tons, and not until the 1770s did Europeans transport 20 thousand tons (Marks 1997).

Trade from the sixteenth to the nineteenth centuries in the East China Sea, bordering Korea, Japan, and the Ryukyus, and the South China Sea around Southeast Asia is illuminated in an essay by Klein (1989). He finds that Europeans never achieved any control, much less domination, or even a partial monopoly. In the East China Sea, trade was exclusively in Asian hands; Europeans hardly entered at all. In the South China Sea, first the Portuguese and then the Dutch Europeans achieved at best a foothold by taking advantage of regional disturbances until the mid-seventeenth century. However, even that was reduced to no more than a toehold (later including the British), with the economic and political recovery of East Asia in the second half of the seventeenth and through the eighteenth centuries. Klein concludes that

The European penetration into the maritime space of the China seas during the sixteenth and seventeenth centuries had only been possible due to the peculiar development of the domestic and regional power relations in the area itself. Its influence on the region's economy had been marginal. Its commercial effects on the world economy had been only temporary, restricting themselves to the rather weak and limited European trading network in Asia. After the region regained a new balance of power in about 1680, its internal maritime trade experienced a new era of growth within a well established framework of traditional institutions. This trade and its institutions were gradually eroded during the later part of the eighteenth century . . . [but included] European commerce . . . [that] also fell prey to disintegration. The establishment of European hegemony in the nineteenth century found no base in what had happened in pre-industrial times . . . [but was based on] entirely new conditions and circumstances.

(Klein 1989: 86–87)

Even at the other, western end of Asia, where commercial access was easier for the Europeans,

> the Arabian seas were part of an ancient, larger network of exchange between China, South-East Asia, India, the Middle East, . . . [where] Europeans were tied to pre-existing arrangements, relating to foreign traders . . . [who] were collaborating with Asians reluctantly, for the degree of mutual trust should not be exaggerated.
>
> (Barendse 1997: chap. 1)

Turning to the significance of Asian trade in world trade as a whole, one of the European historians after van Leur most sympathetic to Asia is Niels Steensgaard (1972). He also agrees that Portugal changed little in the Indian Ocean and that much more important – indeed *the* event of the sixteenth century – was the conquest of Bengal by Akbar in 1576. (Steensgaard 1987: 137).

So it is surprising to read that Steensgaard (1990) regards Asian trade through the Indian Ocean to have been "marginal" and of little importance. "The point may seem like restating the obvious," he adds, dismissing Asian trade by noting Moreland's (1936) and Bal Krishna's estimates of 52,000 to 57,000 tons and 74,500 tons, respectively, of long-distance trade annually at the opening of the seventeenth century. He compares that with half a million or closer to a million tons of shipping capacity in Europe. However, the weight of traded cargoes versus shipping capacity are hardly commensurate measures. Steensgaard himself notes that these Indian Ocean trade figures exclude coastal shipping, which was both greater per se and an integral part of long-distance trade that also relied on relay trade. Yet European ships primarily plied the Baltic and Mediterranean coasts for distances no longer, and mostly less so, than those along the Indian Ocean or the Southeast Asian seas for that matter. So this comparison hardly seems adequate to evaluate the relative weights of India (let alone Asia) and Europe in world trade.

Moreover, [. . .] Asian overland and maritime trade were more complementary than competitive, as Barendse also observes:

> The relation between land and seaborne trade is a complex one: the choice between them partly depended upon the circuits covered, partly on "protection rent." Trade along the caravan roads was not substituted by trade overseas. In some cases seaborne trade might even stimulate caravan trade. In others, commerce partly shifted to the sea routes, particularly where overland trade became dangerous, like in India in the late seventeenth century. . . . Trade on the coast depended on that of the hinterland. Many fairs were mere satellites on the coast of metropolises in the interior: thus Barcelore of Vijayanagara, Dabhul of Bijapur and – as its name indicates – Lahawribandar of Lahore. The centres of both manufacture and government were located in the hinterland; the bulk of the agricultural production was redistributed there.
>
> (Barendse 1997: chap. 1)

We observed [elsewhere] that overland trade also flourished and grew. In India and to and from Central Asia, caravans of oxen, each carrying from 100 and 150 kilograms and numbering 10 to 20 thousand animals, were not uncommon and caravans as large as 40 thousand animals were not unknown (Brenning 1990: 69, Burton 1993: 26). Caravans could also include a thousand or more carts, each drawn by ten to twelve oxen. Caravanserai, rest stops located at a day's distance from each other, accommodated up to 10 thousand travelers and their animals (Burton 1993: 25). In the seventeenth century, just one of the merchant communities, the Banjaras, transported an average of 821 million ton miles over an average of 720 miles a year. By comparison, two centuries later in 1882, all Indian railways carried 2,500 ton miles (Habib 1990: 377).

By all indications, Asia's trade with Europe, though growing over these centuries, still remained a very small share of Asians' trade with each other (even including their long-distance trade). Sir Joshua Childe, the director of the British East India Company, observed in 1688 that from some Indian ports alone Asian trade was ten times greater than that of all Europeans put together (cited in Palat and Wallerstein 1990: 26).

In view of this review of trade in Asia and especially the analysis of trade in the China seas by Klein (1989), it is noteworthy that Carl-Ludwig Holtfrerich (1989: 4) claims, in his introduction to his edited volume of papers in which Klein's work appears, that "Europe dominated throughout the whole period." Holtfrerich goes on to claim (1989: 5, table 1.2) a European share of all world trade at 69 and 72 percent in 1720 and 1750 respectively, leaving only 11 and 7 percent for India in those two years (an additional 12 percent is claimed for Latin America and 8 percent for "Other" during each of the tabulated time periods).

This unabashedly Eurocentric claim is disconfirmed by the evidence discussed in the present book, as well as by Klein's (1989) analysis on Chinese and not European trade in the China seas. Moreover, in the period 1752–1754 according to figures from Steensgaard (1990: 150), the relatively small exports to Europe from Asia (which were a very small share of Asia's trade) remained higher than Europe's imports from the Americas. (European exports to the Americas were higher, but of course the Europeans were still unable to compete successfully with their exports elsewhere, that is in Asia). Indeed, even in 1626 an anonymous Iberian observer wrote a "Dissertation" whose title claims to "Demonstrate . . . the Greater Importance of the East Indies than the West Indies by Virtue of Trade, and therefore we Find the Causes of Why the Oriental Trade is lost and Spain is Reduced to the Abject Poverty that we [now] Witness" (translated from Lourido 1996b: 19).

Terry Boswell and Joya Misra (1995) offer another graphic illustration of how these Eurocentric blinkers not only hide most of the world economy and trade from (Western) view but also distort the perception even of the European "world-economy." First they write that, in Wallerstein's and their view "despite trade connections, Africa and Asia remained external [to the world-system]. Neither logistics not long waves should apply to them." Then they disagree with Wallerstein: "We think it reasonable to consider East Asian trade a leading sector in the world-system, even if Asia itself is external" (Boswell and Misra 1995: 466, 471). So they include "East Asian trade" in their calculations of "global" trade, only to find that "thousands of ships were engaged in the Baltic trade, compared to only hundreds in the Atlantic and Asian." Since the latter journeys were longer, they allot each of them greater weight in their estimations of total "global trade" (Boswell and Misra 1995: 471–2). Alas, their myopia allows them to see and include in their "global" trade only the hundreds of ships in the East–West trade, and not to see nor count any of the thousands in the intra-Asian trade, which Holtfrerich (1989) at least included even if he vastly underestimated them. However, Boswell and Misra also fall into another trap of their own making. First they argue that the observation that "East Asian trade showed a different [cyclical] pattern from the Atlantic and global trades supports considering the latter external" (Boswell and Misra 1995: 472). They do not even consider the possibility that the divergence of "East Asian trade" from East–West trade may be compensatory, as in a see-saw. That would make their observation evidence of the opposite: Asia and its trade would be not "external" but rather internal to the system! Then they argue that their own further investigation of cyclical ups and downs accidentally shows exactly that: "This finding suggests the Asian trade is more central to the capitalist word economy than expected" (Boswell and Misra 1995: 478)! Of course, what they "expected" is a function of their own Eurocentric blinkers, but it turns out that these distort even their own analysis of the "European world-system," as well as of course blinding them to the existence of a much larger world economy and trade in Asia.

In conclusion, the Asian economy and intra-Asian trade continued on vastly greater scales than European trade and its incursions in Asia until the nineteenth century. Or in the words of Das Gupta and Pearson in their *India and the Indian Ocean 1500–1800*,

> a crucial theme is that while the Europeans obviously were present in the ocean area, their role was not central. Rather they participated, with varying success, in an on-going structure. . . . [In] the sixteenth century, the continuity is more important in the history of the Indian Ocean than the discontinuities which resulted from the Portuguese impact.
> (Das Gupta and Pearson 1987: 1, 31)

Even the European(ist) Braudel had long insisted that the world economic center of gravity did not even begin to shift westward until *after* the end of the sixteenth century, and it did not arrive there until the end of the eighteenth century and during the nineteenth. Indeed, "the change comes only late in the eighteenth century, and in a way it is an endogamous game. Europeans finally burst out, and changed this structure, but they exploded from within an Asian context" (Das Gupta and Pearson 1987: 20).

Thus, despite their access to American money to buy themselves into the world economy in Asia, for the three centuries after 1500 the Europeans still remained a small player who had to adapt to – and not make! – the world economic rules of the game in Asia. Moreover, Asians continued to compete successfully in the world economy. How could they do so if, as the received Eurocentric "wisdom" has it, Asians lacked science, technology, and the institutional base to do so? The answer is that Asians did not "lack" any of these and instead often excelled in these areas. So let us turn now to examine the development of science, technology, and institutions in the real world and how they too differ from what Eurocentric mythology alleges.

QUALITIES: SCIENCE AND TECHNOLOGY

Eurocentrism regarding science and technology in Asia

The received Eurocentric mythology is that European technology was superior to that of Asia throughout our period from 1400 to 1800, or at least since 1500. Moreover, the conventional Eurocentric bias regarding science and technology extends to institutional forms, which are examined [elsewhere]. Here I focus on the following questions: (1) Were science and technology on balance more advanced in Europe or in Asia, and until when? (2) After importing the compass, gunpowder, printing, and so on from China, was technology then developed indigenously in Europe but no longer in China and elsewhere in Asia? (3) Was the direction of technological diffusion after 1500 from Europe to Asia? (4) Was technological development only a local and regional process in Europe or China or wherever, or was it really a global process driven by world economic forces as they impacted locally? To preview the answers that will emerge below, all of them contradict or at least cast serious doubt on the received Eurocentric "wisdom" about science and technology.

Technology turns out not to be independently parallel. Instead, technology is rapidly diffused or adapted to common and/or different circumstances. In particular, the choice, application, and "progress" of technology turns out to be the result of rational response to opportunity costs that are themselves determined by world economic and local demand and supply conditions. That is, technological progress here *and* there, even more than institutional form, is a function of world economic "development" much more than it is of regional, national, local, let alone cultural specificities.

Nonetheless an oft-cited student of the subject, J. D. Bernal (1969) attributes the rise of Western science and technology to the indigenous rise of capitalism in the West (which he accounts for in the same terms as Marx and Weber). Robert Merton's now classic 1938 discourse on "Science, Technology, and Society" is entirely Weberian and even linked to the latter's thesis about the Protestant ethic and the "Spirit of Capitalism." That in itself should make his derivative thesis on science and technology suspect, [as argued elsewhere]; for another critical discussion, see Stephen Sanderson (1995: 324 ff.). Coming full circle, Rostow's (1975) "central thesis" on the origins of modern economy is quite explicit: it all began in modern Europe – with the scientific revolution.

The study of the history and role of this scientific and technological revolution seems to be much more ideologically driven than the technology and science that allegedly support it. For instance, Carlo Cipolla (1976: 207) favorably cites one of the Western "experts" on the history of technology, Lynn White, Jr., who asserts that "the Europe which rose to global dominance about 1500 had an industrial capacity and skill vastly greater than that of any of the cultures of Asia . . . which it challenged." We have already seen above that Europe did *not* rise to "dominance" at all in 1500 if only because exactly the opposite of White's Eurocentric claim was true.

The second volume of the *History of Technology* edited by Charles Singer et al. (1957: vol. 2, 756) recognizes and even stresses that from AD 500 to 1500 "technologically, the west had little to bring to the east. The technological movement was in the other direction." Reproduced there is a table from Joseph Needham (1954) that traces the time lags between several dozen inventions and discoveries in China and their first adoption in Europe. In most cases, the lag was ten to fifteen centuries (and twenty-five centuries for the iron plow moldboard); in other cases the lag was three to six centuries; and the shortest time lag was one century, for both projectile artillery and movable metal type. "It was largely by imitation and, in the end, sometimes by improvement of [these] techniques and models . . . that the products of the west ultimately rose to excellence" (Singer et al. 1957: vol. 2, 756).

However, these accounts are themselves also excessively European-focused. There was indeed much technological diffusion; but during the millennium up to 1500 it was primarily back and forth among East, Southeast, South, and West Asia, and especially between China and Persia. Before any of this technology reached Europe at all, most of it had to pass via the Muslim lands, including especially Muslim Spain. The Christian capture of Toledo and its Islamic scholars and important library in 1085 and later of Córdoba significantly advanced technological learning farther "westward" in Europe. The Byzantines and later the Mongols also transmitted knowledge from east to west.

Singer's third volume, covering the period 1500–1750, is explicitly devoted to the West. Without any further comparisons, the assertion is made that "it is certain, however" that the balance had already shifted by 1500, so that "granted the immense European naval and military superiority, European control of the Far East was an almost inevitable consequence." Moreover, it is claimed that there was a "generally higher level of technical proficiency in Europe in the seventeenth century compared with the rest of the globe"; this is attributed to a European and especially British more "liberal social system," being "united in religion" and other such differences in "civilization." Also mentioned is that all this is "in no way inconsistent with an inferiority" in silks and ceramics, but cotton textiles and other industries are not mentioned (Singer et al. 1957: vol. 3, 709–710, 711, 716, 711).

However, this reference to alleged sociocultural superiority is no more than [. . .] Eurocentric prejudice that we [. . .] will have to reject after the examination [elsewhere] of institutions [. . .] . In principle, it could indeed have been the case that Europe lagged behind in the important ceramics, silk, and cotton industries and yet had advanced more in other technologies. However, the *History of Technology* does not offer the slightest comparative evidence for what is taken for "granted," and we will observe below that the evidence from elsewhere does *not* support the suppositions in this multivolume history. Indeed only a quarter of a century later, David Arnold (1983: 40) was already able to observe that "there is now much greater awareness than formerly of the relative narrowness of the technological gap between Europe and China, India and the Muslim world in the fifteenth and sixteenth centuries.

The Eurocentric treatment of the history of science is similar, although there is serious doubt that science, as distinct from inventors working on their own, had any significant impact on technology in the West before the middle of the nineteenth century. The received and excessively Eurocentric treatment of science is illustrated by several well known multivolume histories. A. C. Crombie's (1959) review of medieval and early modern science from the thirteenth to seventeenth centuries does not even mention any science outside of Western Europe. The first volume of Bernal's (1969) *Science in History*, devoted to its emergence up through the Middle Ages, gives some credit to China and less to West Asia. However, Bernal's second volume, which begins with 1440, makes no further reference to science outside Europe. Only in volume 1 does he mention that, thanks to Needham (1954–), "we are beginning to see the enormous importance for the whole world of Chinese technical developments" (Bernal 1969: vol. 1, 311). Alas, when Bernal was writing Needham had only just begun his major work. So in the very next paragraph, Bernal repeats the same old litany, and even cites Needham in support, that "this early technical advance in China, and to a lesser extent in India and the Islamic countries, after a promising start came to a dead stop before the fifteenth century, and . . . resulted in . . . a high but static technical level" (Bernal 1969: vol. 1, 312). Accordingly, Asia disappears from Bernal's second volume. We observe below that the real world evidence is otherwise.

The more recent comprehensive review by H. Floris Cohen, *The Scientific Revolution. A Historical Inquiry* (1994), seems more promising at first sight; but on closer inspection it too is ultimately almost equally disappointing. Cohen does importantly distinguish between science and its use in technology, and he reviews the large body of literature on "the Great Question" of why "The Scientific Revolution" took place in Europe and not elsewhere. Much of his review, of course, reflects the same inquiries cited above as well as others, from Weber and Merton to Bernal and Needham. However, Cohen takes Needham seriously enough to devote sixty-four pages to the discussion of his work and another thirty-nine pages to Islamic and other "nonemergences" of early modern science "outside Western Europe," in a section that takes up one-fifth of his text.

Yet the thread that runs through Cohen's entire review of "the Great Question" is that something about the embedment of science in society was unique in and to Europe. That is, of course, the Weberian thesis and its resurrection by Merton as applied to science. Alas, it was also originally Needham's Marxist and Weberian point of departure. As Needham found more and more evidence about science and technology in China, he struggled to liberate himself from his Eurocentric original sin, which he had inherited directly from Marx, as Cohen also observes. But Needham never quite succeeded, perhaps because his concentration on China prevented him from sufficiently revising his still ethnocentric view of Europe itself. Nor does Cohen succeed.

For, the more we look at science and technology as economic and social activities not only in Europe but worldwide, as Cohen rightly does, the less historical support is there for the Eurocentric argument about the alleged role of the (European!) scientific revolution in the seventeenth or any other century before very modern times. Another interesting and useful example is "Why the Scientific Revolution Did Not Take Place in China – Or Didn't It?" by Nathan Sivin (1982). Sivin examines and effectively rebuts several of the same Eurocentric assumptions about this issue, but he neglects to raise the also crucial question of what impact the scientific revolution had on the development of technology, if any.

Neither does Cohen, whose review of this "revolution" and its role is even more marred by both his point of departure and his final conclusion. To begin with, Cohen seems to accept the proposition that science emerged only in Western Europe and not elsewhere. Therefore, he as much as dismisses Needham's claim that by the end of the Ming dynasty in 1644 there was no perceptible difference between science in China and in Europe. Yet Cohen's own discussion of works by Needham and others about areas outside Europe shows that science existed and continued to develop elsewhere as well. That of course stands to reason if the alleged "East–West" social and institutional differences were far more mythical than real, and it is also confirmed by other evidence cited below. But if there still was science elsewhere as well, then what is the purpose of Cohen's focus on it primarily in Europe?

Maybe even more significant, however, is that Cohen never troubles to inquire if and how science impacted on technology, even though he insists on the distinction between the two. Yet the evidence is that in Europe itself science did not really contribute to the development of technology and industry at all until two centuries after the famed scientific revolution of the seventeenth century.

To inquire into the alleged contribution of Western science to technology in general and to its industrial "revolution" in particular, it is apt to paraphrase the opening sentence of Steven Shapin's (1996) recent study of the subject: "There was no seventeenth century scientific revolution, and [this section of] this book is about it." Authoritative observers from Francis Bacon to Thomas Kuhn conclude that, whether "revolutionary" or not, these scientific advances appear to have had no immediate impact on technology whatsoever and certainly none on the industrial "revolution," which did not even begin until a century later.

Bacon had observed "the overmuch credit that hath been given unto authors in sciences [for alleged contributions to] arts mechanical [and their] first deviser" (cited in Adams 1996: 56). Three centuries later the author of *The Structure of Scientific Revolution* (1970) commented that "I think nothing but mythology prevents our realizing quite how little the development of the intellect need have had to do with that of technology during all but the most recent stage of human history" (Kuhn 1969; cited in Adams 1996: 56–57). All serious inquiries into the matter show that this "stage" did not begin until the second half of the nineteenth century and really not until after 1870, that is two centuries after the scientific "revolution" and one after the industrial "revolution." Shapin himself devotes a chapter to the question of "What was the [scientific] knowledge for?" His subtitles refer to natural philosophy, state power, religion's handmaid, nature and God, wisdom and will, but not to technology other than also to conclude that "It now appears unlikely that the 'high theory' of the Scientific Revolution had any substantial direct effect on economically useful technology in either the seventeenth century or the eighteenth" (Shapin 1996: 140).

Also, Robert Adams's (1996) *Paths of Fire: An . . . Inquiry into Western Technology* reviews any and all relations between technology and science, including the "seventeenth century scientific revolution." He cites numerous observers regarding particular technologies as well as technology and the industrial revolution in general. On the basis of these observers and his own work, Adams concludes on at least a dozen occasions (1996: 56, 60, 62, 65, 67, 72, 98, 101, 103, 131, 137, 256) that scientists and their science made no significant visible contribution to new technology before the late nineteenth century. Adams writes that "few if any salient technologies of the Industrial Revolution can be thought of as science based in any direct sense. They can better be described as craft based in important ways"; and he concludes that "scientific *theories* were relatively unimportant in connection with technological innovation until well into the nineteenth century" (Adams 1996: 131, 101). Adams's most generous conclusion is that "it must be emphasized that scientific discovery was not the only initiating or enabling agency behind waves of technological innovation, nor was it apparently a necessary one" (Adams 1996: 256). Through the eighteenth century in

Britain only 36 percent of 680 scientists, 18 percent of 240 engineers, and only 8 percent of "notable applied scientists and engineers" were at any time connected with Oxford or Cambridge; moreover, over 70 percent of the latter had no university education at all (Adams 1996: 72). Instead, Adams and others trace technological advances primarily to craftsmanship, entrepreneurship, and even to religion. Indeed, Adams credits technology with far more contribution to the advancement of science than the reverse.

Finally, even Nathan Rosenberg and L. E. Birdzell, who attribute the West's growing "rich" only to European developments, recognize that

> evidently the links between economic growth and leadership in science are not short and simple. Western scientific and economic advance are separated not only in time [by 150 or 200 years between Galileo and the beginnings of the industrial revolution], but also by the fact that until about 1875, or even later, the technology used in the economies of the West was mostly traceable to individuals who were not scientists, and who often had little scientific training. The occupational separation between science and industry was substantially complete except for chemists.
>
> (Rosenberg and Birdzell 1986: 242)

On the other hand, Newton believed in alchemy; and in one example of the use of scientific measure in Europe, the Venetian Giovan Maria Bonardo found in his 1589 study, *The Size and Distance of All Spheres Reduced to Our Miles*, that "hell is 3,758 and ¼ miles from us and has a width of 2,505 and ½ miles [while] Heaven is 1,799,995,500 miles away from us" (cited in Cipolla 1976: 226).

So the overwhelming evidence is that the alleged contribution of seventeenth-, eighteenth-, or even early nineteenth-century science to technology or to the industrial revolution is no more than "mythology" as Kuhn aptly termed it. And so what is the relevance of this entire "Great Question" about the seventeenth-century "scientific revolution" to our other "Grand Question" about "the Decline of the East" and "the (temporary) Rise of the West"? Not much, at least not within our present time frame before 1800. Therefore, it is just as well and most welcome that Cohen (1994: 500) himself ends by asking "Is the (fifty year old concept of the) 'Scientific Revolution' going the way of all historical concepts?" "Perhaps" he answers, for "the concept has by now fulfilled its once useful services; the time has come to discard it. After all, historical concepts are nothing but metaphors which one should beware to reify." Amen!

Except alas, not so fast: this Eurocentric mythology still seems to be alive and well also among Asians, whose resulting distortions of developments in science and technology are even more alarming. For instance, Aniruddha Roy and S. K. Bagchi (1986: v) call Irfan Habib a pioneer in medieval technology studies in India. Yet Ahsan Qaisar (1982) records his deep gratitude to Habib for suggesting his own research in *The Indian Response to European Technology and Culture* (AD 1498–1707). Indeed, Habib himself also contributes a chapter on the same theme to the book edited by Roy and Bagchi. Elsewhere, Habib (1969: 1) himself writes that "it would be foolish, even if detailed evidence has not been studied, to deny that India during the seventeenth century had been definitely surpassed by Western Europe [in technology]." Habib does bring some of the evidence, to be examined below. As we observed in chapter 3, Prakash (1994) disputes much of Habib's reasoning and himself disputes many alleged differences between Asia and Europe and avows that Asia played a widely underestimated key role in the early modern world economy. Yet even Prakash (1995: 6) writes that "Europe had an undoubted overall superiority over Asia in the field of scientific and technical knowledge."

Roy MacLeod and Deepak Kumar (1995) also inquire into Western technology and its transfer to India from 1700 to 1947; despite the 1700 date in their subtitle, they explicitly disclaim any attention to the precolonial era; and yet, as we note below, some of their contributors (Inkster, Sanpal) do deal with that period. Even so, the editors permit themselves to introduce their book with unsubstantiated claims that are challenged by the evidence – cited below – from at least one of their own contributors. Yet the editors write that "technological change" in pre-British India "certainly was no match to what was happening in Europe. The whole technical process was skill- and craft-oriented [but not so in Europe, we may ask]; the output was excellent (for example, in steel and textile), but limited to local markets [if so, how then did India dominate world markets, we may ask]. European travellers . . . were wonder-struck by some Indian products, but invariably critical of Indian customs" (MacLeod and Kumar 1995: 11–12). Yet, even their first contributor, Ian Inkster examines and rejects arguments of India's alleged inferiority on cultural grounds. The editors claim that these and other "prefixes" (better prejudices!) "point to the weakness of the Indian economy as compared to proto-industrial Europe, Tokugawa Japan or even Ming China" (MacLeod and Kumar 1995: 12). Alas, they see reality in reverse; for, on all the evidence in the present book, the order of economic "weakness" and strength was the reverse, with China strongest, Europe weakest, and Japan and India in between.

What is noteworthy is that all of these texts by Asian scholars inquire only into technological diffusion from Europe to India and its selective adoption there – not the other way around. Yet as we will note below, diffusion went in *both* directions; and adoption and adaptation in *both* places as well as elsewhere responded to *common* world economic development mediated by local circumstances.

For China, Joseph Needham's (1954–) monumental multivolume *Science and Civilization in China* is well known, although perhaps insufficiently examined because of its large bulk and detail. A four-volume extract has been prepared by Colin Ronan (1986), and Needham (1964) himself has written a summary, "Science and China's Influence on the World." He explicitly challenges the dismissal by others: 'In technological influence before and during the Renaissance China occupies a quite dominating position . . . The world owes far more to the resilient craftsmen of ancient and medieval China than to Alexandrian mechanics, articulate theoreticians though they were" (Needham 1964: 238). Needham lists not only the well-known Chinese inventions of gunpowder, paper and printing, and the compass. He also examines co-fusion and oxygenation iron and steel technology, mechanical clocks, and engineering devices such as drive-belts and chain-drive methods of converting rotary to rectilinear motion, segmental arch and iron-chain suspension bridges, deep-drilling equipment; and paddle-wheel boats, foresails and aft sails, watertight compartments and sternpost rudders in navigation, and many others.

Moreover, Needham insists that scientific investigation was well accepted and supported and that technological innovation and its application continued through the early modern period, also in fields like astronomy and cosmology, and in medical fields like anatomy, immunology, and pharmacology. Needham explicitly denies the European notion that the Chinese only invented things but did not wish to or know how to apply them in practice. Although he examines some apparently parallel developments in East and West, he also speculates on the possible channels and extent of their mutual influence and interchange.

There are also similar studies and findings for India, albeit on a lesser scale than Needham's monumental work. For instance, G. Kuppuram and K. Kumudamani (1990) have published a history of science and technology in India in twelve volumes, and A. Rahman (1984) has edited another collection on the same topic. Both works testify to the continued development of science and technology in India not only before 1500 but also since then. Dharampal (1971) collected eighteenth-century accounts by Europeans, who testify to their interest in and profit from Indian science and technology. Indian mathematics and astronomy were sufficiently advanced for Europeans to import astronomical tables and related works from India in the seventeenth and eighteenth centuries. In medicine, the theory and practice of inoculation against smallpox came from India. The export of Indian science and technology relating to shipbuilding, textiles, and metallurgy are noted below.

Similarly, S. H. Nasr (1976) and Ahmand al-Hassan and Donald Hill (1986) have written and edited histories testifying to the development and diffusion of Islamic science and technology from the earliest to recent times. George Saliba (1996) provides multiple examples of important Arab scientific influences on the Renaissance, not only before and during this period but into the seventeenth century. Only one example from Saliba is that Copernicus knew and had documents about Arab theories, which made crucial inputs to his own "revolution."

So it is not enough to just go on "granting the immense European naval and military superiority," as does Singer, or claiming that it "would be foolish, even if detailed evidence has not been studied, to deny" European technological superiority in other fields, as does Habib. Better to examine the evidence of Asian capacities with a bit more care, as Goody (1996) and Blaut (1997) begin to do, especially in these two fields. Another area of superiority mentioned in Singer's history of technology are coal and iron, while Habib and others also refer to printing and textiles. Upon any inspection, not only will we find that technology was far "advanced" in many parts of Asia, but it continued to develop in the centuries after 1400. That was the case especially in the globally more competitive military and naval technologies. More over, the alleged "Ottoman decline" is contradicted by a comparative examination of technologies in precisely these two areas (Grant 1996) [. . .]. However, advanced technologies were also the case in more "local" arenas such as hydraulic engineering and other public works, iron working and other metallurgy (including armaments and especially steel-making), paper and printing, and of course in other export industries such as ceramics and textiles.

Guns

I say "other" export industries because arms and shipbuilding *were* important export industries. Not for nothing have the Ottomans, Mughals, and the Chinese Ming/Qing been termed "gunpowder empires" (McNeill 1989). They developed the latest and best in armaments and other military technology, which every ruling elite in the world sought to buy or copy it if it could use and afford it (Pacey 1990 [. . .]). Nonetheless, both Cipolla (1967) in his *Guns and Sails* and McNeill (1989) in his *The Age of Gunpowder Empires 1450–1800* repeatedly claim that European guns, especially when mounted on ships, were and remained far superior to any others in the world.

On the other hand, both Cipolla and McNeill themselves bring some contrary evidence. Both discuss the rapid development of Ottoman military technology and power. The Ottomans (but also the Thais) excelled in arms production, as Europeans and Indians recognized and also copied, adapting and reproducing Ottoman small and large arms technology to their own circumstances and needs. "Until about 1600, therefore, the Ottoman army remained technically and in every other way in the very forefront of military proficiency," avers McNeill (1989: 33). Cipolla (1967) acknowledges the same high degree of Ottoman military technology in his Chapter 2, and Jonathan Grant's (1996) comparative examinations confirm it. Although all three authors signal Ottoman military weaknesses (and defeat against Russia) in the seventeenth century, the first two also stress that European development of military technology could not begin to shift the balance of land-based power anywhere in Asia before the second half of the eighteenth century.

On the seas and at the coasts, their naval artillery did give Europeans some military technical advantages, but never enough to impose even a small part of the economic monopoly they sought, as Cipolla and McNeill also recognize. The Ottoman Sultan said that even the 1571 European naval victory at Lepanto only singed his beard (quoted in

Cipolla 1967: 101). The Portuguese sixteenth-century incursions in the Arabian Sea, the Indian Ocean, and the China Sea, using their bases at Hormuz, Goa, and Macao respectively, were only limited and temporary. The seventeenth-century Dutch offensive did much to displace the Portuguese but failed to impose the monopoly they sought in Asian waters, even in "Dutch" Southeast Asia, as we observed above.

Nor did their guns afford the Europeans any significant military impact in or on China and Japan, although there was some reverse diffusion of artillery technology. The Eurocentric fable that Chinese invented gunpowder but did not know how to use it is completely belied by Needham's (1981) evidence. He details widespread Chinese military use of powder for propulsion and also in incendiary devices and flamethrowers since at least AD 1000. Moreover, the Chinese also developed and used rockets with fifty and more projectiles, including two-stage rockets whose second propulsion was ignited after the first stage was in the air. Originally, the rocket launchers were stationary, but then they were made mobile as well. Europeans did not put gunpowder to military use until the late thirteenth century, and then only after they had themselves been victimized by the same in the eastern Mediterranean. Similarly, the Chinese and the Japanese also rapidly adopted and adapted advanced foreign gun technology, as Geoffrey Parker (1991) describes:

> Firearms, fortresses, standing armies, and warships had long been part of the military tradition of China, Korea, and Japan. Indeed, both bronze and iron artillery were fully developed in China before the spread westward to Europe around 1300. However . . . by 1500 the iron and bronze guns of Western manufacture – whether made by Turkish or Christian founders – proved to be more powerful and more mobile than those of the East. . . . they attracted both attention and imitation [when] they may have arrived in China as early as the 1520s, perhaps with one of the numerous Ottoman diplomatic missions to the Ming Court. . . . For most Chinese, Western-style firearms were first encountered in the hands of pirates operating from Japan against Fukien in the late 1540s. . . . European weaponry was adopted on China's northern frontier before 1635.
>
> (Parker 1991: 185, 186)

European "superiority," if any, was limited to naval gunnery and then only temporarily. It may be true, as Governor-General Coen observed in 1614 that "trade cannot be maintained without war, nor war without trade" (cited in Tracy 1991: 180). However, Coen was Dutch, and he was trying to establish control in some small Indonesian islands, where doing so seemed a relatively practical proposition. Yet even there, the Dutch – like the Portuguese before them – never managed to impose economic monopoly control over the spice trade. If and when Europeans had any superiority in land-based military technology, it was not and could not be effectively used anywhere in Asia – without its being immediately copied and adapted. One of the reasons sometimes adduced for the relatively limited European incursions in Asia has been that (in distinction to the Americas and later in Africa) they were militarily incapable of penetrating inland beyond a few coastal ports. That may be true. However, although Tracy (1991) and his contributors like Parker (1991) try to revive this "explanation," it unjustifiably leaves the much greater strength of most Asian economies out of account. Moreover, as is still true today when nuclear arms do not remain a monopoly for long, any and all armaments technology was rapidly diffused to anyone in a position to pay for it.

Ships

Shipbuilding was certainly among the "high-technology" industries of sixteenth-century Europe (Pacey 1990: 72). Yet, no one questions the fact that in earlier centuries Chinese ships were bigger, better, far more numerous, and traveled farther. One case in point is Zheng He's commercial fleets to Africa in the early 1400s. These fleets used much bigger and many times more ships than did either Columbus or Vasco da Gama (who, almost a century later, had to hire an Arab navigator). Another case is the comparison between the Mongol/Chinese fleet that attacked Japan in 1274 and the Spanish "Invincible" armada sent against Britain in 1588. Both were defeated by weather rather than by the defenders, but the Chinese one had over 2,000 ships and the Spanish one 132.

Did European ships outstrip the Chinese, especially after the institution of the official Ming policy to turn away from the sea? The conventional European answer in the affirmative is far from certain. Needham (1964) examines navigation in his fourth volume, which Ronan (1986) summarizes. They quote a European observer who argued in 1669 that "there are more Vessels in China than in all the rest of the known World. This will seem incredible to many Europeans"; but the observer goes on to explain why he is certain of his numbers (Ronan 1986: 89). Also cited in Needham's massive survey and Ronan's summary are various seventeenth- and eighteenth-century European navigators and sailors who register their astonishment at the quality of Chinese ships. In addition there are cataloged a whole series of Chinese nautical, navigational, propulsion, steering, and equipment technologies that matched or were better than, *and* that were being copied and adapted by, other contemporaries. These innovations included the shape of the hull, its compartmentalization into watertight sections, and pumping mechanisms both for bailing water out and for dousing shipboard fires caused in battle. Needham sums up with the following:

> the conclusion that this indicates a clear technical superiority of Chinese seamanship seems almost unavoidable. . . . All that our analysis indicates is that European seamanship probably owes far more than has been generally supposed to the contributions of the sea-going peoples of East and Southeast Asia. One would be ill-advised to undervalue [them].
>
> (Ronan 1986: 210, 272)

Indeed, the Spaniards bought ships in the Philippines and also had their own maintained and repaired there, using technology and workmanship that antedated their arrival (Pacey 1990: 65–68, 123–28). The British East India Company and its servants did the same, although to a lesser extent (Barendse 1997: chap. 1).

The evidence is inescapable that the same is true with regard to South Asian shipbuilders. Unlike Chinese and European shipbuilders, Indian ones did not use iron nails to secure the planks in their oceangoing ships. If only because of the shortage and expense of iron, Indians adopted this technology only sparingly, although they did adopt foreign technology where advisable (Sangwan 1995: 139). They used fiber ties and caulking instead. For that and other reasons, Indian-built ships were more durable, as Europeans of the day certified, praising the quality of Indian-built ships – see for example the quotes in Qaisar (1982: 22) and Sangwan (1995: 140). Moreover, Europeans bought many Indian-built ships for their own use, both because they were more durable and because they were cheaper than European ones, approximately 1,000 pound sterling less for a 500-ton ship in 1619 (Qaisar 1982: 22).

The British East India Company also maintained its own shipyards in Bombay (to which it recruited shipwrights from Surat), building large ships there and elsewhere in India after 1736. The Portuguese and then the Dutch had already done the same before the British;

indeed, Amsterdam protected its own shipbuilding industry by prohibiting Dutch purchase of large ships in India. Shipbuilding costs in India were 30 to 50 percent lower than in Portugal, Holland, and Britain. Moreover, Indian-built ships were better suited for the waters of the Indian Ocean, where their useful life was double and triple that of European-built ships (Barendse 1997: chap. 1). In the last two decades of the eighteenth century, the British EIC *and* the Royal Navy commissioned at least 70 ships to be built there and in the first two decades of the nineteenth century about 300. A contemporary observed:

> We do find many reasons inducing us to build the shipping in this country, where tymber, iron worke, carpenters are very cheape. The building [is] farre more substantial than in England, and more proper for these parts, in regard they will require noe sheeting and chalking more than the decks.
>
> (quoted in Barendse 1997: chap. 1)

Sarpal Sangwan (1995: 140) concludes that "India-built ships of this period were of equal quality, if not superior, to ships built anywhere in the world." Edmond Gosse concurs: "there would be no exaggeration in averring that they build incomparably the best ships in the world" (quoted in Barendse 1997: chap. 1). However, they were less likely to be equipped with guns, though even that increased as competition demanded. To discourage pirates, some Indian ships were built to look like more heavily armored European ships (Barendse 1997: chap. 1). In short, as Pacey observes:

> Asia was thus characterized by superior manufacturing technologies. . . . Some Indian [shipbuilding] techniques were distinctly better than those of their European counterparts by the early eighteenth century. . . . It is striking how eagerly Indians and Europeans learned from each other. . . . The dependence of Europeans on Indian and Filipino shipbuilders is thus part of a pattern in which westerners exploited Asian knowledge and skill.
>
> (Pacey 1990: 67–69)

Despite his skepticism about Indian technology in general, even Habib (1969: 15–16) concedes that India experienced "what is practically an unchronicled revolution" in shipbuilding, which was in some respects superior to that of Europe. Nonetheless, he insists that it did not eliminate the lag he claims it had.

There can be no doubt that Asians also used and adapted European shipbuilding techniques and navigational skills and even personnel. That only shows that in the competitive navigation industry as in various others technological progress and development was worldwide and world-driven economically. Moreover, "as long as there was an 'alternative' or 'appropriate' indigenous technology which could serve the needs of Indians to a reasonable degree, the European counterpart was understandably passed over" (Qaisar 1982: 139).

Printing

Printing is of particular interest not only as an important industry per se, but also as a service industry for the transmission of knowledge, including of course of science and technology, as well as a reflection of some degree of cultural "rationality" and social "openness." It is therefore significant that wood-block printing was invented and used in China up to half a millennium earlier than elsewhere. Color printing began in China in 1340, and five-color printing was in use there in the 1580s and widespread (certainly far more than in the West) in both China and Japan in the seventeenth and eighteenth centuries. Movable metal type came from Korea and was soon introduced elsewhere, though not into the Islamic world for a long time. In China, as Brook (1998) suggests, printing may not have changed much in the strictest technical sense. However, economically and socially speaking, printing, publishing, and literacy expanded enormously and surely had much more widespread effects than in Europe – including even the counterfeiting of paper money until the Ming withdrew it from circulation.

Textiles

A main locus of the industrial revolution of course was the textile industry. We have already observed the Chinese, Persian, and Bengali world economic preeminence in silk and Indian predominance in cotton. They were the highest-quality and lowest-cost producers in the manufacturing industries, competing even more successfully worldwide than in armaments and shipbuilding. As was noted above, textile production also had widespread linkages to the agricultural, machinery, transportation, vegetable dye and mineral-derived chemical industries, not to mention finance. To be a high-quality/low-cost producer and seller of textiles, competitive production in and coordination among all these ancillary industries was necessary. India excelled in all of them.

Moreover, it could not do so by standing still but only by maintaining its competitiveness through continued technological progress and cost reduction. It maintained a competitive lead for at least the four centuries between 1400 and 1800. India also imported new technologies, particularly for dyeing, as well as skilled workmen from Ottoman and Persian sources. A Mughal book listed seventy-seven different processes for producing forty-five shades of color. India also exchanged new technology in the porcelain industry with China and Persia. The British in turn copied their fundamental dyeing techniques from India (Chapman 1972: 12).

Curiously, Habib (1969) denigrates Indian technology and denies its progress even in textiles, although he concedes that there was no built-in resistance to technological change. Yet Vijaya Ramaswamy (1980) examined some evidence regarding particular textile techniques mentioned by Habib and reported that they had been introduced in India long before Habib supposed. Ramaswamy concludes:

> it would be quite erroneous to speak of technological development, at least in the [Indian] textile industry, as having been in spurts and as the result of external agents . . . or [imported] from Europe in the sixteenth–seventeenth centuries. Skill specialization and low labour costs were far from being the only merits of the Indian industry and, as has been demonstrated at some length, there was a gradual development in indigenous textile technology although it was interspersed with certain imported techniques.
>
> (Ramaswamy 1980: 241)

There can or should be no doubt that in the world's most competitive industry, textiles, the choices offered to consumers as well as the selection of the techniques of production anywhere in the world were adopted and were changed in reference to those everywhere else in the world. The incentives for the industrial revolution in Britain, particularly in the textile industry, are further examined [elsewhere].

Suffice it in this regard here to quote Pacey (who in turn is citing Braudel):

> Labour was plentiful in the Indian textile areas and wages were low. There was little incentive, therefore, for Indian merchants to mechanize production. As Braudel puts it, the incentive "worked the other way round." New machines were invented in Britain to try to equal Indian cloth both in cheapness and quality, and there were transfers of dyeing

techniques. . . . Processes which had been in used for centuries in India, Iran and Turkey were extended quite rapidly [in Britain] with many new applications.

(Pacey 1990: 121, 120)

[. . .] [L]ike any Newly Industrializing Economy in East Asia today, Britain began its own industrialization through import substitution for the domestic market by protectionism and other stimulation of the domestic cotton textile industry. Then, Britain proceeded to export promotion to the world market. By 1800, four out of seven pieces of cotton cloth produced in Britain were exported (Stearns 1993: 24); these in turn accounted for one-fourth of all British exports – and for one-half by 1850 (Braudel 1992: 572).

Metallurgy, Coal, and Power

European superiority is widely alleged especially in metallurgy and the associated mining of coal and its use for fuel and mechanical power (including the use of mechanical power in mining coal). To begin with, this development was primarily part and parcel of the industrial revolution only since the nineteenth century. Up through most of the eighteenth century, no one used much coal. As long as charcoal was still widely available and cheap, there was little incentive to replace it by more costly coal, and all the less so in those regions, especially in South Asia, where coal was not readily available. In Britain, the price of charcoal rose significantly during the first half of the eighteenth century while the price of coal dropped until by mid century it became cheaper to smelt iron with coal than charcoal (Braudel 1992: 569).

The Chinese also had coal, and if they mined it less; it was presumably for cost calculations and surely not for lack of appropriate technology. For the Chinese had long since developed and excelled in all sorts of analogous hydraulic engineering and other technology used in the construction and maintenance of their extensive canal system and other public works. Unfortunately for the Chinese and unlike Britain however, ample deposits of coal in China were located very far from the centers of its potential industrial use, as Pomeranz (1997) emphasizes. Moreover, their wood-fueled iron metallurgy had long been centuries ahead of everybody else.

Steel-making was also highly developed in Japan, India, and Persia in the sixteenth and seventeenth centuries. Indeed, there are several accounts of British import of samples of Indian *wootz* steel, which specialized British laboratories found equal to that of Sweden and superior to any made in Britain in 1790. Moreover, among the ten thousand Indian furnaces at the end of the eighteenth century, many still produced comparable iron and steel both faster (in two and a half hours instead of four) and cheaper than the British did in Sheffield (Dharampal 1971, Kuppuram and Kumudamani 1990).

Mechanical devices, also containing metal parts, were developed and put to use where abundant human labor was not cheaper. Watermills were in use in China, India, and Persia; and they supplied power for a variety of irrigation, agricultural, industrial, and other uses. Many regions in Asia excelled in irrigation and other improvements as well as in the clearing and development of agricultural land. Particularly significant for productivity in agriculture was the early development in India and widespread use of the drill plow.

[. . .] [P]roductivity, and by implication appropriate technology, in agriculture was certainly as "advanced" in China and India as anywhere in Europe. Asians were certainly able to feed more people (per hectare of available arable land); and [. . .] southern Chinese agriculture was more efficient than any in Europe.

Transport

Russel Menard (1991: 274) looks for a possible "European transport revolution" between the fourteenth and eighteenth centuries and concludes that there was none. Freight charges hardly fell, and it was cheaper goods, including those from Asia, rather than lower transport costs that made goods more accessible. At the same time, transportation, both by water and overland and also with reliance on mechanical devices, was well developed in many parts of Asia. Pomeranz (1997) can find no European advantages over Asia in overland transport in general and specifically finds that ton miles estimated by Habib for India exceed those estimated by Werner Sombart (1967) for Germany by more than five times in total number and are possibly only a little less per capita.

In 1776, Adam Smith (1937: 637–8) compared Chinese and Indian canal and fluvial low-cost transport with that in Europe and declared the former superior. Asian use of substantial human labor in transport was economical given its availability. However, infrastructural investment in ports, canals, roads, caravanserai, and their maintenance and protection was also large and to all intents and purposes efficient and competitive within China, India, Central Asia, Persia, and in the Ottoman Empire. "International" transport across and around Asia was all the more so developed and competitive; and as we observe again and again [elsewhere], Europeans took advantage of and benefited from this "development" through their own participation.

In short, it is far from established, as is so often supposed, that European "technological superiority" can be dated from 1500 onward. Comparisons of European and Asian technologies certainly cast more than doubt on this Eurocentric thesis.

World technological development

However, this thesis about European superiority is even more doubtful on two other and more important grounds. One is that, as we have noted, there could be no such superiority in Europe or any one other place, if only because of the very substantial diffusion of technology back and forth. This happened through the purchase or theft of items containing technology; their copy and adaptation; the transfer of productive processes and organization through both voluntary and forced (by slavery) displacement and engagement of skilled craftsmen, engineers, and nautical personnel; through publication; and through industrial espionage.

Moreover, to permit increased output and export Asians also needed and fomented technological development. Thus, the fifteenth and early sixteenth centuries witnessed not only growing production and export in China, but also significant increases in productivity and technological progress to support that export production. This occurred especially in the ceramics, silk, and cotton industries, the printing and publishing industry (where copper/lead alloys for casting movable characters were developed), sugar manufacturing, and both irrigated and dry agriculture (including the processing of agricultural products and the introduction of new crops from the Americas). There can be no doubt that India also developed improved technology and increased productivity in the sixteenth and seventeenth centuries, especially in the textile and arms industries, where competition required and stimulated the same.

The other and still more important reason that casts even more than doubt on the thesis of European technological superiority is derivative from the above observations: there was no *European* technology! In the worldwide division of labor in a competitive world economy, national, regional, or sectoral technological superiority could not be maintained as long as at least some other real or potential competitors had sufficient interest and capacity to acquire such technology as well. That is, technological development was a *world economic process*, which took place in and because of the structure of the world economy/system itself. It is true that this world economy/system was and still is structurally unequal and temporally uneven. However, it is not true that technological or any other "development" was essentially determined either locally, regionally, nationally, or culturally; nor that any one place or people had any essential "monopoly" or even "superiority" within this world economy/system. Still less was or is it the case [. . .] that any alleged "superiority" was based on "exceptional" institutions, culture, civilization, or race!

NOTE

* This chapter has been adapted from, Frank, A. G. 1998. "The Global Economy: Comparisons and Relations." Chap. 4 in *ReOrient: Global Economy in the Asian Age*. Berkeley and Los Angeles: University of California Press.

REFERENCES

Adams, Robert McC. 1996. *Paths of Fire: An Anthropologist's Inquiry into Western Technology*. Princeton: Princeton University Press.

Arasaratnam Sinnappah. 1986. *Merchants, Companies and the Commerce of the Coromandel Coast 1650–1740*. Delhi: Oxford University Press.

Arnold, David. 1983. *The Age of Discovery 1400–1600*. London: Methuen.

Bairoch, Paul. 1993. *Economics and World History. Myths and Paradoxes*. Hempel Hempstead, U.K.: Harvester/Wheatsheaf.

——. 1997. *Victoires et déboires II. Histoire économique et sociale du monde du XVIe siècle à nos jours*. Paris: Gallimard.

Bairoch, Paul, and Maurice Levy-Leboyer, eds. 1981. *Disparities in Economic Development since the Industrial Revolution*. London: Macmillan.

Barendse, Rene. 1997. "The Arabian Seas 1640–1700." Unpublished manuscript.

Bennett, M. K. 1954. *The World's Food. A Study of the Interrelations of World Populations, National Diets, and Food Potentials*. New York: Harper.

Bernal, J. D. 1969. *Science in History*. Harmondsworth, England: Penguin.

Bernal, J. D. 1997. "Eight Eurocentric Historians." Chap. 2 in "Decolonizing the Past: Historians and the Myth of European Superiority." Unpublished manuscript.

Boswell, Terry, and Joya Misra. 1995. "Cycles and Trends in the Early Capitalist World-Economy: An Analysis of Leading Sector Commodity Trades 1500–1600/50–1750." *Review* 18, no. 3: 459–86.

Braudel, Fernand. 1991. *The Perspective of the World*. Vol. 3 of *Civilization and Capitalism 15th–18th Century*. Berkeley and Los Angeles: University of California Press.

Brenning, Joseph, A. 1990. "Textile Producers and Production in Late Seventeenth Century Coromandel." In *Merchants, Markets and the State in Early Modern India*, edited by Sanjay Subrahmanyam, 66–89. Delhi: Oxford University Press.

Brook, Timothy, ed. 1998. *The Confusions of Pleasure. A History of Ming China (1368–1644)*. Berkeley and Los Angeles: University of California Press.

Burton, Audrey. 1993. *Bukharan Trade 1558–1718*. Papers on Inner Asia No. 23. Bloomington: Indiana University Institute for Inner Asian Studies.

Carr-Saunders A. M. 1936. *World Population. Past Growth and Present Trends*. Oxford: Clarendon Press.

Chapman, S. D. 1972. *The Cotton Industry in the Industrial Revolution*. London: Macmillan.

Chaudhuri, K.-N. 1978. *The Trading World of Asia and the East India Company 1660–1760*. Cambridge: Cambridge University Press.

——. 1990. *Asia before Europe. Economy and Civilisation of the Indian Ocean from the Rise of Islam to 1750*. Cambridge: Cambridge University Press.

Cipolla, Carlo M. 1967. *Cañones y Velas. La Primera Fase de la Expansión Europea 1400–1700*. Barcelona: Ariel.

——. 1976. *Before the Industrial Revolution. European Society and Economy, 1000–1700*. London: Methuen.

Clark, Colin. 1977. *Population Growth and Land Use*. London: Macmillan.

Cohen, H. Floris. 1994. *The Scientific Revolution. A Historiographic Inquiry*. Chicago: University of Chicago Press.

Crombie, A. C. 1959. *Science in the Later Middle Ages and Early Modern Times: XIII–XVII Centuries*. Vol. 2 of *Medieval and Early Modern Science*. New York: Doubleday.

Das Gupta, Ashin. 1979. *Indian Merchants and the Decline of Surat: c. 1700–1750*. Wiesbaden: Steiner.

Das Gupta, Ashin, and M. N. Pearson, eds. 1987. *India and the Indian Ocean 1500–1800*. Calcutta: Oxford University Press.

Dharampal. 1971. *Indian Science and Technology in the Eighteenth Century. Some Contemporary European Accounts*. Delhi: Impex India.

Durand, John D. 1967. "The Modern Expansion of World Population." *Proceedings of the American Philosophical Society* 3, no. 3: 140–2.

——. 1974. *Historical Estimates of World Population: An Evaluation*. Philadelphia: University of Pennsylvania Population Studies Center.

Goody, Jack. 1996. *The East in the West*. Cambridge: Cambridge University Press.

Grant, Jonathan. 1996. "Rethinking the Ottoman 'Decline': Military Technology Diffusion in the Ottoman Empire 15th–18th Centuries." Paper presented at the World History Association meeting in Pomona, Calif., June 20–22.

Habib, Irfan. 1969. "Potentialities of Capitalistic Development in the Economy of Mughal India." *Journal of Economic History* 29, no. 1 (March): 13–31.

——. 1990. "The Merchant Communities in Pre-Colonial India." In *The Rise of the Merchant Empires. Long-Distance Trade in the Early Modern World, 1350–1750*, edited by James D. Tracy, 371–99. Cambridge: Cambridge University Press.

al-Hassan, Ahmand Y., and Donald R. Hill. 1986. *Islamic Technology. An Illustrated History*. Cambridge and Paris: Cambridge University Press and UNESCO.

Ho Ping-ti. 1959. *Studies on the Population of China, 1308–1953*. Cambridge: Harvard University Press.

Holtfrerich, Carl-Ludwig, ed. 1989. *Interaction in the World Economy, Perspectives from International Economic History*. London: Harvester.

Jones, E. C. 1988. *Growth Recurring. Economic Change in World History*. Oxford: Clarendon Press.

Klein, Peter W. 1989. "The China Seas and the World Economy between the Sixteenth and Nineteenth Centuries: The Changing Structures of World Trade." In *Interaction in the World Economy. Perspectives from International Economic History*, edited by Carl-Ludwig Holtfrerich, 61–89. London: Harvester.

Kollman, Wolfgang. 1965. *Bevölkerung und Raum in Neuerer and Neuester Zeit* (Population and Space in Recent and Contemporary Time). Würzburg.

Kuppuram, G., and K. Kumudamani. 1990. *History of Science and Technology in India*. Delhi: Sundeep Prakashan.

Livi-Bacci, Massimo. 1992. *A Concise History of World Population*. Cambridge, Mass., and Oxford: Blackwell.

Lourido, Rui D'Avila. 1996. "European Trade between Macao and Siam, from its Beginnings to 1663." Florence: European University Institute. Unpublished manuscript.

Mackensen, Rainer, and Heinze Wewer, eds. 1973. *Dynamik der Bevölkerungsentwicklung* (Dynamic of Population Development). München: Hanser Verlag.

MacLeod, Roy, and Deepak Kumar, eds. 1995. *Technology and the Raj. Western Technology and Technical Transfers to India, 1700–1947*. New Delhi: Sage.

Maddison, Angus. 1991. *Dynamic Forces in Capitalist Development. Long-run Comparative View*. Oxford: Oxford University Press.

Marks, Robert B. 1997. *Tigers, Rice, Silk and Silt. Environment and Economy in Late Imperial South China*. New York: Cambridge University Press. Cited from manuscript.

McNeill, William. 1989. *The Age of Gunpowder Empires 1450–1800*. Washington, D.C.: American Historical Association.

Meilink-Roelofsz, M. A. P. 1962. *Asian Trade and European Influence in the Indonesian Archipelago between 1500 and about 1630*. The Hague: Martinus Nijhoff.

Menard, Russel. 1991. "Transport Costs and Long-Range Trade, 1300–1800: Was There a European 'Transport Revolution' in the Early Modern Era?" In *Political Economy of Merchant Empires*, edited by James D. Tracy, 228–75. Cambridge: Cambridge University Press.

Moreland, W H. 1936. *A Short History of India*. London: Longmans, Green.

Mukund, Kanakalatha. 1992. "Indian Textile Industry in the 17th and 18th Centuries. Structure, Organisation, Responses." *Economic and Political Weekly*, 19 September: 2057–65.

Nasr, S. H. 1976. *Islamic Science*. World of Islam Festival.

Needham, Joseph. 1954. *Science and Civilization in China*. Cambridge: Cambridge University Press.

——. 1964. "Science and China's Influence on the World." In *The Legacy of China*, edited by Raymond Dawson. Oxford: Clarendon Press.

——. 1981. *Science in Traditional China. A Comparative Perspective*. Hong Kong: The Chinese University Press.

Pacey, Arnold. 1990. *Technology in World Civilization*. Oxford: Basil Blackwell.

Palat, Ravi Arvind, and Immanuel Wallerstein. 1990. "Of What World System Was Pre-1500 'India' a Part?" Paper presented at the International Colloquium on Merchants, Companies and Trade, Maison des Sciences de l'Homme, Paris, 30 May–2 June, 1990. Revision to be published in *Merchants, Companies and Trade*, edited by S. Chaudhuri and M. Morineau. Forthcoming.

Parker, Geoffrey. 1991. "Europe and the Wider World, 1500–1750: The Military Balance." In *The Political Economy of Merchant Empires*, edited by James D. Tracy, 161–95. Cambridge: Cambridge University Press.

Pearson, M. N. 1987. *The Portuguese in India*. Cambridge: Cambridge University Press.

——. 1989. *Before Colonialism. Theories on Asian-European Relations 1500–1750*. Delhi: Oxford University Press.

Perlin, Frank. 1993. *'The Invisible City'. Monetary, Administrative and Popular Infrastructure in Asia and Europe 1500–1900*. Aldershot, U.K.: Variorum.

Pomeranz, Kenneth. 1997. "A New World of Growth: Markets, Ecology, Coercion, and Industrialization in Global Perspective" Unpublished manuscript.

Prakash, Om. 1994. *Precious Metals and Commerce*. Aldershot. U.K.: Variorum.

——. 1995. *Asia and the Pre-modern World Economy*. Leiden: International Institute for Asian Studies.

Qaisar. Ahsan Jan. 1982. *The Indian Response to European Technology and Culture (AD 1498–1707)*. Delhi: Oxford University Press.

Rahman, Abdur, ed. 1984. *Science and Technology in Indian Culture – A Historical Perspective*. New Delhi: National Institute of Science, Technology and Development Studies.

Ramaswamy, Vijaya. 1980. "Notes on the Textile Technology in Medieval India with Special Reference to the South." *The Indian Economic and Social History Review* 17, no. 2: 227–42.

Raychaudhuri, Tapan, and Irfan Habib, eds. 1982. *The Cambridge Economic History of India*. Vol. 1: *c. 1220–c.1750*. Cambridge: Cambridge University Press.

Ronan, Colin A. 1986. *The Shorter Science and Civilization in China. An Abridgment of Joseph Needham's Original Text*. Vol. 3. Cambridge: Cambridge University Press.

Rosenberg, Nathan, and L. E. Birdzell, Jr. 1986. *How the West Grew Rich. The Economic Transformation of the Industrial World*. New York: Basic Books.

——. 1975. *How it all Began: Origins of the Modern Economy*. New York: McGraw-Hill.

Roy Aniruddha, and S. K. Bagchi. 1986. *Technology in Ancient and Medieval India*. Delhi: Sundeep Prakashan.

Rozman, Gilbert, ed. 1981. *The Modernization of China*. New York: The Free Press.

Saliba, George. 1996. "Arab Influences on the Renaissance." Paper at the Fifth Annual Conference of the World Historical Association, Pomona, Calif., June 21.

Sanderson, Stephen K., ed. 1995. *Civilizations and World Systems. Studying World-Historical Change*. Walnut Creek, Calif.: Altamira.

Sangwan, Satpal. 1995. "The Sinking Ships: Colonial Policy and the Decline of Indian Shipping, 1735–1835." In *Technology and the Raj. Western Technology and Technical Transfers to India, 1700–1947*, edited by Roy MacLeod and Deepak Kumar. New Delhi: Sage.

Shapin, Steve. 1996. *Scientific Revolution*. Chicago: University of Chicago Press.

Singer, Charles et al., eds. 1957. *A History of Technology*. Vols. 2 and 3. Oxford: The Clarendon Press.

Sivin, N. 1982. "Why the Scientific Revolution Did Not Take Place in China – Or Didn't It?" *Explorations in the History of Science and Technology in China. Compiled in Honour of the 80th Birthday of Dr. J. Needham*. Shanghai. Also in *Chinese Science* 5: 45–66; *Transformation and Tradition in the Sciences*, edited by Everett Mendlesohn, 531–54 (Cambridge: Cambridge University Press, 1984); and *Science in Ancient China. Researches and Reflections* (Aldershot, U.K.: Variorum, 1995).

Sombart, Werner. 1967. *Luxury and Capitalism*. Ann Arbor: University of Michigan Press.

Smith, Adam [1776] 1937. *The Wealth of Nations*. New York: Random House.

Stearns, Peter N. 1993. *The Industrial Revolution in World History*. Boulder: Westview Press.

Steensgaard, Niels. 1972. *Carracks, Caravans and Companies: The Structural Crisis in the European-Asian Trade in the Early 17th Century*. Copenhagen: Studentlitteratur.

——. 1987. "The Indian Ocean Network and the Emerging World-Economy (c. 1550 to 1750)." In *The Indian Ocean: Explorations in History, Commerce, and Politics*, edited by S. Chandra, 125–50. New Delhi: Sage.

——. 1990d. "The Growth and Composition of the Long-Distance Trade of England and the Dutch Republic before 1750." In *The Rise of the Merchant Empires. Long-Distance Trade in the Early Modern World, 1350–1750*, edited by James D. Tracy, 102–52. Cambridge: Cambridge University Press.

Subrahmanyam, Sanjay. 1990a. *The Political Economy of Commerce. Southern India 1500–1650*. Cambridge: Cambridge University Press.

Subrahmanyam, Sanjay, ed. 1990b. *Merchants, Markets and the State in Early Modern India*. Delhi: Oxford University Press.

The Times Illustrated History of the World. 1995. Edited by Geoffrey Parker. New York: Harper Collins.

Tracy, James D., ed. 1991. *The Political Economy of Merchant Empires*. Cambridge: Cambridge University Press.

van Leur, J. C. 1955. *Indonesian Trade and Society: Essays in Asian Social and Economic History*. The Hague and Bandung: W. van Hoeve.

Wallerstein, Immanuel. 1989. *The Modern World-System*. Vol. 3, *The Second Era of Great Expansion of the Capitalist World-Economy 1730–1840s*. New York: Academic Press.

Willcox, Walter F. 1931. *International Migrations*. Vol. 2. New York: National Bureau of Economic Research.

——. 1940. *Studies in American Demography*. Ithaca: Cornell University Press.

2

THE BRITISH INDUSTRIAL REVOLUTION*

Eric Hobsbawm

Such works, however their operations, causes, and consequences, have infinite merit, and do great credit to the talents of this very ingenious and useful man, who will have the merit, wherever he goes, of *setting men to think*. . . . Get rid of that dronish, sleepy, and stupid indifference, that lazy negligence, which enchains men in the exact paths of their forefathers, without enquiry, without thought, and without ambition, and you are sure of doing good. What trains of thought, what a spirit of exertion, what a mass and power of effort have sprung in every path of life, from the works of such men as Brindley, Watt, Priestley, Harrison, Arkwright. . . . In what path of life can a man be found that will not animate his pursuit from seeing the steam-engine of Watt?

(Arthur Young, *Tours in England and Wales*[1])

From this foul drain the greatest stream of human industry flows out to fertilize the whole world. From this filthy sewer pure gold flows. Here humanity attains its most complete development and its most brutish, here civilization works its miracles and civilised man is turned almost into a savage.

(A. de Tocqueville on Manchester in 1835[2])

I

Let us begin with the Industrial Revolution, that is to say with Britain. This is at first sight a capricious starting-point, for the repercussions of this revolution did not make themselves felt in an obvious and unmistakable way – at any rate outside England – until quite late in our period; certainly not before 1830, probably not before 1840 or thereabouts. It is only in the 1830s that literature and the arts began to be overtly haunted by that rise of the capitalist society, that world in which all social bonds crumbled except the implacable gold and paper ones of the cash nexus (the phrase comes from Carlyle). Balzac's *Comédie Humaine*, the most extraordinary literary monument of its rise, belongs to that decade. It is not until about 1840 that the great stream of official and unofficial literature on the social effects of the Industrial Revolution begins to flow: the major Bluebooks and statistical enquiries in England, Villermé's *Tableau de l'état physique et moral des ouvriers*, Engels'

Condition of the Working Class in England, Ducpetiaux's work in Belgium, and scores of troubled or appalled observers from Germany to Spain and the USA. It was not until the 1840s that the proletariat, that child of the Industrial Revolution, and Communism, which was now attached to its social movements – the spectre of the Communist Manifesto – walked across the continent. The very name of the Industrial Revolution reflects its relatively tardy impact on Europe. The thing existed in Britain before the word. Not until the 1820s did English and French socialists – themselves an unprecedented group – invent it, probably by analogy with the political revolution of France.[3]

Nevertheless it is as well to consider it first, for two reasons. First, because in fact it 'broke out' – to use a question-begging phrase – before the Bastille was stormed; and second because without it we cannot understand the impersonal groundswell of history on which the more obvious men and events of our period were borne; the uneven complexity of its rhythm.

What does the phrase 'the Industrial Revolution broke out' mean? It means that some time in the 1780s, and for the first time in human history, the shackles were taken off the productive power of human societies, which henceforth became capable of the constant, rapid and up to the present limitless multiplication of men, goods and services. This is now technically known to the economists as the 'take-off into self-sustained growth'. No previous society had been able to break through the ceiling which a pre-industrial social structure, defective science and technology, and consequently periodic breakdown, famine and death, imposed on production. The 'take-off' was not, of course, one of those phenomena which, like earthquakes and large meteors, take the non-technical world by surprise. Its pre-history in Europe can be traced back, depending on the taste of the historian and his particular range of interest, to about AD 1000, if not before, and earlier attempts to leap into the air, clumsy as the experiments of young ducklings, have been flattered with the name of 'industrial revolution' – in the thirteenth century, in the sixteenth, in the last decades of the seventeenth. From the middle of the eighteenth century the process of gathering speed for the take-off is so clearly observable that older historians have tended to date the Industrial Revolution back to 1760. But careful enquiry has tended to lead most experts to pick on the 1780s rather than the 1760s as the decisive decade, for it was then that, so far as we can tell, all the relevant statistical indices took that sudden, sharp, almost vertical turn upwards which marks the 'take-off'. The economy became, as it were, airborne.

To call this process the Industrial Revolution is both logical and in line with a well-established tradition, though there was at one time a fashion among conservative historians – perhaps due to a certain shyness in the presence of incendiary concepts – to deny its existence, and substitute instead platitudinous terms like 'accelerated evolution'. If the sudden, qualitative and fundamental transformation, which happened in or about the 1780s, was not a revolution then the word has no commonsense meaning. The Industrial Revolution was not indeed an episode with a beginning and an end. To ask when it was 'complete' is senseless, for its essence was that henceforth revolutionary change became the norm. It is still going on; at most we can ask when the economic transformations had gone far enough to establish a substantially industrialized economy, capable of producing, broadly speaking, anything it wanted within the range of the available techniques, a 'mature industrial economy' to use the technical term. In Britain, and therefore in the world, this period of initial industrialization probably coincides almost exactly with the period with which this book deals, for if it began with the 'take-off' in the 1780s, it may plausibly be said to be concluded with the building of the railways and the construction of a massive heavy industry in Britain in the 1840s. But the Revolution itself, the 'take-off period', can probably be dated with as much precision as is possible in such matters, to some time within the twenty years from 1780 to 1800: contemporary with, but slightly prior to, the French Revolution.

By any reckoning this was probably the most important event in world history, at any rate since the invention of agriculture and cities. And it was initiated by Britain. That this was not fortuitous, is evident. If there was to be a race for pioneering the Industrial Revolution in the eighteenth century, there was really only one starter. There was plenty of industrial and commercial advance, fostered by the intelligent and economically far from naïve ministers and civil servants of every enlightened monarchy in Europe, from Portugal to Russia, all of whom were at least as much concerned with 'economic growth' as present-day administrators. Some small states and regions did indeed industrialize quite impressively for example, Saxony and the bishopric of Liège, though their industrial complexes were too small and localized to exert the world-revolutionary influence of the British ones. But it seems clear that even before the revolution Britain was already a long way ahead of her chief potential competitor in *per capita* output and trade, even if still comparable to her in total output and trade.

Whatever the British advance was due to, it was not scientific and technological superiority. In the natural sciences the French were almost certainly ahead of the British; an advantage which the French Revolution accentuated very sharply, at any rate in mathematics and physics, for it encouraged science in France while reaction suspected it in England. Even in the social sciences the British were still far from that superiority which made – and largely kept – economics a pre-eminently Anglo-Saxon subject; but here the Industrial Revolution put them into unquestioned first place. The economist of the 1780s would read Adam Smith, but also – and perhaps more profitably – the French physiocrats and national income accountants, Quesnay, Turgot, Dupont de Nemours, Lavoisier, and perhaps an Italian or two. The French produced more original inventions, such as the Jacquard loom (1804) – a more complex piece of apparatus than any devised in Britain – and better ships. The Germans possessed institutions of technical training like the Prussian *Bergakademie* which had no parallel in Britain, and the French Revolution created that unique and impressive body, the *Ecole Polytechnique*. English education was a joke in poor taste, though its deficiencies were somewhat offset by the dour village schools and the austere, turbulent, democratic universities of Calvinist Scotland which sent a stream of brilliant, hard-working, career-seeking and rationalist young men into the south country: James Watt, Thomas Telford, London McAdam, James Mill. Oxford and Cambridge, the only two English universities, were intellectually null, as were the somnolent public or grammar schools, with the exception of the Academies founded by the Dissenters who were excluded from the (Anglican) educational system. Even such aristocratic families as wished their sons to be educated, relied on tutors or Scottish universities. There was no system of primary education whatever before the Quaker Lancaster (and after him his Anglican rivals) established a sort of voluntary mass-production of elementary literacy in the early nineteenth century, incidentally saddling English education forever after with sectarian disputes. Social fears discouraged the education of the poor.

Fortunately few intellectual refinements were necessary to make the Industrial Revolution.[4] Its technical inventions were exceedingly modest, and in no way beyond the scope of intelligent artisans experimenting in their workshops, or of the constructive capacities of carpenters, millwrights and locksmiths: the flying shuttle, the spinning jenny, the mule. Even its scientifically most sophisticated machine, James Watt's rotary steam-engine (1784), required no more physics than had been available for the best part of a century – the proper *theory* of steam engines was only developed *ex post facto* by the Frenchman Carnot in the 1820s – and could build on several generations of practical employment for steam engines, mostly in mines. Given the right conditions, the technical innovations of the Industrial Revolution practically made themselves, except perhaps in the chemical industry. This does not mean that early industrialists were not often interested in science and on the look-out for its practical benefits.[5]

But the right conditions were visibly present in Britain, where more than a century had passed since the first king had been formally tried and executed by his people, and since private profit and economic development had become accepted as the 'supreme objects of government policy. For practical purposes the uniquely revolutionary British solution of the agrarian problem had already been found. A relative handful of commercially-minded landlords already almost monopolized the land, which was cultivated by tenant farmers employing landless or smallholders. A good many relics of the ancient collective economy of the village still remained to be swept away by Enclosure Acts (1760–1830) and private transactions, but we can hardly any longer speak of a 'British peasantry' in the same sense that we can speak of a French, German or Russian peasantry. Farming was already predominantly for the market; manufacture had long been diffused throughout an unfeudal countryside. Agriculture was already prepared to carry out its three fundamental functions in an era of industrialization: to increase production and productivity, so as to feed a rapidly rising non-agricultural population; to provide a large and rising surplus of potential recruits for the towns and industries; and to provide a mechanism for the accumulation of capital to be used in the more modern sectors of the economy. (Two other functions were probably less important in Britain: that of creating a sufficiently large market among the agricultural population – normally the great mass of the people – and of providing an export surplus which helps to secure capital imports.) A considerable volume of social overhead capital – the expensive general equipment necessary for the entire economy to move smoothly ahead – was already being created, notably in shipping, port facilities, and the improvement of roads and waterways. Politics were already geared to profit. The businessman's specific demands might encounter resistance from other vested interests; and as we shall see, the agrarians were to erect one last barrier to hold up the advance of the industrialists between 1795 and 1846. On the whole, however, it was accepted that money not only talked, but governed. All the industrialist had to get to be accepted among the governors of society was enough money.

The businessman was undoubtedly in the process of getting more money, for the greater part of the eighteenth century was for most of Europe a period of prosperity and comfortable economic expansion; the real background to the happy optimism of Voltaire's Dr Pangloss. It may well be argued that sooner or later this expansion, assisted by a gentle inflation, would have pushed some country across the threshold which separates the pre-industrial from the industrial economy. But the problem is not so simple. Much of eighteenth-century industrial expansion did not in fact lead immediately, or within the foreseeable future, to industrial *revolution*, i.e. to the creation of a mechanized 'factory system' which in turn produces in such vast quantities and at such rapidly diminishing cost, as to be no longer dependent on existing demand, but to create its own market.[6] For instance the building trade, or the numerous small scale industries producing domestic metal goods – nails, pots, knives, scissors, etc. – in the British Midlands and Yorkshire, expanded very greatly in this period, but always as a function of the existing market. In 1850, while producing far more than in 1750, they produced in substantially the old manner. What was needed was not any kind of expansion, but the special kind of expansion which produced Manchester rather than Birmingham.

Moreover, the pioneer industrial revolutions occurred in a special historical situation, in which economic growth emerges from the criss-crossing decisions of countless private entrepeneurs and investors, each governed by the first commandment of the age, to buy in the cheapest market and to sell in the dearest. How were they to discover that maximum profit was to be got out of organizing industrial revolution rather than out of more familiar (and in the past more profitable) business activities? How were they to learn, what nobody could as yet know, that industrial revolution would produce an unexampled acceleration in the expansion of their markets? Given that the main social foundations of an industrial society had already been laid, as they almost certainly had in the England of the later eighteenth century, they required two things: first, an industry which already offered exceptional rewards for the manufacturer who could expand his output quickly, if need be by reasonably cheap and simple innovations, and second, a *world* market largely monopolized by a single producing nation.[7, 8]

These considerations apply in some ways to all countries in our period. For instance, in all of them the lead in industrial growth was taken by the manufacturers of goods of mass consumption – mainly, but not exclusively, textiles[9] – because the mass market for such goods already existed, and businessmen could clearly see its possibilities of expansion. In other ways, however, they apply to Britain alone. For the pioneer industrialists have the most difficult problems. Once Britain had begun to industrialize, other countries could begin to enjoy the benefits of the rapid economic expansion which the pioneer industrial revolution stimulated. Moreover, British success proved what could be achieved by it, British technique could be imitated, British skill and capital imported. The Saxon textile industry, incapable of making its own inventions, copied the English ones, sometimes under the supervision of English mechanics; Englishmen with a taste for the continent, like the Cockerills, established themselves in Belgium and various parts of Germany. Between 1789 and 1848 Europe and America were flooded with British experts, steam engines, cotton machinery and investments.

Britain enjoyed no such advantages. On the other hand it possessed an economy strong enough and a state aggressive enough to capture the markets of its competitors. In effect the wars of 1793–1815, the last and decisive phase of a century's Anglo-French duel, virtually eliminated all rivals from the non-European world, except to some extent the young USA. Moreover, Britain possessed an industry admirably suited to pioneering industrial revolution under capitalist conditions, and an economic conjuncture which allowed it to: the cotton industry, and colonial expansion.

II

The British, like all other cotton industries, had originally grown up as a by-product of overseas trade, which produced its raw material (or rather one of its raw materials, for the original product was *fustian*, a mixture of cotton and linen), and the Indian cotton goods or *calicoes* which won the markets that the European manufacturers were to attempt to capture with their own imitations. To begin with they were not very successful, though better able to reproduce the cheap and coarse goods competitively than the fine and elaborate ones. Fortunately, however, the old-established and powerful vested interest of the woollen trade periodically secured import prohibitions of Indian calicoes (which the purely mercantile interest of the East India Company sought to export from India in the largest possible quantities), and thus gave the native cotton industry's substitutes a chance. Cheaper than wool, cotton and cotton mixtures won themselves a modest but useful market at home. But their major chances of rapid expansion were to lie overseas.

Colonial trade had created the cotton industry, and continued to nourish it. In the eighteenth century it developed in the hinterland of the major colonial ports, Bristol, Glasgow but especially Liverpool, the great centre of the slave trades. Each phase of this inhuman but rapidly expanding commerce stimulated it. In fact, during the entire period [. . .] slavery and cotton marched together. The African slaves were bought, in part at least, with Indian cotton goods; but when the supply of these was interrupted by war or revolt in and about India, Lancashire was able to leap in. The plantations of the West Indies, where the slaves were taken, provided the bulk of the raw cotton for the British industry, and in return the planters bought Manchester cotton checks in appreciable quantities. Until shortly before the 'take-off' the overwhelming bulk of Lancashire cotton exports went to the combined African and American markets.[10] Lancashire was later to repay its debt to slavery by preserving it; for after the 1790s the slave plantations of the Southern United States were extended and maintained by the insatiable and rocketing demands of the Lancashire mills, to which they supplied the bulk of their raw cotton.

The cotton industry was thus launched, like a glider, by the pull of the colonial trade to which it was attached; a trade which promised not only great, but rapid and above all unpredictable expansion, which encouraged the entrepreneur to adopt the revolutionary techniques required to meet it. Between 1750 and 1769 the export of British cottons increased more than ten times over. In such situations the rewards for the man who came into the market first with the most cotton checks were astronomical and well worth the risks of leaps into technological adventure. But the overseas market, and especially within it the poor and backward 'under-developed areas', not only expanded dramatically from time to time, but expanded constantly without apparent limit. Doubtless any given section of it, considered in isolation, was small by industrial standards, and the competition of the different 'advanced economies' made it even smaller for each. But, as we have seen, supposing any one of the advanced economies managed, for a sufficiently long time, to monopolize *all* or almost all of it, then its prospects really were limitless. This is precisely what the British cotton industry succeeded in doing, aided by the aggressive support of the British Government. In terms of sales, the Industrial Revolution can be described except for a few initial years in the 1780s as the triumph of the export market over the home: by 1814 Britain exported about four yards of cotton cloth for every three used at home, by 1850 thirteen for every eight.[11] And within this expanding export market, in turn, the semi-colonial and colonial markets, long the main outlets for British goods abroad, triumphed. During the Napoleonic Wars, when the European markets were largely cut off by wars and blockades, this was natural enough. But even after the wars they continued to assert themselves. In 1820 Europe, once again open to free British imports, took 128 million yards of British cotton; America outside the USA, Africa and Asia took 80 millions; but by 1840 Europe took 200 million yards, while the 'under-developed' areas took 529 millions.

For within these areas British industry had established a monopoly by means of war; other people's revolutions and her own imperial rule. Two regions deserve particular notice. *Latin America* came to depend virtually entirely on British imports during the Napoleonic Wars, and after it broke with Spain and Portugal [. . .] it became almost an economic dependency of Britain, being cut off from any political interference by Britain's potential European competitors. By 1820 this impoverished continent already took more than a quarter as much of British cotton cloths as Europe; by 1840 it took almost half as much again in Europe. The East Indies had been, as we have seen, the traditional exporter of cotton goods, encouraged by the East India Company. But as the industrialist vested interest prevailed in Britain, the East India mercantile interests (not to mention the Indian ones) were pressed back. India was systematically deindustrialized and became in turn a market for Lancashire cottons: in 1820 the subcontinent took only 11 million yards; but by 1840 it already took 145 million yards. This was not merely a gratifying extension of Lancashire's markets. It was a major landmark in world history. For since the dawn of time Europe had always imported more from the East than she had sold there; because there was little the Orient required from the West in return for the spices, silks, calicoes, jewels, etc., which it sent there. The cotton shirtings of the Industrial Revolution for the first time reversed this relationship, which had been hitherto kept in balance by a mixture of bullion exports and robbery. Only the conservative and self-satisfied Chinese still refused to buy what the West, or western-controlled economies offered, until between 1815 and 1842 western traders, aided by western gun-boats, discovered an ideal commodity which could be exported *en masse* from India to the East: opium.

Cotton therefore provided prospects sufficiently astronomical to tempt private entrepreneurs into the adventure of industrial revolution, and an expansion sufficiently sudden to require it. Fortunately it also provided the other conditions which made it possible. The new inventions which revolutionized it – the spinning jenny, the water-frame, the mule in spinning, a little later the power-loom in weaving – were sufficiently simple and cheap, and paid for themselves almost immediately in terms of higher output. They could be installed, if need be piecemeal, by small men who started off with a few borrowed pounds, for the men who controlled the great accumulations of eighteenth-century wealth were not greatly inclined to invest large amounts in industry. The expansion of the industry could be financed easily out of current profits, for the combination of its vast market conquests and a steady price inflation produced fantastic rates of profit. 'It was not five per cent or ten per cent,' a later English politician was to say, with justice, 'but hundreds per cent and thousands per cent that made the fortunes of Lancashire.' In 1789 an ex-draper's assistant like Robert Owen could start with a borrowed £100 in Manchester; by 1809 he bought out his partners in the New Lanark Mills for £84,000 *in cash*. And his was a relatively modest story of business success. It should be remembered that around 1800 less than 15 per cent of British families had an income of more than £50 per year, and of these only one-quarter earned more than £200 a year.[12]

But the cotton manufacture had other advantages. All its raw material came from abroad, and its supply could therefore be expanded by the drastic procedures open to white men in the colonies – slavery and the opening of new areas of cultivation – rather than by the slower procedures of European agriculture; nor was it hampered by the vested interests of European agriculturists.[13] From the 1790s on British cotton found its supply, to which its fortunes remained linked until the 1860s, in the newly-opened Southern States of the USA. Again, at crucial points of manufacture (notably spinning) cotton suffered from a shortage of cheap and efficient labour, and was therefore pushed into mechanization. An industry like *linen*, which had initially rather better chances of colonial expansion than cotton, suffered in the long run from the very ease with which cheap, non-mechanized production could be expanded in the impoverished peasant regions (mainly in Central Europe, but also in Ireland) in which it mainly flourished. For the *obvious* way of industrial expansion in the eighteenth century, in Saxony and Normandy as in England, was not to construct factories, but to extend the so-called 'domestic' or 'putting-out' system, in which workers – sometimes former independent craftsmen, sometimes former peasants with time on their hands in the dead season – worked up the raw material in their own homes, with their own or rented tools, receiving it from and delivering it back to merchants who were in the process of becoming employers.[14] Indeed, both in Britain and in the rest of the economically progressive world, the bulk of expansion in the initial period of industrialization continued to be of this kind. Even in the cotton industry such processes as weaving were expanded by creating hosts of domestic handloom weavers to serve the nuclei of mechanized spinneries, the primitive handloom being a rather more efficient device than the spinning-wheel. Everywhere weaving was mechanized a generation after spinning, and everywhere, incidentally, the handloom weavers died a lingering death, occasionally revolting against their awful fate, when industry no longer had any need for them.

III

The traditional view which has seen the history of the British Industrial Revolution primarily in terms of cotton is thus correct. Cotton was the first industry to be revolutionized, and it is difficult to see what other could have pushed a host of private entrepreneurs into revolution. As late as the 1830s cotton was the only British industry in which the factory or 'mill' (the name was derived from the most widespread pre-industrial establishment employing heavy power-operated machinery) predominated; at first (1780–1815) mainly in spinning, carding and a few ancillary operations, after 1815 increasingly also in weaving. The 'factories' with which the new Factory Acts dealt were, until the 1860s, assumed to be exclusively textile factories and predominantly cotton mills. Factory production in other textile branches was slow to develop before the 1840s, and in other manufactures was negligible. Even the steam engine, though applied to numerous other industries by 1815, was not used in any quantity outside mining, which had pioneered it. In 1830 'industry' and 'factory' in anything like the modern sense still meant almost exclusively the cotton areas of the United Kingdom.

This is not to underestimate the forces which made for industrial innovation in other consumer goods, notably in other textiles,[15, 16] in food and drink, in pottery and other household goods, greatly stimulated by the rapid growth of cities. But in the first place these employed far fewer people: no industry remotely approached the million-and-a-half people directly employed by or dependent on employment in cotton in 1833.[17] In the second place their power to transform was much smaller: *brewing*, which was in most respects a technically and scientifically much more advanced and mechanized business, and one revolutionized well before cotton, hardly affected the economy around it, as may be proved by the great Guinness brewery in Dublin, which left the rest of the Dublin and Irish economy (though not local tastes) much as it was before its construction.[18] The demand derived from cotton – for more building and all activities in the new industrial areas, for machines, for chemical improvements, for industrial lighting, for shipping and a number of other activities – is itself enough to account for a large proportion of the economic growth in Britain up to the 1830s. In the third place, the expansion of the cotton industry was so vast and its weight in the foreign trade of Britain so great, that it dominated the movements of the entire economy. The quantity of raw cotton imported into Britain rose from 11 million lb. in 1785 to 588 million lb. in 1850; the output of cloth from 40 million to 2,025 million yards.[19] Cotton manufactures formed between 40 and 50 per cent of the annual declared value of *all* British exports between 1816 and 1848. If cotton flourished, the economy flourished; if it slumped, so did the economy. Its price movements determined the balance of the nation's trade. Only agriculture had a comparable power, and that was visibly declining.

Nevertheless, though the expansion of the cotton industry and the cotton-dominated industrial economy 'mocks all that the most romantic imagination could have previously conceived possible under any circumstances',[20] its progress was far from smooth, and by the 1830s and early 1840s produced major problems of growth, not to mention revolutionary unrest unparalleled in any other period of recent British history. This first general stumbling of the industrial capitalist economy is reflected in a marked slowing down in the growth, perhaps even in a decline, in the British national income at this period.[21] Nor was this first general capitalist crisis a purely British phenomenon.

Its most serious consequences were social: the transition to the new economy created misery and discontent, the materials of social revolution. And indeed, social revolution in the form of spontaneous risings of the urban and industrial poor did break out, and made the revolution of 1848 on the continent, the vast Chartist movement in Britain. Nor was discontent confined to the labouring poor. Small and inadaptable businessmen, petty-bourgeois, special sections of the economy, were also the victims of the Industrial Revolution and of its ramifications. Simple-minded labourers reacted to the new system by smashing the machines which they thought responsible for their troubles; but a surprisingly large body of local businessmen and farmers sympathized profoundly with these Luddite activities of their labourers, because they too saw themselves as victims of a diabolical minority of selfish innovators. The exploitation of labour which kept its incomes at subsistence level, thus enabling the rich to accumulate the profits which financed industrialization (and their own ample comforts), antagonized the proletarian. However, another aspect of this diversion of national income from the poor to the rich, from consumption to investment, also antagonized the small entrepreneur. The great financiers, the tight community of home and foreign 'fund-holders' who received what all paid in taxes [. . .] – something like 8 per cent of the entire national income[22] – were perhaps even more unpopular among small businessmen, farmers and the like than among labourers, for these knew enough about money and credit to feel a personal rage at their disadvantage. It was all very well for the rich, who could raise all the credit they needed, to clamp rigid deflation and monetary orthodoxy on the economy after the Napoleonic Wars; it was the little man who suffered, and who, in all countries and at all times in the nineteenth century demanded easy credit and financial unorthodoxy.[23] Labour and the disgruntled petty-bourgeois on the verge of toppling over into the unpropertied abyss, therefore shared common discontents. These in turn united them in the mass movements of 'radicalism', 'democracy' or 'republicanism' of which the British Radicals, the French Republicans and the American Jacksonian Democrats were the most formidable between 1815 and 1848.

From the point of view of the capitalists, however, these social problems were relevant to the progress of the economy only if, by some horrible accident, they were to overthrow the social order. On the other hand there appeared to be certain inherent flaws of the economic process which threatened its fundamental motive-force: profit. For if the rate of return on capital fell to nothing, an economy in which men produced for profit only must slow down into that 'stationary state' which the economists envisaged and dreaded.[24]

The three most obvious of these flaws were the trade cycle of boom and slump, the tendency of the rate of profit to decline, and (what amounted to the same thing) the shortage of profitable investment opportunities. The first of these was not regarded as serious, except by the critics of capitalism as such, who were the first to investigate it and to consider it as an integral part of the capitalist economic process and as a symptom of its inherent contradictions.[25] Periodic crises of the economy leading to unemployment, falls in production, bankruptcies, etc. were well known. In the eighteenth century they generally reflected some agrarian catastrophe (harvest failures, etc.) and on the continent of Europe, it has been argued, agrarian disturbances remained the primary cause of the most widespread depressions until the end of our period. Periodic crises in the small manufacturing and financial sectors of the economy were also familiar, in Britain at least from 1793. After the Napoleonic Wars the periodic drama of boom and collapse – in 1825–6, in 1836–7, in 1839–42, in 1846–8 – clearly dominated the economic life of a nation at peace. By the 1830s, that crucial decade in our period of history, it was vaguely recognized that they were regular periodic phenomena, at least in trade and finance.[26] However, they were still commonly regarded by businessmen as caused either by particular mistakes – e.g. overspeculation in American stocks – or by outside interference with the smooth operations of the capitalist economy. They were not believed to reflect any fundamental difficulties of the system.

Not so the falling margin of profit, which the cotton industry illustrated very clearly. Initially this industry benefited from immense advantages. Mechanization greatly increased the productivity (i.e. reduced the cost per unit produced) of its labour, which was in any case abominably paid, since it consisted largely of women and children.[27] Of the 12,000 operatives in the cotton mills of Glasgow in 1833, only 2,000 earned an average of over 11s. a week. In 131 Manchester mills average wages were less than 12s., in only twenty-one were they higher.[28] And the building of factories was relatively cheap: in 1846 an entire weaving plant of 410 machines, including the cost of ground and buildings, could be constructed for something like £11,000.[29] But above all the major cost, that of raw material, was drastically cut by the rapid expansion of cotton cultivation in the Southern USA after the invention of Eli Whitney's cotton-gin in 1793. If we add that entrepreneurs enjoyed the bonus of a profit-inflation (i.e. the general tendency for prices to be higher when they sold their product than when they made it), we shall understand why the manufacturing classes felt buoyant.

After 1815 these advantages appeared increasingly offset by the narrowing margin of profit. In the first place industrial revolution and competition brought about a constant and dramatic fall in the price of the finished article but not in several of the costs of production.[30] In the second place after 1815 the general atmosphere of prices was one of deflation and not inflation, that is to say profits, so far from enjoying an extra boost, suffered from a slight lag. Thus, while in 1784 the selling-price of a pound of spun yarn had been 10s. 11d., the cost of its raw material 2s. (margin, 8s.11d.), in 1812 its price was 2s. 6d., its raw material cost 1s. 6d. (margin 1s.) and in 1832 its price 11¼d., its raw material cost 7½d., and the margin for other costs and profits therefore only 4d.[31] Of course the situation, which was general throughout British – and indeed all advanced – industry, was not too tragic. 'Profits are still sufficient', wrote the champion and historian of cotton in 1835, in extreme understatement, 'to allow of a great accumulation of capital in the manufacture.'[32] As the total sales soared upwards, so did the total of profits even at their diminishing rate. All that was needed was continued and astronomic expansion. Nevertheless, it seemed that the shrinking of profit-margins had to be arrested or at least slowed down. This could only be done by cutting costs. And of all the costs *wages* – which McCulloch reckoned at three times the amount per year of the raw material – were the most compressible.

They could be compressed by direct wage-cutting, by the substitution of cheaper machine-tenders for dearer skilled workers, and by the competition of the machine. This last reduced the average weekly wage of the handloom weaver in Bolton from 33s. in 1795 to 14s. in 1815 to 5s. 6d. (or more precisely a net income of 4s. 1½d.) in 1829–34.[33] And indeed money wages fell steadily in the post-Napoleonic period. But there was a physiological limit to such reductions, unless the labourers were actually to starve, as of course the 500,000 handloom weavers did. Only if the cost of living fell could wages also fall beyond that point. The cotton manufacturers shared the view that it was kept artificially high by the monopoly of the landed interest, made even worse by the heavy protective tariffs which a Parliament of landlords had wrapped around British farming after the wars – the *Corn Laws*. These, moreover, had the additional disadvantage of threatening the essential growth of British exports. For if the rest of the not yet industrialized world was prevented from selling its agrarian products, how was it to pay for the manufactured goods which Britain alone could – and had to – supply? Manchester business therefore became the centre of militant and increasingly desperate opposition to landlordism in general and the Corn Laws in particular, and the backbone of the Anti-Corn Law League of 1838–46. But the Corn Laws were not abolished until 1846, their abolition did not immediately lead to a fall in the cost of living, and it is doubtful whether before the age of railways and steamers even free food-imports would have greatly lowered it.

The industry was thus under immense pressure to mechanize (i.e. to lower costs by labour-saving), to rationalize and to expand its production and sales, thus making up by the mass of small profits per unit for the fall in the margins. Its success was variable. As we have seen, the actual rise in production and exports was gigantic; so, after 1815, was the mechanization of hitherto manual or partly-mechanized occupations, notably weaving. This took the form chiefly of the general adoption of existing or slightly improved machinery rather than of further technological revolution. Though the pressure for technical innovation increased significantly – there were thirty-nine new patents in cotton spinning, etc. in 1800–20, fifty-one in the 1820s, eighty-six in the 1830s and a hundred and fifty-six in the 1840s[34] – the British cotton industry was technologically stabilized by the 1830s. On the other hand, though the production per operative increased in the post-Napoleonic period, it did not do so to any revolutionary extent. The really substantial speed-up of operations was to occur in the second half of the century.

There was comparable pressure on the rate of interest on capital, which contemporary theory tended to assimilate to profit. But consideration of this takes us to the next phase of industrial development – the construction of a basic capital-goods industry.

IV

It is evident that no industrial economy can develop beyond a certain point until it possesses adequate capital-goods capacity. This is why even today the most reliable single index of any country's industrial potential is the quantity of its iron and steel production. But it is also evident that under conditions of private enterprise the extremely costly capital investment necessary for much of this development is not likely to be undertaken for the same reasons as the industrialization of cotton or other consumer goods. For these a mass market already exists, at least potentially: even very primitive men wear shirts or use household equipment and foodstuffs. The problem is merely how to put a sufficiently vast market sufficiently quickly within the purview of businessmen. But no such market exists, e.g. for heavy iron equipment such as girders. It only comes into existence in the course of an industrial revolution (and not always then), and those who lock up their money in the very heavy investments required even by quite modest ironworks (compared to quite large cotton-mills) before it is visibly there, are more likely to be speculators, adventurers and dreamers than sound businessmen. In fact in France a sect of such speculative technological adventurers, the Saint-Simonians [. . .] , acted as chief propagandists of the kind of industrialization which needed heavy and long-range investment.

These disadvantages applied particularly to metallurgy, especially of iron. Its capacity increased, thanks to a few simple innovations such as that of puddling and rolling in the 1780s, but the non-military demand for it remained relatively modest, and the military, though gratifyingly large thanks to a succession of wars between 1756 and 1815, slackened off sharply after Waterloo. It was certainly not large enough to make Britain into an outstandingly large producer of iron. In 1790 she out-produced France by only forty per cent or so, and even in 1800 her output was considerably less than half of the combined continental one, and amounted to the, by later standards, tiny figure of a quarter of a million tons. If anything, the British share of world iron output tended to sink in the next decades.

Fortunately they applied less to mining, which was chiefly the mining of *coal*. For coal had the advantage of being not merely the major source of industrial power in the nineteenth century, but also a major form of domestic fuel, thanks largely to the relative shortage of forests in Britain. The growth of cities, and especially of London, had caused coal mining to expand rapidly since the late sixteenth century. By the early eighteenth it was substantially a primitive modern industry, even employing the earliest steam engines (devised for similar purposes in non-ferrous metal mining, mainly in Cornwall) for pumping. Hence coal mining hardly needed or underwent major technological revolution in our period. Its innovations were improvements rather than transformations of production. But its capacity was already immense and, by world standards, astronomic. In 1800 Britain may have produced something like ten million tons of coal, or about 90 per cent of the world output. Its nearest competitor, France, produced less than a million.

This immense industry, though probably not expanding fast enough for really massive industrialization on the modern scale, was sufficiently large to stimulate the basic invention which was to transform the capital goods industries: the railway. For the mines not only required steam engines in large quantities and of great power, but also required efficient means of transporting the great quantities of coal from coalface to shaft and especially from pithead to the point of shipment. The 'tramway' or 'railway' along which trucks ran was an obvious answer; to pull these trucks by stationary engines was tempting; to pull them by moving engines would not seem too impractical. Finally, the costs of overland transport of bulk goods were so high that it was likely to strike coal-owners in inland fields that the use of these short-term means of transport could be profitably extended for long-term haulage. The line from the inland coalfield of Durham to the coast (Stockton–Darlington 1825) was the first of the modern railways. Technologically the railway is the child of the mine, and especially the northern English coalmine. George Stephenson began life as a Tyneside 'engineman', and for years virtually all locomotive drivers were recruited from his native coalfield.

No innovation of the Industrial Revolution has fired the imagination as much as the railway, as witness the fact that it is the only product of nineteenth-century industrialization which has been fully absorbed into the imagery of popular and literate poetry. Hardly had they been proved technically feasible and profitable in England (*c.* 1825–30), before plans to build them were made over most of the Western world, though their execution was generally delayed. The first short lines were opened in the USA in 1827, in France in 1828 and 1835, in Germany and Belgium in 1835 and even in Russia by 1837. The reason was doubtless that no other invention revealed the power and speed of the new age to the layman as dramatically; a revelation made all the more striking by the remarkable technical maturity of even the very earliest railways. (Speeds of up to sixty miles per hour, for instance, were perfectly practicable in the 1830s, and were not substantially improved by later steam-railways.) The iron road, pushing its huge smoke-plumed snakes at the speed of wind across countries and continents, whose embankments and cuttings, bridges and stations, formed a body of public building beside which the pyramids and the Roman aqueducts and even the Great Wall of China paled into provincialism, was the very symbol of man's triumph through technology.

In fact, from an economic point of view, its vast expense was its chief advantage. No doubt in the long run its capacity to open up countries hitherto cut off by high transport costs from the world market, the vast increase in the speed and bulk of overland communication it brought for men and goods were to be of major importance. Before 1848 they were economically less important: outside Britain because railways were few, in Britain because for geographical reasons transport problems were much less intractable than in large landlocked countries.[35] But from the perspective of the student of economic development the immense appetite of the railways for iron and steel, for coal, for heavy machinery, for labour, for capital investment, was at this stage more important. For it provided just that massive demands which was needed if the capital goods industries were to be transformed as profoundly as the cotton industry had been. In the first two decades of the railways (1830–50) the output of iron in Britain rose from 680,000 to 2,250,000, in other words its trebled. The output of coal between 1830 and 1850 also trebled from 15 million tons to 49 million tons. That dramatic rise was due primarily to the railway, for on average each mile of line required 300 tons of iron merely for track.[36] The industrial advances which for the first time made the mass production of steel possible followed naturally in the next decades.

The reason for this sudden, immense, and quite essential expansion lay in the apparently irrational passion with which businessmen and investors threw themselves into the construction of railways. In 1830 there were a few dozen miles of railways in all the world – chiefly consisting of the line from Liverpool to Manchester. By 1840 there were over 4,500 miles, by 1850 over 23,500. Most of them were projected in a few bursts of speculative frenzy known as the 'railway manias' of 1835–7 and especially in 1844–7; most of them were built in large part with British capital, British iron, machines and know-how.[37] These investment booms appear irrational, because in fact few railways were much more profitable to the investor than other forms of enterprise, most yielded quite modest profits and many none at all: in 1855 the average interest on capital sunk in the British railways was a mere

3.7 per cent. No doubt promoters, speculators and others did exceedingly well out of them, but the ordinary investor clearly did not. And yet by 1840 £28 millions, by 1850 £240 millions had been hopefully invested in them.[39]

Why? The fundamental fact about Britain in the first two generations of the Industrial Revolution was that the comfortable and rich classes accumulated income so fast and in such vast quantities as to exceed all available possibilities of spending and investment. (The annual investable surplus in the 1840s was reckoned at about £60 millions.[40]) No doubt feudal and aristocratic societies would have succeeded in throwing a great deal of this away in riotous living, luxury building and other uneconomic activities.[41] Even in Britain the sixth Duke of Devonshire, whose normal income was princely enough, succeeded in leaving his heir £1,000,000 of debts in the mid-nineteenth century (which he paid off by borrowing another £1,500,000 and going in for the development of real estate values).[42] But the bulk of the middle classes, who formed the main investing public, were still savers rather than spenders, though by 1840 there are many signs that they felt sufficiently wealthy to spend *as well as* to invest. Their wives began to turn into 'ladies', instructed by the handbooks of etiquette which multiply about this period, their chapels began to be rebuilt in ample and expensive styles, and they even began to celebrate their collective glory by constructing those shocking town halls and other civic monstrosities in Gothic and Renaissance imitations, whose exact and Napoleonic costs their municipal historians recorded with pride.[43]

Again, a modern socialist or welfare society would no doubt have distributed some of these vast accumulations for social purposes. In our period nothing was less likely. Virtually untaxed, the middle classes therefore continued to accumulate among the hungry populace; whose hunger was the counterpart of their accumulation. And as they were not peasants, content to hoard their savings in woollen stockings or as golden bangles, they had to find profitable investment for them. But where? Existing industries, for instance, had become far too cheap to absorb more than a fraction of the available surplus for investment: even supposing the size of the cotton industry to be doubled, the capital cost would absorb only a part of it. What was needed was a sponge large enough to hold all of it.[45]

Foreign investment was one obvious possibility. The rest of the world – mostly, to begin with, old governments seeking to recover from the Napoleonic Wars and new ones borrowing with their usual dash and abandon for indeterminate purposes – was only too anxious for unlimited loans. The English investor lent readily. But alas, the South American loans which appeared so promising in the 1820s, the North American ones which beckoned in the 1830s, turned only too often into scraps of worthless paper: of twenty-five foreign government loans sold between 1818 and 1831, sixteen (involving about half of the £42 millions at issue prices) were in default in 1831. In theory these loans should have paid the investor 7 or 9 per cent; in fact in 1831 he received an average of 3.1 per cent. Who would not be discouraged by experiences such as those with the Greek 5 per cent loans of 1824 and 1825 which did not begin to pay any interest at all until the 1870s?[46] Hence it is natural that the capital flooding abroad in the speculative booms of 1825 and 1835–7, should seek an apparently less disappointing employment.

John Francis, looking back on the mania from 1851, described the rich man who:

saw the accumulation of wealth, which with an industrial people always outstrips the ordinary modes of investment, legitimately and justly employed . . . He saw the money which in his youth had been thrown into war loans and in his manhood wasted on South American mines, forming roads, employing labour and increasing business. [The railway's] absorption of capital was at least an absorption, if unsuccessful, in the country that produced it. Unlike foreign mines and foreign loans, they could not be exhausted or utterly valueless.[47]

Whether it could have found other forms of home investment – for instance in building – is an academic question to which the answer is still in doubt. In fact it found the railways, which could not conceivably have been built as rapidly and on as large a scale without this torrent of capital flooding into them, especially in the middle 1840s. It was a lucky conjuncture, for the railways happened to solve virtually all the problems of the economy's growth at once.

V

To trace the impetus for industrialization is only one part of the historian's task. The other is to trace the mobilization and redeployment of economic resources, the adaptation of the economy, and the society which were required to maintain the new and revolutionary course.

The first and perhaps the most crucial factor which had to be mobilized and redeployed was *labour*, for an industrial economy means a sharp proportionate decline in the agricultural (i.e. rural) and a sharp rise in the non-agricultural (i.e. increasingly in the urban) population, and almost certainly (as in our period) a rapid general increase in population. It therefore implies in the first instance a sharp rise in the supply of food, mainly from home agriculture – i.e. an 'agricultural revolution'.[48]

The rapid growth of towns and non-agricultural settlements in Britain had naturally long stimulated agriculture, which is fortunately so inefficient in its pre-industrial forms that quite small improvements – a little rational attention to animal husbandry, crop-rotation, fertilization and the lay-out of farms, or the adoption of new crops – can produce disproportionately large results. Such agricultural change had preceded the industrial revolution and made possible the first stages of rapid population increases, and the impetus naturally continued, though British farming suffered heavily in the slump which followed the abnormally high prices of the Napoleonic Wars. In terms of technology and capital investment the changes of our period were probably fairly modest until the 1840s, the period when agricultural science and engineering may be said to have come of age. The vast increase in output which enabled British farming in the 1830s to supply 98 per cent of the grain for a population between two and three times the mid-eighteenth-century size,[49] was achieved by general adoption of methods pioneered in the earlier eighteenth century, by rationalization and by expansion of the cultivated area.

All these in turn were achieved by social rather than technological transformation, by the liquidation of medieval communal cultivation with its open field and common pasture (the 'enclosure movement'), of self-sufficient peasant farming, and of old-fashioned un-commercial attitudes towards the land. Thanks to the preparatory evolution of the sixteenth to eighteenth centuries this uniquely radical solution of the agrarian problem, which made Britain a country of a few large landowners, a moderate number of commercial tenant farmers and a great number of hired labourers, was achieved with a minimum of trouble, though intermittently resisted not only by the unhappy rural poor but by the traditionalist country gentry. The 'Speenhamland System' of poor relief, spontaneously adopted by gentlemen-justices in several counties in and after the hungry year of 1795, has been seen as the last systematic attempt to safeguard the old rural society against the corrosion of the cash nexus.[50] The Corn Laws with which the agrarian interest sought to protect farming against the post-1815 crisis, in the teeth of all economic orthodoxy, were in part a manifesto against the tendency to treat agriculture as an industry just like any other, to be judged by the criteria of profitability alone. But these were doomed rearguard actions against the final introduction of capitalism into the countryside; they were finally defeated in the wave of middle-class radical advance after 1830, by the new Poor Law of 1834 and the abolition of the Corn Laws in 1846.

In terms of economic productivity this social transformation was an immense success; in terms of human suffering, a tragedy, deepened by the agricultural depression after 1815 which reduced the rural poor to demoralizing destitution. After 1800 so enthusiastic a champion of enclosure and agricultural progress as Arthur Young was shaken by its social effects.[51] But from the point of view of industrialization these also were desirable consequences; for an industrial economy needs labour, and where else but from the former non-industrial sector was it to come from? The rural population at home or, in the form of (mainly Irish) immigration, abroad, were the most obvious sources supplemented by the miscellaneous petty producers and labouring poor.[52] Men must be attracted into the new occupations, or if – as was most probable – they were initially immune to these attractions and unwilling to abandon their traditional way of life[53] – they must be forced into it. Economic and social hardship was the most effective whip; the higher money wages and greater freedom of the town the supplementary carrot. For various reasons the forces tending to prise men loose from their historic social anchorage were still relatively weak in our period, compared to the second half of the nineteenth century. It took a really sensational catastrophe such as the Irish hunger to produce the sort of massive emigration (one and a half millions out of a total population of eight and a half millions in 1835–50) which became common after 1850. Nevertheless, they were stronger in Britain than elsewhere. Had they not been, British industrial development might have been as hampered as that of France was by the stability and relative comfort of its peasantry and petty-bourgeoisie, which deprived industry of the required intake of labour.[54]

To acquire a sufficient number of labourers was one thing; to acquire sufficient labour of the right qualifications and skills was another. Twentieth-century experience has shown that this problem is as crucial and more difficult to solve. In the first place *all* labour had to learn how to work in a manner suited to industry, i.e. in a rhythm of regular unbroken daily work which is entirely different from the seasonal ups and downs of the farm, or the self-controlled patchiness of the independent craftsman. It had also to learn to be responsive to monetary incentives. British employers then, like South African ones now, constantly complained about the 'laziness' of labour or its tendency to work until it had earned a traditional week's living wage and then to stop. The answer was found in a draconic labour discipline (fines, a 'Master and Servant' code mobilizing the law on the side of the employer, etc.), but above all in the practice where possible of paying labour so little that it would have to work steadily all through the week in order to make a minimum income [. . .]. In the factories, where the problem of labour discipline was more urgent, it was often found more convenient to employ the tractable (and cheaper) women and children: out of all workers in the English cotton mills in 1834–47 about one-quarter were adult men, over half women and girls and the balance of boys below the age of eighteen.[55] Another common way of ensuring labour discipline, which reflected the small-scale, piecemeal process of industrialization in this early phase, was sub-contract or the practice of making skilled workers the actual employers of their unskilled helpers. In the cotton industry, for instance, about two-thirds of the boys and one-third of the girls were thus 'in the direct employ of operatives' and hence more closely watched, and outside the factories proper such arrangements were even more widespread. The sub-employer, of course, had a direct financial incentive to see that this hired help did not slack.

It was rather more difficult to recruit or train sufficient skilled or technically trained workers, for few pre-industrial skills were of much use in modern industry, though of course many occupations, like building, continued practically unchanged. Fortunately the slow semi-industrialization of Britain in the centuries before 1789 had built up a rather large reservoir of suitable skills, both in textile technique and in the handling of metals. Thus on the continent the locksmith, one of the few craftsmen used to precision work with metals, became the ancestor of the machine-builder and sometimes provided him with a name, whereas in Britain the millwright, and the 'engineer' or 'engineman' (already common in and around mines) did so. Nor is it accidental that the English word 'engineer' describes both the skilled metal-worker and the designer and planner; for the bulk of higher technologists could be, and was, recruited from among these mechanically skilled and self-reliant men. In fact, British industrialization relied on this unplanned supply of the higher skills, as continental industrialism could not. This explains the shocking neglect of general and technical education in this country, the price of which was to be paid later.

Beside such problems of labour supply, those of capital supply were unimportant. Unlike most other European countries, there was no shortage of immediately investable capital in Britain. The major difficulty was that those who controlled most of it in the eighteenth century – landlords, merchants, shippers, financiers, etc. – were reluctant to invest it in the new industries, which therefore had often to be started by small savings or loans and developed by the ploughing back of profits. Local capital shortage made the early industrialists – especially the self-made men – harder, thriftier and more grasping, and their workers therefore correspondingly more exploited; but this reflected the imperfect flow of the national investment surplus and not its inadequacy. On the other hand, the eighteenth-century rich were prepared to sink their money in certain enterprises which benefited industrialization; most notably in transport (canals, dock facilities, roads and later also railways) and in mines; from which landowners drew royalties even when they did not themselves manage them.

Nor was there any difficulty about the technique of trade and finance, private or public. Banks and banknotes, bills of exchange, stocks and shares, the technicalities of overseas and wholesale trade, and marketing, were familiar enough and men who could handle them or easily learn to do so, were in abundant supply. Moreover, by the end of the eighteenth century, government policy was firmly committed to the supremacy of business. Older enactments to the contrary (such as those of the Tudor social code) had long fallen into desuetude, and were finally abolished – except where they touched agriculture – in 1813–35. In theory the laws and financial or commercial institutions of Britain were clumsy and designed to hinder rather than help economic development; for instance, they made expensive 'private acts' of Parliament necessary almost every time men wished to form a joint-stock company. The French Revolution provided the French – and through their influence the rest of the continent – with far more rational and effective machinery for such purposes. In practice the British managed perfectly well, and indeed considerably better than their rivals.

In this rather haphazard, unplanned and empirical way the first major industrial economy was built. By modern standards it was small and archaic, and its archaism still marks Britain today. By the standards of 1848 it was monumental, though also rather shocking for its new cities were uglier, its proletariat worse off, than elsewhere,[56] and the fog-bound, smoke-laden atmosphere in which pale masses hurried to and fro troubled the foreign visitor. But it harnessed the power of a million horses in its steam-engines, turned out two million yards of cotton cloth per year on over seventeen million mechanical spindles, dug almost fifty million tons of coal, imported and exported £170 millions worth of goods in a single year. Its trade was twice that of its nearest competitor, France: in 1780 it had only just exceeded it. Its cotton consumption was twice that of the USA, four times the French. It produced more than half the total pig-iron of the economically developed world, and used twice as much per inhabitant as the next-most industrialized country (Belgium), three times as much as the USA, more than four times as much as France. Between £200 and £300 million of British capital investment – a quarter in the USA, almost a fifth in Latin America – brought back dividends and orders from all parts of the world.[58] It was, in fact, the 'workshop of the world'.

And both Britain and the world knew that the Industrial Revolution launched in these islands by and through the traders and entrepreneurs, whose only law was to buy in the cheapest markets and sell without restriction in the dearest, was transforming the world. Nothing could stand in its way. The gods and kings of the past were powerless before the businessmen and steam-engines of the present.

NOTES

* This chapter has been adapted from, E. Hobsbawm, 'The Industrial Revolution', in E. Hobsbawm (ed.) *The Age of Revolution (1789–1848)*, (London, Abacus Books 1962, Reprinted 1999), pp. 42–72.

1 Arthur Young, *Tours in England and Wales*, London School of Economics edition, p. 269.

2 A. de Tocqueville, *Journeys to England and Ireland*, ed. J. P. Mayer (1958), pp. 107–8.

3 Anna Bezanson, The Early Use of the Term Industrial Revolution, *Quarterly Journal of Economics*, XXXVI, 1921–2, p. 343, G. N. Clark, *The Idea of the Industrial Revolution* (Glasgow 1953).

4 'On the one hand it is gratifying to see that the English derive a rich treasure for their political life, from the study of the ancient authors, however pedantically this might be conducted; so much so that parliamentary orators not infrequently cited the ancients to good purpose, a practice which was favourably received by, and not without effect upon, their Assembly. On the other hand it cannot but amaze us that a country in which the manufacturing tendencies are predominant, and hence the need to familiarize the people with the sciences and arts which advance these pursuits is evident; the absence of these subjects in the curriculum of youthful education is hardly noticed. It is equally astonishing how much is nevertheless achieved by men lacking any formal education for their professions.' W. Wachsmuth, *Europaeische Sittengeschichte* 5, 2 (Leipzig 1839), p. 736.

5 cf. A. E. Musson & E. Robinson, Science and Industry in the late Eighteenth Century, *Economic History Review*, XIII. 2, Dec 1960, and R. E. Schofield's work on the Midland Industrialists and the Lunar Society *Isis* 47 (March 1956), 48 (1957), *Annals of Science* II (June 1956) etc.

6 The modern motor industry is a good example of this. It is not the demand for motor-cars existing in the 1890s which created an industry of the modern size, but the capacity to produce cheap cars which produced the modern mass demand for them.

7 Only slowly did purchasing power expand with population, income per head, transport costs and restraints on trade. But the market was expanding, and the vital question was when would a producer of some mass consumption goods capture enough of it to allow fast and continuous expansion of their production.[8]

8 K. Berrill, International Trade and the Rate of Economic Growth, *Economic History Review*, XII 1960, p. 358.

9 W. G. Hoffmann, *The Growth of Industrial Economies* (Manchester 1958), p. 68.

10 A. P. Wadsworth & J. de L. Mann, *The Cotton Trade and Industrial Lancashire* (1931), chapter VII.

11 F. Crouzet, *Le Blocus Continental et l'Economie Britannique* (1958), p. 63, suggests that in 1805 it was up to two-thirds.

12 P. K. O'Brien, British Incomes and Property in the early Nineteenth Century, *Economic History Review*, XII, 2 (1959), p. 267.

13 Overseas supplies of wool, for instance, remained of negligible importance during our entire period, and only became a major factor in the 1870s.

14 The 'domestic system', which is a universal stage of manufacturing development on the road from home or craft production to modern industry, can take innumerable forms, some of which can come fairly close to the factory. If an eighteenth-century writer speaks of 'manufactures' this is almost invariably and in all western countries what he means.

15 In all countries possessing any kind of marketable manufactures, textiles tended to predominate: in Silesia (1800) they formed 74 per cent of the value of all manufacture.[16]

16 Hoffmann, op. cit., p. 73.

17 Baines, *History of the Cotton Manufacture in Great Britain* (London 1835). p. 431.

18 P. Mathias, *The Brewing Industry in England* (Cambridge 1959).

19 M. Mulhall, *Dictionary of Statistics* (1892), p. 158.

20 Baines, op. cit., p. 112.

21 cf. Phyllis Deane, Estimates of the British National Income, *Economic History Review* (April 1956 and April 1957).

22 O'Brien, op. cit., p. 267.

23 From the post-Napoleonic Radicalism in Britain to the Populists in the USA, all protest movements including farmers and small entrepreneurs can be recognized by their demand for financial unorthodoxy: they were all 'currency cranks'.

24 For the stationary state cf. J. Schumpeter, *History of Economic Analysis* (1954), pp. 570–1. The crucial formulation is John Stuart Mill's (*Principles of Political Economy*, Book IV, chapter iv): 'When a country has long possessed a large production, and a large net income to make saving from, and when, therefore, the means have long existed of making a great annual addition to capital; it is one of the characteristics of such a country, that the rate of profit is habitually within, as it were, a hand's breadth of the minimum, and the country therefore on the very verge of the stationary state. . . . The mere continuance of the present annual increase in capital if no circumstances occurred to counter its effect would suffice in a small number of years to reduce the net rate of profit (to the minimum.)' However, when this was published (1848) the counteracting force – the wave of development induced by the railways – had already shown itself.

25 The Swiss Simonde de Sismondi, and the conservative and country-minded Malthus, were the first to argue along these lines, even before 1825. The new socialists made their crisis-theory into a keystone of their critique of capitalism.

26 By the radical John Wade, *History of the Middle and Working Classes*, the banker Lord Overstone, *Reflections suggested by the perusal of Mr J. Horsley Palmer's pamphlet on the causes and consequences of the pressure on the Money Market* (1837), the Anti-Corn Law campaigner J. Wilson, *Fluctuations of Currency, Commerce and Manufacture; referable to the Corn Laws* (1840); and in France by A. Blanqui (brother of the famous revolutionary) in 1837 and M. Briaune in 1840. Doubtless also by others.

27 E. Baines in 1835 estimated the average wages of all the spinning and weaving operatives at 10s. a week – allowing for two unpaid weeks holiday a year – and of the handloom weavers at 7s.

28 Baines, op. cit., p. 441. A. Ure & P. L. Simmonds, *The Cotton Manufacture of Great Britain* (1861 edition), p. 390 ff.

29 Geo. White, *A Treatise on Weaving* (Glasgow 1846), p. 272.

30 M. Blaug, The Productivity of Capital in the Lancashire Cotton Industry during the Nineteenth Century, *Economic History Review* (April 1961).

31 Thomas Ellison, *The Cotton Trade of Great Britain* (London 1886), p. 61.

32 Baines, op. cit., p. 356.

33 Baines, op. cit., p. 489.

34 Ure & Simmonds, op. cit., Vol. 1, p. 317 ff.

35 No point in Britain is more than 70 miles from the sea, and all the chief industrial areas of the nineteenth century, with one exception, are either on the sea or within easy reach of it.

36 J. H. Clapham, *An Economic History of Modern Britain* (1926), p. 427 ff.; Mulhall, op. cit., pp. 121, 332, M. Robbins, *The Railway Age* (1962), p. 30–1.

37 In 1848 one third of the capital in the French railways was British.[38]

38 Rondo E. Cameron, *France and the Economic Development of Europe 1800–1914* (1961), p. 77.

39 Mulhall, op. cit., 501, 497.

40 L. H. Jenks, *The Migration of British Capital to 1875* (New York and London 1927), p. 126.

41 Of course such spending also stimulates the economy, but very inefficiently, and hardly at all in the direction of industrial growth.

42 D. Spring, The English Landed Estate in the Age of Coal and Iron, *Journal of Economic History*, (XI, I, 1951).

43 A few cities with eighteenth-century traditions never ceased public building; but a typical new industrial metropolis like Bolton in Lancashire built practically no conspicuous and non-utilitarian structures before 1847–8.[44]

44 J. Clegg, *A chronological history of Bolton* (1876).

45 The total capital – fixed and working – of the cotton industry was estimated by McCulloch at £34 millions in 1833, £47 millions in 1845.

46 Albert M. Imlah, British Balance of Payments and Export of Capital, 1816–1913, *Economic History Review V* (1952, 2, p. 24).

47 John Francis, *A History of the English Railway* (1851), 11, 136; see also H. Tuck, *The Railway Shareholder's Manual* (7th edition 1846), Preface, and T. Tooke, *History of Prices II*, pp. 275, 333–4 for the pressure of accumulated Lancashire surpluses into railways.

48 Before the age of railway and the steamship – i.e. before the end of our period – the possibility of importing vast quantities of food from abroad was limited, though Britain became on balance a net importer of food from the 1780s.

49 Mulhall, op. cit., p. 14.

50 Under it the poor were to be guaranteed a living wage by subsidies from the rates where necessary; the system, though well-intentioned, eventually led to even greater pauperization than before.

51 *Annals of Agric.* XXXVI, p. 214.

52 Another view holds that the labour supply comes not from such transfers, but from the rise in the total population, which as we know was increasing very rapidly. But this is to miss the point. In an industrial economy not only the numbers, but the *proportion* of the non-agricultural labour force must increase steeply. This means that men and women who would otherwise have stayed in the village as their forefathers did, *must* move elsewhere at some stage of their lives, for the towns grow faster than their own natural rate of increase, which in any case tended normally to be lower than the villages. This is so whether the farming population actually diminishes, holds its numbers, or even increases.

53 Wilbert Moore, *Industrialisation and Labour* (Cornell 1951).

54 Alternatively, like the USA, Britain would have to rely on massive immigration. In fact she did rely on the immigration of the Irish.

55 Blaug, loc. cit., p. 368. Children under 13, however, declined sharply in the 1830s.

56 'On the whole the condition of the working class seems distinctly worse in England than in France in 1830–48,' concludes a modern historian.[57]

57 H. Sée, *Histoire Economique de la France*, Vol. II, p. 189 n.

58 Mulhall, op. cit.; Imlah, loc. cit., II, 52, pp. 228–9. The precise date of this estimate is 1854.

SECTION 2: ECONOMIC AGENTS

INTRODUCTION

In a market economy, there are three important kinds of decision-makers: households, firms and government. In this section, we examine the role and behaviour of households and firms – the role of government is investigated later in section 4.

Chapter 3, *Households* by Wheelock explores the role of households in a market economy, in particular their role as consumers. She begins by exploring the factors that impact upon the consumption and saving behaviour of households, and then proceeds to investigate in greater depth the various influences on consumer demand for individual commodities. In her analysis, she emphasises both the economic influences on consumer behaviour such as the role of income distribution and price, as well as the socio-cultural influences such as peer pressure, fashion and advertising. With regard to the latter, she refers to the pioneering work of Veblen, Duesenberry and Galbraith, who stressed that consumption is as much a social and cultural process as an economic one. 'Keeping up with the Joneses' and ceremonial consumption to signal wealth, status or success have often been powerful influences on consumption behaviour in many societies throughout history.

Chapter 4, *More on consumer demand* by Atkinson and Miller carries the study of consumer behaviour forward by exploring the concept of elasticity of demand. The elasticity of demand is a measure of the degree to which various factors such as price or income influence the demand for a product. The chapter discusses how one can calculate the various demand elasticities such as price elasticity, income elasticity and cross-elasticity of demand. The concept of demand elasticity has great practical value in business decision making, and the chapter demonstrates how the different measures of demand elasticity can be used to inform business decision making such as in understanding the relationship between a product's price and the revenue generated by selling the product.

Chapter 5, *Organizations* by Costello discusses the nature and functioning of organisations in general and firms in particular. Firms are formal organisations that are responsible for organising a great deal of productive activity in a market economy. Costello begins by exploring the distinction between firms and markets and asking why sometimes firms decide to carry out certain activities internally while in other cases they choose to carry these out via market transactions. He then investigates how firms can efficiently transform inputs into outputs and explores how costs behave as a firm increases the level of production.

Firms, however, cannot simply be viewed as least-cost transformers of inputs into outputs: firms are social organisations that may harbour diverse objectives and cultures. The chapter concludes by looking at some of the issues relating to the varying objectives, structures and cultures that different organisations and firms may possess and pursue.

HOUSEHOLDS*

Jane Wheelock

INTRODUCTION

This chapter looks at how people, and the households they live in, behave as economic agents. The focus is on what we do to live on a day-to-day basis: what economists call 'consumption'. The household is a very important economic institution because it links significant economic activities – consumption, production and distribution - through the activities of its members. Indeed, [. . .] households [are] crucial agents in the circular flow process of the national economy (see Figure 3.1).

It is people in households who make decisions about whether to take work in the labour market or to do unpaid work in the home or elsewhere. Paid work may involve the production of commodities which are sold on the market. Work in the home also maintains women and men in the current workforce. Bringing up children to reproduce a future labour force is work. Decisions about spending are also made by the members of a household; this involves decisions about who is going to get what, and therefore about distribution. The household is thus a significant economic institution whose activities require investigation.

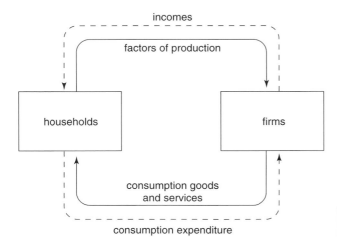

Figure 3.1 Households in the simple circular flow of income

This chapter will look at how people and households behave in individual markets: for example, when they make decisions about buying leaded or unleaded petrol. This is what economists call *micro* level behaviour.

Economists are also interested to see how household behaviour affects activity in the economy in general, at the *macro* level, for example in terms of the total amount of money that is saved or spent in the country.

How people live together in households can vary a lot. For example, the form that the household takes may be culturally specific, and depends on whether the household is in an urban or a rural setting. The form of the household has also changed over the course of history. Furthermore, households have different structures: for example, they may be single-person households or made up of a family with one or two parents, or a group of unrelated people, as with a student household. Households may also have different social characteristics, such as the class, race, gender or generation to which members of the household belong. The economic characteristics of households are what interest economists most: whether the household is rich, poor, in work, retired, unemployed, and so on.

Consumption, and the purchasing power of people in households, depends above all on levels of income. A recurring theme of this chapter is the relationship between spending and the demand for goods and services, and how rich or poor households are. But as I shall try to show throughout this chapter, consumption is a social as well as an economic process. The effects of cigarette advertising on encouraging children to smoke, or the urge to 'keep up with the Joneses' are just two examples of this.

The structure of the chapter is as follows. The next section [. . .] looks at the (macro) behaviour of people and households in the economy as a whole, to gain an understanding of the relationship between income, expenditure and savings. [. . .] The following section moves to the micro level asking why households purchase particular commodities bearing in mind that there are some things which individuals cannot buy on the market, like a clean environment or non-material things such as spiritual fulfilment. [. . .]

THE PERSONAL SECTOR OF THE ECONOMY: INCOME EXPENDITURE AND SAVINGS

The personal sector

In this section I want to examine the behaviour of people and households in the economy as a whole, to gain an understanding of their importance for the macro economy. A useful way to start doing this is by looking at what those concerned with measuring the macro economy call the personal sector, to see its role in economic terms. [We have elsewhere] introduced you to the idea of national income accounting. In national income accounting terms, a sector is an aggregate of economic agents. When we talk about economic agents, the group that most often springs to mind is firms and other organizations which aim to make a profit. What is special about the personal sector is that the households which constitute the overwhelming bulk of the sector are by and large family units. Family units are not primarily formed to make a profit, and so it is often said that their purpose is fundamentally non-economic. This difference in micro-level behaviour is the basis for putting households in a separate sector.

In the national accounts, the personal sector is a complicated aggregate of economic transactors: it is essentially a non-government, non-firm rag-bag. In this section I shall focus on households as by far the most important part of the personal sector. [. . .] [T]he easiest way to understand what the personal sector does in economic terms is to take an overview of the sector as a series of accounts, starting with an income and expenditure account, then looking at the capital account. Table 3.1 does this for the UK. The income and expenditure

Table 3.1 The personal sector in the UK: income, expenditure and savings, 1991 (£m)

(a) Personal sector income and expenditure account

Income before deduction of tax

Income from employment	329 808
Income from self-employment	57 507
Rent, dividends, net interest	56 874
State benefits	71 767
Transfers from overseas, etc.	2 788
Total income	518 744

Expenditure

Consumers' expenditure	367 853
UK taxes on income including social security contributions	111 098
Total current expenditure	478 951
(Unmeasured: social consumption, consumption of the environment)	
Balance on income and expenditure account: savings	39 793

(b) Personal sector capital account

Receipts

Gross savings (from income and expenditure account)	39 793
Capital transfers	3 966

Expenditure

Physical assets, predominantly houses	26 195
Acquisition of financial assets	17 564

Source: United Kingdom National Accounts (1992) Tables 3.1, 4.1, 4.2

account tracks where household incomes come from and what they are spent on. The focus here is on consumption.

When we look at the aggregate behaviour of households, we see that a relatively large proportion of income is not spent, so there is a substantial flow of savings as a balance on the income and expenditure account. It is this flow of savings that is the main source of receipts for the capital account – that is, the 'adding to wealth' account of households. Personal sector savings distribute purchasing power over time through the purchase of physical and financial assets. Housing, superannuation and life assurance are respectively the most significant of these; they are shown as expenditure on the capital account.

Households in the personal sector must have an income before they can spend it, and Table 3.1 indicates hat there are two types of source. First, members of households sell productive services in the market. Some receive wages and salaries from selling their power to work, whether with their manual or intellectual skills; others gain income from self-employment, or from rents, dividends or interest through ownership of property or money capital in whatever form. The largest tranche of household income, 64 per cent in 1991, derives from employment: 11 per cent came from self-employment and 11 per cent from rents, dividends and net interest. The remaining 14 per cent came from the second type of source: transfer payments. These are paid by government as part of the welfare state, and are seen as 'unrequited' payments in that they are not made in respect of an immediate service rendered.

Question

In 1972 wages and salaries made up 69 per cent of household income, income from self-employment 10 per cent, income from rent dividends and interest 10 per cent, and state benefits 11 per cent (*UK National Accounts*, 1980, Table 4.1). Compare these with the 1991 proportions. What do you think are the reasons for the changes in the different sources of household income over these twenty years?

First, unemployment has risen substantially, so wage income has fallen relatively. This also means that more is paid out in state benefits. Furthermore, the post-war downward trend in self-employment has been reversed, at least partly due to the pressure of unemployment.

Personal sector expenditure

As Table 3.1 indicates, there are three main ways in which households use their incomes. Consumer expenditure for day-to-day living uses up by far the largest part - more than two-thirds of income. Economically this is very important because it ensures that people are in a fit state to produce what the economy needs. Of course, day-to-day living may mean very different things to different households, and [. . .] consumption behaviour is affected by level of income.

Households in aggregate live within their means, so that as well as consuming goods here and now, the personal sector also distributes its purchasing power over time through savings. Once we start looking at what households do with their savings, we have moved on to the capital account. Households put savings to two main uses in adding to their wealth. First, they provide security for the family in the future. In this case savings are used to buy financial assets, particularly superannuation or private pension contributions. The other main use for savings is to provide shelter, and here physical assets are purchased, notably houses. The capital account as an adding-to-wealth account is concerned with the stream of future benefits to be obtained from these financial and physical assets.

The third major element in household spending is tax. Only taxes on income - income tax and national insurance payments - show up in the personal sector income and expenditure account. Nowadays, an increasing proportion of tax in the UK is levied on expenditure, mainly Value Added Tax (VAT). However, since VAT is a tax on consumers' expenditure, it is not a separate item in the personal sector accounts.

Essentially, tax is used by governments in two main ways. Governments use taxes to pay for social consumption, such as education, health, defence and roads, on behalf of households. Social consumption provides goods and services on a collective basis, in part because of the difficulties of making them available through the market mechanism. In addition to their money income, households thus receive an income in kind, sometimes known as the 'social wage'. The other main way in which tax can be used is to redistribute purchasing power between households. Tax is thus a rather special form of household spending in that people have no legal choice but to pay it.

Consumer expenditure

Let us now look in more detail at consumption expenditure. Table 3.2 gives a breakdown of the different elements of consumer expenditure in selected countries of the European Community (now the European Union) for 1989. You can see that food (with beverages and tobacco) and housing (including expenditure on fuel and power) make up the single largest parts of the broad categories of expenditure listed in the table. It is interesting to note that the proportion of household expenditure which went on food, beverages and tobacco varied quite substantially within Western Europe, from a low of 16.6 per cent in what was then the Federal Republic of Germany to nearly 40 per cent in the Republic of Ireland. There are also fairly large differences in proportional expenditure on housing.

Question

Why do you think there are such variations in the proportion of expenditure on food, beverages and tobacco in different European countries?

Table 3.2 Percentage of household expenditure on selected commodities in selected European countries, 1989

	Food, beverages, and tobacco	Clothing and footwear	Rent, fuel and power	Furniture, furnishings, household equipment	Transport and communication	Recreation, entertainment, education, culture	Miscellaneous goods and services	Total
UK	21.1	6.2	19.5	6.9	17.7	9.5	19.1	100
France	19.4	6.9	18.9	8.1	16.8	7.3	23.1	100
Germany (Federal Republic)	16.6	7.7	18.4	8.8	15.1	9.0	24.5	100
Irish Republic	39.0	6.9	10.9	7.0	12.6	11.1	12.6	100
Italy	21.7	9.6	14.3	8.9	12.9	9.1	23.6	100
Spain	22.0	9.1	12.6	6.6	15.7	6.5	27.6	100

Source: Social Trends, no. 22 (1992)

It is well known that poor households spend a greater proportion of their income on basic items like food. The Republic of Ireland and Spain are the poorest nations in Table 3.2, while Germany has the highest income per head. Like individual households, less well-off nations spend proportionately more on basics than the better-off.

Food for thought: some anomalies of definition

Before leaving this overview of personal sector expenditure, it is worth pointing out some anomalies in the way the personal sector accounts are drawn up. These anomalies have rather important economic implications.

Consumption, or investment in people?

This anomaly relates to the difficulty of making hard-and-fast distinctions between consumption and 'adding to wealth', or production. As already suggested, at its simplest consumption expenditure is eating in order to live. But it is living people who undertake productive work in the economy, so expenditure on consumption can also be viewed as maintaining the working people and the domestic carers who are essential to the productive functioning of the economy. In developed countries it is usually taken for granted that the workforce is in a fit state to work. Yet back at the turn of the century, the British establishment was horrified to discover that many of the working-class men who were recruited for the Boer War were too unfit to join the army. With substantial proportions of the populations of Third World countries suffering from malnutrition, many commentators argue that these countries do not so much need investment in capital resources requiring savings, but in people, requiring consumption expenditure. Undernourished people cannot work as hard, and so add less to value. If incomes were redistributed to the poorest groups, households would have more to spend on food, and so would be fit enough to produce more in agriculture and in other sectors of the economy. There is therefore a sense in which consumer expenditure adds to wealth, the wealth incorporated in human beings, where people provide a stream of services throughout their working life.

Consuming the environment

It must be remembered that households, in the process of using what they have purchased, in the process of consuming, are also using up the environment. Cars pollute the air, rubbish uses up landfill sites, roads use open land, and so on. Degradation of the environment is generally not paid for by consumers out of their income, and so is not included in the accounting process. People are therefore made even less aware of it than they are of the social wage. However, just as a mortgage on your house is a debt to a bank or other lender, so degradation of the environment can be seen as a debt owed to future generations. Environmental degradation is a liability which the present generation is leaving to others to deal with.

In summary, then, the personal sector accounts show households dividing their income between expenditure and savings. Indeed, people could be pictured as going through a two-stage budgeting process: deciding how much to save and then deciding how the remainder should be spent. But as with every accounting convention, there are anomalies in the definitions used which have considerable economic significance.

[. . .]

HOUSEHOLD DEMAND FOR PARTICULAR COMMODITIES

Demand and income

I now want to turn to how households behave as economic agents in the micro economy - that is, in the market for individual commodities. What determines how much butter or petrol households will buy, or how many visits to the cinema they will make, haircuts they will have, or holidays abroad, they will take? [. . .] Income is unequally distributed between households in all countries, though it is more unequally distributed in some than others. A hierarchy of income distribution means a hierarchy of patterns of consumption between poor and rich. The unequal distribution of purchasing power therefore affects the market for individual products. If a country's national income goes up, its households in the aggregate have more purchasing power, and more commodities of most types will be bought. For example, the effects of rising national income on car purchases are readily observable: roads become more crowded, cities become more polluted, rush hours extend. But it can still be noticeably easier to find parking spaces in poorer residential districts than in rich ones. This gives us the first rule about the relationship between level of income and what economists call the demand (or amount purchased) for different sorts of goods: *those with higher incomes will purchase more of most commodities.*

Table 3.3 Weekly income and expenditure on selected items per household, UK, 1991 (£)

Gross normal weekly income			Alcoholic drink	Tobacco	Clothing & footwear	Leisure services
	<	60	2.57	2.47	2.39	3.23
60	<	80	2.42	2.96	3.67	4.37
80	<	100	3.24	3.77	4.67	5.17
100	<	125	3.91	3.95	5.93	6.74
125	<	150	3.94	4.53	7.78	8.28
150	<	175	4.85	4.78	7.86	8.48
175	<	225	6.97	5.38	9.59	11.27
225	<	275	9.32	6.06	13.21	15.15
275	<	325	10.46	6.00	14.26	15.23
325	<	375	10.82	5.30	15.84	24.36
375	<	425	13.44	5.55	20.57	21.11
425	<	475	13.16	6.57	19.66	21.18
475	<	550	15.73	6.34	22.84	29.17
550	<	650	17.31	6.10	27.24	38.57
650	<	800	18.95	5.71	30.46	43.65
		800+	27.99	5.24	36.77	82.07
	All		10.83	5.15	15.80	22.20

Source: Family Expenditure Survey (1992)

Table 3.3 shows how the amount spent on alcoholic drink, tobacco, clothing and footwear and on leisure services goes up (with one or two small 'blips' – a non-technical term widely used by finance ministers) across the income brackets. [. . .]

Studies of households in poverty show their very limited purchases. There are some products, such as basic foodstuffs, or black and white television sets, where fewer items will be purchased as income rises. For example, as poor households in the Third World get richer, they will be able to substitute beans, meat or fish for part of their basic grain diet of rice, maize or millet. Less rice will therefore be purchased. The same goes for black and white television sets in a country like Britain, where incomes are now high enough for most households to purchase a colour television instead. When less of a commodity is purchased as incomes go up, they are called inferior goods. This gives us our second relationship between income and demand, qualifying the first one: *the rich and the poor may buy different sorts of things, so that in the case of so-called inferior goods, those with higher incomes actually buy less of them.*

Exercise 3.1

Draw up two columns, one of commodities that you think would be 'inferior goods' in the rich economies of the developed world, the other of inferior goods in a poor Third World economy.

Food for thought: some insights from socio-economics on other influences on demand

Being less easy to quantify than income or price (I deal with price [on page 67] below), what might be called the socio-economic influences on demand are often forgotten by economists. Let me provide some examples of such influences.

What is available on the market?

What we buy is inevitably influenced by what is available for purchase. This may seem rather a curious thing to say in the post-yuppie era of the 1990s. Isn't everything available on the market today? True, I may be able to buy all sorts of gadgets and gizmos, but it is not possible to live in a city and purchase clean air, or even clean streets. As touched upon [earlier], there is frequently no market for environmental goods, and therefore need cannot be expressed in the form of market demand. Indeed, Joan Robinson, one of the few prominent women economists, once asked where it was possible to find the pricing system that offers consumers a fair choice between air to breathe and cars to drive around in (Robinson, 1978).

It is also interesting that with hindsight we realize that the restrictions of wartime rationing of food in Britain gave rise to healthier patterns of eating! Indeed an increase in availability can actually have an undesirable effect. Food aid to Third World countries has brought about shifts in households' tastes from foods based on local whole grains, such as sorghum or millet, to processed wheat-based products like white bread. This then has a knock-on effect on local farmers who find it more difficult to sell their grains.

The influence of technology

It may seem simple enough to say that everyone has a need for clean clothes, for example, but the socio-economist Jonathan Gershuny (1978) has shown that the connection between psychological need and economic demand is not a direct one - it is one that is mediated by technology. How do we actually clean our clothes? Back in the 1950s, working-class households in Scottish cities went to the 'steamie' or municipal public wash-house, where hot running water and washboards were available for women to do the week's wash (and where you could also get a bath if you were one of the many households without a bathroom). During the 1960s, innovatory automatic washing machines became available in privately run launderettes, and the steamie slipped out of use as more and more households also got their own bathrooms. Then family incomes rose and the technology used in automatic washers became cheaper. Household investment in automatic washing machines replaced private investment in launderettes, and nowadays people do not even use their section of the drying green for each tenement, but another consumer durable, the electric dryer.

This is just one example of how the means of satisfying a need changes. An important part of this is the response to technological change in its broader sense. Thus, technology in this example includes the institutional framework of publicly owned steamie, privately owned launderette, or household-owned washing machine, and a mass market of consumer durables, as well as the innovation of the automatic washing machine.

Gershuny calls this a socio-technical innovation, when the means by which a need is satisfied changes. A socio-technical innovation like a video-recorder, as a means of providing entertainment, can also lead to changes in the structure of household demand: not only do households purchase video-recorders, but families may stay in to watch hired videos instead of going out to the cinema.

There is an interesting furthest dimension to the process of socio-technical innovation, for the purchase of more consumer durables means that the work of using them is being undertaken by household members in their unpaid capacity. If you buy a car to go to work, rather than using public transport, then the work of driving the car becomes the private, unpaid responsibility of each commuter, instead of being the paid work of the bus driver. Gershuny calls this the self-service economy, where households service themselves using their own consumer durables, rather than buying the service on the market. As we shall see in the final section of this chapter socio-technical innovations raise some interesting gender issues. Who within the household undertakes the work and/or enjoys the fruits of such innovations?

Reflection

Before you read on, consider what has been the impact of socio-technical innovations in food provision, entertainment or transport on the structure of household demand in your own household.

Social influences

Commentators from a number of disciplines have examined aspects of the socio-economic impact of advertising on demand, from a number of different perspectives. J.S. Duesenberry, an American economist, suggested that demand for particular commodities, as well as consumption expenditure in general, is affected by a 'demonstration effect', where people feel social pressures to purchase what others have. J.K. Galbraith, another North American economist, talks of a dependence effect, where wants are dependent on the very process by which they are satisfied, as producers use advertisements and salesmanship to persuade us to purchase what they are making. There is a feedback loop here.

Back at the turn of the century, Thorstein Veblen, the American institutional economist, paid much attention to the cultural influences on consumption. His ideas remain highly pertinent today. He argued (Veblen, 1912) that at every phase of culture, consumption behaviour has related on the one hand to a system of work and livelihood, and on the other to what he called a system of exploit, status and ceremonial adequacy. He therefore made a distinction between two sorts of consumption: instrumental, and ceremonial or wasteful consumption. In the latter case, possession of wealth becomes honourable in itself and so it becomes important to show off your wealth by means of conspicuous consumption. The rich therefore pursue a high-profile lifestyle, with demand for what in 1980s Britain were called 'yuppie products'.

Demand and price

I turn now to the final major influence on how much of a particular commodity will be purchased by individuals and households in an economy, namely its price. Price is generally considered by economists as one of the most important variables.

Perhaps the greatest virtue of the market system is that it allows people choice in terms of the price they are prepared to pay for individual items. The responsible consumer-cum-citizen in a market economy shops around for the cheapest bargain in meat, which incidentally may mean that there is still enough money left to buy an additional vegetable for the meal. If the price of meat falls, then the household may choose to have a meat meal more often, and more meat is purchased: if the price rises, they may decide to eat more fish and buy less meat. Of course, as we saw above on page 64, income is also a constraint on demand. It is sometimes argued (particularly on the right of the political spectrum) that the distribution of income is something that a market economy should not do anything about. If your household has a lower income, then you may choose to become a vegetarian, still enjoying a healthy diet, but avoiding expensive foods like meat, and instead buying cheaper pulses and vegetables. However as we saw above, social influences may also affect demand: concern for heart disease may mean that some people cut back on their purchase of fatty meat in particular.

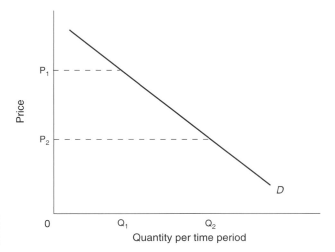

Figure 3.2 A demand curve for commodity x

Let us, for the moment, concentrate on the effects of price, abstracting from the other things that influence demand. The relationship between demand and price can be represented in the form of a diagram, known as a demand curve. The market demand curve (which may in practice be a straight or a curved line) for a commodity like milk depicts buyers' willingness to purchase milk, depending on its price. The amount of milk purchased in an economy is not necessarily the amount that people need, but what they are willing and able to purchase. (Free milk was provided to children in British schools with the introduction of the welfare state after the Second World War, partly because it was thought that some households would not be able to afford it, but also because it was thought that the nation needed healthy children.) Figure 3.2 shows the relationship between market demand and price, based on the intuitively acceptable assumption that if the price falls - say from P_1 to P_2 - it will mean that (other things remaining equal) more is purchased - Q_2 rather than Q_1. It is important to remember to specify a time period within which the amount is purchased.

This inverse relationship between the price of a commodity and the quantity demanded (shown by the demand curve sloping downwards and to the right) is known as the 'law of demand'. However, our earlier discussion may have alerted you to some exceptions to this law.

If we follow Veblen in making a distinction between instrumental and wasteful consumption then conspicuous consumption is a means of showing off wealth. This means that luxury items like exclusive jewellery, cars or designer clothes may be in greater demand at higher prices. Luxury items whose demand behaves in this way are known as *Veblen goods*.

At the lower end of the scale, consumers in very poor countries may actually spend less on an inferior good like rice when its price falls. This is because they can use the spending power released by the fall in the price of the basic foodstuff to purchase a greater variety. Such goods are called *Giffen goods* because the influential economist Alfred Marshall, apparently in error, gave Sir Robert Giffen credit for this exception to the general law of demand.

[. . .]

Movements along the demand curve and shifts of the demand curve

We have so far been looking at the market demand curve on the assumption that other things remain equal. What happens if we relax this assumption (which economists refer to as the *paribus ceteris*). Figure 3.3 shows a hypothetical British market demand curve for a seasonal product, strawberries, whose price varies at different times of the year. It shows that at the height of the British strawberry season, when prices are as low as £1.20 a kilo, six million kilos are purchased (point A). In early May, prices are higher at, say, £2.40 a kilo, since strawberries are being imported from southern Europe, with higher handling costs implied. *Ceteris paribus*, [all other things remaining equal] we can find out how many strawberries will be purchased by moving along the demand curve to point B, where the quantity demanded will be four million kilos. Around the new year, strawberries cost £4 a kilo, and people only buy small quantities to add colour to a fruit salad. We move along the demand curve to point C, and see that one and a third million kilos are purchased.

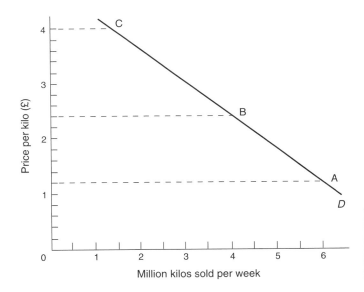

Figure 3.3 Hypothetical market demand curve for strawberries, showing movements along the demand curve

Returning again to point A on the demand curve, let us suppose that one of the other influencing factors changes. If real national income falls, one would expect everyone to spend less on all goods. The market demand for strawberries will therefore decrease at all prices. This means that we now have a new relationship between quantity demanded and price, and this is shown by the new demand curve, D_1, in Figure 3.4, lying to the left of the original one, D. A change in any of the variables other than price causes a *shift* in the whole demand curve, because the *ceteris paribus* assumption has been dropped. The shift may be to the left or right, depending on the cause of the change. However, if all other variables remain the same and it is price alone that changes, then there is movement *along* the given demand curve.

Here is an exercise to help you think about demand curve shifts.

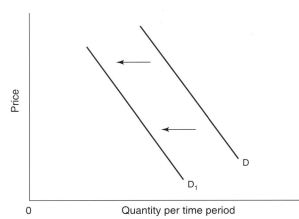

Figure 3.4 A shift of
the demand curve

Exercise 3.2

Think for a few minutes about how other things besides price may *not* remain equal in the market for strawberries. Work out what effect each will have on the demand curve. Then see if you can complete Table 3.4 below.

Table 3.4 Shifts in the demand curve for strawberries

Change in variable	Effect on demand curve
Decrease in national income.	Decrease in demand for strawberries at all prices. Demand curve shifts to the left.
Increase in national income.	
Rise in price of substitute goods (e.g. raspberries, or cherries).	
Fall in price of substitute goods.	
Rise in price of complementary goods (e.g. cream).	
Fall in price of complementary goods.	
Change in socio-economic preferences in favour of strawberries (e.g. advertising campaign).	
Change in socio-economic preferences away from strawberries (e.g. due to pollution of crops).	

I hope that you now understand the difference in principle between a shift along the demand curve and a shift of the curve itself, though you should realize that in practice it is not so easy to disentangle the variables.

[. . .]

ANSWERS TO EXERCISES

Exercise 3.1

Examples of 'inferior goods' might include the following:

Developed world	**Third World**
Black and white televisions	Basic foodstuffs such as rice and millet
Public transport	Bicycles
Public housing	Traditional forms of housing
Matches	

Exercise 3.2

Your completed table should read as follows:

Table 3.4 Shifts in the demand curve for strawberries *(completed)*

Change in variable	Effect on demand curve
Decrease in national income.	Decrease in demand for strawberries at all prices. Demand curve shifts to left.
Increase in national income.	Increase in demand for strawberries at all prices. Demand curve shifts to right.
Rise in of substitute goods (e.g. raspberries or cherries).	Demand curve shifts to right price.
Fall in price of substitute goods.	Demand curve shifts to left.
Rise in price of complementary goods (e.g. cream).	Demand curve shifts to left.
Fall in price of complementary goods.	Demand curve shifts to right.
Change in socio-economic preferences in favour of strawberries (e.g. advertising campaign).	Demand curve shifts to right.
Change in socio-economic preferences away from strawberries (e.g. due to pollution of crops).	Demand curve shifts to left.

NOTE

* This chapter has been adapted from, The Open University (1995) D216 *Economics and Changing Economies*, Book 1 *The Market System*, Chapter 3 'People and households as economic agents', Milton Keynes, The Open University.

REFERENCES

Serials

Family Expenditure Survey, London, HMSO for Central Statistical Office (annual).
Social Trends, London, HMSO for Central Statistical Office (annual).
United Kingdom National Accounts, London, HMSO for Central Statistical Office (annual).

Other references

Gershuny, J. (1978) *After Industrial Society*, London, Macmillan.
Robinson, J. (1978) *Economic Philosophy*, Harmondsworth, Penguin.
Veblen, T. (1912) *The Theory of the Leisure Class*, London, Macmillan.

4

MORE ON CONSUMER DEMAND*

Brian Atkinson and Robin Miller

THE CONCEPT OF ELASTICITY

Elasticity of demand

We have seen that there are numerous factors which can affect the level of demand. **Elasticity of demand** measures the *extent* to which a change in these factors influences the level of demand. The main measures that we shall look at are **price elasticity of demand**, **income elasticity of demand** and **cross-elasticity of demand**, although the concept can also be applied to examine the extent to which other factors (e.g. advertising expenditure) affect demand.

Price elasticity of demand

In the vast majority of cases, there is an inverse relationship between price and the quantity demanded. If a firm puts the price of its product up, other things remaining equal, it can expect sales to fall, while if it lowers price, it can expect sales to rise.

However, a firm will want to know more than this. It will want to know the *extent* to which demand changes as price changes. In other words, how sensitive is the demand for its product to changes in price?

Consider for example two products, salt and chocolate biscuits. If the price of salt were to rise by 50 per cent, or even fall by 50 per cent, one would not expect there to be a very significant change in the demand for salt. However, if the price of chocolate biscuits were to rise or fall to the same degree, one might predict a significant change in the quantity demanded because people would buy other kinds of biscuits. The demand for salt, in the above example, is therefore said to be price inelastic, as demand does not respond much to changes in price, while the demand for chocolate biscuits is said to be price elastic, as a change in price causes a sizeable change in the quantity demanded.

A convenient way to illustrate price elasticity of demand is through the gradient of the demand curve. In Figure 4.1 a small change in price from P_1 to P_2 has resulted in a significant change in the quantity demanded, thus illustrating demand that is price elastic, while in Figure 4.2 a fairly substantial price change from P_1 to P_2 has had little effect on the quantity demanded, thus illustrating demand that is price inelastic.

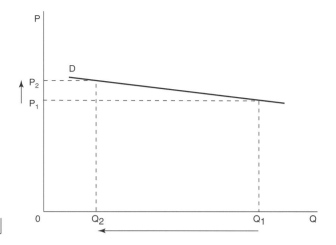

Figure 4.1 Elastic demand

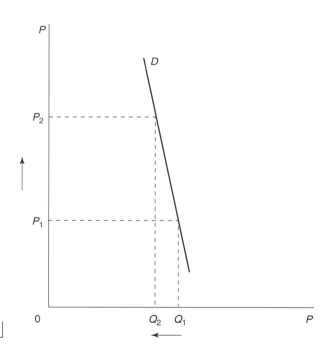

Figure 4.2 Inelastic demand

However, diagrams can be misleading, because, for example, the slope depends on the scale of the axes used in the diagram [. . .]. An alternative is to calculate elasticity mathematically.

Measurement of price elasticity of demand

Price elasticity of demand can be measured through using the formula:

$$\text{Price elasticity of demand} = \frac{\text{Percentage change in quantity demanded}}{\text{Percentage change in price}}$$

or, using symbols:

$$\frac{\Delta Q}{Q} \div \frac{\Delta P}{P}$$

where:

ΔQ = change in quantity;
Q = original quantity;
ΔP = change in price; and
P = original price.

If the value for price elasticity is greater than one, then demand is said to be price elastic, while if the value is less than one, demand is said to be price inelastic. The higher the value of price elasticity, the more elastic demand is said to be. Note that as there is an inverse relationship between price and the quantity demanded, the value for price elasticity of demand will be negative. However, for brevity the minus sign is often omitted.

Consider the following examples. A firm raises the price of its product from £2 to £2.20 and as a result, sales fall from 400 per week to 320. What is the price elasticity of demand? Using the formula:

$$\frac{\text{Percentage change in quantity demanded}}{\text{Percentage change in price}}$$

price elasticity of demand:

$$= \frac{(-)20\% \quad \text{(a decrease from 400 to 320)}}{(+)10\% \quad \text{(an increase from £2 to £2.20)}}$$

$$= (-)2$$

Thus demand is elastic over this price range.

However, when the firm raises the price of another product, from £1 to £1.10, sales fall from 1,000 per week to 960 per week. In this case, the price elasticity of demand:

$$\frac{(-)4\% \quad \text{(a decrease from 1,000 to 960)}}{(+)10\% \quad \text{(an increase from £1 to £1.10)}}$$

$$= (-)0.4$$

In this case demand is price inelastic.

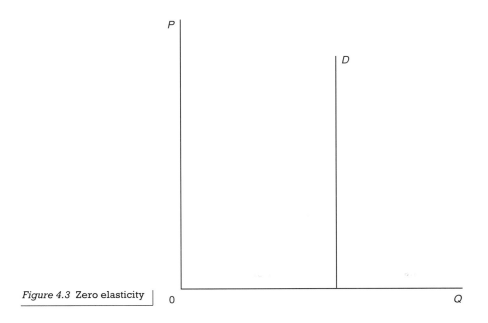

Figure 4.3 Zero elasticity

If price elasticity of demand has a value of one, then demand is said to have unit elasticity. (A demand curve of unit elasticity is illustrated in Figure 4.8.) The two extreme cases are where the price elasticity of demand is equal to zero (perfectly inelastic) or is equal to infinity (perfectly elastic). These are illustrated in Figures 4.3 and 4.4).

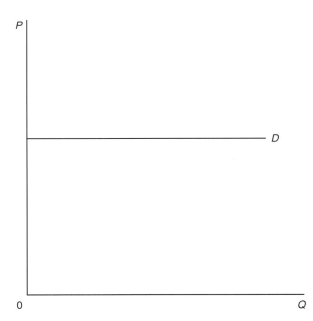

Figure 4.4 Infinite elasticity

Factors influencing price elasticity of demand

There are several factors which may determine the price elasticity of demand of a product. The *availability of substitutes* will have an influence. If there are many close substitutes or alternative products available, then demand is likely to be price elastic, but if there are few alternative products, as in the case for salt, then demand is likely to be price inelastic. Note, however, that the demand for petrol can be considered to be price inelastic as there are no substitutes available, but the demand for a particular brand of petrol will be elastic.

Whether the product is a *necessity* or a *luxury* will also have an influence on the price elasticity of demand. If the product is a luxury, as in the case of chocolate biscuits, consumers may decide to forgo the product following an increase in price, but if the product is a necessity they may still continue to demand the product despite a price increase. This explanation, however, produces the problem of defining what is a necessity and what is a luxury. Products do not always fall neatly into these two categories: for instance, food is clearly a necessity and the demand for this as a whole is therefore inelastic, but the demand for fillet steak is elastic. The *proportion of a person's income* spent on a product will also influence the price elasticity of demand. If the price of a box of matches were to double, the demand is not likely to change much as, despite the 100 per cent increase in price, it represents such a small proportion of a person's budget. If a product taking up a much larger proportion of one's budget increased in price, it is likely that demand for this product would have to be reduced considerably. Goods which are bought through *habit*, or which have *addictive properties*, will tend to be price inelastic.

Time can also have an effect on price elasticity of demand. When the price of cigarettes is raised in the budget, many smokers decide to cut back on demand, unwilling to pay the higher price. However, as time passes, people become accustomed to the higher price and demand reverts back to its original pre-budget level. In this example, the passing of time has made demand less price elastic. However, time also provides consumers with more time to search for alternative products. Thus, for example, if the price of petrol rises, motorists have little choice but to continue buying petrol at the higher price as their car will not function on any other fuel. But over time, there is the opportunity to switch to a diesel-engine car, so in time the demand for petrol may fall in response to the higher price. In this example, the passing of time has made demand more price elastic.

The relationship between price elasticity of demand and revenue

The sales revenue of a firm is determined by multiplying the price of the product by the number of units sold, and this can be illustrated by the rectangle shown in Figure 4.5.

The effect on a firm's revenue of a change in price depends on the price elasticity of demand for its product. When demand is elastic, an increase in price will lead to a fall in the firm's revenue, while a reduction in price will lead to an increase in revenue (see Figure 4.6). [. . .] If demand, on the other hand, is inelastic, a rise in price results in an increase in the firm's revenue, while a decrease in price results in a fall in revenue, as illustrated in Figure 4.7.

If demand has unit elasticity over a price range, a change in price will leave revenue unchanged. This is illustrated in Figure 4.8, which shows a demand curve that has unit elasticity along its entire length. This curve is called a rectangular hyperbola. Whatever the price charged, the revenue remains the same, so that the area bounded by OP_1AQ1 is the same as that bounded by OP_2BQ_2.

Knowledge of the price elasticity of demand for their product is therefore important for firms when considering their pricing policy. The argument that a firm needs to raise price

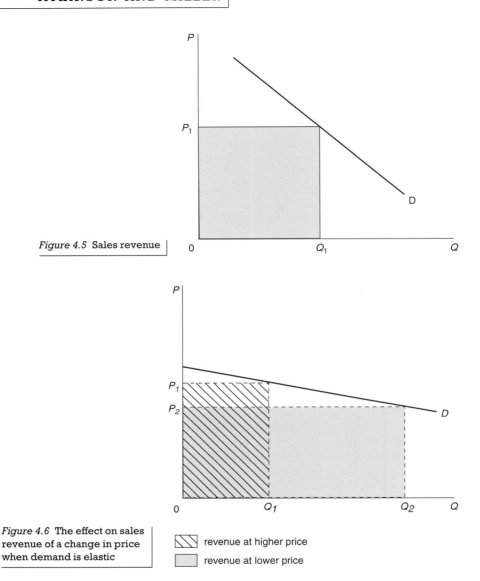

Figure 4.5 Sales revenue

Figure 4.6 The effect on sales revenue of a change in price when demand is elastic

◿◿ revenue at higher price

▢ revenue at lower price

in order to increase revenue does not hold true if the demand for the product is elastic; a better policy may actually be to lower price. If demand is inelastic, however, there is little to be gained from a price cut.

Knowledge of the price elasticity of demand for products is also important for the Chancellor of the Exchequer, who needs to know the effect that a change in tax rates will have on the demand for products when calculating total tax yields. If the aim of the Chancellor is to raise as much revenue as possible from indirect taxes, then he or she would be advised to tax products which have an inelastic demand, as consumption will remain high, despite the imposition of a sales tax.

[. . .]

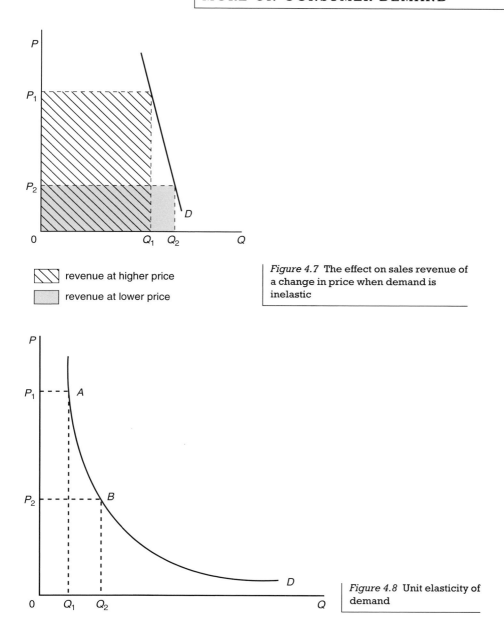

Figure 4.7 The effect on sales revenue of a change in price when demand is inelastic

◩ revenue at higher price

▨ revenue at lower price

Figure 4.8 Unit elasticity of demand

Income elasticity of demand

We have seen when discussing demand that income is an important factor influencing the level of demand. In most cases, an increase in income leads to an increase in the demand for a product. However, it would be useful to know the *extent* to which demand changes as income changes. Income elasticity of demand measures the sensitivity of demand to changes in income. If consumers get an increase in income, their demand for some products may rise substantially, but their demand for other products may rise only very slightly, if at all.

Income elasticity of demand can be measured by using the formula:

Percentage change in quantity demanded

Percentage change in income

If the value is more than one, demand is said to be income elastic, and if the answer is between zero and one, demand is said to be income inelastic. Most goods will fall into this range: that is, their income elasticity of demand will be positive, and the higher the value of the income elasticity of demand, the stronger the relationship is between changes in income and changes in demand. Luxury products tend to have a high income elasticity, while necessities have a low income elasticity. Thus the demand for foreign holidays or eating out is likely to be fairly responsive to changes in income, but the demand for bread is unlikely to change by much as income changes.

For some products, however, the income elasticity of demand is negative, and these are referred to as inferior products. For these products there is an inverse relationship between income and demand, and an increase in income will lead to a fall in demand. The explanation for this is that as their income rises, consumers substitute better products in place of the 'inferior' products. Typical examples are public transport or cheap cuts of meat.

Knowledge of the income elasticity of demand is important as it can help us to predict what will happen to demand as income levels change. Over time, living standards and the level of income have a tendency to rise. Using data on the income elasticity of demand for products, we can predict changes in spending patterns. We can expect to see a rise in spending on those products which have a high income elasticity of demand, such as eating out, electrical goods, foreign holidays and leisure activities, whereas for those products which have a low income elasticity of demand - for example, necessities such as bread, toothpaste, washing-up liquid - demand will rise only slightly. Expenditure on those products which have a negative income elasticity will fall. Thus the demand for public transport may fall as people switch to private cars.

Firms may therefore want to consider selling products with high income elasticities of demand, as when living standards are rising, peoples' expenditure on these goods will be rising more rapidly than on those goods with low income elasticities of demand. On the other hand, those firms which produce goods with low income elasticities of demand will be less affected in times of recession as, despite the fall in income levels, demand for these products will remain fairly stable.

A particular problem for the UK economy is that many of the products which it imports have a high income elasticity of demand. Therefore, as the level of national income rises, this leads to an influx of imports. The products which the UK exports, however, tend to have a much lower income elasticity of demand, and so, as world income rises, the level of exports does not increase to the same extent, which results in balance of payments problems for the UK.

In practice, it might be difficult to calculate accurately the elasticity of demand for a product. A firm could attempt to determine the price elasticity of demand for its product by varying the price it charges and examining the extent to which demand changes. In the UK, the Ministry of Agriculture, Food and Fisheries has estimated the price elasticities and income elasticities for various food products, and these are shown in Table 4.1. The figures demonstrate that the demand for bread, milk and potatoes is inelastic with respect to price, and that they are 'inferior' products, as their income elasticity of demand is negative, while the demand for fruit, cheese, beef and veal is price elastic and has a positive income elasticity of demand.

Table 4.1 Price and income elasticities for various food products

	Price elasticity of demand	Income elasticity of demand
Bread	−0.09	−0.25
Milk	−0.19	−0.02
Potatoes	−0.21	−0.48
Fruit	−1.05	+0.48
Cheese	−1.20	+0.19
Beef and veal	−1.25	+0.08

Cross-elasticity of demand

Cross-elasticity of demand examines the nature and the extent of the relationship between two products. In particular, it examines the extent to which a change in the price of one product affects the demand for another product. To measure the cross-elasticity of demand, we can use the formula:

Percentage change in demand for product X
───
Percentage change in price of product Y

The value of the cross-elasticity of demand may be positive or negative, depending on the nature of the relationship between the two products. If the value is positive, this indicates that the two products are substitutes. Thus, a 10 per cent increase in the price of gin might lead to a 5 per cent increase in the demand for whisky. Using the formula above, the cross-elasticity of demand:

$$= \frac{+5\%}{+10\%}$$

$$= +0.5$$

However, if the cross-elasticity of demand between two products is negative, this indicates that they are in joint demand or complementary products. Thus a 10 per cent increase in the price of gin might lead to a 5 per cent decrease in the demand for tonic water. Using the formula, the cross-elasticity of demand in this case:

$$\frac{-5\%}{+10\%}$$

$$= -0.5$$

The further the value is away from zero, either positive or negative, the stronger the relationship is between the two products. If, however, the value of the cross-elasticity of demand between two products is zero, then this indicates that there is no apparent relationship between the two products. Thus one would expect the demand for bread to remain unchanged following an increase in the price of gin.

As well as helping us to forecast the effect on demand of a change in the price of another product, cross-elasticity of demand can also be used to help assess the extent of competition in an industry. If the cross-elasticity of demand between two products is high, this indicates that the products are close substitutes and are competing within the same market. This might then influence whether the government feels it is necessary to intervene to ensure competition. [. . .]

NOTE

* This chapter has been adapted from, Atkinson, B. and Miller, R. (1998) *Elasticity of Demand*, New York, Addison Wesley Longman, pp. 87–98.

5

ORGANIZATIONS*

Neil Costello

INTRODUCTION

Chapter 3 considered the activities of households as economic agents in the economy, focusing particularly on consumption but also acknowledging the household as a site of productive activity. This chapter explores production more explicitly by concentrating on the other main set of economic agents in the circular flow model, namely firms (see Figure 5.1).

My objective in this chapter is to develop several models of firms as producing organizations in an effort to understand how firms operate in the economy. From an economic point of view, perhaps the single most important fact about firms is that they are formal organizations. They have defined organizational structures, often hierarchical, and they usually have a legal identity and status. The relationships *within* firms are rarely market relations but rather relations of command and/or co-operation. Just as economic analysis has shifted between, on the one hand, treating the household as an unproblematic consuming unit, and, on the other, exploring relations within households, so economists have shifted between treating firms as unproblematic profit-seeking units, and exploring the

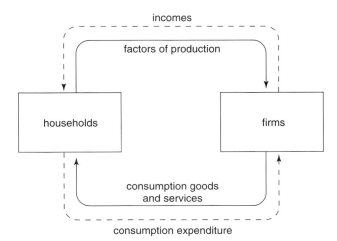

Figure 5.1 Firms in the simple circular flow of income

economic relationships within them. At present there is a renewed interest among economists in the internal culture and organization of firms.

Before looking at firms in detail, however, I want to emphasize that not all production takes place in private firms. As you know, some takes place in households, while other formal organizations also produce goods and services and play an influential role as economic agents: their activity influences the development of the economy.

Question

Try to think of formal organizations, other than private firms, which produce goods and services and therefore exercise an influence on economic life.

It's not difficult to come up with a list, but where do you stop? Which are important? Did you include any of the organizations in the list below? If you did, think briefly about why. If you did not include them, pause for a moment and consider whether or not they could constitute economic agents.

- The Church of England
- The Open University
- The parks and recreation department of your local authority
- Save the Children Fund
- Voluntary helping organizations at your local hospital
- The parent–teacher association (PTA) at your local school
- The local athletics club
- Your local public library
- Pension funds

Some of these are large and influential producers of services. The Church of England, through its extensive investments, the salaries it pays to its employees, and the day-to-day upkeep of its buildings, is clearly an economic agent in a very full sense, though it might not be the first organization we think of when we are trying to work out how the economy works.

The Open University, with budgets of well over £120 million in 1993, is also a service producer and an economic agent. Its objectives are different from those of, say, major grocery chains, but it is certainly significant in economic terms.

What about the four voluntary organizations in the list: Save the Children Fund, helpers in a hospital, the local PTA and the local sports club? This is more difficult. All of them expend money, and whilst the latter three are certainly not major players, the economy could not function well without them in the sense of providing variety and services which people value. Save the Children Fund, on the other hand, is a sizeable economic agent. In 1990–91 it was the sixth largest charity in the UK, with a total voluntary income of nearly £39 million. In that year the total income of the 171434 charities registered in England and Wales was £16.18 billion or 3.4 per cent of GDP (Posnett, 1992).

Pension funds control an enormous proportion of financial investments in capitalist economies. For example, in the UK in 1991, 31 per cent of equities – that is, shareholdings in private companies – were held by pension funds (Dibben, 1993). But pension funds have different overriding objectives from, say, a typical small business such as a computer software company, because their horizons are very long-term.

If we are to make sense of the economy, we have to examine the nature of the economic agents that make up the economy. Their diversity is enormous: from the local corner shop to vast enterprises like the Pentagon (the US defence establishment); international corporations producing, for example, motor vehicles or pharmaceuticals; major multi-product organizations which are bigger on most measures of size than many nation states; universities and hospitals; small high-tech companies at the forefront of technology; market traders selling vegetables or cheap clothing. The list is potentially endless and extraordinarily diverse. How can we begin to make sense of an array of institutions like this?

One way is to consider formal organizations as institutions which have histories. Their evolution is driven both by their interactions and by changes in the social world. Their interactions are governed partly by socially defined rules. For example, there are clear, formally defined legal obligations which public companies in the UK must follow in their financial accounts, and the laws of contract prescribe the required behaviour in many activities related to buying and selling goods and services. More important in many respects, these institutions adhere to informal rules in-relation to other firms or individuals such as customers, employees or suppliers. Wherever organizations sit in the spectrum of size or influence, they are, like the households you considered in Chapter 3, socially constructed.

Economists therefore try to understand the socially constructed rules that influence firms' behaviour. Later chapters focus on the relationships between economic agents and in particular how those relationships are managed through one form of social institution with its own set of informal rules – the market. This chapter, by contrast, considers the nature of the institutions themselves. As you will see, this cannot be separated from the organization's environment, but my focus will be on the organization. This will enable you to understand a good deal more about such organizations and give a background on which to base your subsequent analysis of such issues as inter-firm rivalry and market behaviour.

Most of the chapter concentrates on private firms. These have an existence which is in many respects independent of other social institutions, and they have been extraordinarily successful at creating wealth and a range of products undreamt of in our grandparents' generation. At the same time they are seen by some people as sources of divisiveness and inequality in society. They are seen to possess power greater than that of many national governments and, it is claimed, to ride roughshod over social and personal needs. For some they are the crowning glory of modern civilization; for others they are the source of exploitation and discontent. They are controversial, important, and a fascinating part of any attempt to understand economic behaviour.

Markets and firms

One question that economists have repeatedly asked is, why are some activities carried out within one firm which in other circumstances might be carried out via market transactions? For example, my employer has its own finance department with accountants and other financial experts. At one time I ran a small consultancy, but all my financial dealings were carried out using an accountancy firm whose time and expertise I hired through the market. So why does my employer organize its accounts internally rather than using the market? The same question can be asked of virtually every function carried out by any organization.

One answer relates to the cost of transacting through the market compared with the cost of the same transaction within the firm. If the market is cheaper and I am a profit-seeking firm, I will use the market rather than carry out the transaction myself. However, the issue is not entirely straightforward. Why don't we carry out all transactions through the market, or conversely why do markets exist when many activities are planned and co-ordinated within firms more effectively than they could be through the market? Why in particular do both systems coexist – why does my employer employ accountants, whereas it was more efficient for me to use market transactions?

This is an area of current economic controversy. Potential answers relate to such things as the 'lumpiness' of the activity: for example, I had no need for a full-time accountant but my employer has sufficient work for several. Furthermore, accountants use knowledge of their employer's business which is acquired over time. There are issues about the certainty that someone will be available when needed to carry out the work, and possibly questions of confidentiality. So cost, knowledge and security of supply influence the 'make or buy' decision, and this differs for organizations which have different objectives.

In addition, market transactions also differ, and companies use the market in different ways. For example, I recently discussed company strategy with the Morgan Motor Company, the UK specialist sports car manufacturer. The company prefers to build long-term relationships with its suppliers but is aware that not all suppliers are prepared to develop such an approach. Consequently the company buys some supplies from a variety of sources, but is prepared to limit itself to a single source for other materials. In the former case the market provides an immediate and relatively impersonal source; in the latter, it is an institution within which to develop trust and to avoid taking advantage of short-term opportunities. Such varied behaviour is typical of a wide range of firms and other organizations. Sometimes market transactions are replaced by firms' internal processes – that is, firms and their suppliers merge when the objective of the firms and the cost conditions they face make that an appropriate action.

[. . .]

Economics of organization

Economists have recently recognized anew the importance of considering the institutional structures of firms. Firms are not homogeneous black boxes which we need never look inside. The internal organization of firms, the ways in which their objectives are determined, and a recognition of their complexity have returned to prominence. It has become clear that firms cannot be considered simply as efficient organizers of production – a model discussed below on pages 96–106. [. . .] European and US firms have been outcompeted by Asian firms, and Asian cultures and organizational features are different from those of the West. Is there a particular kind of organizational structure towards which all firms should strive? An answer depends on the nature of the organization we are considering and the kind of environment in which it finds itself. These issues are taken up [below on pages 107–112].

In looking at such questions a helpful distinction is sometimes made between the passive and active behaviour of firms (Hay and Morris, 1991). Passive behaviour begins with constraints facing the firm, for example particular cost conditions, and then assumes that the firm will try to fulfil its objectives within those constraints. Active behaviour, conversely, would be that engaged in by the firm in order to try to change the constraints it faced. This might include merger with a competitor, or research and development in an attempt to reduce costs. Passive and active behaviour are frequently complementary, but they highlight a major difference in approaches to economic policy. A view that firms are largely passive tends to be associated with a belief in the efficacy of markets to achieve policy goals. A perspective that emphasizes the active role of firms will be associated with a tendency to downgrade the importance of industrial structure and to concentrate on the economic power of the corporate sector. The approaches adopted in [the final two main sections of the chapter] can model both active and passive behaviour.

Before that, [. . .] I shall consider a financial model of firms' behaviour which is neither active nor passive but primarily descriptive. As [the 'Firms and finance' section below] shows, the description depends on assumptions about the nature of the firm and its relationship with other actors in the economy.

However, I shall begin [. . .] with an empirical focus, in order to provide background material for you to get a sense of the place of firms in the economy and to provide us with some material that will be valuable later in the chapter.

FIRMS: A BACKGROUND

I am going to start with the story of one real-life firm, Protoscan Software Services Ltd. Protoscan is a firm of its time. It is almost a parable for the 1980s and 1990s. It is a high-tech company, based in the UK, which thrived and was subsequently taken over by a Japanese conglomerate. The case study includes some of the complexity of the real world and gives us a flavour of the issues and priorities facing firms during the 1990s. It tries to capture some of the excitement involved in running a firm, as well as the extent to which the firm is at the mercy of its environment – the passive view – or is able to control and change events – the active view. The case study is included here to exemplify some of the issues raised in the last section and as a resource for examples in subsequent sections.

Questions

As you read through Protoscan's story, try to assess the primary constraints it faced and those things that were major influences on its behaviour. For later consideration try also to pick out its major goals and think about the way in which it approached its business. You should also consider how the people who ran Protoscan related to each other – for example, did they see themselves in hierarchical terms or perhaps as a team of equals?

The Protoscan story

Protoscan was set up by Mike Hall and Andy Eltis in November 1987. It showed spectacular growth. At the end of its first year it employed six people. In March 1992 it employed 35 professional staff and 60 unskilled, casual staff. During the first three years sales turnover virtually tripled, from £1.2 million in 1988 to £3.4 million in 1990.

Mike Hall has a sales, marketing and general management background. Andy Eltis is a highly skilled computing expert. The combination of Andy's exceptional technical talents and Mike's business experience has been a fundamental strength in the development of their company. They initially developed proposals for a new business venture in their previous company but were turned down. Ultimately they decided to go it alone, and on 1 November 1987 they set themselves up as Protoscan in the back room of Mike's house.

The early weeks were characterized by many of the features reported by other high-tech start-ups. A very rapid response rate for customers was a way in which they could establish themselves in the market-place, and they found themselves working a shift system, four hours on and four hours off. Mike spent much of his time following up contacts and knocking on doors. Equipment was borrowed because of their severely limited financial resources.

But then the story begins to change. Unlike many first-generation high-tech companies, Protoscan did not involve a technical breakthrough looking for a market. It had been conceived as a result of an awareness of a gap in the market and from the beginning organized itself around the needs of its customers, not around the technical virtuosity of its product. Its product was technically advanced, but that was not the reason for the company's existence. In addition, Mike Hall's business experience plus the business plan they had developed meant that commercial disciplines were already at the forefront of their thinking.

They took advice from local contacts and sought support from the major high street banks. At this time they wanted to retain total control of the company but had no assets apart from their houses plus limited savings. The local bank was impressed and decided to support them.

There followed two years of very rapid growth. The company's product was a technical service. Mike Hall realized that turning round a simple product very quickly was not enough. The company had to offer potential customers something their competitors did not. Fortuitously 16-bit computers hit Europe at the time Protoscan was developing. Such machines require far more complex and costly programming than the simple 8-bit machines they replaced and, in addition, the computer games market was becoming very sophisticated. Games suppliers would pay thousands of dollars for the licence to produce a game based on, for example, a popular TV programme. Mike describes their entry into this market as partly accidental: 'We didn't deliberately go into the leisure market . . . but because of what Andy did we were dragged into it'. Basically Andy devised 'Protec', a system for protecting disks. It is impossible to produce a foolproof protection system, since expert hackers can always take out the protective code. However, 'Protec' protected disks from easy copying by end-users. Protoscan thus provided a protection for disks as well as a copying service, and had moved into a mass market rather than simply a small, specialized technical market.

Early in 1990 Protoscan expanded further. It bought out a competitor to become Protoscan Europe plc. Protoscan's portfolio was expanded and the amount of equipment at their disposal significantly increased. Expansion brought with it difficulties. Profits had been ploughed back and the basic company was very healthy, but their dramatic growth rate, effectively doubling every year, created cash flow problems and a severe risk of over-trading – that is, essentially, a risk of taking on more business than they had the capacity to provide. Mike Hall tried to slow down the company's expansion, though this was difficult. With the help of Lloyds Bank and Coopers & Lybrand he produced a three-year business plan with the aim of attracting venture capital from the City. He had spent over three months developing this strategy when Protoscan received a cold call from a major Japanese corporation with interests in the disk-copying market, Kao Corporation.

Kao Corporation is a large Japanese conglomerate. Their interests are primarily in chemicals, but a by-product of their operations provides the raw materials for manufacturing computer disks. They had set up major operations in Europe during the 1980s, and they also had extensive facilities in California. Kao had realized, like Protoscan, that only low margins are possible on disks, so that to make significant returns it was necessary to find some way of adding value. Kao were also keen to establish a sizeable base in Europe in anticipation (subsequently realized) of restrictive trade arrangements from the European Community's anti-dumping laws. Kao's manufacturing base in Barcelona could provide a European duplicating company with its disk requirements, and it seemed to Kao that potential synergies existed between themselves and European duplicators. Kao had reviewed the 24 companies then competing in the trade duplicating market in Europe, and Protoscan had come out at the top of the list.

It was clear that Kao were not prepared to take a minor stake in Protoscan. Given the size of Kao, the original owners could not hope to match the investment that Kao were proposing and the deal became very clear: sell the company or go it alone. Negotiations were protracted, as is the Japanese style, and eventually an offer was put to Protoscan which Kao believed would allow all the parties concerned to feel satisfied. However, for Andy the offer was too low. Mike believed it to be acceptable, but his respect for Andy and the nature of their working relationship meant that, after discussion, the proposal was rejected.

The Japanese negotiators were completely floored. It was outside their experience for negotiations to fall at the last hurdle. They had sensed the acceptability of their proposed solution inaccurately and were now in disarray. Protoscan worked hard to maintain contact and eventually an alternative arrangement was struck in July 1990. Until the end of March 1993 Protoscan was to become Kao Protoscan Software Services. Mike and Andy received a financial consideration and had three years to provide themselves with a significant return. Kao did not interfere during this period. (Such arrangements are often referred to as an 'earn out'.) The recession of the early 1990s affected Protoscan's profitability, but at the end of the earn-out Mike and Andy finished with a good return, though less than they had originally hoped for.

Interpreting the case

The Protoscan story includes the messy detail of the real world, and it is not completely straightforward to work out answers to the questions that were suggested to you.

The major constraints faced by Protoscan were primarily financial. The company had to convince the banks early on that it was a worthwhile investment. Then, as expansion took place, the company, like many innovative small firms, found itself in a position where its short- to medium-term cash flow problems were a major hurdle in achieving its longer-term potential. Help was sought in the City, and Kao's provision of a solution to these problems was unexpected. Other major influences include the histories and the skills, in technical and managerial terms, of the two principals. In the external environment the rapidly changing nature of the high-tech world was also influential, in particular the change in the complexity of computers to 16-bit machines and the growth of the games market. These features significantly affected Protoscan's market in technical terms and in size.

The major goals of the company are not at all obvious. Much of the founders' motivation was implicity to determine their own life chances. A certain amount of financial return was clearly required, but that did not appear to be the only or even the primary motive. Profit was a major motivating factor but does not appear to be *the* prime mover in this case. In cases like this firms are producing satisfactory rather than maximum profits. Such an objective is usually referred to as *satisficing*.

Protoscan was a small entrepreneurial company. Like many organizations with this structure, it approached its business by responding quickly to environmental change and was itself able to generate changes in the environment in the way it responded to challenges. It was flexible and sought out new opportunities. This is particularly evident in the way it responded to the opportunity presented by the games market.

Mike and Andy clearly saw themselves as a team. They each played a different role in the company and for them the combination of their skills was successful. This was partly the reason for their ability to respond effectively to change such as that presented by the games market and ultimately by Kao. Particularly in large organizations, such structures are sometimes considered to be unstable and less easy to control, but they can be very effective, as this case shows.

What is confirmed by the Protoscan example is the importance of recognizing the complexity of the real world and the need to look at a wide range of phenomena if we are to undertake a rich, detailed analysis. However, there are many features that apply to many cases. In looking at those general features we move away from the rich detail but give ourselves the opportunity to make broader and tentative generalizations. We shall come back to Protoscan. Now we need to explore some more empirical background on firms.

Background: the place of firms in the economy

Let us look at some evidence on the place of firms in the economy, taking the UK first. Table 5.1 shows the proportion of UK gross domestic product (GDP) contributed by different industrial sectors. Manufacturing (which in 1990 included Protoscan) is an important sector, though the growth of service industries, which include transport, communication, banking and finance, health and education – basically anything which cannot be dropped on your foot – is a feature of modern, advanced, western economies.

Table 5.1 Industry output as a percentage of UK gross domestic product, 1980, 1985 and 1990

	1980	*1985*	*1990*
Agriculture, forestry and fishing	2.1	1.9	1.5
Energy and water supply	9.7	10.7	5.1
Manufacturing	26.7	24.0	22.4
Construction	6.1	5.8	7.6
Service industries	55.1	57.7	63.4

Source: Great Britain Annual Abstract of Statistics (1992) Table 14.7

An examination of manufacturing is revealing, however, and detailed data are available on that. The *Census of Production*, produced by the Central Statistical Office, is a major source of data on firms in the UK. The most recent census, carried out in 1990, breaks up the manufacturing sector by size of firm, and Table 5.2 summarizes those findings.

Table 5.2 is a simplified version of the census data. I have also added three columns of percentages which I hope make the data easier to interpret. The table indicates a number of interesting features of the manufacturing sector.

Question

Examine Table 5.2 yourself before you read my commentary. Pick out what you see as the most important features.

Table 5.2 Numbers of enterprises according to numbers employed, their employment totals and contribution to net output, United Kingdom manufacturing sector, 1990

Size by total employment	*Number of enterprises*	*Percentage of enterprises*	*Employment (thousands)*	*Percentage of employment*	*Net output (£ million)*	*Percentage of net output*
1–99	127 998	96.28	1 203.7	25.0	26 682.2	19.2
100–999	4 362	3.28	1 156.6	24.0	30 545.5	22.0
1000–4999	469	0.35	944.7	19.7	29 201.6	21.0
5000–49 999	107	0.08	1 192.4	24.8	42 133.9	30.3
50 000 and over	4	0.003	311.3	6.5	10 420.3	7.5

Source: based on Central Statistical Office (1992) Table 12

By far and away the largest number of enterprises are small firms – 96.28 per cent – and they employ a quarter of the manufacturing workforce. Protoscan was one of these firms in 1990. In contrast, larger firms provide the greater part of total output. I added firm sizes together so that each size band (except the biggest) represents around a fifth to a quarter of total employment. As you can see, for firms with up to 5000 employees, each of the bands produces around one-fifth of net output. The largest firms, only three one-thousandths of 1 per cent of the total number of firms, employ over 6 per cent of manufacturing workers and produce 7.5 per cent of net output. Clearly, big firms are more important in terms of total output than they are collectively in terms of employment, and much more important than would be indicated by their proportion of all firms. On the other side of the coin, it is perhaps surprising, in a world which sometimes seems to be dominated by huge impersonal bureaucracies, to see the significance of firms that employ less than 100 people. With 25 per cent of employment and 19.2 per cent of net output, small firms made a sizeable contribution to the economy. Remember these data refer to manufacturing – they do not include the local corner shop or hairdressing salon.

The figures in this table refer to *enterprises*. The census also gives figures for *businesses*. In census terms enterprises refer to ownership. One enterprise can own several businesses. When analysed using an enterprise base, the figures for the number of businesses show an increasing concentration as we move from smaller to larger enterprises. For small firms the number of enterprises and businesses is roughly the same – in other words each business is a separate enterprise. However, as we move to bigger and bigger enterprises the position changes. The 4 enterprises that employ over 50000 people – the really large part of the manufacturing sector – own 135 separate businesses.

The census does not reveal information about individual companies, in order to avoid compromising their competitive position, so it is not possible to discover who those four enterprises are. However, we can obtain information about the world's largest companies from other sources; the figures for Europe in the same year as the UK census are given in Table 5.3.

According to the *Census of Production*, in 1990 the gross output of all UK production enterprises was roughly £380 billion. As you can see from Table 5.3, the turnover figures for Royal Dutch Shell Petroleum and BP are each around £38 billion, or the rough equivalent of 10 per cent of the gross production of UK production enterprises. (Production in this context means energy and manufacturing. The census definition uses a standard convention adopted in official statistics about the economy and does not include primary products such as agriculture, fishing or mining nor services under the heading of

Table 5.3 Top European companies, 1990 (ranked by turnover, £m)

	Company	Country of origin	Turnover
1	Royal Dutch Shell Petroleum Company	Netherlands	38867.0
2	British Petroleum	United Kingdom	37394.0
3	Daimler Benz AG	Germany	26245.7
4	Shell Transport and Trading	United Kingdom	25912.0
5	Fiat SpA	Italy	24377.8
6	IRI (state holding company)	Italy	23064.8
7	Volkswagen AG	Germany	22452.7
8	Siemens AG	Germany	21001.5
9	Nestlé SA	Switzerland	19447.0
10	Deutsche Bundespost	Germany	18038.6

Source: based on Allen (1990)

'production'.) The turnover of these companies is not generated totally within the UK, and gross output is not quite the same thing as turnover – turnover is essentially sales – but the comparative size indicated by such figures is revealing.

Protoscan could never have reached such a size as a producer of a specialized technical product, as the demand for its product is simply too small. Large and small firms are therefore likely to coexist. However, as with Kao and Protoscan, when potential synergies are seen to exist, one firm, in this case Kao, preferred to incorporate the smaller firm into its own organization rather than continue to operate through markets: Kao was in a sufficiently powerful position to put this preference into practice. As the census shows, many small firms are owned by major corporations, and the potential power of these corporations on an international scale is enormous.

Firms therefore have an almost infinite variety, from the small high-tech world of a firm like Protoscan to massive organizations such as Royal Dutch Shell which cross national boundaries and are by any standard immense.

FIRMS AND FINANCE

We now turn to some different perspectives on firms, which provide different ways of modelling them. The model that is most commonly used in day-to-day conversation to explain firms' behaviour is that based on accounting conventions. The primary focus of this model is the firm as a money processor. The firm uses its money to buy materials and labour which enable it to make more money. This model is important for firms in both the public and private sectors, since without finance they would not exist. The model is also valuable because it simplifies our view of the firm: instead of the firm being a complex organization, it becomes a vehicle for processing money.

In order to operate, the firm has to be able to raise finance. In the case of Protoscan finance was a major constraint throughout its existence. The two partners borrowed from one of the commercial banks using their houses as security and made use of their limited savings. This is a very common way for firms to get started.

However, it is unusual for a firm of any scale to have access to sufficient funds simply through reinvestment of profits or bank loans. Large firms are, therefore, frequently *joint stock companies*, which enables them to raise funds by selling shares to the public or borrowing through the sale of bonds. The establishment of joint stock companies in England in the middle of the nineteenth century (primarily to provide sufficient financial resources for the large industrial developments of the day, in particular the growth of railways) represents a major step in the history of private enterprise. The significant feature of a joint stock company is that it is regarded, in law, as a separate entity from the individuals who own it. It can enter into debt, issue contracts, own property, sue and be sued in its own right. It is the company, not its owners, that incurs legal obligations. The owners' responsibilities are limited to the amount of money they have invested in the company through purchasing shares. The owners will not be liable to lose their personal assets in order to meet the liabilities of the company. This is the concept of *limited liability* (in the UK this is the reason for the 'limited' descriptor in plc, public limited company). It means that share ownership can be undertaken by literally millions of small investors and that they will have complete knowledge of the maximum risks they are taking – namely the loss of money they have invested, and no more. Funds raised through the sale of shares are usually referred to as *equity*. Equity does not have to be repaid. Equity holders invest their money in order to share in the firm's profits. For the large firms described [on page 91], raising funds in this way can be a major preoccupation, though the companies in Table 5.3 also include organizations which are (or have recently been) funded by national governments, for example IRI, and one which is privately funded, Nestlé.

Borrowing through debenture capital or bonds is also possible for joint stock companies. The people who purchase bonds are not owners of the firm, they are creditors. The firm promises to pay interest on the loan each year and to repay the loan at some stated future date. These sums must be paid by law whether or not the firm makes a profit, and bondholders have first call on the company's assets if it is unable to pay. They can force the firm into liquidation; that is, they can require the firm to make its assets liquid – to sell them off – in order to pay its creditors. For the firm, therefore, bonds can be less attractive than equity, since they require payment and can sometimes force firms which are in only temporary difficulty into liquidation. On the other hand equity dilutes the amount of control that any one individual can exert, since shareholders have rights over the company's activities through shareholders' meetings and the opportunity to appoint directors.

The consequences of widespread share ownership are profound. In particular there is frequently a *separation of ownership from control*. Control is commonly exercised by the company's managers or its technostructure (this is a term sometimes used to describe the skilled managers and professionals who work for the company and are knowledgeable about its markets and other aspects of its environment in a way that a single shareholder could never hope to be).

Question

Think about organizations familiar to you in which ownership of the organization is separated from control. What do you think are the implications of this separation of ownership and control?

In these circumstances the owners' interests become only one feature of the firm's objective function. Managers can try to exert control in their own interests but must maintain sufficient return to equity to keep shareholders satisfied – remember this is called satisficing. When ownership and control are separated, it is possible for many groups to exert an influence subject to the owners being satisfied. Such groups are often called *stakeholders*.

One limitation on the ability of the company's technostructure to do whatever it wishes is the legal requirement to maintain adequate accounts. In order for any organization to function efficiently it must maintain adequate records. Without a system that provides for the maintenance of such records, the stakeholders will have, at best, incomplete information. Owners will not receive satisfactory summaries of the company's activities, and managers will be unable to take effective decisions as a result of the lack of relevant information. But the people who may have an interest in accounting information are not limited to the obvious categories of owners and managers. Other people and institutions have a genuine interest too.

Government needs information about the economy as a whole, and such information can only be accumulated by organizations contributing their own individual pieces of the jigsaw. The tax authorities also require information for taxation purposes.

Creditors require information on which the level of creditworthiness may be judged. The company's accounts are the basis for such judgements.

The information needs of employees have also become more widely recognized. Many companies now recognize their employees' rights to know about the viability of the organization they work for, particularly those which include share options of various kinds in their remuneration packages.

There are a number of other groups which have interests but which at present are not normally included in the formal reporting processes. These include the customers of the organization and the local community in which it functions. Their information needs may be linked with social and economic issues, or with environmental concerns, for example. At present such groups are not formally included in accounting procedures, though they can get access to the accounts of public companies since such accounts have to be made publicly available. It is important to recognize that different people have different opportunities to pick up issues, and their interests will be dealt with in different ways depending on their position in relation to the firm. The items that are included in accounts, and those that are excluded, reflect the interests which are seen as most important by the firm, the accounting professions and the legal authorities, and this in itself raises interesting issues about the appropriate spread of interests and property rights. These stakeholders are effectively determining the way in which the company is seen by defining those items that are seen as important and those that are not.

The picture of a firm that is drawn via its accounts is displayed basically in three main statements which are available for economists to scrutinize: the balance sheet, the profit statement, and the funds flow statement.

The structure of company accounts

The balance sheet

The balance sheet depicts the financial position of an organization at a particular moment, for example at the year end, by listing and attributing values to items owned (assets) and amounts owed (liabilities). The balance sheet will not normally show the economic value of assets and liabilities – what something is 'worth' in economic terms. It simply shows the values of the assets and liabilities as shown in the records of the organization. Here is an example.

OPEN ENTERPRISES

Balance Sheet

31 December 1995

Assets	£	Liabilities	£
Cash	80 000	Accounts payable	180 000
Accounts receivable	140 000	Salaries payable	100 000
Inventories	100 000	Mortgage	150 000
Buildings (original value £250 000)	200 000	Bank loan	80 000
			510 000
Other equipment	220 000		
		Net worth	230 000
	740 000		740 000

Assets are what the firm owns. They are shown on the left. Open Enterprises has some cash in the bank. It is also owed money, called 'accounts receivable', by customers and has large inventories in its warehouses. In addition it owns buildings which originally cost £250 000 but are now worth only £200 000 because of depreciation. Its other equipment has also depreciated and is now worth £220 000. The total value of Open Enterprises' assets is £740 000.

Liabilities are what a firm owes. They are shown on the right. They include unpaid bills and salaries, the mortgage, and a bank loan for short-term cash needs. The total value of debts is £510 000. The net worth of Open Enterprises is £230 000 – in other words, this is the excess of its assets over its liabilities.

Net worth is shown on the liabilities side. The firm is owned by the shareholders and the net worth is one of the resources to which the firm, as an organization, has access. But the net worth does not belong to the firm; it belongs to the shareholders. It is therefore a liability of the firm to the shareholders.

The profit statement

The profit statement (sometimes called an income statement or profit-and-loss account) tells us about the flow of money during a given year. The profit statement shows how the profit for a particular period has been determined by listing revenues and expenses. It does not just measure the difference between cash received and cash expended. It measures the difference between monetary values earned for providing goods or services and the monetary values incurred in generating such earnings. This is an important distinction in accounting. For example, in the consultancy firm with which I was involved, our accounting year ended on 31 March. If we carried out activities for a client in March and billed the client in the same month, we would not expect to receive payment until May or June of our next accounting year. However, the fact that the cash would not be received until the next accounting year would not stop us from including the relevant earnings on the profit statement relating to the year in which the money was earned. The profit statement is not measuring cash received or cash paid out. It is measuring economic values earned and the economic values associated with the generation of such earnings.

UNIVERSAL SECURITY SERVICES

Profit statement

Year ending 31 March 1995

Revenue (£)		2 000 000
Expenses (£)		
Wages	1 400 000	
Rent	100 000	
Advertising	100 000	
Other expenses	200 000	
		1 800 000
Profits before tax		200 000
Taxes paid		50 000
Profits after tax		150 000

Universal Security Services (USS) is a firm that provides security personnel to other organizations. It charges £20 per hour for each security officer and pays each officer £14 per hour. During 1995 it provided 100 000 hours worth of security services and thus spent £1 400 000 on wages. Business expenses came to £400 000. All expenses therefore came to £1 800 000. Profits equal revenue minus costs, so taking costs from revenue gives a profit before tax of £200 000.

The funds flow statement

The funds flow statement shows where and how funds have come into an organization during a period, and what has happened to those funds. This statement would show the earnings in my consultancy firm mentioned above for March as flowing into the firm in May or June.

In the case of USS at the end of 1995, we can expect that it has not yet been paid for all the services it provided during the year. There will also be bills it owes which have not been paid. This will have implications for the firm's cash flow (which would be shown on the funds flow statement). Cash flow is the net amount of money actually received during the period. Profitable firms may have a poor cash flow when customers are slow to pay their bills or when new equipment has been purchased.

Depreciation was discussed [elsewhere] in relation to national accounts [. . .] Essentially the same rules apply to private firms. The basic idea is that the cost of *using* rather than buying a piece of capital equipment should be treated as costs within the year. When a piece of equipment is first acquired there is a large cash outflow, which is larger than the depreciation cost of using the equipment during its first year. Profits may be high but cash flow low. In subsequent years no further cash outlay is required, but depreciation is still calculated as an economic cost since the resale value of the equipment will decline each year. Cash flow will now be higher than profit (assuming unpaid bills remain much the same).

PRODUCTION, COSTS AND PROFITS

The conventional approach adopted by economists is not to model the firm as a money processor, though that is clearly an important perspective, but to regard firms fundamentally as producers of goods and services. This has similarities to the previous model. It uses related categories, but here the *expenses* (which appeared in the USS profit statement) are called *costs* and are looked at in a rather different way. The analytical framework set out below is logically consistent and internally coherent and can be applied to *all* firms. A theory that applies to all firms in general is unlikely to be able to explain the detailed day-to-day behaviour and strategic development of a particular company, but in abstracting from that detail it provides powerful results which have been very insightful.

The starting point for this basic approach is to emphasize the firm as an efficient organizer of inputs – that is, an organization which always tries to minimize costs of production. It may have other objectives too, but provided it is concerned to minimize costs the analysis will hold.

I shall also assume that the firm can purchase all the inputs it needs from the relevant 'factor' markets (a factor market is simply the place where the inputs required for production are bought and sold). The market for labour is a factor market, and has many subsets, of course. Thus there is a market for different kinds of skilled labour, for strategic planners and for cleaners. From each of these the firm can buy just the amount of each kind of labour necessary for it to produce efficiently. Similarly it can enter the market for capital equipment and will invest in whatever machinery it requires; it can enter the market for land and raw materials and buy the relevant quantities there, and so on.

The production function

The production function[1] summarizes the most efficient relationship between inputs and outputs, i.e. between the amount of product the firm wishes to produce and the factors of production it requires to produce that output. The production function is defined for a given state of technology.

For example, a restaurateur needs premises and raw materials (food), up-to-date capital equipment (good ovens, mixers, microwaves, and so on), skilled labour (the chef and chief waiter), plus various other forms of semi-skilled and unskilled labour (cleaners, kitchen porters, etc.). The restaurateur will buy amounts of these factors so that the required output – the number of meals per day – can be produced.

We can express this production function in an algebraic form [. . .]:

$$Q = f(F_1, F_2, \ldots F_n)$$

This means that Q is a function of $F_1, F_2 \ldots F_n$ (where Q is the quantity of meals required and the Fs refer to the factors of production: there are up to 'n' of them and the size of 'n' will vary, depending on the particular production process under consideration.) In other words the number of meals of a given quality that a restaurant can produce depends on the different factors of production that the restaurant possesses.

The factors can be combined in different ways. If we had more skilled chefs we might need fewer raw materials because they would waste less, or we might need a different kind of equipment. In general each of the Fs can be combined in many different ways with each of the other Fs. The limitation to this is the current state of technological knowledge. The production function is only concerned with efficient processes, however – that is, processes which will use more of one factor only if they use less of a second factor. This is known as technical efficiency.[2] The production function is not concerned with processes that use more of all factors.

If technological improvements take place, then we would find that for any given Q we would need fewer Fs – fewer people to make the same number of meals, for example, or we might combine the Fs in rather different ways. When microwave ovens were invented it became possible to prepare more food prior to the time of consumption and to heat it up quickly in the microwave. This meant that skilled chefs could be used more effectively and perhaps less skilled people would carry out the reheating.

[. . .]

Different states of technology allow labour to be divided up to a greater or lesser extent. For example, in the case of motor vehicle production, the original motor vehicles produced by Gottlieb Daimler at the end of the nineteenth century were manufactured by small groups of skilled workers who hand-crafted every component. Those small teams could produce more vehicles per month than would have been the case if every single component had been made by the same person, but their output levels were completely outstripped by the mass-production methods introduced by Henry Ford in the 1920s, when each worker took on only a small part of the total production process. Using the division of labour in this way was seen as more efficient. Greater output could be produced with the same resources, and the limits to the division of labour were seen to be primarily the demand for the firm's product. These are powerful arguments and they begin to touch on issues relating directly to the organization of firms which we shall come to in [the final section of this chapter].

The short and the long run

The dividing up of work in this way is something that is very familiar to us. The flexibility that is possible with such work organization will be different depending on the time scale. In the short-run[3] the firm is unable to build new factories or bring new machinery on line, and so the division of labour is limited to dividing workers up between the different processes in the existing workplaces and with existing equipment. In the long-run[4] new investment can take place and new buildings can be acquired. The range of options thus available is significantly greater, and completely new ways of working can be adopted.

To express this more generally, we would say that in the short run the firm's land and capital are fixed – they are fixed factors of production – whilst labour is variable. In the long run all factors are variable.

The short run and the long run will be different lengths of time depending on the particular processes we are talking about. Steelworks, for example, take much longer to set up than sandwich shops. It takes over five years to build a modern steelworks, so for steel the short run lasts five years. Its capital is fixed for five years. For a sandwich shop the short run is only a few weeks.

Exercise 5.1

To check your understanding try to answer the following questions without skipping forward to the answers and, if possible, without going back to the earlier text. [. . .]

1 What is the production function?
2 Define the phrase 'division of labour'.
3 What is meant by 'the short run'?

The cost function

The cost function shows the relationship between output and costs. More specifically it shows the cost associated with any particular output level, assuming the method of production chosen is the lowest-cost method available. It relates to the production function since it identifies the least-cost method available from all the efficient options indicated by the production function.

Long-run costs

Let us look first at long-run costs. Remember that in the long run all factors are variable, so they can be combined in the least-cost way possible.

Question

Suppose for the moment that the firm can obtain all the *F*s it needs at current factor prices. How will its total costs change as it increases its output? Another way of asking this question is to say, 'What will its cost function look like?'

We can say with absolute confidence that the firm's total costs will rise. Every time it increases output by one unit it will need to buy extra raw materials and labour hours, and so it will incur extra costs. The total costs it incurs get bigger.

Question

If output increases, total costs will rise, but will they rise exactly in proportion with the increase in output? Try to think through what this means. Is it necessary for costs to rise by exactly the same amount every time output increases by one unit?

The answer to this question is no, but why? The explanation lies in something with which we are very familiar. I think many people take it for granted that when a firm produces more of any product its costs per unit fall in the long run. The example of Ford is instructive again. When Henry Ford was able to expand to a scale that enabled him to employ mass production methods, his costs per unit fell significantly. By using the potential of the division of labour he could reduce the costs he incurred from increasing output and thus make cheaper cars. Even though his *total costs* were rising, his average costs[5] were falling.

This phenomenon – unit or average costs falling as output expands – is often referred to as the effect of economies of scale.[6]

Some are called *internal* economies of scale because they are internal to the firm. All important internal economy is the potential of the division of labour which Henry Ford used so effectively. A second internal economy of scale arises because of a simple geometric relationship. The best example is that of the storage tank. The cost of a storage tank is largely determined by the area of the material used to construct its sides. If the sides of a tank are doubled in length, say from 2 metres to 4 metres, and each square metre of material costs £10, then this doubling in its dimensions increases costs from £40 per side ($2 \times 2 \times £10$) or £240 for the tank since the tank has 6 sides, to £160 per side ($4 \times 4 \times £10$) or £960 for the tank. That is a large increase: costs have quadrupled. However, the volume of the tank has increased from 8 cubic metres ($2 \times 2 \times 2$) to 64 cubic metres ($4 \times 4 \times 4$); there has thus been an eightfold increase in capacity (see Figure 5.2).

There are, therefore, substantial economies of scale available in such circumstances since capacity is increasing twice as quickly as costs. It is this simple relationship that results in enormous oil tankers which have to manoeuvre for port hundreds of miles out to sea, and the same relationship creates the pressure to allow increasingly large lorries on our roads.

External economies of scale also exist. These are the reductions in costs which a firm experiences as a result of the expansion of the industry. For example, Protoscan almost

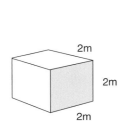

volume = 8 cu. metres

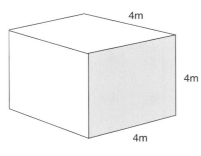

volume = 64 cu. metres

Figure 5.2
Technical economies of scale

certainly gained some external economies by being located in Huntingdon, close to Cambridge. The 'Cambridge phenomenon' – the concentration of numerous innovative high-tech companies in the Cambridge area – undoubtedly led to some factors relevant to such firms being available more cheaply and easily than for companies elsewhere (Segal, 1957).

There is a limit to economies of scale. Even Henry Ford eventually found that there was a level of output after which the extra cost of one more unit was pretty much the same as the costs incurred on the previous unit. This level of output is often referred to as the *minimum efficient scale* because it is the size or scale of the production process at which all economies of scale have been taken up. In terms of average costs it means that average costs are constant – total costs are still rising but the average cost per unit remains the same. These are likely to be the circumstances which prevail for most firms. In the long run most firms experience constant average costs for significant ranges of output.

The possibility that average costs rise as output increases beyond a certain point does not seem likely in many industries, except perhaps at a massive scale. What this means is that if we assume that the firm can obtain all the factors it wants at existing prices, it will not find that its costs per unit increase as it expands until it reaches a very large scale indeed. We can, however, envisage limits to expansion in organizational terms if no others: eventually a firm can become so cubersome that it starts to cost increasingly large amounts to manage effectively. The break-up of ICI into ICI and Zenica in 1993 is a good example of this kind of behaviour.

We can draw the relationship between output and cost per unit in the long run as a graph which will look something like Figure 5.3.

Note how the curve falls, showing average costs falling until minimum efficient scale is reached. There is then a flat section of constant average costs and the possibility that average costs rise at very high output levels. In the rest of this text you will find that we often draw long-run average cost curves 'L' shaped, ignoring the occasions when they may rise at high levels of output.

Short-run costs

In the short run, remember, the supply of some factors is fixed, so that the firm cannot increase its use of all factors as it expands. Realistically a firm will be unable to buy and install new plant and equipment except over a substantial period of time. In the short run,

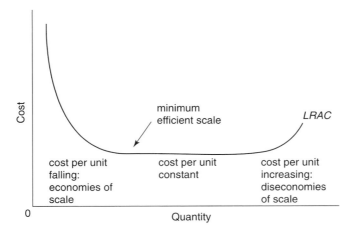

Figure 5.3 Long-run average cost (LRAC) curve

therefore, it is realistic to consider the firm having a *fixed* stock of plant, machinery, premises and equipment, but that it is able to *vary* the amount of labour it uses relatively easily either through overtime or through employing more staff.

Question

What happens to its costs in these circumstances as output changes?

The lowest cost level it can reach at any output level is that represented by the long-run cost curve. The long-run cost curve shows what we might call the optimum combination of factors. This is often referred to as economic efficiency.[7] It is, of course, possible for the firm to produce at a point above its long-run cost curve, but at that point it would be using factors inefficiently and would be able to reduce costs by becoming more economically efficient. (The firm may be combining factors in a way that is *technically* efficient but still be inefficient economically. This would arise if it was using large amounts of expensive factors and small amounts of cheaper factors. It would be more economically efficient to switch to a technique which used fewer expensive factors and more cheap factors. I shall come back to this point in a moment.) However, if the firm wishes to expand in the short run, it must do so without being able to obtain more of its fixed factors. It can vary only its labour input.

Think about Protoscan again. In the first few months of its existence it was housed in the back room of Mike Hall's house. The company copied disks using a shift system. There was very little equipment available and that equipment was the major determinant of output. At first the addition of labour to this fixed piece of equipment would enable output to rise and average costs to fall, as say eight hours' labour was increased to ten. The equipment costs would remain virtually the same – the same rental, insurance and maintenance – but for a little extra electricity, more blank disks and two hours' extra labour, the output of the machine would rise by 25 per cent (two hours' additional output to the eight already worked).

Eventually the machine worked 24 hours a day (less whatever time was necessary for routine checking and maintenance). The addition of extra labour then would still increase output a little: the disks could be sorted and boxed more quickly and efficiently; the distribution to customers could be faster; and more time could be spent with customers checking their needs. All this could be enhanced by increasing the amount of labour working alongside the limited equipment available. However, the cost per unit – the average cost – would now be increasing quite fast as the extra labour costs were borne by an output level which was very close to the maximum possible – determined by the continuous operation of the machine and its maximum output. This relationship – output increasing but by smaller increments each time more of the variable factor is added – is referred to as *diminishing returns* to the variable factor of production.

The short-run average cost curve which illustrates what is happening in these circumstances is shown in Figure 5.4.

In such circumstances we can envisage a number of short-run average cost curves contained in the long-run average cost curve. Each short-run curve represents a particular size or combination of equipment and premises which is fixed in the short term. Figure 5.5 illustrates this point. In the circumstances in which a firm finds itself working on the rising part of the short-run average cost curve ($SRAC_1$), such as output level Q, for any significant period of time it will wish to invest in new equipment in order to expand its operation to the new economically efficient level, shown by a move from $SRAC_1$ to $SRAC_2$. Conversely,

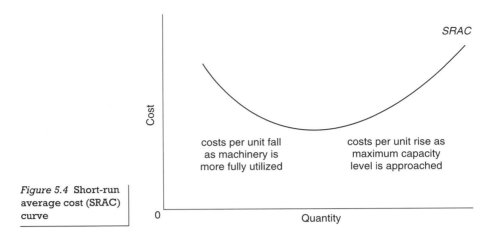

Figure 5.4 Short-run average cost (SRAC) curve

in periods of decline it may wish to scrap equipment or sell it to other companies in order to avoid incurring the maintenance and other charges associated with it. Each of the short-run curves is tangential to the long-run curve – they do not cross it. If they did, that would imply that costs in the short run could be lower than the optimum long-run position, which is impossible by definition. Note, furthermore, that while I have drawn the *SRAC* curves as 'U' shaped, they may not take that precise form; they may have a flat bottom section where average costs per unit level out before output starts to approach the capacity of the equipment.

A summary of the differences between some technical terms

I have been using a number of terms which appear to be very similar but mean different things. Sometimes the differences are subtle, sometimes wider, and I would like to pause at this stage to clarify the different usages.

- *Economies of scale* are the *reductions* in costs associated with expansion in output in the long run.

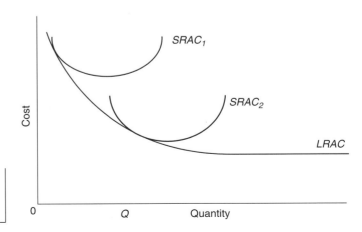

Figure 5.5 The relationship between long-run and short-run average cost curves

- *Internal economies of scale* are those which arise within the firm, through such things as the division of labour.
- *External economies of scale* are economies which the *firm* gains as a result of the expansion of the *industry*.
- *Diseconomies of scale* are increases in cost associated with expansion of output in the long run.
- *Returns to scale* can be *increasing, constant* or *decreasing*. They reflect the technological effects of expansion or contraction in the long run. So the increase in capacity brought about by expanding the size of an oil tanker exhibits increasing returns to scale, as illustrated in Figure 5.2. If such expansion brings about a big increase in the price of the metal used in oil tanker construction, it might be that bigger oil tankers actually cost the oil companies more per litre of oil carried than before the expansion took place. But the process still exhibits increasing returns to scale.

   Constant returns to scale implies that expansion or contraction does not have a technological effect on the cost per unit. Decreasing returns occur when the technological implications of expansion produce an increase in the cost per unit.
- *Diminishing returns* are not the same as decreasing returns to scale. Diminishing returns are a *short-run* phenomenon. As more of the variable factor (usually labour) is added to the fixed factor(s) (usually capital or land), the increase in output for every extra increment of the variable factor gets smaller. Diminishing returns to the variable factors set in on all pieces of equipment eventually, and prompt growing firms to invest in new capacity so that they can move to a more economically efficient plant in the long run. This is illustrated in Figure 5.5.

Variable factor prices

To simplify matters I have not yet considered what happens when factor prices change. If you recall the Protoscan case, it is unlikely that its initial recruitment of labour had any impact on the going rate for the job. However, when it expanded, it is possible that it may have been unable to recruit at its original rate. It was established then in a small town, Huntingdon, and may well have had to attract workers with the relevant skills from other companies and nearby towns. In those circumstances it would probably offer higher rates and would not have been able to satisfy its needs for labour at the pre-existing rate.

   What will happen in such circumstances, when firms face an increase in their factor prices?

Question

What do you think will happen? Think about the behaviour of organizations with which you are familiar. The answer is straightforward, but now we can describe it in terms of cost curves. What would you expect to happen to the cost curves?

The first answer is that if factor prices go up, then total costs go up. The average cost curve would shifts upwards at any given output level to reflect a general increase in costs (shown in Figure 5.6). I expect your answer is clear on that.

   But we need to consider a wider range of possibilities than an across-the-board increase in factor costs. What if the price of only one factor goes up? The outcome then depends on the production function and the extent to which it is possible to substitute one factor for another. If factors have to be used in fixed proportions, for example each pan needs a lid

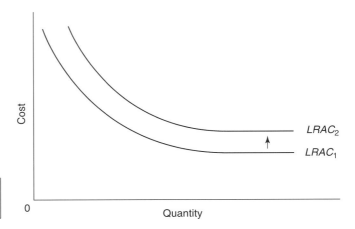

Figure 5.6 Upward shift of the long-run average cost curve

and each chef needs a grill, then an increase in the price of one factor has a similar effect as an across-the-board increase. However, factors do not usually need to be combined in such fixed ways. Pans can share lids, plates can double up as lids, and chefs can share grills. In such circumstances firms will use more of the factor which has not increased in price and less of the factor which is now more expensive. This is known as *factor substitution*.

The long-run average cost curve will then have changed so that each point on it, which remember is an optimal point, will represent a factor combination using less of the relatively expensive factor and more of those factors that can be substituted for it. The curve will be higher than the original curve, since costs have increased, but not so high as in the circumstances where factor proportions are fixed.

Marginal costs

There is one more concept in relation to costs that is used a great deal by economists. It is known as marginal cost.[8] You need to be clear about this and then you are all set: you will have the basic armoury of cost concepts that you need to undertake this kind of economic analysis.

Marginal cost is one of those concepts that is simple when you know what it is but can be a bit of a struggle to get the hang of. It is essentially the cost of the additional unit produced. If average costs are constant, then the extra cost incurred by producing one more unit is the same as the average cost. If average costs are falling, however, the cost of the last unit must be less than the average. In effect the firm is still moving down its average cost curve and reaping the benefits of expansion. The extra cost of one more unit in these circumstances is less than the extra cost incurred by the unit before it. Conversely, if average costs are rising, marginal costs will be above average costs. The relationship between average costs and marginal costs is shown in Figure 5.7.

The concept can probably be understood more easily if we use a numerical example. The example in Table 5.4 shows the change in cost as the firm expands its output from one unit per day to four units per day. The total cost of the first unit is £100. Since only one unit is produced, the cost of the last unit – the marginal cost – is also £100 and the average cost, i.e. total cost divided by number of units produced, is also £100.

To expand output by one unit the firm has to employ more labour, buy in extra raw materials, and perhaps incur bigger maintenance charges, but some costs do not increase, for example building rental. Expanding from one to two units a day is, nevertheless, a

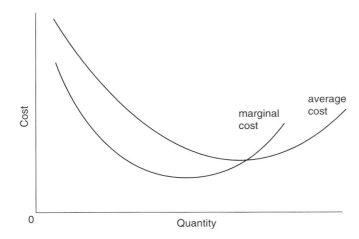

Figure 5.7 Average costs and marginal costs

Table 5.4

Level of output (no. of units per day)	Total cost (£)	Average cost (£)	Marginal cost (£)
1	100	100	100
2	180	90	80
3	240	80	60
4	300	75	60

significant expansion, and the extra cost incurred is £80. This is the marginal cost. The total cost is £180, and the average cost £90 per unit.

A further expansion to three units per day can be undertaken without taking on more labour. The existing workforce has to work longer hours, but many costs do not change. The extra unit costs £60 to produce. Total costs are now £240 and average costs are £80 per unit.

Expansion from three to four units costs just as much as the previous expansion. More overtime has to be worked at the same rate as before and the marginal cost is £60 again. Total costs are still rising, of course, but the average cost per unit is still falling and is now £75.

Question

What will happen to the average cost per unit if the firm expands to five units per day and can still finance the expansion simply by extending overtime?

I hope you found this easy. The fifth unit would cost an additional £60, so the marginal cost is £60. Total costs are now £360, so the average cost per unit will be £72.

As you can see, average costs are falling but by a smaller amount each time as they get nearer to the marginal cost. At some point we would expect marginal costs to rise. The firm is unlikely to be able to expand solely by increasing overtime. It will probably have to take on extra staff, even if only part time. The firm may also find that it is becoming somewhat cramped in its premises, even though it may have moved equipment around and created storage areas. Let's say the sixth unit costs the company an additional £72 to produce. Total costs are thus £432 and average costs remain at £72. Average costs and marginal costs are now equal. If we carried on with this numerical example we would find that extra units begin to cost the company increasingly large amounts as it squeezes more labour into its premises and works the limited amount of equipment continuously. In other words, marginal costs would be rising rapidly. Average costs would also be rising but would not be as high as marginal costs. If you sketch this numerical example, you will see that the marginal cost curve turns up, to cut the average cost curve at the minimum level of average costs.

A note on smooth curves

You will notice that whenever I draw cost curves I have drawn them as smooth curves. In general, curves are drawn in this way in economics. But in doing that we must bear in mind a number of issues, so that we are clear about the implications of what we are doing:

- If I graphed the marginal and average cost curves from the *actual* costs incurred by a specific firm – as I have just suggested you do for the numerical example above – they would not come out as smooth curves, but would have lots of corners in them. The data would be in discrete amounts and the cost curve would simply join up the relevant points.
- However, smoothing them out is not just to make them look pretty. The smooth curves used in much theoretical work in economics imply that output or cost or whatever we are graphing is infinitely variable – that is, it can be changed by infinitesimally small amounts so that all the corners – the lumpiness – of realistic discrete changes disappear. In a theoretical model this has the major advantage of making it amenable to a range of powerful mathematical techniques, in particular differential calculus. We don't use those techniques in this text, but they are used a good deal in advanced economic theory and occur frequently in the economic literature.
- *Estimated curves*, based on an examination of actual data, also look smooth but these are drawn as a line of best fit through identified points. They are smoothed out by statistical techniques. You need to recognize the difference between theoretical smooth curves and the estimated curves calculated by economic statisticians.

[. . .]

Marginal costs are important for the firm because they measure the precise impact on the firm's costs of producing one extra item. If a firm knows what its marginal costs are, it is in a strong position to maximize its profits. Overall, however, if it is to remain profitable the firm must cover its total costs; that is, it must receive revenue per unit which is at least equal to cost per unit (or average cost). We shall be referring to this in much more detail in subsequent chapters. For now it is important that you feel comfortable with the cost concepts discussed so far. Have a go at the following exercise.

Exercise 5.2

Attempt the following questions in order to check your understanding of the important concepts we have just discussed.

1 Draw a long-run average cost curve. What does it show?
2 Why do short-run average costs differ from long-run average costs?
3 Draw the relationship between the long-run average cost curve and short-run average cost curves.
4 What happens to long-run average costs if the price of a factor rises and factors are substitutable for each other?
5 Complete the figures in Table 5.5.

Table 5.5

Level of output (no. of units per day)	Total cost (£)	Average cost (£)	Marginal cost (£)
1			50
2	90		
3		50	
4			70

ORGANIZATIONAL STRUCTURES, CULTURES AND GOALS

Firms' objectives

Models of firms as essentially producers of goods and services or as processors of money provide a sound framework, but in abstracting from the complexity of *social* institutions, what is missing are the human dimensions and the sense of excitement and uniqueness, evident for example in the Protoscan case. Furthermore, in emphasizing impersonal features, the histories of firms and the sense of them as institutions are pushed to one side as if irrelevant to the structures under analysis. The problem is that if we concentrate on the detail, the task of explaining changes and relationships can become so large that we finish up with a series of case studies but no overall sense of the dynamics driving firms and other organizations. But it is important to tackle this level of analysis. It is possible to identify categories and trends that enable us to flesh out the broader theories and which give us major insights into the behaviour of particular market relationships or particular companies. If we wish to have a deep understanding of the organizations which act as economic agents, we have to tackle their complexity and not just abstract from it.

> **Question**
>
> Firms' objectives are an important part of the analysis. After all, if we can identify objectives, then, in principle, we can devise methods by which they can be achieved. What would you expect to be the primary objectives of firms?

Once we get inside the organization we find that it can be intensely difficult to understand. It may not be easy to identify the firm's objectives. Whilst it is true that there may be an underlying acceptance of the simple objective of minimizing costs, that will be a means to achieving other goals and not the prime motivator in its own right. Liebenstein (1966) indicates that firms usually work above their long-run average cost curves unless forced down to the cost curve by their environments. Important features of the environment relate to internal motivation, he argues, not just external pressures. This accords with our observation of the world around us, that neither individuals nor firms always work as hard as they could, but this may be a legitimate objective for the organization and may be compatible with other long-term goals. So even something as simple as cost minimization may be an aspiration rather than a measurable standard to be achieved.

As part of the objective function (the interrelated set of objectives of a firm) there will frequently be some kind of *profit constraint* – a minimum level of profit that is acceptable to the oganization's owners, the *satisficing* level – but alongside this, other objectives appear. Some organizations regard *sales volumes* as a major objective. Others appear to see *growth* as their major objective.

Many Japanese firms appear to value growth highly. Conversely, other firms claim to eschew profits except as a way of maintaining their business. For example, BUPA (a private health services company) claims that all their profits are reinvested into health care. But it is misleading to concentrate on single objective for most companies. Their objectives will change as the environment changes. If the environment becomes very tough, survival may become the sole concern. On the other hand, in an easier environment other priorities may appear. One priority can be the wish to gain some control over the environment in order to provide opportunities for more discretion in the way the firm can actively engage with it. In many organizations different parts will have different priorities, and the organization's behaviour will be centred around some kind of *coalition* which may vary over time. Thus we find that the company will be attempting to achieve several objectives simultaneously and from time to time may have to trade off one objective against another.

A number of economic models have been devised using, for example sales or revenue as the major objective, but the objective that is usually assumed in economics is profit. Firms are assumed to be *profit maximizers*, though even in this case the concept is not unambiguous since short-run profit maximization – screwing as much as possible out of the immediate situation – may be incompatible with long-run profit maximization when the maintenance of a loyal customer base may be more important. Nevertheless, in analysis using the kinds of models set out in [the previous section of this chapter], profit maximization is frequently assumed in order to clarify its implications for a firm's decision making. Profit is likely to be an important feature of all private firms' objective function, but as I've argued earlier, it is unlikely to be the sole objective.

Organizational cultures

In order to understand the ways in which multiple objectives are determined, as well as to gain insight into the internal complexity of organizations and thus the ways in which those objectives might be fulfilled, it is valuable to consider organizational culture. Internal structures are often pictured using a simple mechanical analogy which assumes that, like simple mechanical devices, if one bit of the machine is moved, a second piece will move until an inevitable and easily predictable outcome is reached. In practice I think you will know that most, if not all, organizations do not react like that. There are frequently features that appear to be mechanical, but these are usually combined with much more complex forms reflecting the kinds of people employed by the organization, their own personal goals and values, power systems, information processing limitations, and much more.

Different cultures will have different taken-for-granted assumptions about the world and will respond in different ways to environmental stimuli, depending on the meanings perceived by actors within the organization, and to the importance of the culture of the organization and the symbols that are used as part of that culture. Non-cultural features are vital, of course – for example the context, the objective conditions faced by the organization, the knowledge and understanding of the organization's members, and the network of potential and actual collaborators – but the culture of the organization will interpret these in different ways. Different outcomes will arise depending on the balance of features. The organization's *history* bears heavily on its interpretation of events. The organization will have *developed ideologies* and possess particular *organizational structures* and distinctive *competences*. Thus the way in which any organization responds to changes in its environment, such as changes in competitors' behaviour or newly perceived opportunities, will be determined by a complex web of cultural features which interpret the new environment and indicate appropriate directions in which the organization might move.

For example, Cadbury, the chocolate manufacturer, has a long tradition of concern for the welfare and community-related aspects of its work. This dates back to the company's origins as a Quaker family firm. More recently the company has undergone a number of significant changes, and its founding values have been important:

> Cadburyism remained a strong ideology in the consciousness of family members, managers and workers, who all perpetuated it. It appears to have been both a benchmark for change and a force mediating that change. As a benchmark it provoked key change agents deliberately to set out their case against the fundamentals of the tradition. For example, the Cadbury (later group) technical director twice put up proposals to evacuate production out of Bournville, the centre and very essence of the Cadbury tradition. He argued that Bournville was too large and too institutionalized. He claimed that his intention on the second occasion was to spur the two leading family directors into a commitment to radical change. . . . At the same time, the company was able to invoke elements of the ideology and remould these in different circumstances. . . . In short, a dominant traditional corporate ideology should not necessarily be seen merely as an obstacle to transformation. For many it may encourage a clearer articulation of alternatives the more highly developed it is, and if reshaped or re-applied flexibly it may provide an important legitimatory bridge for the transition from one organizational policy configuration to another.
>
> (Child and Smith, 1987, pp.584–5)

What this amounts to is that to understand how firms react to changes we need to have a full analysis of the kind of organization we are dealing with, including a knowledge of its history and its interpretation of the objective conditions that it faces, as well as an understanding of the many competencies the firm may have. A decision to move from Bournville in order to maintain competitive strengths involved fundamental discussions about the nature of the company, and was connected to the existence of multiple objectives, including concerns about community values. At any given time Cadbury's goals were a kind of negotiated consensus in which ideas about the nature of the company and its history were influential.

Organizations, like Cadbury, also engage actively with their environments. In many respects they create or 'enact' their own environments (Weick, 1979). The idea of enactment questions the assumption that we can think of an organization and its environment as two quite separate things. It makes the point that a firm that is operating in a particular market is able to influence that market by the way in which it responds to market changes or tries to initiate changes itself – the extent to which it is active or passive. Many firms are important players in their own markets. Some firms will have more impact on the environment than others, but all will influence it, so that sometimes it is difficult to say precisely where the organization ends and the environment begins.

Organizational configurations

We can make connections between the firm, its cultural features and its environment, though these will change as the environment and culture change and interact. What we are considering here is a framework for understanding firms in a changing or dynamic world, not simply the static picture of [the *Production, costs and profits* section of this chapter]. Firms are likely to be attempting to minimize costs alongside other (sometimes incompatible) objectives. In a changing world the minimization of costs *now* may be less important than a longer-term objective and the need to create an organizational structure flexible enough to cope with expectations about change. Much of this is indeterminate.

Firms' organizational structures can be categorized in different ways. The main distinction in industrial economics has been between the U form and the M form. The U, for unitary, form refers to the archetypal form of business organization with a hierarchical structure in which different divisions report to a chief executive officer (CEO) or managing director. The M, or multi-divisional, form is generally larger and has a central office to which several operating divisions report, each of which has a structure like the U form and each of which is likely to have its own CEO. During the last century there has been a move first to large U form organizations, and then to M form organizations as the unitary structure became difficult to manage. This distinction highlights an important feature of recent economic history, namely the growth of firms into massive institutions. In looking at the complexity of firms it is useful to break down these distinctions further and to relate them to the kinds of environments in which they might thrive and the kinds of cultures which seem suited to particular configurations (Mintzberg, 1989). Firms move between configurations as their environments and cultures change and interact, but I shall set out different configurations for consideration separately for ease of exposition.

Firms usually begin their lives as *entrepreneurial organizations*. They are simple small units which can be flexible and responsive. They are in many ways the models for the firms analysed by the more abstract forms of economic theory in [the previous section of this chapter]. They are vulnerable in a dynamic economy because they rely on the expertise of a few individuals and do not have easy access to substantial financial resources. Protoscan was a company of this kind. Through its takeover by Kao it became part of a *machine organization* or *bureaucracy*. In this configuration jobs are specialized and standardized, the organization has elaborate administrative structures, and it is frequently controlled by a technostructure of experts. The expertise of the technostructure gives it a good deal of informal and formal power because it possesses the skill and information necessary to the organization's success. These machine organizations are essentially the U form. In the West, their cultures are typically Fordist and they tend to thrive in circumstances where the product is *standardized* and the environment is *stable*. In Japan their cultures seem to be more flexible (Best, 1990).

When the environment becomes *complex*, standardized procedures may not respond adequately and a more appropriate configuration may be the *professional organization*. This is made up of individuals who are highly skilled. They frequently work independently and autonomously. Their expertise is regulated through professional bodies. They are expensive in comparison with the standardized workers in the bureaucratic form, and they are supported by an administration which is itself professional. 'Scientific management' is not appropriate in such circumstances. Project-based firms in relatively stable environments, such as engineering consultancies, take this form, and hospitals and universities are organizations of this type. Such organizations are typically small autonomous units working within a more bureaucratic framework. They will respond to environmental changes and try to enact environmental changes in a very different manner from, say, the world of the entrepreneurial firm.

The organizational forms discussed so far find it difficult to respond to complexity and instability. In these circumstances the *innovative organization* or '*adhocracy*' is important. Such organizations are typified by team working and project groups which break up and re-form according to the particular needs of the moment. Aerospace, many forms of computing, consulting, and 'creative' occupations such as film-making usually take on this organizational form. Protoscan had elements of this form. Adhocracy is typically an organic structure relying on extensive liaison and co-ordination. The term *matrix organization* is sometimes used for this kind of structure. Environments that are complex and dynamic, requiring sophisticated innovative activity which calls for the co-operative effort of many different experts, are ones in which adhocracies flourish. They tend to be small or part of bigger *diversified organizations*.

Diversified organizations are typical of the world's largest organizations and are usually a loose coupling of other organizational forms under a broad umbrella. In essence this is the M form. The headquarters of such organizations rely on performance control systems to try to ensure that each part of the diversified form plays its role effectively. Because they are so large such organizations can be fascinating in their own right. Table 5.6 gives some background information on the world's biggest industrial groupings. It is based on *The Times 1000*, which is one of an increasing number of publications that list the world's biggest companies by various measures of size.

As you can see, the top ten is dominated by Japanese companies, thus confirming the importance of Asian companies. [. . .] *Sogo shoshas* are vast umbrella organizations providing integrated services to member companies. Until quite recently they were unique to Japan, but they are now developing in other Asian countries. The scale of these companies is truly enormous. Sumitomo's £80500 million worth of sales, or roughly $140 billion, is bigger, for example, than the GNP of one of Europe's wealthiest nations, Denmark, which had a GNP of $113.5 billion in 1990. GNP and sales are not the same thing, but organizations of such scale are potentially enormously powerful. It is not surprising that many industrial economists are fascinated by this configuration. Kao's takeover of Protoscan is part of the trend highlighted by this table. It represents a shift towards Pacific rim economies and change in the institutional and cultural forms that firms take.

If we wish to understand better the behaviour of particular companies, the use of such organizational configurations can be helpful. We no longer assume that all companies respond in the same way, but try to analyse their heterogeneity. An entrepreneurial organization will respond to changes differently from a large diversified company (whose preoccupation will sometimes be trying to hold the disparate parts together and to deal

Table 5.6 The world's top ten industrial groupings in 1990

Company	Headquarters	Main activity	Sales (£m)
1 Sumitomo	Japan	Sogo shosha	80 520.7
2 C Itoh	Japan	Sogo shosha	77 244.5
3 Mitsui & Co.	Japan	Sogo shosha	76 369.2
4 General Motors	USA	Vehicle manufacturer	71 571.4
5 Marubeni	Japan	Sogo shosha	68 650.2
6 Mitsubishi	Japan	Sogo shosha	62 502.2
7 Nissho Iwai	Japan	Sogo shosha	56 608.9
8 Ford	USA	Vehicle manufacturer	54 212.3
9 Exxon Corporation	USA	Oil and natural gas	54 173.3
10 Royal Dutch/Shell Group	Netherlands/UK	Oil industry	44 003.0

Source: Allen (1990)

with their differing objectives) and different again from an innovative organization. We can also see that different cultures will thrive better in different environments and that these are linked to the kind of configuration adopted. These will change as the environment changes and the culture shifts.

CONCLUSION

This chapter has started from the position that firms are complex social institutions. In trying to understand their behaviour a number of strategies are open to us. We can abstract from the detail and concentrate on particular features, as do the financial models and the abstract theoretical models. Such models produce powerful insights which enable us to make general statements about firms' behaviour. The nature of firms as institutions cannot be ignored, however. It raises questions about the nature of the market itself – whether markets or firms are the most appropriate way to organize production – and it forces us to recognize the heterogeneity of firms and to consider the richness of the detail. There is no right or wrong way to approach these issues. Our approach depends on the level of analysis appropriate to the questions we are asking. However, it is important to recognize the significance of each of the different approaches adopted here to the full understanding of the behaviour of organizations as economic agents.

[. . .]

ANSWERS TO EXERCISES

Exercise 5.1

1 The production function summarizes the relationship between inputs and outputs. For a given state of technology it shows the maximum output that can be produced from different combinations of inputs.
2 In the context of firms' production activities, division of labour means the dividing up of any work process into specialized activities undertaken by different people in order to increase the quantity of output available from given inputs.
3 The short run is the period in which not all factors of production are variable. The long run, in contrast, is the period in which all factors of production can be varied.

Exercise 5.2

1 The long-run average cost curve (see Figure 5.8) shows the lowest unit costs that can be obtained at all the relevant levels of output. This can be thought of as representing the optimum combination of factors of production.
2 Short-run average costs differ from long-run average costs because in the short run some factors of production are fixed in quantity.
3 See Figure 5.9. $SRAC_n$ indicates that there are many short-run average cost curves bounded by the $LRAC$.
4 In these circumstances long-run average costs rise, but because cheaper factors can replace the more expensive factors, long-run average costs do not rise by the full amount of the increase in the factor price.
5 The figures in Table 5.5 should be as shown below.

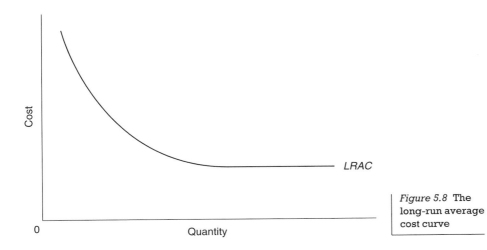

Figure 5.8 The long-run average cost curve

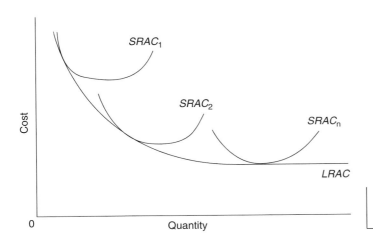

Figure 5.9 The relation between short-run and long-run average costs

Table 5.5 (completed)

Level of output (no. of units per day)	Total cost (£)	Average cost (£)	Marginal cost (£)
1	50	50	50
2	90	45	40
3	150	50	60
4	220	55	70

NOTES

* This chapter has been adapted from, The Open University (1995) D216 *Economics and Changing Economies*, Book 1 *The Market System*, Chapter 4 'Organizations as economic agents', Milton Keynes, The Open University.

1 The production function identifies the maximum output that can be produced from different combinations of inputs with a given technology.

2 A production process is technically efficient if it is not possible to produce a given quantity of goods or services with less of one factor of production without using more of another factor of production.

3 In the short run the firm is unable to vary its use of at least one of its factors of production.

4 In the long run the use of all factors of production is variable.

5 Average costs are costs per unit – that is, total costs divided by the number of units produced.

6 Economies of scale are reductions in average costs associated with expansion in output in the long run. Internal economies of scale are those which arise within the firm, as a result, for example, of taking advantage of opportunities for division of labour; external economies of scale are those which the firm gains because of the expansion of its industry.

7 A firm is economically efficient if it is working at a point on its long-run average cost curve.

8 Marginal cost is the change in total costs incurred by changing production by one unit. It reflects the extra amount of resources that the firm must lay out as it expands, or the resources saved as it contracts, and is the specific cost associated with changing output by one unit. It does not include overheads or other costs which are incurred whatever the level of output.

REFERENCES

Serial

Great Britain Annual Abstract of Statistics, London, Central Statistical Office (annual).

Other references

Allen, M. (ed.) (1990) *The Times 1000: 1990–91*, London, Times Books Ltd.

Best, M.H. (1990) *The New Competition: Institutions of Industrial Restructuring*, Cambridge, Polity Press.

Central Statistical Office (1992) *Business Monitor PA 1002: Report on the Census of Production 1990*, summary volume, London, HMSO.

Child, J. and Smith, C. (1987) 'The context and process of organizational transformation – Cadbury Limited in its sector', *Journal of Management Studies*, vol.24, no.6, pp.565–93.

Dibben, M. (1993) 'Fair deals from the counter revolution', *The Observer*, 7 November.

Hay, D.A. and Morris, D.J. (1991) *Industrial Economics and Organization: Theory and Evidence*, Oxford, Oxford University Press.

Liebenstein, H. (1966) 'Allocative efficiency and X-efficiency', *American Economic Review*, vol.56, pp.392–415.

Mintzberg, H. (1989) *Mintzberg on Management: Inside our Strange World of Organizations*, New York, Free Press.

Posnett, J. (1992) 'Income and expenditure of charities in England and Wales', *Charity Trends*, HMSO.

Segal, N. (1987) 'The Cambridge phenomenon', in Ferguson, D. *et al.*, *Cambridge*, Cambridge, Covent Garden Press.

Weick, K.E. (1979) *The Social Psychology of Organizing*, 2nd edn, Reading, Mass., Addison Wesley.

SECTION 3: HOW MARKETS WORK

INTRODUCTION

This section explores how markets work, and the nature of competition and power in markets.

Chapter 6, *Competition and power in markets* by Brown presents a diversity of perspectives on how markets work, and what is meant by market competition and market power. Brown draws upon various traditions of economic thought and demonstrates how different schools emphasise different aspects of the market process. For Schumpeter, the most significant form of market competition is that concerned with innovation in products and processes. Firms that continually innovate are successful, those that do not go bust: this process of 'creative destruction' is for him the hallmark of competition in capitalist economies. Large firms may have an advantage over their smaller rivals in circumstances where large investments are required for generating and appropriating rewards from innovation. Consequently, in the Schumpetarian tradition, dynamic market competition over the long period may be consistent with a market structure dominated by giant firms and with elements of monopoly in the shorter period. In contrast to the Schumpetarian model, the neoclassical or the perfect competition model of market competition tries to demonstrate that markets work best in the absence of corporate power. The neoclassical model assumes the existence of a large number of firms all of whom individually supply such a small share of a homogeneous product that none can have an impact on the product's price. The perfect competition model then demonstrates that in such a world, the interaction of the forces of demand and supply leads to the determination of an equilibrium price such that all firms produce in the least-cost fashion (assuming given and unchanging technology) and make just enough profits to keep them in business. This ensures that the interests of consumers and producers are harmonised. The neoclassical model thus embodies a more static view of competition in contrast to the Schumpetarian model. It is also rather weak in explaining the *process* of competitive price formation. This is a point emphasised by Hayek, who offers an alternative model of how markets work. In the Hayekian tradition, the real value of the process of market competition lies not in the fact that it may generate equilibrium outcomes but in that prices and changes in prices help in transmitting useful information between agents in a market. By responding to the change in prices, producers and consumers are led to adjust to economic change in an appropriate way. For Hayek, the market serves another useful purpose as well: it guarantees individual freedoms. This view, however, is contested by Sen. Sen's model of markets does not assume any automatic harmonisation of interests through the market mechanism. The distribution of the benefits from a market transaction depend upon the relative economic power of the transacting parties. In Sen's model, the market is seen as a 'power balance', and conflict of interests is seen as an inescapable feature of the market process.

6

COMPETITION AND POWER IN MARKETS*

Vivienne Brown

INTRODUCTION

In the realm of economic policy-making, one of the striking features of the recent period has been a renewed interest in the market and an increasing scepticism about the value of government involvement in the economy. In the UK we tend to associate this revival of economic liberalism with the policies of Mrs Margaret Thatcher's administrations following her first election victory in 1979. This trend towards economic liberalism has been evident around the globe: in the United States, it was associated with President Ronald Reagan (President from 1980-88), and, in the USSR, it was associated with Mr Mikhail Gorbachev's policy of perestroika and glasnost introduced in 1985. In Europe, these ideas can be seen behind some aspects of the move towards European integration, in particular behind the move towards setting up the single European market in 1992.

In this [chapter] we shall concentrate on examining arguments about the way that markets work, and their strengths and weaknesses. This links up with the [a] more general concern with the 'health' of the economy, and with its efficiency and productiveness. In this [chapter] the focus of enquiry will be on the different ways that market competition can contribute towards efficiency, producing at the lowest cost the range of goods that consumers wish to buy.

In the course of examining these different arguments we shall find that, underlying them, are different concepts of competition and different models of the market. [We shall be discussing] different meanings of 'competition' where we shall see that this is linked up with different models of the competitive market. In this way, I shall be illustrating [that] our models of the market are not given to us as automatic or straightforward effects of our day to day experiences. Instead these models of the market have to be built or constructed, and we shall see that different economists have approached this in different ways. [. . .]

In this [chapter], we will also examine how the revival of modern economic liberalism draws on a number of these different models of competitive markets. We shall [also] be looking at some important policy issues connected with the operation of competitive markets [. . .].

In summary, the aims of this [chapter] are:

- to examine the links between 'liberalism' and markets;
- to examine how different models of the market are used in debates about the working of the market;
- to examine some policy debates about the market.

COMPETITIVE MARKETS AND THE LIBERAL TRADITION

On 5 February 1989, the first of Sky Television's six satellite television channels was beamed into 600,000 homes in the UK and Irish Republic via cable television or home dishes, and a jubilant Mr Rupert Murdoch proclaimed that: 'Sky Television will bring competition; choice and quality to British Television. The monopoly is broken' (*The Times*, 6 February 1989).

Mr Murdoch's claim here represents what is perhaps a familiar understanding of markets: left unhindered, markets promote competition and this is good for the consumer. Competition promotes 'choice and quality' and very often, it is thought, lower prices too. Here competition is contrasted with monopoly, its opposite, where producers who are protected from competition become inefficient and do not provide choice, quality or low price for the consumer.

Just how competitive television may become over the next decade is something we shall have to wait to see. It is worth noting though that the event being celebrated by Mr Murdoch here is the increase in the number of suppliers by one; himself, in the person of Sky Television. Also note that until British Satellite Broadcasting launched their own satellite service in 1990, Mr Murdoch's own Sky Television had a true monopoly of satellite broadcasting as it was the one and only supplier. Note too that when BSB competes against Sky Television, satellite television is supplied by two producers (what economists call a duopoly) just as broadcast television had previously been supplied under duopoly conditions (BBC and ITV).

These details suggest that we should be wary when we read striking claims about 'competition' as opposed to 'monopoly' since these terms (as we shall see again later) are open to a range of meanings. But what Mr Murdoch's statement does illustrate is the commitment to competitive markets that can be traced back to the origins of the liberal tradition in the eighteenth century and the writings of Adam Smith in *The Wealth of Nations*. [. . .]

[W]ithin liberal thought, self-interested behaviour best promotes the wealth of nations through the free and undisturbed play of market forces. Here the market is seen as an efficient co-ordinator of the activities of free individuals, where the interplay of demand and supply in a competitive market is the 'key to prosperity' for everyone.

This liberal view of competitive markets, together with Adam Smith's own writings within this tradition, have played a powerful role in shaping modern thinking on markets. But, as with any fertile tradition of thought, we shall find that there are different interpretations of the benefits deriving from competitive markets, and also different degrees of scepticism as to how far markets alone may be relied upon to provide these benefits. In the course of this [chapter] we shall be looking at a number of 'models' of the market, models which provide different interpretations of Adam Smith's legacy and the liberal attachment to markets.

Summary

- Mr Murdoch's statement about the advent of Sky Television illustrates the commitment to competitive markets that is characteristic of the liberal tradition of thoughts.
- This liberal tradition of thought has given rise to a number of different models of the competitive market.

COMPETITIVE MARKETS AND INNOVATION

The first model of the competitive market that I would like to look at is one that emphasizes the importance of competition in stimulating *innovation in new products and new processes*. As an example of such an innovation we could think of the case of microcomputers whose production was revolutionized during the 1970–80s. Just a little while before, computers were bulky and expensive items, the preserve only of large institutions who could afford to buy them and accommodate them. By the end of the 1980s, microcomputers were everywhere in the office and frequently at home too. In 1987, 18 per cent of all households contained a home computer, and for larger families this figure was as high as 44 per cent, although it seems that it is boys rather than girls who use the computers. The price of these computers had fallen dramatically in relation to household budgets, and a large and profitable market for home computers had developed such that a new generation of micros with their attendant software programs were being directed specifically at this household market. Children were now growing up with microcomputers both as toys and visibly at use in the home and the school. It seemed that the age when computers were mysterious and inaccessible pieces of technical equipment was one that had existed long, long ago.

The process of creative destruction

This story of the introduction of microcomputers is one that accords well with the view of competition that sees it primarily in terms of the pressure to introduce *innovations*, that is, new products using new processes of production. This view of competition was put forward by Joseph Schumpeter in the early part of this century, when he set up a model of competitive markets characterized by competition over new products and new processes of production. In this way Schumpeter emphasized the changing structure of the economy, as firms are forced to try to move ahead faster than their rivals. In describing this process, Schumpeter refers to it as an evolutionary process, emphasizing its constantly changing and adaptive nature. This was how he put it in a book first published in Britain in 1943:

> The essential point to grasp is that in dealing with capitalism we are dealing with an evolutionary process. . . . Capitalism, then, is by nature a form or method of economic change and not only never is but never can be stationary. . . . The fundamental impulse that sets and keeps the capitalist engine in motion comes from the new consumers' goods, the new methods of production or transportation, the new markets, the new forms of industrial organization that capitalist enterprise creates . . . the history of the productive apparatus of a typical farm, from the beginnings of the rationalization of the crop rotation, plowing and fattening to the mechanized thing of today – linking up with elevators and railroads – is a history of revolutions. So is the history of the productive apparatus of the iron and steel industry from the charcoal furnace to our own type of furnace, or the

history of the apparatus of power production from the overshot water wheel to the modern power plant, or the history of transportation from the mail-coach to the airplane. The opening up of new markets, foreign or domestic, and the organizational development from the craft shop and factory to such concerns as US Steel illustrate the same process of industrial mutation – if I may use that biological term – that incessantly revolutionizes the economic structure *from within*, incessantly destroying the old one, incessantly creating a new one. This process of Creative Destruction is the essential fact about capitalism. It is what capitalism consists in and what every capitalist concern has got to live in.

(Schumpeter, 1976, pp.82–3)

In this passage, Schumpeter outlines his view of the evolutionary nature of capitalism where firms are forced to innovate in order to stay in the race. Those firms which do not do this, or which fall behind in the race to innovate, will go out of business. Schumpeter refers to this competitive process of 'innovate or go bust' as one of 'creative destruction'. Many firms are destroyed in the competitive race, but the outcome for the economic system as a whole is a creative one, Schumpeter argues, as it is this that forces the pace of innovation that has improved living standards over the years.

This is a view of competitive markets as a dynamic process of continuous change. The key to this process is the introduction of innovations, new products and new processes which revolutionize factories and offices and the work that goes on within them. As examples we could cite the case of the motor car, which brought with it the assembly line method of production, and the microcomputer which transformed office work. [. . .] [W]e could [also] cite the case of the fast-food industry. These products such as cars, microcomputers and fast-food, also transform the everyday lives of their consumers: motor cars open up possibilities for leisure travel and also for commuting to work; microcomputers increase the scope for the home-office and affect leisure activities, and fast food has changed family eating habits. In these ways, competition between firms transforms the products on sale in the shops, the types of shops selling the products, and the ways people spend their time outside working hours.

Summary

- Schumpeter's model of dynamic competition emphasizes competition over innovations in both products and processes.
- In the process of competition over innovations, firms innovate or go bust, this is the process of creative destruction.
- Innovations often depend on advances in technological knowledge.

Efficiency and costs

One of the points that Schumpeter emphasizes about competition is that it is competition over innovations that reduces costs and improves product quality. It is in these cost and product improvements that Schumpeter sees the progressive consequences of competitive activity. It is worth pausing for a moment to examine these cost reductions more closely. One crucial source of cost reduction that Schumpeter emphasizes is that arising from *technological advances*. This means that costs are reduced because advances in technological knowledge enable new production processes to be used that are cheaper than the old, sometimes creating entirely new products on the way. These cost reductions are often referred to as examples of *dynamic efficiency*. In the case of the motor car, the new technology of the internal combustion engine, combined with the new assembly line method of production, enabled the mass production of relatively cheap cars. In the case of microcomputers, the development of the microchip was an essential ingredient in the technological changes that enabled microcomputers to be both technically possible and relatively cheap to produce.

In addition, another source of cost reductions are *economies of scale* which relate to the scale of operations of the firm; here the argument is that it is the large firms which can produce most cheaply because they can spread the fixed costs or overhead costs over a larger scale of output. [. . .] Fixed costs are those costs that remain constant whatever the level of output; these are usually the cost of buildings, land and equipment. If fixed costs are spread over a larger output, then the average cost per unit produced will fall. (The average cost or unit cost is calculated by dividing the total costs by the number of units of output produced.) For example, a doubling of output may not require a doubling of the factory size and a doubling of all machinery costs. In this case, the unit cost reductions arising from the large scale of operation by the firm are known as economies of scale as the rate of output increases proportionately more than costs.

Perhaps here this point could be illustrated using a numerical example. For example, if an increase in output of 20 per cent required an increase in costs of 10 per cent, then the firm is operating under economies of scale as unit costs would fall with an increase in output.

Question 1

Just to check that you understand the idea of economies of scale, consider the case if output were to double and total costs were to increase threefold? Would you say that the firm here is operating under economies or diseconomies of scale?

In this case, there are diseconomies of scale; this is because total costs would increase proportionately faster than output, and this means that unit costs would rise with an increase in output.

To recap this section so far; we have seen that there are two possible sources of cost reductions that support Schumpeter's arguments about the efficiency of dynamic competition. There are cost reductions arising from new technological knowledge, and there are cost reductions arising from economies of scale. Although we can easily separate these two kinds of cost reductions at a conceptual level, in practice they are often combined as the new methods of production are feasible only if operated on a large scale. For example, the introduction of assembly line production was feasible only at certain high levels of production; similarly, microchip production also yields economies of large scale production.

One implication of this view of dynamic competition is that it is the large corporations and their entrepreneurial managers that are significant for the competitive health of the economy. It is only the large corporations who have the financial resources to fund large research departments, set up the innovations and carry out the large scale marketing and advertising necessary to sustain the large production runs. In this way, Schumpeter bases his model of competition on a market structure dominated by the large corporations; he also argues that these large corporations hold the technological key to the future dynamism of the economy, although he also expresses the concern that the institutional structure of large corporations may have the effect of stunting entrepreneurial initiative.

[. . .]

> ### Summary of Schumpeter's views
>
> - Competition is over innovation, new products and new processes.
> - In this process costs are reduced by new technology and by economies of scale.
> - Large firms are important in this evolutionary process of the economy.

Monopolies in the market

We have seen that, in Schumpeter's account, it is the large corporations that have the competitive edge in introducing innovations, deriving the benefits of dynamic efficiency and economies of scale, although he also feared that entrepreneurial initiative might suffer. [. . .] But this then raises a question as to the extent to which the competitive market itself produces such agglomerations of corporate power and monopolistic tendencies that the competitive process undermines itself. In this case, the presence of monopoly could lead to inefficient production with high costs and prices.

Competition in Schumpeter's sense of dynamic competition does seem to include some of the characteristics that could be associated with monopoly situations in the short period. For example, a substantial market share of sales is sometimes thought to be indicative of some degree of monopoly power. The most concentrated industrial sectors in Europe are motor vehicles, aerospace and computers/office equipment; in each of these industries the top five firms accounted for nearly two thirds of sales. At the other end of the scale, in industries such as food textiles, printing and metal goods, the top five firms account for a low proportion of sales, about 10 per cent or less.

Schumpeter, however, argued that we need to take a longer view of the time period necessary for competitive forces to work themselves out. He argued that, if we take a longer historical perspective, firms will have to innovate and be forward-looking, and it is this that ensures that costs will constantly be reduced with the technological advances that accompany the innovation process. A corner shop, for example, may have a monopoly of the local neighbourhood trade in that it has a high market share, but in time there will be competition from the supermarket and the hypermarket. Schumpeter argues that it is this kind of competition between the corner shop and the hypermarket, encompassing new ways of selling and including a wider range of goods, that is the significant form of competition, rather than the competition between a number of corner shops all selling the same range of goods and vying for the local custom. Thus, as long as there is freedom of entry, even local 'monopolies' in the short period will have to face competition from innovative, forward looking firms in the longer run.

Many governments, however, are obliged to be concerned with shorter time horizons than Schumpeter, and have introduced legislation in an attempt to control the growth of monopolies and cartel agreements. In the UK, the Monopolies and Mergers Commission makes reports on proposed mergers that are referred to it. One of the issues covered in the Commission's Reports is the extent to which a monopoly situation could result from the proposed merger. This kind of government concern would be an example of a situation where the 'free' competitive market needs the intervention of the state in order to protect it and maintain its 'freedom'. Monopolies here are considered harmful because they have less incentive to be efficient in the absence of effective rivals. They may have higher costs, and prices to the consumer are higher than they need be. In addition, the quality of the product or service may decline.

A related difficulty is posed by the existence of what are termed 'natural monopolies'. In this case, an industry has such large economies of scale that the market cannot support more than one supplier, as this single firm can undercut all its rivals. Network industries such as the telephone service or the railway are examples of natural monopolies. In this case, it may well be efficient for there to be only one firm supplying the market. The problem, however, is that there is little incentive for the firm to be efficient if it faces no competition from rival firms. Many natural monopolies have in the past been taken into public ownership in order to try to overcome this problem. The public utilities such as gas, electricity, water, rail and telephones have at various times come into this category.

With the privatizations of the 1980s, however, and the planned transfer of many of these corporations into the private sector, alternative methods of control had to be devised. It was discovered that a monopoly in the private sector may well not operate any more 'efficiently' than a monopoly in the public sector. For this reason it was argued by many economists that the issue of the ownership of the utility is less significant than the issue of the degree of competition facing it. As a result, along with privatization went a need to 'regulate' the performance of the industry in order to ensure that it did not abuse its position of power in the market. In this way, attempts were made to 'mimic the market' and make the privatized monopoly industry behave as if it were more like a competitive industry.

For example, British Telecom and British Gas are natural monopolies. When they were privatized in 1984 and 1986 respectively, they became privately owned monopolies rather than publicly owned monopolies, and so some additional regulation was proposed to encourage these firms to be efficient, improving quality and service while keeping costs to a minimum. Here, regulation took the form of price regulation, and pricing formulas were developed that had to be adhered to by the newly privatized industries. This too presents another example of state intervention in attempting to safeguard the conditions for the operation of a 'free' market, as it was the state that set up the regulatory bodies OFTEL and OFGAS. In the case of industries transferred to the private sector, a form of external control was needed in order to try to prevent the industries from abusing their market power. [. . .]

Summary

- Schumpeter's emphasis on the importance of dynamic competition over a long period of time may be consistent with elements of monopoly in the shorter period.
- Government policies often include an attempt to regulate monopolies; these policies include the Monopolies and Mergers Commission, nationalization and regulation.
- In the 1980s, regulation and private ownership replaced nationalization for natural monopolies such as British Telecom and British Gas.

Conclusion

Schumpeter's model of competition as innovative competition between corporate giants may well present a picture of capitalist competition that seems 'realistic' to us, but it is nonetheless a specific model of competitive behaviour. It concentrates on the longer term aspects of competition and it focuses on competition over products, markets and processes. Schumpeter argues that dynamic competition and creative destruction are beneficial because innovations provide the most effective way of reducing costs and prices. Thus, Schumpeter is offering not only a model of what competition is and how it works; he is also offering an argument as to why competition (in his sense) is to be welcomed and promoted. Note here that Schumpeter's concept of competition is a very wide one. For example, it includes

Table 6.1 Schumpeter's model

model of competition	dynamic competition, i.e. forward-looking competition over innovations in products and processes
source of efficiency	
organizations	

instances that are sometimes understood as monopolistic where a small number of large firms dominate the market for that product.

As a way of summarizing the different models of the market, it would be helpful to keep a grid illustrating the main points of similarity and difference. I have started the grid for you in [Table 6.1]. There is a complete grid at the end of the [chapter] for you to compare with your own as you progress through the [chapter].

COMPETITIVE MARKETS AND EQUILIBRIUM

In Schumpeter's model of competitive innovation and creative destruction, we saw that the innovating firms were seen as powerful organizations in the market. An opposing model of competition is one which identifies competition with the *absence* of such corporate power in the market. According to this neoclassical model of competitive equilibrium or perfect competition, there is such a large number of firms that each one can be seen as a miniscule, insignificant atom that has no influence.

In this case, a greater role is ascribed to 'the market' itself in securing certain competitive outcomes, rather than the activities of forward-looking corporations, and this role is what we shall be examining in this section. Crucial to this way of thinking is the importance attached to price. In Schumpeter's model, innovations were the hallmark of healthy competitive activity; in the neoclassical model of competitive equilibrium it is the determination of price that registers the extent to which a market is competitive. According to this model of competition, prices are determined impersonally in the market, and this secures equality between those demanding the good and those supplying the good.

Balancing of demand and supply

The neoclassical model of competitive equilibrium examines the influences on the price of a commodity by grouping them into two broad categories – those influences on the side of supply and those on the side of demand. On the side of *supply* are included all those influences on the production of a commodity, such as the availability of the right kind of labour, raw materials, machinery, power, and also the technology in use at the time. On the side of *demand* are included all those influences which affect consumers' demand for a commodity, such as income, lifestyle, age, and the social conventions and expectations that can all be summed up as consumers' tastes. The activity below gives some illustrations.

Question 2

- As a result of an increase in food poisoning alleged to be related to the consumption of eggs, consumers wish to buy fewer eggs at any given price. In this case there has been a change on the *demand* side. The demand for eggs has fallen.
- Because of a world shortage of oil, less petrol is produced at any given price. In this case there has been a change on the supply side; the supply has fallen.

Now try some exercises for yourself: would the following changes affect the demand or supply side of the market?

1 Manufacturers develop a more economical process for making washing machines.
2 Producers introduce an extensive advertising campaign for a product.

In the first example, if manufacturers develop a more economical process for making washing machines, there would be a change on the supply side of the market. In the second example, if an extensive advertising programme is introduced by the producers this will be aimed at making the product more attractive to consumers. If the advertising campaign is successful, demand for the product will increase.

In this way, all the influences on price can be grouped either on the side of demand or on the side of supply. But what is the relation between demand, supply and price? One way of understanding this is to see the neoclassical competitive market as a *balancing mechanism* that balances demand and supply. In this mechanism, price has a crucial role to play as it is the price that secures a balance – or equilibrium – between demand and supply. If demand is greater than supply, then the new price must be higher than the original price in order for demand and supply to be in balance again; if demand is less than supply, then the new price must be lower than the original one in order to restore balance. These results are summarized in Table 6.2.

Table 6.2 The balancing of demand and supply

if D is less than S, then P would have to fall for D and S to be in equilibrium

if D is more than S, then P would have to increase for D and S to be in equilibrium

---

Question 3

The results in Table 6.2 may have a certain plausibility, but do you feel you can explain them in your own words?

My own explanation would be along the following lines. In the first example, if demand is less than supply at the original price, this means that there are unsold supplies on the market. If these unsold supplies are to find a buyer, then the price would have to be lower. At a lower price, more would be demanded both because consumers could afford to buy more and because, compared with other goods whose price has not fallen, this good is now a better buy. Similarly, at a lower price, less would be supplied because it is now less financially attractive for firms to produce the good if their objective is to make as much profit as possible. The combined effect of the increase in quantity demanded and the fall in the quantity supplied, would ensure that demand and supply are in equilibrium at the lower price.

In the second example, if demand is greater than supply at the original price, this means that there are consumers in the market who would like to make purchases at the going price, but who are unable to do so. If demand and supply are to be in equilibrium again, there would have to be an increase in the price which would reduce the quantity demanded and increase the quantity supplied.

This neoclassical model has been an important one for economics. This may be seen by reading the following extract from Professor Kenneth Arrow's Nobel Prize Lecture delivered in 1972. Professor Arrow subscribes to the neoclassical model of competition, and he looks back to Adam Smith for an early statement of the importance of the notion of a balance or equilibrium between demand and supply:

> From the time of Adam Smith's *Wealth of Nations* in 1776, one recurrent theme of economic analysis has been the remarkable degree of coherence among the vast numbers of individual and seemingly separate decisions about the buying and selling of commodities. In everyday, normal experience, there is something of a balance between the amounts of goods and services that some individuals want to buy and the amounts that other, different individuals want to sell. Would-be buyers ordinarily count correctly on being able to carry out their intentions, and would-be sellers do not ordinarily find themselves producing great amounts of goods that they cannot sell. This experience of balance is indeed so widespread that it raises no intellectual disquiet among laymen; they take it so much for granted that they are not disposed to understand the mechanism by which it occurs.
>
> (Arrow, 1974, p.253)

In this passage, Arrow refers to the balance between the amounts that people wish to buy and sell. In other words, Arrow is describing the balance between demand and supply. As he says, there is a 'remarkable degree of coherence' among producers' and consumers' decisions, and this coherence is achieved by the operation of the price 'mechanism'.

Summary

- In a neoclassical model of competitive equilibrium (or perfect competition), demand and supply are in balance at the equilibrium price.
- If demand is greater than supply, then price has to rise for demand and supply to be equal; if demand is less than supply, then price has to fall for demand and supply to be equal.

Equilibrium price

As a way of exploring the demand and supply model, we could take further our image of the price system as a *balancing* mechanism where the equality of demand and supply is represented as a balancing of demand and supply. One way of doing this is to represent an individual market as a 'balance' or as a pair of weighing scales, scales that have been replaced in our shops now by electronic weighing machines. In Figure 6.1 there is a diagram of such a pair of scales, and here the pans represent demand and supply.

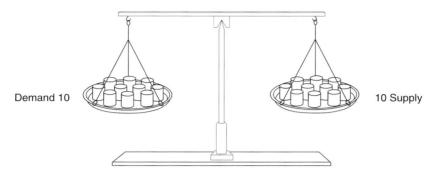

Figure 6.1 A representation of the competitive market as the balancing of demand and supply

In Figure 6.1, the demand and supply pans are in balance, or in equilibrium. In this case, demand and supply are equal and everything is at rest; the market price is said to be the *equilibrium price*.

In Figure 6.2, the demand pan is lighter than the supply pan. In this case, demand has fallen (i.e. has become lighter) whilst supply has remained unchanged (and so has become relatively heavier). Consumers have switched their expenditure away from this good for some reason; this would be the case with the example of food poisoning allegedly associated with eggs that we saw earlier on.

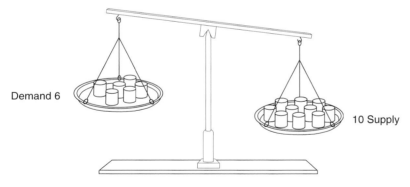

Figure 6.2 A fall in demand relative to supply at the existing market price

In the case shown in Figure 6.2, demand is lighter than supply, so that to make them balance again we have to increase demand relative to supply. One way of achieving this is to reduce the price of the good. This reduction in price would have two effects. It would increase the quantity demanded, as the lower price would both encourage and enable more people to consume more of the good. In addition, it would reduce the quantity supplied, as the good would become less profitable for suppliers to produce. The new equilibrium price would be such that the net effect of the reduced demand and the increased supply is that demand and supply once again balance. This is shown in Figure 6.3. At a lower equilibrium price, demand and supply are again in balance.

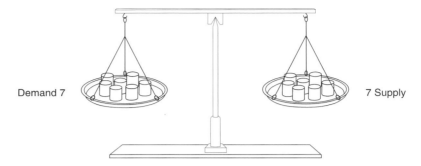

Demand 7   7 Supply

Figure 6.3 Restoration of equilibrium at a reduced market price following an initial reduction in demand

In Figure 6.3, demand and supply are again in balance, at the lower price, but note that the actual quantities demanded and supplied are smaller than in the original equilibrium position.

Question 4

What do you think would happen in the opposite case where supply fell for some reason? Do you think that the final equilibrium price would be higher or lower than the original equilibrium price?

If supply were less than, i.e. lighter than, demand, then an increase in the price would be needed to increase the quantity supplied and decrease the quantity demanded. A higher price would make the good more profitable for firms to produce. The higher price would also mean that consumers would be discouraged from buying the good, and that it would now compare less favourably with other goods available for sale on the market. If supply were to increase and demand fall, this means that the supply pan would become heavier and the demand pan would become lighter until the two pans are in balance again. In other words, if the price increases, the quantity supplied would increase and the quantity demanded would fall until they are once again in balance at the new higher equilibrium price.

Question 5

In Question 2, you may remember, we looked at the way that events can affect demand and supply, but we did not follow this through to see how these changes in demand and supply would affect the equilibrium price.

It is worth referring back to Question 2 now, and checking how the equilibrium price would change in the examples there.

The first example in Question 2 was the eggs case. If the demand for eggs falls, there would have to be a fall in the equilibrium price of eggs for demand and supply to be in balance again. In the second case, if there is a world shortage of oil, this means that supply has fallen at any given price, and so the equilibrium price would have to rise for supply to balance demand. (Remember the OPEC price rises of 1974 and 1979, and effects of the Gulf crisis breaking out in 1990.) The third case involved a cheapening of the production of washing machines; here the increase in supply means that the equilibrium price would have to fall for demand to equal supply. In the final example, consumer demand increases as a result of the advertising campaign. Here the equilibruim price would have to rise.

We have seen in this section how changes in the equilibrium price can secure a balance between demand and supply. In this way, price changes provide incentives to both consumers and suppliers, whose independent reactions then result in a new balancing of the market where there are no unsatisfied customers and no frustrated sellers. Consumers economize on goods that become more expensive, and suppliers will have an incentive to produce more of those goods whose price rises. In this way, the price mechanism works by balancing demand and supply without any central direction, relying only on individual consumers and suppliers acting in their own interests. As a model of the decentralized co-ordination of many independent consumers and suppliers, this model of the competitive market has gained many admirers and has stimulated an enormous amount of very sophisticated theoretical work from economists such as Kenneth Arrow.

I wonder if you've noticed, however, that I haven't said anything yet as to *how* prices are formed in the market. What I showed was that, *if* prices were changed in a particular way, then there would be equilibrium in the market where demand and supply were equal. But we have not actually considered the *process* of price adjustment. Using the balance diagram to illustrate demand and supply has focussed our attention on how demand and supply are balanced *if* price were to be changed, but it also turned our attention away from the actual process of changing the equilibrium price. We just took it for granted. In examining Figure 6.3, I 'announced' the new price which then determined the quantities on the measuring pans. In this way, my guiding presence was necessary for the new equilibrium to emerge. This may reinforce the notion that there is an 'invisible hand' whose presence guarantees the successful operation of competitive markets.

But how is the market price changed? In the neoclassical model of competitive equilibrium, each supplier and consumer is so small relative to the market as a whole that everyone has to accept the price as given. In this case, there is so much competition and so many producers that no individual producer has any effect on price at all. We say that the producers are *price-takers* because they have to accept the market price whatever it is.

Now we are ready to answer our question: how is the market price changed? And here we come to a result that may appear paradoxical to you. If all firms and consumers are price-takers, who is it then who marks down the price of the commodity when supply is greater than demand? And who is it that marks up the price when demand is greater than the supply? The answer to this is that it is 'the market', the result of the general market process. But this still provides no answer since there is no such thing as 'the market', only a large number of individual consumers and producers.

Economists summarize this result by explaining that the model of a perfectly competitive market is essentially a model for demonstrating the properties of a market that is in equilibrium where demand and supply are equal at the equilibrium price. It enables us to investigate the properties of a competitive equilibrium, but it does not describe a process of adjustment from one equilibrium to another. Just as the weighing scales needed a hand to equilibrate the demand and supply pans, so the neoclassical competitive model needs a hand (an invisible hand?) to find the right set of prices to equilibrate demand and supply. And as the pans 'naturally' come into balance again, so the market process of price changes is seen as a natural process detached from any individual's influence. One of the best examples of the model of competitive equilibrium in practice is the market for fixing the price of gold. Here, telephone contact with the dealers establishes the equilibrium price where demand equals supply. No actual trade takes place until the equilibrium price has been announced.

Summary

- The neoclassical model of competitive equilibrium (or perfect competition) has been enormously influential and has been at the root of many discussions about the effectiveness of competitive markets.
- The strength of the neoclassical model is that it shows the equilibrium properties of a competitive market.
- Demand equals supply at the equilibrium price.

Competition and efficiency again

What is the link between competition and efficiency in this neoclassical model of competition? As firms are price-takers, they cannot influence the market price. This means that if a firm wants to make profits, it must reduce its costs as much as possible. But all firms are doing this, and so costs for the entire market are pushed down to the minimum level. When costs are at the minimum possible level for any given state of technology, we say that firms are *productively efficient*.

Competition between firms also means that the equilibrium price is pushed down to the minimum level that is consistent with the continued survival of the firms in the market. If any firm's costs rise as a result of being inefficient, profits will be eliminated and the firm will be driven out of business. If costs of production fall, say because the cost of raw materials has fallen, this will result in a fall in the equilibrium price. Why do you think this will happen?

Question 6

It is worth spending some time thinking about this question.

At the original equilibrium price, profits increase because the cost of raw materials has fallen. (Or you could consider the case where profits have increased because demand has increased).

What do you think are likely to be the longer term consequences if other firms are free to enter the market, attracted by the higher profits? If you are not sure about this, you could look back at questions 2–5 and consider the effects of an increase in supply.

Note that there is a clue in the last sentence where I suggested you might think about an increase in supply.

If new firms enter the market in pursuit of higher profit, then this means that supply will increase and this will imply a reduction in the equilibrium price. As long as the price is high enough for exceptional profits to persist, then new entrants into the market may be expected. But once the equilibrium price is at a level where the going rate of profit is being made, then the flow of new firms entering the market will cease. With this new equilibrium price, there is a larger output than before and firms once again earn the going, or normal, rate of profit.

In this [part of the chapter], we have seen that firms in the neoclassical model of competition are productively efficient, that is, costs are at the minimum known level given the state of technology. In addition, prices are at the minimum possible level.

Summary

- In the neoclassical model of competitive equilibrium (or perfect competition), costs are reduced to the minimum, given existing technology: i.e. firms are productively efficient.
- Equilibrium prices are at the minimum level that is consistent with the continued survival of firms in the market.

Conclusion

I have outlined the basic neoclassical model of competitive equilibrium, and we have seen how changes in the equilibrium price can balance demand and supply. If demand is greater than supply, then the equilibrium price will have to increase in order for balance to be restored; if supply is greater than demand, then the equilibrium price will have to fall. In this way, price changes can restore equilibrium in the market in an apparently natural or impersonal manner, as no one individual consumer or trader has any influence in the market. This is a very powerful model of the market. Its main weakness is that it models the competitive *outcome*, i.e. equilibrium, rather than the competitive *process*. In this case, the model makes sense by imagining an external presence such as an auctioneer or invisible hand, which would set the correct equilibrium price in the full knowledge of the state of demand and supply. The fixing of the price of gold, using telephone contact amongst the dealers to agree an equilibrium price, is a rare example of this 'auctioneer principle' at work. In practice, the demand and supply model is widely used in economic analysis of real markets. [. . .]

This would be a good moment to fill in the main points about the neoclassical model of competition on your [table]. My own contribution is provided below:

Table 6.3 Neoclassical model

model of competition	competitive equilibrium or perfect competition: at the equilibrium price, demand and supply are equal
source of efficiency	
organizations	

[. . .]

COMPETITIVE MARKETS AND INFORMATION

Some economists who admire the basic idea of the neoclassical model of perfect competition, argue that its main weakness is its lack of emphasis on the *process* of competitive price formation. Here they point out that the crucially important feature of competition is the process of market adjustment, and its ability to generate the right sort of information to facilitate this adjustment.

Prices as signals

One economist who has been associated with this approach is F.A. Hayek, a major influence on the revival of free market thinking and Mrs Margaret Thatcher's policies during the 1980s. The main issue that the competitive equilibrium model ignores, Hayek argues, is the fact that individuals never have complete information when responding to economic changes. Hayek's argument is that it is of crucial significance that individuals do not have complete information, and that it is the crowning achievement of the competitive market that it succeeds in transmitting relevant information to the appropriate people at a surprisingly low cost to society. Thus, he argues that equilibrium economics is largely irrelevant compared with the process of competitive price adjustment for economies experiencing change.

Question 7

Consider a change in tastes such that consumers decide they no longer wish to eat crops and fruits sprayed with chemicals. How do you think this vital information can be conveyed to the growers of crops and fruits?

Perhaps here you could think back to the neoclassical model of competition [in the previous section of this chapter], and consider what would happen to the equilibrium price if consumers switch over from food produced with the aid of chemical fertilizers to food produced organically.

If consumers switch over from conventionally produced to organically produced food, then there is a fall in demand for conventionally grown food and an increase in demand for organically grown food. From the section on competitive markets and equilibrium we know that the new equilibrium price of organic food will be higher than the old one, and conversely that the new equilibrium price of the other food must be lower.

Hayek's approach, however, is to emphasize the importance of the *process* of competitive price changes. Instead of emphasizing the equilibrium outcome as in the neoclassical model based on price-taking behaviour, he emphasizes the process of adjustment where demand and supply are out of equilibrium. If the demand for organic food increases, this means that the price of organic food increases; although organic food producers need know nothing about the general state of demand for their product, they do notice that the price of their product has increased. This increased price acts as an incentive for them to produce more, and they increase the rate of output until the price stops rising. When the price is no longer rising, then demand and supply are equal once again and the ruling price is once again the equilibrium price. But, because Hayek emphasizes the process of change rather than the equilibrium outcome, he accepts that the final equilibrium may never actually take place. This does not in his view weaken his account of markets as a process of adjustment to changed conditions. As another example of this process, we could consider the increase in the price of oil and petrol in 1990 following the Gulf crisis. The increased price reflected oil's increased scarcity and encouraged consumers to economize in its use.

Notice here then that Hayek sees changing competitive prices as a *signal*, a mechanism for transmitting information between individuals in the market. By responding to these changed prices, producers and consumers are led to respond in an appropriate way to economic change. In this way, vital information about the availability of goods is transmitted throughout the economy to those producers and consumers who are affected by it. When we take into account that such changes are taking place constantly throughout a market system, Hayek argues, the amount of information transmitted is truly incredible.

Thus, in Hayek's model of the competitive market, changes in competitive prices are the signals by which information is transmitted to those who need to know it. Competitive prices are seen as a kind of 'machine' for sending out information. Hayek describes it in this way:

> We must look at the price system as such a mechanism for communicating information if we want to understand its real function – a function which, of course, it fulfils less perfectly as prices grow more rigid . . . It is more than a metaphor to describe the price system as a kind of machinery for registering change, or a system of telecommunications which enables individual producers to watch merely the movement of a few pointers, as an engineer might watch the hands of a few dials, in order to adjust their activities to changes of which they may never know more than is reflected in the price movement.
>
> (Hayek, 1976, pp.86–7)

Hayek argues that this competitive process of price change is the best method available for transmitting necessary information about consumers' tastes and production possibilities. Though not perfect, and though it may never result in equilibrium, Hayek argues that it is better than the alternative which he sees as state planning. His economic argument here against state planning largely relies upon the informational difficulties involved once the competitive market process is laid aside. Changes in prices convey information which the state would somehow have to discover by other means, and Hayek's argument is that the informational problems involved here are insuperable.

Hayek's point about the transmission of information using the price system is an important one, and we have seen a hypothetical example of this at work in the case of the switch to organic produce, and the real example of the oil price rise in 1990. But markets are not a costless way of transmitting information. Firms have to calculate costs and prices, and this information has to be processed and transmitted. Thus the actual creation and communication of this vital information is carried out by institutions and has a real resource cost. Indeed, the explosion in information technology in recent years underlines the point that this is in itself big business.

Summary

- Hayek emphasizes the importance of the process of competition rather than the end result of equilibrium.
- Information about changes in consumers' tastes or in the conditions of production, is transmitted by changes in prices.
- In this competitive process, Hayek emphasizes the importance of the price system as a decentralized mechanism for transmitting information; prices are information signals.

Prices and information

We need to remember, however, that prices do not always transmit the correct information, and that sometimes the information is impossible to get. When I was writing this [chapter], there were a number of food scares where it suddenly became public knowledge (as reported in the newspapers) that the chemicals that had for years been sprayed on food crops had now been associated with an increased incidence of cancer. It was argued that the chemical Alar sprayed on apples had been identified as carcinogenic, although this finding was vigorously disputed by the Growers' Associations. As a result of these reports, I went into my local greengrocer to ask if she had any apples that had not been sprayed by Alar. This information was not available.

Thus, prices cannot always be relied upon to provide the necessary signals and incentives to allocate resources to their best uses. An example is where market prices may not transmit all the relevant information because they include only the costs borne by the individual producer and exclude the wider effects on society. Similarly, prices may reflect only the individual consumer's satisfaction and exclude the wider benefits to society as a whole. One example of this as we have seen is the case of the excessive use of chemicals on food products. The private cost of this is the cost of the chemicals to the food producer, who balances it against the increased crop yield and its resistance to crop diseases. But, if the wider effect is to contaminate the food chain and to harm consumers, this is a social cost which is not reflected in the cost of the chemical as such. These *social costs*, which are not borne as private costs and so are not transmitted by the changing prices of goods, are known as *externalities*. The presence of externalities therefore indicates that prices are failing fully to reflect all the appropriate information. Similarly, *social benefits* are another source of externalities which are not included in prices; for example, my pleasure in another's well-landscaped garden will not be included in its price.

To give you a better idea of the range of externalities in practice, it might be helpful if I run through a list of different externalities. These may include: the health effect on others of smoking cigarettes, the effect on others of driving a car while drunk, the effect on others' health if contagious diseases receive proper medical treatment, the 'tender loving care' provided by hospital domestic services prior to the privatization of these services [. . .], the effect on industry of an efficient school system, the effect on the environment and public health of intensive farming methods, the effect on a local economy of providing a modern transport system, the effect on the environment of industrial pollution, the effect on global temperatures of carbon dioxide and other gas emissions, the effect of 'accidents' involving nuclear power generators, the effect on world peace of antagonistic economic systems, etc., etc.

As you can see, the list of externalities could be a very long one and would include items of varying importance. The point is that, if externalities are present and they will detract from the informational properties of competitive prices. The difficulty is to know how to quantify them in practice.

The presence of externalities has provided one set of potential reasons for state involvement in the economy including environmental policies, health programmes, educational provision, public transport, industrial support, and regulations concerning standards and safety that we take for granted until something goes wrong. A relatively new issue that has been causing increased concern is that of the 'greenhouse effect' where the earth's temperature is thought to be increasing as a result of the emission of carbon dioxide, chlorofluorocarbons (CFCs), methane, and nitrous oxide into the atmosphere. Scientific estimates differ, but the consensus is that the increase of greenhouse gas concentrations from their pre-industrial revolution levels will involve an increase in average world temperatures. One implication of this global warming is that the earth's oceans are warming and the ice caps melting, with consequential risks of flooding in low-lying coastal areas. In addition, the regional climatic effects of such a warming are likely to be extensive although they are difficult to predict. The evidence on global warming has raised again in a particularly acute form the question of the extent to which free market solutions can be found for environmental problems.

In July 1989, the all-party Commons Energy Select Committee published a Report, *Energy Policy Implications of the Greenhouse Effect* which argued against the Government's preferred policy of a free market solution. The Report stated that 'Our witnesses were virtually unanimous in conceding that market mechanisms unaided would not produce an adequate response to global warming' (para. 134). The Report urged a combination of policy measures such as tax measures, direct regulatory measures and financial incentives in order to reduce the emissions of harmful gases and to improve energy efficiency.

Summary

- The price mechanism is not a costless way of transmitting information.
- Sometimes prices do not transmit the correct information; externalities are present when prices do not convey all the social costs and social benefits arising from an economic activity; but externalities are themselves extremely difficult to quantify.
- Environmental pollution and the greenhouse effect are examples of externalities, as these are social costs arising from economic activities that are not reflected in market prices.

Hayek and individual freedom

[. . .] [M]any proponents of the free market have argued that the free market economy is the best way of guaranteeing individual freedom, and Hayek too has put forward this argument [. . .]. Hayek's own political philosophy places an over-riding emphasis on individual liberty. This concept of individual liberty is associated with a strand in liberal political thought which has constructed a concept of liberty as the freedom from interference in pursuing one's own ends, sometimes known as *negative freedom*. Hayek writes: ' . . . a condition of liberty in which all are allowed to use their knowledge for their purposes, restrained only by rules of just conduct of universal application, is likely to produce for them the best conditions for achieving their aims . . . ' (Hayek, 1976, vol.1, p.55).

This concept of freedom finds a clear expression in the view of the 'market' as the site of the exchange of goods and services by free agents pursuing their own aims. As the market order produces outcomes that are 'natural' and not the result of human intention, these outcomes cannot be an encroachment on individual freedom. The basis of Hayek's argument here is that there are two different ways of making a distinction between the natural and the social. One way is to distinguish between natural outcomes and those outcomes which are the unintended result of human *action*, and the other is to distinguish between natural objects and those which are the result of intended human *design*. According to Hayek's approach, the crucial point about social and economic outcomes is that they are the unintended result of individual human *action* but not the intended result of human *design*. Hayek also traces his approach to the writings of the eighteenth century, including Adam Smith's famous metaphor of the invisible hand, and so here again we can see the authority of Adam Smith's writings for twentieth century economics. This crucial distinction allows Hayek to claim that economic outcomes that are the unintended consequences of human action are 'natural' outcomes; these natural outcomes have not been 'designed' but are the product of a process of evolution responding to the necessity of the situation.

Hayek also argues that it is inappropriate to ask of spontaneous, natural outcomes, such as market outcomes, whether the results are just or not. For Hayek, the concept of 'justice' is an attribute of *intentional* human conduct, and so cannot be applied to the unintended results of human action such as the market order: 'Justice . . . clearly has no application to the manner in which the impersonal process of the market allocates command over goods and services to particular people: this can be neither just nor unjust because the results are not intended or foreseen, and depend on a multitude of circumstances not known in their totality to anybody' (Hayek, 1976, vol.2 p.70). This means that it is inappropriate to ask whether market outcomes are just or not; such outcomes are the result of individuals' luck and judgment.

Returning to our earlier case of an increased demand for organically grown products, we saw that here would be a change in the incomes and employment of those involved. There would be an increase in income and employment for those involved in organic farming and a fall in the incomes and employment of those involved in conventional farming and the production of chemical fertilizers. From a Hayekian viewpoint, the change in incomes resulting from the change in demand is caused by the spontaneous and natural process of the market, and is necessary to bring about the movement of resources from one form of farming into another. But Hayek's further point is that this desirable outcome is brought about in such a way that no one individual's liberty is impaired, as everyone in the two agricultural sectors is able to pursue his or her own ends, restrained only by the rules of just conduct.

Summary

- A decentralized market system is seen as a way of guaranteeing individual freedoms.
- Market outcomes are seen as natural outcomes because they are the result of human action but not human design.
- Market outcomes can neither be said to be just nor unjust; they are the result of luck and judgment on the part of individuals.

Conclusion

Hayek's approach has been an important contributory factor in the revival of economic liberalism and free market movements of the 1980s. In this approach, Hayek has emphasized both the economic gains from the operation of free competitive markets and the political gains for individual freedom. The economic basis of this model is its emphasis on competition as a decentralized process of adjustment in the absence of full information. The virtue of the price system here is that prices are seen as signals which transmit information, and it is this that enables a decentralized system of decision making to be as well coordinated as it is. Critics of the Hayekian view of the price system (as well as of the neoclassical view) have emphasized that prices do not always convey the correct information (externalities).

This is the moment to fill in some more items on your summary chart of the different models of competition. Below are my own suggestions.

COMPETITIVE MARKETS AND POWER

We saw that in Hayek's model, arguments about justice and injustice are not relevant to the outcomes of market events. But not all economists accept this, including many economists working within a broadly liberal framework of analysis as well as those working within a social reformist approach. Such economists accept that the competitive market provides a way of exploiting 'congruent interests' where both parties to an exchange may

Table 6.4 Hayek's model

model of competition	competition is a process of responding to change; prices are signals disseminating information to consumers and producers
source of efficiency	
organizations	
freedom	

benefit and where there is an overriding 'harmony of interests'. But these economists emphasize that markets are often characterized by conflicting interests, and they are concerned about the distributional outcomes of these cases.

Markets and conflict

Concern has been expressed about those cases where there is a conflict of interest in the market transaction, and it is argued that the distribution of the benefits from the market transactions will reflect the power of the transacting parties. Here then we have a model of the competitive market as a 'power balance'. This view has been expressed by [Nobel Laureate] Professor Amartya Sen:

> The market mechanism, with each person pursuing his self-interest, is geared to making sure that the congruent interests are exploited, but it does not offer a mechanism for harmonious or fair resolution of the problem of conflict that is inoperably embedded in the congruent exercise. The 'presumed harmony' . . . stands for, at best, a half-truth. The market division of benefits tends to reflect, roughly speaking, the economic 'power balance' of different individuals and groups.
>
> (Sen, 1989, p.111)

Later on in the same piece Sen adds: 'The "invisible hand" in the form of the market mechanism is geared to the congruence exercise, with the conflict problem unaddressed and essentially left to the equilibrium of relative powers and muscles' (p.121). Here Sen is using the metaphor of balance and equilibrium that we met in [the section on competitive markets and equilibrium], but instead of seeing a balancing of demand and supply by the autonomous and impersonal market mechanism, Sen is saying that the balancing is of powers and muscles, and in such a contest the weak must inevitably come off worst. (By the way, Adam Smith also made similar statements in *The Wealth of Nations*; Smith could also be very cynical about the self-interest of the market-place and about the vanity of personal ambition.) This approach thus puts on the agenda issues such as the distribution of income and wealth arising from market allocations, regional differences in economic welfare, and the opportunities available for improving life chances.

This approach to the market is using a different concept of 'freedom' from that employed by Hayek. [. . .] [F]or Hayek and many other free market writers, the concept of freedom may be described as a 'negative freedom' because it is seen as a freedom *from* interference [. . .]. The concept of freedom appropriate to an approach such as Sen's would on the other hand be a concept of freedom as enabling powers or capabilities. As this concept of freedom emphasizes the actual opportunities available for people to act upon, it is sometimes referred to as *positive freedom*.

As an example of the difference between positive and negative freedom, consider a person's freedom to take an Open University course. Everyone is free to take such a course, free in the negative sense that the state does not directly intervene to prevent people from taking the course. But the actual conditions attaching to the successful completion of such a course mean that some students do have greater access to such courses and are better placed to complete them successfully. Conditions such as the payment of a fee, a quiet place to study undisturbed and the support of family and friends are all factors which will affect a person's actual ability to attempt a course of intensive study, and so they can all be seen as factors affecting a person's positive freedom to study. Here, the attitudes of employers towards study leave and state policy on the charging of fees will also have a significant effect on people's freedom to undertake courses of study. It is because the concept of negative freedom seemed too narrow to reflect people's ability to actually exercise their notional freedoms, that the concept of positive freedom was developed. It tends to focus on the extent to which people are able in a material sense to exercise the rights included under negative freedom. It thus attaches considerable importance to the distribution of material and economic life-chances, as it sees these as important in determining a person's ability to make choices.

Summary

- Sen's approach argues that the neoclassical emphasis is on balance and harmony of interest obscures the conflict of interest in market transaction.
- Most market situations are accompanied by large imbalances in power ('equilibrium of relative powers and muscles').
- Interpretation of freedom as 'positive freedom' where material powers underlying the capability to make choices are also significant.

Markets and inequality

The approach represented by Sen's writings raises some large questions about the distribution of the benefits arising from competitive markets and technological advances. Sen has been involved in examining the occurrence of famines and he has argued against the Food Availability Decline (FAD) approach by stressing that these famines were not always the result of absolute food shortages. [. . .] Instead Sen has argued that the famines were the result of the inadequate command or 'entitlement' that individuals were able to exercise over the marketed food output in their country. Even in the richer market-based economies of the West, he argues, it is recognized that individuals cannot be left to survive on market entitlements only. In all these Western countries, social security payments

Table 6.5 European Gross Domestic Product per head (European 12 = 100)

	1960	1970	1980	1990(est)
Belgium	95.4	98.6	104.5	103.0
Denmark	118.6	115.4	109.0	107.2
West Germany	117.2	112.5	113.8	113.4
Greece	38.4	51.2	58.2	53.6
Spain	59.2	73.3	73.4	76.3
France	104.3	109.1	111.9	108.6
Republic of Ireland	61.4	60.7	64.5	67.3
Italy	91.2	100.4	102.5	105.2
Luxembourg	134.5	120.8	115.6	128.7
Netherlands	117.8	115.0	111.0	103.1
Portugal	37.3	47.1	54.2	55.4
UK	127.6	107.1	101.1	103.7
European 12	100.0	100.0	100.0	100.0

Source: European Economy, No.42, Table 9, November 1989, p. 239

cushion the less fortunate from the vagaries and shocks of the market system, and this basic welfare proposition is subscribed to in principle by free market writers such as Hayek too.

Sen, however, is concerned to point to the unevenness with which the benefits of the competitive market are distributed to the individuals involved, and the ways in which this contrains positive freedom for many people. [. . .] The benefits of the market may also be unevenly distributed across different countries or across different regions within a single country. Table 6.5 shows the extent of differences in Gross Domestic Product (GDP) per head within the European Community over the period 1960 to 1990. Figures showing GDP are often taken to be indicative of general living standards. The base for each year is the average of all twelve countries; this means that an index number of 100 for any country indicates that the GDP per head for that country coincides with the European GDP per head. If a country has an index greater than 100, this means that its GDP is above the European average, whilst a number below 100 means that the GDP is below the European average. In this table, then, we are able to compare each country's GDP per head with that of all other European countries and the average of all the countries; and we are able to make this comparison for years spanning a period of thirty years.

In this table, we can see that there is considerable variation between the income levels in different countries. For example, looking at the [. . .] data for 1990, the richest country Luxembourg (128.7) has an income level that is nearly two-and-a-half times that of the poorest country Greece (53.6). But, if we compare this with the data for 1960, we find that in that year the richest country, again Luxembourg (135.7), had an income level just over three-and-a-half times that of the poorest countries, Portugal (37.3) and Greece (38.4). This suggests that there has been a slight narrowing of income differentials across countries over the thirty year period, although the four poorest countries hardly improved their relative position during the 1980s. It is one of the stated economic and social objectives of EC policy to reduce these disparities and promote a convergence towards high levels of income.

But disparities *within* the European countries remain very large, and these are not shown in the table. For example, the level of income in Italy has been close to the European average, but the per capita income level in southern Italy is 30 per cent below the Community average while the income level in the north-western regions is 30 per cent above. This means of course that the income level in the north-western regions is double that in southern Italy.

Table 6.6 UK regions: Gross Domestic Product per head (UK=100)

	1977	1980	1984	1988
European 12	96.4	99.1	97.1	93.1
UK	100.0	100.0	100.0	100.0
North	93.0	90.7	89.1	86.4
Yorks & Humberside	93.7	92.0	90.1	89.9
East Midlands	95.4	95.4	95.0	93.3
East Anglia	96.6	95.4	100.4	97.6
South East	114.8	118.2	118.7	121.5
South West	91.8	92.8	95.3	95.2
West Midlands	96.3	92.0	90.1	89.8
North West	96.0	95.9	93.7	92.4
Wales	85.1	82.6	83.0	82.6
Scotland	96.7	94.5	95.6	93.0
Northern Ireland	78.0	75.9	76.6	74.5

Source: Data supplied by the statistical office of the European Communities, Luxembourg

In the case of the UK, the per capita income level expressed as a percentage of the European average fell, though unevenly, from 1960 to 1990. This means that in 1960 the average UK income level was 27.6 per cent higher than the average European level, but by 1990 this had fallen to a level that was only 3.7 per cent above the European average. Whereas the UK level was the second highest in 1960, this had fallen to sixth place by 1990. Note though that there has been some improvement since 1980, a low point for the UK.

If Sen's argument links market transactions with inequalities, we might want to know whether inequalities within the UK grew more marked during the 1980s with the move towards more market oriented policies at a national level.

[It has been shown elsewhere] how poverty was unevenly distributed across the regions of the UK with the heaviest unemployment and social security dependence in Northern Ireland, the North, Scotland and Wales, and the lowest in the South East. [. . .] [Table 6.6] shows per capita GDP figures for the UK regions and for Wales, Scotland and Northern Ireland for 1977, 1980, 1984 and 1988.

In this table, the average UK figure is taken as a 100 and is higher than the European average for each of the four years shown in the table. But, when we look at the individual regions, we see a varied picture. The South East is clearly the richest region and has prospered over this period compared with both the UK average and the European average. Northern Ireland is the poorest region with only about three quarters of the GDP per head of the UK taken as a whole, and Wales is the next poorest region with an average GDP level of just over four-fifths of the UK as a whole.

Have regional differences and the North–South divide become more acute from the late 1970s to the late 1980s? Looking at the figures for Northern Ireland, Wales, and Scotland we can see that regional disparities seemed to be more pronounced by 1988. Of the English regions it was the North, Yorks and Humberside, West Midlands and the North West whose position deteriorated, while the South East and the South West improved their position.

Within these UK regions, however, there is a considerable range of incomes, so that another measure we could use is that of the distribution of income across all households. Here we can rank household incomes in 5 groups each representing 20 per cent of household incomes (these are known as 'quintile groups'); these 5 groups are ranked from the bottom 20 per cent of incomes to the top 20 per cent of incomes. [Table 6.7 gives us some figures on the distribution of income by household.]

Table 6.7 Percentage distribution of original and final income by quintile group, 1979 and 1986

	1979	1986	1979	1986
	Original income		Final income	
Bottom quintile	0.5	0.3	7.1	6.3
2nd	9	6	12	11
3rd	19	16	18	17
4th	27	27	24	24
top	45	51	38	42
All households	100	100	100	100

Source: Economic Trends, No. 422, Table 10, Dec 1988, p. 114

In 1979, the bottom quintile, that is the bottom 20 per cent of households, received 0.5 per cent of all original income, but by 1986 this had been reduced to 0.3 per cent. The share received by the next two quintiles also fell. At the top of the income scale, in 1979 the top 20 per cent of households received 45 per cent of original income, but by 1986 this had increased to 51 per cent. From this we can see that inequality worsened during the period 1979 to 1986.

The figure for final income shows the effect of taxes and welfare benefits on the distribution of income. The effect of the tax and welfare system is to reduce inequality throughout the range, for example, the top 20 per cent received 51 per cent of all original income in 1986, but 42 per cent of final income in that year. Here too, when measured in terms of final income, the degree of inequality was greater in 1986 than in 1979 as the lower quintiles received a smaller percentage of final income and the top quintile received a larger share of final income in 1986 compared with 1979.

Summary

- Imbalances of market power mean that income is distributed unequally across the population.
- This inequality of income is reduced somewhat by the operation of the welfare system in the UK.
- Between the period 1979 and 1986, inequality in the UK increased, and this increased inequality remains even after the equalizing tendency of the tax and benefit system is taken into account.

Conclusion

The approach to the market that we have been considering in this section emphasizes that the issue of the distribution of economic power is also present whenever we analyse the market and that distributional outcomes may be very unevenly balanced. Although there may be a balance between demand and supply, this approach points out that other dimensions of market societies are out of balance. Building on the income and wealth data that you have already studied in earlier parts of the course, we have looked at some data summarizing inequalities of income within the UK and within Europe. We saw that the evidence suggests that the UK became a more unequal society between 1979 and 1986 when viewed in terms of its household distribution of income. We also examined the changes in income per head across the UK regions where we saw that regional inequalities have also become more marked over this period. These data help to illustrate Sen's argument that economic power is distributed unevenly and that this too is an aspect of competitive market relations.

Remember to fill in the major points from this section in your overall grid of the models. My own summary is provided in [Table 6.8].

Table 6.8 Sen's model

model of competition	competition as a power struggle: markets characterized by conflict rather than by harmony of interest; uneven distribution of the benefits
source of efficiency	
organizations	
freedom	

CONCLUSION

In [the first section] of this chapter, we looked at the introduction of Sky Television as an example of a move towards a more competitive environment. Now that we have looked at a range of different models of competitive markets, what do you think you might have learnt about the case of Sky Television? Do you think it corresponds more to the Schumpeterian case of dynamic competition or to the neoclassical case of perfect competition? Do you think that price can include all the relevant costs and benefits connected with TV programmes or are there significant externalities for TV programmes? What are your views about the balance of powers in connection with the production and transmission of television programmes, and in the wider UK society of the 1980s and 1990s of which the move to increased market competition was a part.

[. . .]

Table 6.9 Grid: Summary of models of the market

	Schumpeter's model	*Neoclassical model*	*Hayek's model*	*Sen's model*
model of competition	dynamic competition forward-looking competition over innovations in products and processes	perfect competition/ competitive equilibrium, equilibrium price where demand = supply	competition as a process of adjustment to change; prices are signals which transmit information	competition as a power struggle markets characterized by conflict rather than by harmony of interests
source of efficiency	dynamic efficiency – innovations arising from technological advances and economies of scale result in lower prices and costs	productive efficiency – prices and costs at the minimum level given existing technology	the decentralized price mechanism transmits information about changing preferences and conditions of production	emphasis here not on efficiency whose gains may accrue to all, but on the unequal nature of the gains and losses
organizations	large corporations with their entrepreneurial managers	firms are price-takers	firms respond to price signals in an environment where they cannot have all the information	economic organizations are part of the struggle for economic power
freedom	–	–	price system guarantees individual freedom; market outcomes are neither just nor unjust; freedom as negative freedom	emphasis on freedom as enabling powers and capabilities (positive freedom), but markets do not ensure this for all

NOTE

* This chapter has been adapted from, The Open University (1991, 1995) D103 *Society and Social Science*, Block 3 *Work, Markets and the Economy*, Unit 11 'Competitive markets', Milton Keynes, The Open University.

REFERENCES

Arrow, K. J. (1974) 'General economic equilibrium: purpose, analytic techniques, collective choice', *American Economic Review*, vol. 64.

Hayek, F.A. (1973) *Law, Legislation and Liberty*, London, Routledge & Kegan Paul.

Hayek, F.A. (1976) 'The use of knowledge in society' (first published in 1945), reprinted in *Individualism and Economic Order*, pp.77–91, London, Routledge & Kegan Paul.

Schumpeter, J. A. (1976) *Capitalism, Socialism and Democracy* (first published in GB in 1943), London, George Allen & Unwin.

Sen, A. (1989) 'The profit motive' (first published 1983), reprinted in 'The market on Trial', *Lloyds Bank Annual Review*, vol.2, pp.106–24, London, Pinter Publishers.

Smith, A. (1976) *An Inquiry into the Nature and Causes of the Wealth of Nations* (first published in 1776), reprinted as vol.2 of *The Glasgow Edition of the Works and Correspondence of Adam Smith*, Oxford, Clarendon Press, reprinted by Liberty Classics, Indianapolis, USA.

SECTION 4: MARKET FAILURE

INTRODUCTION

Markets are not infallible: they can fail to organise economic activity in a socially desirable fashion.

Chapter 7, *When Markets Fail* by Lipsey and Chrystal explores the various sources and dimensions of market failure. Markets may fail to generate socially efficient outcomes and may fail to deliver equitable outcomes. Various factors may lead to social inefficiency: these include externalities, public goods, the behaviour of monopolies and oligopolies, "inappropriate" consumer preferences, lack of information, uncertainty and the immobility of factors of production. Inequitable outcomes may be generated by an inequitable initial distribution of resources, unequal access to career advancing opportunities or an unequal distribution of bargaining power. Lipsey and Chrystal investigate whether and how some of these market failures can be remedied, and what role can the government play in this process. The state may potentially use a wide array of instruments to correct market failure, such as the use of taxes and subsidies, provision of missing information, the creation or alteration of property rights, the establishment of laws and bodies to regulate economic behaviour and the direct provision of certain goods and services. State intervention is not without its problems though. Just as markets can fail, so can governments. 'Government failure' may be caused by a range of factors, such as the costs involved in gathering the required information, the inefficiency that may result due to lack of market incentives and the absence of adequate accountability. In recent years, many countries have reduced the degree of state intervention in their economies as a consequence of such considerations. They have also experimented with newer forms of state intervention, such as trying to regulate the production of certain goods and services rather than providing them directly through public enterprises. The results of this experimentation have been mixed, and the challenge remains as how to devise an appropriate mix of market and non-market mechanisms that helps achieve socially desired objectives.

7

WHEN MARKETS FAIL

Richard G. Lipsey and K. Alec Chrystal

An unkind critic of economics once said that economists have two great insights: *markets work* and *markets fail*. An unkind critic of politics once added that economics was thus a step ahead of both the political left and the political right, each of which accepts only one of these insights. Whatever may be true of other disciplines, we will see in this [chapter] how economists attempt the critical step of showing when each of these insights applies, and why.

In this chapter we first look at the basic functions that all governments have undertaken since the dawn of history. These are providing security of life, limb, and property. We see that if those functions are reasonably well performed, the free-market economy will allocate resources with relative efficiency. We go on to see that [. . .] markets fail to do an efficient job under a number of well-defined circumstances, including common property resources, public goods, harmful externalities, and excessive market power. These market failures provide the potential for government intervention to improve market efficiency. We see what government policies could do this job under ideal circumstances. [We then] study how well or poorly actual governments do this job.

BASIC FUNCTIONS OF GOVERNMENT

Governments are as old as organized economic activity. They arose shortly after the neolithic agricultural revolution turned people from hunter–gatherers into settled farmers. An institution that has survived that long must be doing something right! Over the intervening 100 centuries the functions undertaken by government have varied enormously. But through all that time the function that has not changed is to provide what is called a *monopoly of violence*. Violent acts can be conducted by the military and the civilian police arms of government, and through its judicial system the government can deprive people of their liberty by incarcerating them or, in extreme cases, by executing them. This is a dangerous monopoly that is easily abused, as is any monopoly, but with more serious consequences than when monopolies over production are abused. For these reasons satisfactory societies have systems of checks and balances designed to keep the government's monopoly directed to the general good rather than to the good of a narrow government circle.

The importance of having a monopoly of violence can be seen in those countries whose governments do not have it. Somalia in recent decades and China in the 1920s provide examples of countries in which individual warlords commanded armies that could not vanquish each other. Colombia, and to some extent Russia, provide examples of organized crime having substantial power to commit violence that the government cannot control. In extreme cases where many groups have almost equal ability to exert military violence, power struggles can create havoc with normal economic and social life. Life then becomes 'nasty, brutish, and short' – to use the words of the seventeenth-century English political philosopher Thomas Hobbes.

The importance of having checks on the arbitrary use of its monopoly by a selfish government is seen in the disasters that ensue in the many dictatorships that misuse their power. The USSR under Stalin, Uganda under Idi Amin, Nigeria under Sanni Abacha, and Cambodia under Pol Pot are a few of the many modern-day examples.

> When the government's monopoly of violence is secure and functions with reasonable restraints against its arbitrary use, citizens can safely carry on their ordinary economic and social activities.

So governments are, as they always have been, institutions to which people give over a monopoly of violence in return for the enforcement of 'law and order'. A related government activity is to provide security of property. Governments define and enforce property rights that give people a secure claim to the fruits of their own labour. These property rights include clear definition and enforcement of the rights and obligations of institutions such as joint-stock companies, banks, insurance companies, and stock exchanges.

As the founder of British classical economics, Adam Smith, put it a long time ago:

> The first duty of the sovereign [is] that of protecting the society from the violence and invasion of other independent societies. . . . The second duty of the sovereign [is] that of protecting, as far as possible, every member of the society from the injustice or oppression of every other member of it.[1]

In a modern complex economy, providing these 'minimal' government services is no simple task. Countries whose governments are not good at doing these things have seldom prospered economically.

[. . .]

[MARKET FAILURE]

The term market failure describes the failure of the market economy to achieve an efficient allocation of resources. [. . .]

There are several important circumstances under which markets fail to allocate resources with reasonable efficiency:

[. . .]

1. where there are resources that can be used by everyone but belong to no one – called common property resources
2. where there are goods whose consumption cannot be restricted to those who are willing to pay for them – called public goods
3. where people not party to some market bargain are none the less significantly affected by it – called externalities
4. where one party to a market transaction has fuller knowledge of its consequences than is available to the other party – a situation referred to as asymmetric information
5. where needed markets do not exist.
6. where substantial monopoly power [exists] . . .

Coping with these market failures provides governments with major functions in addition to the law and order functions discussed earlier. In the rest of this chapter we study these sources of market failure and how government policies could conceivably alleviate them. [We also] study how well government policies actually work in coping with market failures and in achieving all the other goals that governments set for themselves.

NON-RIVALROUS AND NON-EXCLUDABLE GOODS

Economies must allocate resources between the production and consumption of the four major classes of goods and services that are shown in Table 7.1. A good is **rivalrous** if no two persons can consume the same unit. For example, if you buy and eat an apple, no one else can buy and eat that same apple. A good is **excludable** if people can be prevented from obtaining it. Excludability requires that an owner be able to exercise effective property rights over the good or service in order to determine who uses it – typically only those who pay for the privilege.

Table 7.1 Four types of goods

	Excludable	Non-excludable
Rivalrous	*Normal goods*	*Common property*
	Apples	Fisheries
	Dresses	Common land
	TV sets	Wildlife
	Computers	Air
	A seat on an aeroplane	Streams
Non-rivalrous (up to capacity)		*Public goods*
	Art galleries	Defence
	Museums	Police
	Fenced parks	Public information
	Roads	Broadcast signals
	Bridges	Some navigation aids

Markets cope best with rivalrous excludable goods. The table gives examples of items in each of the four categories. The market can produce goods that are excludable but non-rivalrous. Goods that are non-excludable but rivalrous are common property resources, which get overused by free markets. Goods that are non-rivalrous and non-excludable are public goods, which will usually not be produced at all by the free market.

Most of the goods and services that you and I buy are rivalrous and excludable. If I buy a chocolate bar and eat it, no one else can buy and eat that bar, and the owner can prevent me from having it if I am unwilling to pay for it (unless I steal it). If an airline sells you a seat on a particular flight, it cannot let more than one person occupy that seat.

Obvious though these characteristics may seem, there are important classes of goods and services that lack one or both of them. Goods and services are **non-rivalrous** when the amount that one person consumes does not affect the amount that other people can consume. They are **non-excludable** when, once produced, there is no way to stop anyone from consuming them.

Rivalrousness is usually fixed once and for all by the nature of the good or service. An apple is rivalrous; a work of art is not. In contrast, excludability depends on the specific circumstances and the state of technology.

Circumstances The Fastnet lighthouse guides all shipping making a landfall on southwest Ireland and there is no way to force passing ships to pay for its services. The New Brighton lighthouse illuminates the entrance to the River Mersey and the Port of Liverpool, and if its operators had turned it off (prior to the invention of radar), many ships would have passed on to another, better-lit harbour entrance. In this case private owners could sell the lighthouse's services, not to passing ships, but to the port authorities, who knew they needed it in order to compete with rival ports.

Technology Early TV programmes were all broadcast openly to anyone who had a set. But the development of satellites, encoded signals, and cable transmission allowed some forms of TV signals to be provided only to those who pay for the service. The programmes are still nonrivalrous in the sense that there is no limit to the number of people who can watch a given programme. But the new technologies made them excludable so that private companies would provide them. For another example, until recently it has been impracticable to charge tolls for the use of urban roads and exclude non-payers because of the excessive costs involved in the many tollbooths needed to service a road in a densely populated urban area. Today it is possible to implant in each car a device that tracks its location at very small cost. Fees for the use of urban roads can now be assessed and non-payers denied use of the roads.

Cost In some cases it is technically possible to make a good excludable but too costly to do so. One could put a fence around the Lake District National Park and charge hikers a fee for walking in the area, but the cost of erecting and policing the fence makes it uneconomic to exclude non-payers.

In what follows we look at the characteristics of goods and services that fall into the four possible combinations of excludable and non-excludable and rivalrous and non-rivalrous as shown in Table 7.1.

Excludable goods

Private agents who produce goods and services for sale on the free market must be able to prohibit consumption of their output by those who will not pay for the privilege. Otherwise the producers cannot gain the revenue they need to cover their production costs.

So excludability is necessary for a good to be produced by a firm for sale on the market.

Ordinary goods: excludable and rivalrous

The market works best when goods and services are rivalrous and excludable. Private firms can produce and sell them. [. . .]

Non-excludable goods

This class provides [. . .] two sources on our list of major market failures, those associated with common property resources and public goods.

Common property: non-excludable but rivalrous

If you catch a fish in the open ocean, I cannot catch it, so it is rivalrous. But in a free market there is no way for you to exclude me from catching it, so it is non-excludable. This is the [first] reason on our list of causes of market failures. A **common property resource** is one that is rivalrous but non-excludable. No one has an exclusive property right to it, and it can be used by anyone. No one owns the ocean's fish until they are caught. No one owns common grazing land. The world's international fishing grounds are common property for all fishermen, as is common grazing land for all livestock owners. If, by taking more fish, one fisherman reduces the catch of other fishermen, he does not count this as a cost, although it is a cost to society. If, by grazing her own sheep, a peasant reduces the feed available for other people's goats, she does not count this as a cost. The result has been called *the tragedy of the commons* – the tendency for commonly held property to be overexploited, often to the extent of destruction.

It is socially optimal to add to a fleet that is fishing any given fishing area until the last boat increases the *value of the fleet's total catch* by as much as it costs to operate the boat. Similarly, it is optimal to add another sheep to the flock that grazes on the commons as long as the total supply of meat (and milk) is increased by as much as the cost of maintaining the extra animal. These are the sizes of fishing fleet and flock of sheep that a social planner [. . .] would choose.

> The socially optimal exploitation of a common property resource occurs when the marginal cost of the last user equals the value of the marginal addition to total output.

The free market will not, however, produce that result. Consider the fishery. Potential new entrants will judge entry to be profitable if the *value of their own catch* is equal to the costs of operating their boats. But a new entrant's catch is *partly* an addition to total catch and *partly* a reduction of the catch of other fishermen – because of congestion each new boat reduces the catch of all other boats. Thus, under competitive free entry there will be too many boats in the fleet and too many sheep on the common.

[. . .]

With common property resources the level of output will be too high because each new entrant will not take account of the cost that he or she imposes on existing producers.

[. . .]

> Fishing grounds, common pastures, and other common property resources often show a pattern of overexploitation.

This is true of almost all of today's fishing grounds, except where the catch is effectively regulated by government intervention. Box 7.1 discusses this case in more detail.

BOX 7.1 ENDANGERED FISH

The fish in the ocean are a common property resource, and theory predicts that such a resource will be overexploited if there is a high enough demand for the product and suppliers are able to meet that demand. In past centuries there were neither enough people eating fish nor efficient enough fishing technologies to endanger stocks. Over the last fifty years, however, the population explosion has added to the demand for fish and advances in technology have vastly increased the ability to catch fish. Large boats, radar detection, and more murderous nets have tipped the balance in favour of the predator and against the prey. As a result the overfishing prediction of common property theory has been amply borne out. Today fish are a common property resource; tomorrow they could become no one's resource.

continued . . .

Overfishing

Since 1950 the world's catch has increased fivefold. The increase was only sustained by substituting smaller, less desirable fish for the diminishing stocks of the more desirable fish and by penetrating ever further into remote oceans. Today, all available stocks are being exploited, and now even the total tonnage is beginning to fall. The UN estimates that the total value of the world's catch could be increased by nearly $30 billion if fish stocks were properly managed by governments interested in the total catch, rather than exploited by individuals interested in their own catch.

The developed countries have so overfished their own stocks that Iceland and the European Union could cut their fleets by 40 per cent and catch as much fish as they do today. This is because more fish would survive to spawn, allowing each boat in a smaller fleet to catch about 40 per cent more than does each boat in today's large fishing fleet.

The problem has become so acute that Canada shut down its entire Atlantic cod fishing industry in 1985 and its Pacific salmon industry in 1988. Tens of thousands of Newfoundland residents lost their livelihoods in the demise of what had been the province's largest industry – the catching, freezing, and canning of fish – an industry that had flourished for five centuries. Canada and the European Union have since been in conflict over what Canada claims is predatory overfishing by EU boats just outside Canadian territorial waters.

The Mediterranean has been so overfished that seafood that was once the staple for the poor is now an expensive luxury eaten mainly by rich tourists.

Policy response

The European Union has a common fishing policy covering the Atlantic territorial waters of its member countries. Since 1983, total allowable catches for all main species have been set annually and divided up into catch quotas for each member country. Minimum mesh size on nets and other ways of protecting young fish are also imposed. Inspection and monitoring measures are rigorously applied to give force to the regulations. So far, however, the regulations apply only to the Atlantic. There is no equivalent set of policies to protect the seriously overfished Mediterranean.

Some developing countries are following similar lines, but the majority are encouraging rapid expansion of their own fishing fleets with the all-too-predictable results that their domestic waters will soon be seriously overfished.

Worldwide action saved most species of whales. It remains to be seen how many types of fish will be caught to extinction and how many will recover as individual nations slowly learn the lesson of economic theory. Common property resources need central management if they are not to be overexploited to an extent that risks extinction.

One solution to the common property problem is to agree on the optimal level of use and then police the resource to reduce its use to that level. This is done with such items as fishing quotas and hunting licences. The problem here is to enforce the restrictions. It is possible to control the number of fish caught in the high seas, but doing so is difficult and costly, as attested by the frequent international disputes over alleged quota violations.

Another method is for the state to create property rights that make the resource excludable. Its private owners then have an incentive to exploit it efficiently. The English enclosure movement that peaked between 1793 and 1815 did just that. Although those who had previously used the common grazing land were hurt by the measure, the land was much more efficiently used under private ownership. Issuing licences for the use of each particular wavelength can control the airwaves. State forests which are being destroyed by excessive wood gathering can be sold to private owners. Property rights to wildlife can be given to local villages. And so on. This last case is controversial and is further discussed in Box 7.2.

BOX 7.2 BUFFALOES, COWS, AND ELEPHANTS

For centuries North American bison – commonly called buffaloes – were a common property resource for the Plains Indians, whose populations were small enough that they could kill all they needed without endangering the ability of the herds to reproduce themselves. In a little over a decade following the end of the American Civil War in 1865, white hunters decimated the herds. Buffalo Bill Cody may have been a folk hero, but he, and those like him, were the buffalo's executioners.

The buffalo was replaced by cattle, which did not follow the buffalo into extinction. The difference was that cattle were the private property of the ranchers. Rustlers and other predators attacked the herds, but the self-interest of ranchers made it worthwhile for them to protect their cattle.

Many people, watching the decimation of wildlife in Africa and Asia, have argued that property rights should be used to turn these animals from the modern equivalent of the buffalo into the modern equivalent of cattle. Wildlife is a common property resource. When it becomes endangered, laws are passed to prevent predatory hunting. But no one has any profit motive in enforcing these laws. Government officials are employed to do this job, but they are often few in number and poorly paid. Some become corrupted by the large sums poachers are willing to pay to avoid enforcement. Others find the policing job impossible, given the inadequate resources that their governments devote to enforcement.

Some African governments have dealt with the problem by giving ownership of the wild animals to local villages and allowing them to use the animals as a commercial asset. The animals are the subjects of camera safaris whose organizers pay the locals for the privilege. They are also prey for hunters who pay large sums for licences to kill a selected number of animals. Local tribesmen control poachers and keep the licensed kill rate below the reproduction rate because they have a profit motive in protecting what has become their very valuable property.

These schemes have many opponents as well as many supporters. Some opponents object to any permissible 'sports hunting' and other commercial use of wild animals. They argue for more effective public enforcement of anti-poaching laws. Supporters counter that leaving the animals as common property is bound to result in their extinction. Farming them is, they argue, better than presiding over their extinction.

All of these cases show the common problem of a tradeoff between efficiency and equity. When a common property resource is 'privatized', the efficiency of its use typically rises but the former users typically suffer. The difficult issue of trading off efficiency of the resource's use against justice for the present users has no easy resolution. What is sure, however, is that if the resource is being exploited to the point of destruction, little is achieved for either equity or efficiency by preserving its common property status.

Public goods: non-excludable and non-rivalrous

Goods that are neither excludable nor rivalrous are called **public goods**, or sometimes **collective consumption goods**. They are the [second] reason on our list of causes for market failure. The classic case is national defence. An army of a given size protects all the nation's citizens equally no matter how many citizens there are and whether or not a particular individual pays taxes to support it. Similarly, a police force that keeps the streets safe protects all of the street's users, no matter how many there are. If some do not pay their share of the costs, they cannot be denied protection as long as they continue to use the safe street. Information is often a public good. It is clearly non-rivalrous and often non-excludable. Suppose a certain food additive causes cancer. The cost of discovering this needs to be borne only once. The information is then of value to everyone who might have used the additive. Once it is in the public domain, no one can be stopped from learning about the information. Other public goods include lighthouses (in most but not all circumstances) and weather forecasts.

Because public goods are non-excludable, private firms will not provide them.

The obvious remedy in these cases is for the government to provide the good and pay for its provision out of general tax revenue.

When should a public good be provided? To illustrate the basic principle, consider a community composed of just two consumers. The government is considering whether or not to provide a park. Arthur is prepared to pay up to £200 for use of the park, while Julia is willing to pay up to £100. The total value to the two individuals of having the park is £300. If it can be produced for £225, there is a £75 gain on its production since it provides services that the community values at £300 at a cost of only £225.

[. . .]

The practical problem in using any formula based on what people are willing to pay for the public good lies in getting people to reveal their preferences. Suppose, for example, that the government is considering building a public park to serve a community of 1,000 people. It asks each of them how much he or she is prepared to pay. If I am one of those 1,000, it is in my interests to understate my true valuation, as long as everyone else does not do the same. Indeed, I might say I valued the park at zero, while others reported enough value to cover the costs. The public good would then be produced, and I would get the use of it for no payment at all.

The **free rider problem** refers to each person's motivation to understate the value of a non-rivalrous good in the hope that others will end up paying for it. This motivation makes it difficult to cover the costs of such goods by any formula based on people's individual valuations.

The free rider problem can be avoided by covering the costs of public goods out of tax revenue.

Goods such as national defence, weather forecasts, navigation aids, police, and fire protection are typically paid for from tax revenue and provided free to all users. This allows the goods to be produced above the levels at which the free market would produce them (often the free market would produce nothing) [. . .] Those who value a particular good higher than the average valuation gain more than those who value it below the average valuation. The hope is that, over a large number of public goods, these individual differences will cancel out. Everyone will then gain on balance as a result of the government's provision of public goods out of tax revenue.

EXTERNALITIES

[. . .] **Externalities** are costs or benefits of a transaction that are incurred or received by other members of the society but not taken into account by the parties to the transaction.

They are also called *third-party effects* and sometimes *neighbourhood effects*, because parties other than the primary participants in the transaction (the consumers and the producers) are affected. Externalities are the [third] item on our list of causes of market failure.

Externalities arise in many different ways, and they may be beneficial or harmful. A harmful externality occurs, for example, when a factory generates pollution. Individuals who live and work in the neighbourhood bear costs arising from the factory's production, including adverse health effects and clean-up costs. Profit-maximizing factory owners do not take these effects into account when they decide how much to produce. The element of social cost that they ignore is external to their decision-making process.

A beneficial externality occurs, for example, when I paint my house and enhance my neighbours' views and the values of their properties. Other cases arise when some genius – an Einstein, a Mozart, a Van Gogh – gives the world discoveries and works of art whose worth is far in excess of what he or she is paid to create them.

Externalities create a divergence between the private benefits and costs of economic activity and the social benefits and costs. **Private costs** are those costs that are incurred by the parties directly involved in some economic activity. When a good is produced, the private costs are those borne by the producing firm. **Social costs** are the costs incurred by the whole society. These are the private costs *plus* any costs borne by third parties. **Private benefits** are the benefits received by those involved in the activity. In the case of a marketed good these are the utilities obtained by buyers. **Social benefits** are the benefits to the whole society. They are the private benefits *plus* any benefit to third parties.

Society's resources are optimally allocated when social marginal cost equals social marginal benefit.

When this is so, there can be no social benefit in reallocating resources among different lines of production. Free markets will not produce social optimality when there are discrepancies between private and social costs and private and social benefits. [. . .]

Two important results follow:

1. The outputs of firms that create harmful externalities will exceed the socially optimal levels.

[. . .]

2. The outputs of firms that create beneficial externalities will be less than the socially optimal levels.

[. . .]

The control of pollution

In this section we illustrate government policies with respect to negative externalities in the context of one of their most important applications, environmental damage caused by pollution. Steel plants produce heat and smoke in addition to steel. Farms produce chemical runoff as well as food. Household consumption produces human waste and refuse. Indeed, there are few human activities that do not produce some negative pollution externalities.

[. . .]

Pollution control through direct regulation

Direct controls are a common method of environmental regulation. For example, UK car emissions standards must be met by all new cars, and by cars over three years of age when they take their annual MOT test. Many cities and towns prohibit the private burning of leaves and other rubbish because of the air-pollution problem that the burning would cause. The 1956 UK Clean Air Act obliged people to switch from coal to smokeless fuels. Similarly, the government gradually reduced the amount of lead allowed in petrol and provided tax incentives for drivers to switch to unleaded petrol. Since the mid-1970s, petrol consumption has increased by about 50 per cent while lead emissions have fallen by about 75 per cent.

[. . .]

Control through emissions taxes

The great British economist A. C. Pigou (1877–1959),who did path-breaking work on externalities of all sorts, was a pioneer in developing public policy tools for their control. His name is associated particularly with pollution taxes, which provide an alternative method to direct controls. The advantage of such taxes is that they **internalize the externality**, which means increasing the firm's private cost by the amount of the external cost. This makes private and social costs the same, with the result that efficient outcomes can result from decentralized decisions made by individual producers.

[. . .]

Emissions taxes in practice Emissions taxes can work only if it is possible to measure emissions accurately. In some cases this does not pose much of a problem, but in many other cases there are no effective measuring devices that can be installed at reasonable cost. One important example is automotive pollution. It would be very expensive to attach a reliable monitor to every car and lorry and then to assess taxes based on readings from the monitor. In this case, as in many others, direct controls are the only cost-effective method.

[. . .]

Asymmetric information

Markets work best when everyone is well informed. People cannot make maximizing decisions if they are poorly informed about the things they are buying or selling. Lack of relevant information is the [fourth] item on our list of reasons for market failure.

Rules requiring that products and prices be described correctly are meant to improve the efficiency of choices by providing people with correct and relevant information. In many cases where the consequences of errors are not dramatic, consumers can be left to discover, through trial and error, what is in their own best interests. In other cases, however, the results of error can be too drastic to allow consumers to learn from their own experiences which products are reliable and which unreliable. For example, botulism, caused by poorly preserved foods, can cause death. In such cases the state intervenes to impose standards and testing requirements in the consumers' own best interests.

Standards are also set in the workplace. Some people argue that firms should be left to set their own safety standards. High-risk firms would then have to pay wage premiums to induce workers to accept these risks voluntarily. Those who favour government regulation of work standards argue it on two grounds. First, firms are often better informed than workers on changing safety conditions in work, particularly in small factories. Government regulation then compensates for the inefficiencies caused by this unequal access to information. Second, people who are desperate for work will take risks that are socially unacceptable, or that their own desperation causes them to assess imperfectly. In this case the purpose of government intervention is either to impose social values not held by specific individuals or to act paternalistically in the belief that the state can assess the self-interests of the workers better than the workers can do for themselves.

In some situations governments cannot easily remove the differences in information available to buyers and sellers. The party with the superior knowledge can then use it to change the nature of the transaction itself. For example, doctors, lawyers, and other specialists typically know much more than their clients about what they are doing. They can, therefore, influence the demand for their services by what they do and do not tell their clients. In countries where doctors are paid for on a fee-for-service basis – whether by the government, private insurers, or individual patients – elective surgery is often observed to vary with doctors' other workloads. It is low in regions where doctors are busy and high in regions where doctors are underemployed. The explanation lies not in the different needs of patients in these various areas, but in the varying demands for these services created by the different advice that doctors give to their patients.

[. . .]

BOX 7.3 POLICIES FOR ENVIRONMENTAL REGULATION

Governments throughout the world are experimenting with many of the methods of environmental control discussed in the text. Here is a sampling of some of these policies:

- In the United Kingdom the Environmental Protection Act of 1989 lays down minimum standards for all emissions from thousands of chemical, waste incineration, and oil-refining factories. Performance is monitored by HM Inspectorate of Pollution, the costs of which are paid for by the factory owners themselves. The release of genetically engineered bacteria and viruses is also regulated. Strict regulations are imposed on waste-disposal operations and on most forms of straw and stubble burning. Litterers are subject to on-the-spot fines of up to £1,000.
- The 'Environmental Action Programmes' of the European Union set specific standards for minimum acceptable levels of water quality for drinking and for bathing. Bathing beaches are regularly monitored.
- In the 1992 Copenhagen Agreements nearly 100 countries agreed to phase out chloro-fluorocarbons (CFCs) by the year 1996, four years earlier than had previously been agreed. The Copenhagen Agreements also regulated other ozone-damaging substances, such as methyl bromide, used in preserving fruit and grain, the output of which was to be held at 1991 levels by the year 1995.
- The Kyoto Protocol signed in 1998 called for major reductions in greenhouse gas emissions over the next fifteen years. [. . .] Many observers wondered if the reductions agreed to by some of the developed nations could be realized at an acceptable cost. [. . .]
- Under the United States Clean Air Act utilities must cut emissions of sulphur dioxide from a national total of 19 million tonnes to 9 million tonnes by the year 2000. This is being accomplished by issuing 9 million tonnes worth of tradable permits to pollute.

[. . .]

Missing markets

In the 1950s two American economists, Kenneth Arrow and Gerard Debreu, who were subsequently awarded Nobel Prizes in economics studied necessary conditions for optimality in resource allocation. One of the conditions is that there must exist a separate market in which each good and service can be traded to the point where the marginal benefit equals the marginal cost. Missing markets are the [fifth] item on our list of causes of market failure.

Not only do markets not exist for such prominent things as public goods and common property resources; they are also absent in a number of less obvious but equally important cases.

One important set of missing markets involves risk. You can insure your house against its burning down. This is . . . because the probability of your house burning down is normally independent of the probability of other houses burning down.

If you are a farmer, you cannot usually insure your crop against bad weather. This is because the probabilities of yours and your neighbour's crop suffering from bad weather are interrelated. If the insurance company has to pay you, the probabilities are it will also have to pay your neighbour and everyone else in the county – perhaps even throughout the country. An insurance company survives by pooling independent risks. It cannot survive if the same event affects all its clients in the same way. (This is why, although you can insure your house against a fire from ordinary causes, you cannot insure it against fires caused by war.)

[. . .]

Another set of missing markets concerns future events. You can buy certain well-established and unchanging products, such as corn or oil, on futures markets. But you cannot do so for most manufactured products, such as cars and TV sets, because no one knows the precise specifications of future models. Futures markets for these products are missing, so there is no way that the costs and benefits of planned future expenditure on these products can be equated by economic transactions made today.

PUBLIC POLICY TOWARDS MONOPOLY AND COMPETITION

The [sixth] and last item on our list of reasons for market failure concerns market power. Cartels and price-fixing agreements among oligopolists, whether explicit or tacit, have long met with public suspicion and official hostility. These, and other non-competitive practices, are collectively referred to as monopoly practices. Note that these are not just what monopolists do. They include non-competitive behaviour of firms that are operating in other market structures such as oligopoly [a market structure in which the market is supplied only by a few firms]. The laws and other instruments that are used to encourage competition and discourage monopoly practices make up competition policy and are used to influence both the market structure and the behaviour of individual firms.

The goal of controlling market power provides rationales both for competition policy and for economic regulation. Competition can be encouraged and monopoly practices discouraged by influencing either the *market structure* or the *market behaviour* of individual firms. By and large UK competition policy has sought to create more competitive market structures where possible. Where such structures could not be established, policy has sought to discourage monopolistic practices and to encourage competitive behaviour. In addition the government employs economic regulations, which prescribe the rules under which firms can do business, and in some cases determine the prices that businesses can charge for their output.

We study three aspects of these policies: the direct control of natural monopolies, the direct control of oligopolies, and the creation of competitive conditions. The first is a necessary part of any competition policy, the second has been important in the past but is less so now, and the third constitutes the main current thrust of UK competition policy.

Direct control of natural monopolies

The clearest case for public intervention arises with a natural monopoly, an industry in which economies of scale are so dominant that there is room for only one firm to operate at the minimum efficient scale. UK policymakers have not wanted to insist on the establishment of several smaller, less efficient producers whenever a single firm would be much more efficient; neither have they wanted to give a natural monopolist the opportunity to restrict output, raise prices, and reap monopoly profits.

One response to natural monopoly is for government to assume ownership of the single firm, setting it up as a nationalized industry. The government appoints managers who are supposed to set prices guided by their understanding of the national interest. Another response has been to allow private ownership but to regulate the monopoly firm's behaviour. Until the 1980s, and particularly after the Second World War, UK policy favoured public ownership. Recently such industries have been privatized – that is, sold to members of the public – and then to some extent regulated. Examples are telecommunications, gas, water, and electricity. Whichever choice the government makes, it will exert an influence on the behaviour of these industries.

[. . .]

The very long run

Natural monopoly is a long-run concept, meaning that, given existing technology, there is room for only one firm to operate profitably. In the very long run, however, technology changes. Not only does today's competitive industry sometimes become tomorrow's natural monopoly, but also today's natural monopoly sometimes becomes tomorrow's competitive industry.

A striking example is the telecommunications industry. Not long ago the transmissions of voice and hard-copy messages were thought to be natural monopolies. Now technological developments such as satellite transmission, electronic mail, the Internet, and fax machines have made these activities highly competitive. Also, new firms can be given access to existing infrastructure such as cables, thus greatly lowering set-up costs and encouraging competition from new entrants. As a consequence in many countries an odd circumstance arose: nationalized industries, such as the UK Post Office and the telephone system, sought to maintain their profitability by prohibiting entry into what would otherwise have become a fluid and competitive industry. Since it has the full force of the legal system behind it, the public firm may be more successful than the privately owned firm in preserving its monopoly long after technological changes have destroyed its 'naturalness'.

Government policies need to be adjusted frequently to keep them abreast with more or less continuous technological change.

When the UK telephone system was privatized to become British Telecom, it was given a near monopoly for five years, with Cable and Wireless, another privatized company, as its only competitor. This legal restriction of competition was presumably designed to raise the value of the shares that the government sold to the public.

Regulation of natural monopolies

Now that most UK nationalized industries have been privatized, those that are natural monopolies are being regulated by newly formed public regulatory authorities, such as OFTEL (telephones), OFGAS (gas), and OFWAT (water). In the United States, such regulatory bodies were often captured by the firms they were supposed to regulate and ended up working against the interests of consumers (see Box 7.4). An opposite pitfall that some worry about in the United Kingdom is that prices may be pushed so far down in the short-term interests of consumers that the regulated industries will have little incentive to invest in technological innovations. In response to this worry firms were given the right to appeal if they feel prices are being pushed too low. In today's world of rapid technological change this could work to the long-term disadvantage of consumers.

BOX 7.4 REGULATION AS PROTECTION AGAINST COMPETITION

North American regulatory bodies have all too frequently protected firms rather than consumers. For example, Canadian and American railroad rates were originally regulated in order to keep profits down by establishing schedules of maximum rates. By the 1930s, however, concern had grown over the railroads' depressed economic conditions and the emerging vigorous competition from road transportation. The regulators then became the protectors of the railroads, permitting them to establish minimum rates for freight of different classes . . . and encouraging other restrictive practices. Moreover, the regulators became leading advocates of including road haulage under the regulatory umbrella, restricting entry and setting *minimum* rates for the large road transport firms. As a result, the big firms lost out to small, unregulated road haulage firms, who could cut rates and draw away customers without fear of retaliation. To eliminate the rate competition, regulation was extended to the small firms. The only reason for regulating the highly competitive road carriers was to control their competition with the railroads.

Airline regulation provides another example. When US airline routes and fares were first regulated, there was arguably so little demand that competition could not have been effective. By the mid-1960s, however, the regulations were plainly designed to shield the major North American carriers from competition. (Unlike Europe, where most carriers have been government-owned, North America is served by many competing privately owned airlines.) In the 1970s most US regulation, except for safety and other related matters, was swept away. Fares tumbled. Fierce competition broke out. Many small airlines arose and were then absorbed into the big airlines. Some big airlines went under or were absorbed by competitors. The end result, however, was fares on competitive routes that are often less than half those paid by the average air traveller in Europe, where regulations are only slowly being relaxed, decades after they were swept away in the USA.

Why did American regulatory bodies shift from protecting consumers to protecting firms? One thesis, championed by the American Nobel Prizewinner George Stigler (1911–91), is that the firms they were supposed to regulate gradually captured the regulatory commissions. In part this capture was natural enough. When regulatory bodies were hiring staff, they needed people who were knowledgeable in the industries they were regulating. Where better to go than to people who had worked in these industries? Naturally, these people tended to be sympathetic to firms in their own industries. Also, since many of them aspired to go back to those industries once they had gained experience within the regulatory bodies, they were not inclined to arouse the wrath of industry officials by imposing policies that were against the firms' interests.

This worry is often raised in connection with the so-called RPI – X formula, which has been used to regulate the prices charged by privatized firms. The permitted price increase is the increase in the retail price index (RPI) minus some amount designed to pass on some of the firm's cost reductions to its customers. For example, if X is 2 per cent and the price index rises by 5 per cent, the firm can raise its prices by 3 per cent. This is all very well, provided X is not set too high or adjusted too rapidly whenever the firm succeeds in cutting its costs. Large profits provide the incentive to spend money and take risks in developing new cost-cutting innovations. If prices are forced down as soon as the cost reductions are effective, the incentive to innovate will quickly be dissipated.

The UK water industry is being regulated under an RPI + K formula, rather than RPI – X. This is to allow for the fact that the water companies have an obligation to undertake significant expenditures on capital projects, both to improve the reliability and quality of tap water and to reduce pollution of rivers and beaches. The *K* factor, announced by Ian Byatt, head of OFWAT, in July 1994 for the rest of the decade, was an average of 1.5 per cent. (It was different for each company.) This means that water companies will be permitted to raise the price charged to consumers each year by an average of 1.5 per cent above the rate of increase of retail prices.

UK regulation of privatized industries is still in its early days. One can only hope that the regulators will remain flexible as experience accumulates and will avoid, as far as possible, excessively favouring either firms or consumers at the expense of the other.

Direct control of oligopolies

Governments have from time to time intervened in industries that were oligopolies, rather than natural monopolies, seeking to enforce the type of price and entry behaviour that was thought to be in the public interest. Such intervention has typically taken two distinct forms. In the United Kingdom from 1945 to 1980 it was primarily nationalization of whole oligopolistic industries such as airlines, railways, steel, and coalmining, which were then run by government-appointed boards. In the United States firms in such oligopolistic industries as airlines, railways, and electric power were left in private hands, but their decisions were regulated by government-appointed bodies that set prices and regulated entry.

Deregulation and privatization

The last two decades of the twentieth century witnessed a movement in virtually all advanced industrial nations, and the vast majority of less developed nations as well, to reduce the level of government control over industry. As a result nationalized industries are being sold to private sector buyers throughout the world. Also, privately owned oligopolies are being subjected to much less detailed control than they were only a couple of decades ago.

Causes

A number of forces had been pushing in this direction:

- Regulatory bodies often sought to reduce, rather than increase, competition (as discussed in Box 7.4).
- Expectations that nationalized industries would be superior to private firms in the areas of efficiency, productivity growth, and industrial relations were falsified by experience.
- Falling transportation costs, and the information and communications revolutions, are exposing local industries to much more international competition than they have previously experienced domestically. This has lowered concern over high national concentration ratios.
- [. . .] Oligopolistic market structures [have] provided much of the economic growth of the twentieth century. New products, and new ways of producing old products, have followed each other in rapid succession, all leading to higher living standards and higher productivity. Many of these innovations have been provided by firms in oligopolistic industries such as motor cars, agricultural implements, steel, petroleum refining, chemicals, and telecommunications. As long as governments can keep oligopolists competing with each other rather than cooperating to produce monopoly profits, most economists see no need to regulate such things as the prices at which they sell their products and the conditions of entry into their industries.

The worldwide movement towards privatization and deregulation is part of a growing belief among policymakers that private firms operating in free markets are more efficient producers and innovators than governments.

The call is for a diminished role of government in resource allocation – but not for a zero role. Although the belief that government intervention has been excessive is almost worldwide, there are many reasons why the public interest may still require significant intervention. Externalities and other market failures are some of the reasons why it is not necessarily efficient to leave the free market to decide all issues of resource allocation.

The natural outcome of these revised views has been the privatization of nationalized industries and the deregulation of privately owned ones. This latter policy was intended, among other things, to return price-setting and entry decisions to market determination.

Privatization has gone a long way in the United Kingdom. The majority of the nationalized industries, both those containing a few large firms and those containing many smaller firms, have been returned to private ownership. Some details are given in Box 7.5.

BOX 7.5 PRIVATIZATION IN THE UNITED KINGDOM

Privatization has been a complex development in the United Kingdom. Some nationalized industries were sold outright; in others, the government maintained substantial holdings while selling off the rest of its shares. In yet other cases, profitable parts of unprofitable enterprises were separated off and sold. In still other cases, the government sold shares that it held in private companies that had never been nationalized.

The first step towards UK privatization was the sale of council houses, which began in 1979. Over the succeeding decade there was a major reduction in the stock of publicly owned housing, with almost 700,000 dwellings being sold to their occupiers.

The next phase covered a number of relatively small operations in markets where competition was strong. These included the British Sugar Corporation, British Rail Hotels, Sealink Ferries, British Ports, Jaguar, and British Aerospace. These companies have operated successfully, under relatively competitive conditions, since their privatization.

The third phase covered the great industrial giants. It began with British Telecom in 1984 and continued with British Gas in 1986, British Airways in 1987, and British Steel in 1988. Sale of shares in the publicly owned electricity industry began in 1990, with water following soon thereafter. Sale of the remaining coal pits was completed in 1994. The privatization of British Rail was completed by 1997, with the track going to Railtrack and the train services going to several private operators.

The evidence on the effects of privatization is largely encouraging. Prices have fallen markedly in the gas, electricity, and telecommunications industries. At the same time all have had rising stock market values. Some former state-owned companies have become world leaders in a manner that would have been unlikely under state control. The most obvious examples are BT, Cable and Wireless, and British Airways. Many have been attractive targets for takeover bids by foreign utilities. All of this is strong evidence that their performance has been improved by being transferred to private ownership.

Privatization has also spread to other EU countries. For example, Deutsche Telekom was privatized in 1996. Part of the pressure to privatize has come from stiff competition from efficient foreign firms and part from the Maastricht Treaty, which limits public spending and government borrowing. There has also been a trend towards deregulation of many markets. Major pressure in this direction has been exerted by the Single Market Act [. . .]. A notable example is air travel, where state-imposed restrictions, often designed to protect state-owned national airlines, are being phased out. Many new private carriers are entering the industry, such as Easyjet based in the UK. The ensuing competition is pushing many fares down, although they still have a long way to go to reach the low fares per mile achieved by the highly competitive US airline industry.

Criticisms

Only a minority of economists today support public over private ownership in industries that can support several competing firms. There is more disagreement, however, over natural monopolies such as gas and electricity. Supporters of privatization argue that there are no natural monopolies in the very long run and that private ownership will encourage the technological dynamism that will erode any natural monopoly. They argue that in the meantime the private firms can be prevented from charging monopoly prices by effective regulation. Opponents argue that a privately owned monopoly will not be more technologically progressive and will behave more like a monopolistic profit-maximizer than would a publicly owned firm. There is no simple resolution to this part of the debate. The behaviour probably depends on the relative abilities of the managements of the publicly owned and privately owned firms, and on the nature of the regulations to which they are subjected.

Intervention to keep firms competing

The least stringent form of government intervention is designed to create conditions of competition by preventing firms from merging unnecessarily or from engaging in certain anti-competitive practices such as colluding to set monopoly prices. Such policies seek to create the most competitive market structure possible and then to prevent firms from reducing competition by engaging in certain forms of co-operative behaviour.

Why worry?

For some time up until the early 1990s industrial concentration increased in Britain, with the percentage of industrial production accounted for by the five largest firms growing steadily. Two major causes were the growth of large firms at the expense of smaller ones and mergers of existing firms. Although more recent data are difficult to come by – the last Census of Production was in 1990 – those that exist suggest that recent developments have been mixed. Concentration increased, for example, in pharmaceuticals when Glaxo merged with Wellcome. In other industries, however, large firms have been broken up by their owners, reducing concentration ratios.

Globalization – the growing internationalization of competition – is one reason why this increasing domestic concentration in production has not necessarily implied less market competition. The size of most markets now extends well beyond the boundaries of a single nation as a result of such developments as the removal of almost all trade barriers within the European Union, the decline in world transportation costs, and the steady reduction of worldwide tariffs under the auspices of the GATT and its successor, the World Trade Organization (WTO). A firm with an apparent monopoly in the United Kingdom may well be operating in a highly competitive international market that includes German, French, and Japanese firms. None the less, some intervention to keep firms competing rather than colluding is still thought necessary in most countries.

UK competition policies

Ultimate responsibility for competition policy in the United Kingdom lies with the Secretary of State for Trade and Industry. For many years key elements of monitoring and enforcement have been delegated to three important institutions: the Restrictive Practices Court (RPC), the Office of Fair Trading (OFT), and the Monopolies and Mergers Commission (MMC). At the end of 1998 proposals for reform were under active consideration including abolishing the MMC and merging its functions with the OFT.

There is an important difference between the legislation affecting restrictive practices and that affecting the potential creation of a monopoly by a merger. Restrictive practices must be registered and demonstrated to be in the public interest. The OFT can investigate cases that are not already approved and refer them to the RPC for judgement. By contrast, the onus is entirely on the authorities to prove that a merger is not in the public interest; otherwise it must be permitted to proceed. Here decisions are made by the Secretary of State on the basis of recommendations made by the MMC.

[. . .]

The future of competition policy

Even though governments on the whole are no longer in the business of owning industries or tightly controlling their pricing and output decisions, they are certainly not indifferent to industry performance. Government has an important role as both rule-maker and referee of the market economy. So long as monopoly and restrictive practices continue to be seen as a threat to the efficient working of the economy, governments will regard the behaviour of firms as something that requires appropriate monitoring and occasional control. [. . .]

GOVERNMENT OBJECTIVES

Governments have multiple objectives, only some of which we have studied above. [. . .] The main ones are as follows:

1. to protect life and property by exercising a monopoly of violence and establishing property rights
2. to improve economic efficiency by addressing the various causes of market failure
3. to achieve some accepted standard of equity
4. to protect individuals from others and from themselves
5. to influence the rate of economic growth
6. to stabilize the economy against income and price level fluctuations

The first two of these objectives were considered [above]. The next three are considered [below]. The last is a major subject of macroeconomic theory and policy [and is covered elsewhere].

Policies for equity

Markets generate reasonably efficient allocations of the nation's resources because, most of the time, the information that they need to perform well is derived from agents' desires to improve their private circumstances. No one should be surprised, therefore, that markets do not efficiently allocate resources towards achieving such broad social goals as establishing an 'equitable' distribution of income and promoting shared community values. Markets do not directly foster these goals, precisely because individuals do not seek to achieve them by purchasing goods and services in markets. Instead we look to the political system to achieve desired results in these directions.

The distribution of income

An important characteristic of any market economy is the *distribution* of income that it determines. People whose skills are scarce relative to supply earn large incomes, whereas people whose skills are plentiful relative to supply earn much less.

As we have seen [elsewhere], differentials in earnings serve the important function of motivating people to adapt. The advantage of such a system is that individuals can make their own decisions about how to alter their behaviour when market conditions change. The disadvantage is that temporary rewards and penalties are dealt out as a result of changes in market conditions that are beyond the control of the affected individuals. The resulting differences in incomes will seem inequitable to many – even though they are the incentives that make markets work.

Concerns about equity have two dimensions, horizontal and vertical equity. **Horizontal equity** means that persons in similar circumstance should be treated similarly. Although this type of equity appeals to many people as desirable, it is not always a goal of government policies. For example, people who are exposed to similar natural risks are given more government assistance when they are planting crops than when they are mining ore, cutting trees, or extracting oil. This may be because farmers have more political power than others, or it may stem from a gut feeling on the part of the electorate that food production is more basic than any other economic activity. **Vertical equity** means the different treatment of people in different economic situations in order to reduce inequalities between them.

Redistributive policies are of two general types. Some, such as the progressive income tax [a progressive income tax is one that taxes higher incomes at a higher rate], are concerned with vertical equity. They seek to alter the size distribution of income in quite general ways. High marginal rates of income tax, combined with a neutral expenditure system that benefits all income groups more or less equally, will narrow income inequalities.

Other policies seek to mitigate the effects of markets on particular individuals. They do not seek to narrow income gaps in general but to deal with specific unfortunate events. Should heads of households be forced to bear the full burden of their misfortune if they lose their jobs through no fault of their own? Even if they lose their jobs through their own fault, should they and their families have to bear the whole burden, which may include starvation? Should the ill and the aged be thrown on the mercy of their families? What if they have no families? Policies designed to deal with such situations usually seek horizontal equity in treating similarly all those who fall into some group.

Both private charities and a great many government policies are concerned with modifying the distribution of income that results from such things as one's parents' abilities, luck, and how one fares in the labour market.

The distribution of wealth

It is sometimes argued that egalitarian economic policy should devote more concern than it does to the distribution of wealth and less to the distribution of income. Wealth confers economic power, and wealth is more unequally distributed than is income. Heavy estate duties in the United Kingdom, however, caused a gradual reduction in the inequality of wealth distribution during the twentieth century. The trend has slowed, if not reversed, over the last two decades, but largely because of the buildup of pension wealth in the hands of 50–70-year-olds. None the less, in the mid-1990s just less than 20 per cent of all marketable wealth was held by the top 1 per cent of people in the UK wealth distribution, and an impressive 93 per cent of all marketable wealth by those in the top half of the distribution.

There are two main ways in which inequalities in the distribution of wealth can be reduced. The first is to levy taxes on wealth at the time that wealth is transferred from one owner to another, either by gifts during the lifetime of the owner or by bequest after death. In Britain such transfers used to be subject to a capital transfer tax. The rate of tax was progressive and rose to 60 per cent on taxable transfers in excess of £2 million. Currently, however, gifts among individuals during their lifetime are potentially exempt from tax. They become taxable if made within seven years of the donor's death. In 1998 inheritance tax was set at the rate of 40 per cent on all estates over £233,000.

The second method is an annual tax on the value of each person's wealth. A wealth tax of this sort has been considered in the past but it has not been actively debated since 1979.

[. . .]

Policies to protect individuals

Protection from others   People can use and even abuse other people for economic gain in ways that the members of society find offensive. Child labour laws and minimum standards of working conditions are responses to such actions. Yet direct abuse is not the only example of this kind of market failure. In an unhindered free market, the adults in a household would usually decide how much education to buy for their children. Selfish parents might buy no education, while egalitarian parents might buy the same education for all of their children, regardless of their abilities. The members of society may want to interfere in these choices, both to protect the child of the selfish parent and to ensure that some of the scarce educational resources are distributed according to ability rather than the family's wealth. All households are forced to provide a minimum of education for their children, and a number of inducements are offered – through public universities, scholarships, and other means – for talented children to consume more education than they or their parents might choose if they had to pay the entire cost themselves.

Protection from oneself Members of society, acting through the government, often seek to protect adult (and presumably responsible) individuals not from others, but from themselves. Laws prohibiting the use of heroin, crack cocaine, and other drugs, and laws prescribing the installation and use of car seat belts, are intended primarily to protect individuals from their own ignorance or shortsightedness. This kind of interference in the free choices of individuals is called **paternalism**. Whether such actions reflect the wishes of the majority in society or whether they reflect the interference of overbearing governments, there is no doubt that the market will not provide this kind of protection. Buyers do not buy what they do not want, and sellers have no motive to provide it.

Paternalism is often closely related to **merit goods**. Merit goods are goods that society, operating through the government, deems to be especially important or that those in power feel individuals should be encouraged to consume. Housing, education, health care, and certain cultural activities are often cited as merit goods. Critics argue that the concept is merely a way of imposing the tastes of an elite group on others.

Policies to promote social obligations

In a free-market system if you can persuade someone else to clean your house in return for £20, both parties to the transaction are presumed to be better off. You prefer to part with £20 rather than to clean the house yourself, and the person you hire prefers to have £20 than to avoid cleaning your house. Normally society does not interfere with people's ability to negotiate mutually advantageous contracts.

Most people do not feel this way, however, about activities that are regarded as social obligations. For example, during major wars when military service is compulsory, contracts similar to the one between you and your housekeeper could also be negotiated. Some persons, faced with the obligation to do military service, could no doubt pay enough to persuade others to do their tour of service for them. By exactly the same argument as we just used, we can presume that both parties will be better off if they are allowed to negotiate such a trade. Yet such contracts are usually prohibited as a result of widely held values that cannot be expressed in the marketplace. In times of major wars, of the sort that were experienced twice in the twentieth century, military service by all healthy males is held to be a duty that is independent of an individual's tastes, income, wealth, or social position.

Military service is not the only example of a social obligation. Citizens are not allowed to buy their way out of jury duty or to sell their votes, even though in many cases they could find willing trading partners. Even if the price system allocated goods and services with complete efficiency, members of a society do not wish to rely solely on the market for all purposes, since they have other goals that they wish to achieve.

Policies for economic growth

Over the long haul economic growth is the most powerful determinant of living standards. Whatever their policies concerning efficiency and equity, people who live in economies with rapid rates of growth find their living standards rising on average faster than those of people who live in countries with low rates of growth. Over a few decades these growth-induced changes tend to have much larger effects on living standards than any policy-induced changes in the efficiency of resource allocation or the distribution of income.

For the last half of the twentieth century most economists viewed growth mainly as a macroeconomic phenomenon related to total savings and total investment. Reflecting this view, most textbooks do not even mention growth in the chapters on microeconomic policy.

More recently there has been a shift back to the perspective of earlier economists, who saw technological change as the engine of growth, with individual entrepreneurs and firms as the agents of innovation. This is a microeconomic perspective, which is meant to add to, not replace, the macroeconomic stress on total savings and total investment.

Although most basic textbooks have not yet caught up with the change to a microeconomic perspective on growth, governments have. Today few microeconomic policies escape being exposed to the question 'Even if this policy achieves its main goal, will it have unfavourable effects on growth?' Answering yes is not a sufficient reason to abandon a specific policy. But it is a sufficient reason to think again. Is it possible to redesign the policy so that it can still achieve its main objective, while removing its undesirable side-effects on growth?

THE COSTS OF GOVERNMENT INTERVENTION

We have seen that governments have many reasons to take action. We also know that governments have many tools that may help them to achieve their goals. This, however, is not the end of the story. To evaluate government intervention, we need to consider costs as well as benefits.

Large potential benefits do not necessarily justify government intervention, nor do large potential costs necessarily make it unwise. What matters are net benefits – the balance between benefits and costs.

Three types of cost of government intervention need to be considered. These are costs that are internal to the government, costs that are external to the government but directly paid by others in the sector where the intervention occurs, and costs that are external to the government and felt more generally throughout the entire economy.

Internal costs

Everything the government does uses resources. It costs money when government inspectors visit plants to check on compliance with government-imposed health standards, industrial safety, or environmental protection. The inspectors and their support staff must be paid and their offices maintained. The salaries of the judges, the clerks, and the court reporters that are needed when an anti-monopoly case is heard are costs imposed by the regulation.

Armies of clerks, backed up by computers and other modern equipment, keep track of income tax and VAT receipts. Inspectors take the field to enforce compliance, and the courts deal with serious offenders. Unemployment and supplementary benefits must be administered. The size of the body of public employees at the national and local levels attests to the significant resource costs of government activity, costs that need to be set against the benefits produced. In 1996 the income payments made in the three major parts of the UK public sector expressed in billions of pounds and as percentages of GDP were as follows: public corporations £26bn (3.5 per cent), central government £27bn (3.5 per cent), and local authorities £38bn (5.1 per cent), which sums to £91bn or 12.1 per cent of GDP. These are not inconsiderable figures.

Direct external costs

External costs are costs that the government's action imposes on others; they may be either direct or indirect. Direct external costs fall on agents with whom the government is directly interacting.

Increases in production costs   Regulation and control often add directly to the costs of producing goods. For example, firms must inspect machinery to ensure that it meets government safety standards.

Costs of compliance   Much business activity is devoted to understanding, reporting, and contesting regulatory provisions. Occupational safety and environmental control have increased the number of employees not working on the shop floor. The legal costs of a large company can run to large sums each year. The same can be said of the costs of complying with tax laws. Firms, and wealthy individuals, spend substantial sums on lawyers and accountants. These advisers help them to comply with tax laws. They also assist in choosing tax-minimizing courses of action. These resources have alternative uses. So do firms' time and planning energies, whose social product might be higher if devoted to maximizing growth potential rather than minimizing their tax payments.

Losses in productivity   Quite apart from the actual expenditures, government intervention may reduce the incentive for experimentation, innovation, and the introduction of new products. Requiring advance government clearance before introducing a new method or product (on grounds of potential safety hazards or environmental impact) can reduce the incentive to develop it. New lines of investment may be chosen more for their tax implications than for their potential for reducing production costs and so contributing to productivity growth.

Indirect external costs

Indirect external costs are costs of the government's action that spread beyond those immediately affected by it – sometimes to the entire economy. [. . .]

Externalities

Ironically, government intervention to offset adverse externalities can create new adverse externalities. For example, government regulations designed to ensure the safety of new drugs delay the introduction of all drugs, including those that are safe. The benefits of these regulations are related to the unsafe drugs kept off the market. The cost includes the delayed availability of new safe drugs.

[. . .]

GOVERNMENT FAILURE

So far we have dealt with a government that is trying its best to achieve the goals that we laid out [earlier]. It may impose costs, some expected and some unexpected, but it is seeking, as best it can, to achieve socially acceptable goals.

Is this too naïve a view of government and the political process? Today, many observers of the political scene, including not a few economists, would answer with an emphatic yes.

Without doubt governments are far from perfect. This is not because bureaucrats and politicians are worse than other people, more stupid, more rigid, or more venal. Instead it is because they are like others, with flaws as well as virtues and with motives of their own. So having found potential net benefits from perfect but costly government intervention, the final issue is whether the imperfect governments that we encounter in the real world would achieve some of these benefits. Where they do not succeed in achieving potential benefits that exceed the full direct and indirect costs, we speak of **government failure**.

Governments may sometimes make isolated mistakes just as private decision-makers do. What is interesting, however, are the reasons why governments tend, under certain circumstances, to be more systematically in error than would unhindered markets. Here are a few of the many possible causes of systematic government failure.

Rigidities

Rules and regulations, tax rates, and expenditure policies are hard to change. Market conditions, however, change continually and often rapidly. A rule requiring the use of a certain method to reduce pollution may have made sense when the cost of that method was low. It may, however, become a wasteful rule when some alternative becomes a less costly method.

Today's natural monopolies are often made into tomorrow's competitive industries by technological innovations. For example, the near monopoly of the early railways was eliminated by the development of cheap road transport, and the falling cost of air transport is currently providing potent competition for surface transport in the movement of many products. One danger of government intervention is that it will be too slow in adapting to a constantly changing environment.

> A centralized decision-taking body has difficulty in reacting to changing conditions as fast as decentralized decision-takers react to market signals.

As well as rigidities in reacting to changing market conditions, governments are often slow to admit mistakes even when they become aware of them. It is often politically easier to go on spending money on a project that has turned sour than to admit fault. A classic example was the development of Concorde. Successive governments realized it was an enormous money-loser, but went on supporting it long after any chance of commercial success was gone.

Markets are much harsher in judging success. When people are investing their own money, the principle that bygones are bygones is usually followed. No firm could raise fresh financial capital for what was currently a poor prospect just because the prospects had seemed good in the past. Nor could it do so because much money had already been spent on it, or because those who supported it in the past would lose face if it were now dropped.

Decision-makers' objectives

By far the most important cause of government failure arises from the nature of the government's own objectives. Until recently, economists did not concern themselves greatly with the motivation of government. The theory of economic policy implicitly assumed that governments had no objectives of their own. As a result economists only needed to identify places where the market functioned well on its own, and places where government intervention could improve the market's functioning. Governments would then stay out of the former markets and intervene as necessary in the latter.

This model of government behaviour never fitted reality, and economists were gradually forced to think more deeply about the motivation of governments. Why was economists' advice followed closely in some cases, while it was systematically ignored in others? Today economists no longer assume that governments are faceless robots doing whatever economic analysis shows to be in the social interest. Instead they are modelled just as are producers and consumers – as units with their own objectives, which they seek to maximize.

Governments undoubtedly do care about the social good to some extent, but public officials have their careers, their families, and their prejudices as well. Public officials' own needs are seldom wholly absent from their consideration of the actions they will take. Similarly, their definition of the public interest is likely to be influenced heavily by their personal views of what policies are best. [. . .]

Modelling governments as maximizers of their own welfare, and then incorporating them into theoretical models of the working of the economy, was a major breakthrough. One of the pioneers of this development was the American economist James Buchanan, who was awarded the 1986 Nobel Prize in economics for his work in this field. The theory that he helped to develop is called *public choice theory*.

The key breakthrough was to view the government as just another economic agent engaging in its own maximizing behaviour. When this view is adopted, there is still room for many competing theories, depending on what variables are in the government's preference function (i.e. what things the government cares about). Consider the other two main decision-taking bodies in orthodox economics. Firms have only profits in their utility functions, and they seek to maximize these. Consumers have only goods and services in their utility functions, and they seek to maximize their satisfactions from consuming them. An analogous theory of the government allows only one variable in its utility function, the variable being votes! Such a government takes all its decisions with a view to maximizing its votes at the next election.

Public choice theory

Full-blown public choice theory deals with three maximizing groups. Elected officials seek to maximize their votes. Civil servants seek to maximize their salaries (and hence their positions in the hierarchy). Voters seek to maximize their own utility. To this end, voters look to the government to provide them with goods and services and income transfers that raise their personal utility. No one cares about the general interest!

On the one hand this surely is not a completely accurate characterization of motives. Elected statesmen have acted in what they perceive to be the public interest, hoping to be vindicated by history even if they know they risk losing the next election. Some civil servants have exposed inside corruption even though it cost them their jobs. And some high-income individuals vote for the political party that advocates the most, not the least, income redistribution.

On the other hand the characterization is close to the mark in many cases. Those who have seen the UK TV series *Yes Minister* have seen civil servants that fit the public choice model very well. Most of us have read of politicians whose only principle is 'What will get me most votes?' And many voters ask only 'What is in it for me?' This is why the theory can take us a long way in understanding what we see, even though real behaviour is more complex.

[. . .]

The ability of elected officials and civil servants to ignore the public interest is strengthened by a phenomenon called **rational ignorance**. Many policy issues are extremely complex. For example, even the experts are divided when assessing the pros and cons of the UK's decision to stay out of the first wave of membership in the euro, the common European currency. Much time and effort is required for a layperson even to attempt to understand the issue. Similar comments apply to the evidence for and against capital punishment or lowering the age of criminal liability. Yet one person's vote has little influence on which party gets elected or on what they really will do about the issue in question once elected. So the costs are large, the benefits small. Thus a majority of rational, self-interested voters will remain innocent of the complexities involved in most policy issues.

Who will be the informed minority? The answer is those who stand to gain or lose a lot from the policy, those with a strong sense of moral obligation, and those policy junkies who just like this sort of thing.

GOVERNMENT INTERVENTION TODAY

Do governments intervene too little, or too much, in response to market failure? This question reflects one aspect of the continuing debate over the role of government in the economy.

The role of analysis

Economics can help to eliminate certain misconceptions that cloud and confuse the debate. We have [elsewhere] noted one such misconception: the optimal level of a negative externality such as pollution is not, as some urge, zero.

Another mistake is to equate market failure with the greed of corporations. Externalities do not require callous, thoughtless, or deliberately deceptive practices on the part of private firms. Externalities occur whenever the signals to which rational decision-takers respond exclude significant benefits and costs. Local authorities and nationalized industries pollute just as much as privately owned industries when they neglect externalities in their operations, as they often do. Most dramatically, pollution in the centrally planned former Soviet Union vastly exceeded the pollution in any industrialized Western market economy.

A third mistake is to think that industrial profits are related to externalities. Both profitable industries such as chemicals, and unprofitable ones such as coal, are capable of spending too little on pollution control or on safety. They may also spend too much. The existence of profits provides no clue one way or the other.

The role of ideology

While positive analysis has a part to play, there are reasons why ideology plays a large role in evaluating government intervention. First, measuring the costs of government intervention is difficult, particularly with respect to indirect costs, because some of the trade-offs are inherently uncertain. How important and how unsafe is nuclear power? Does the ban on some pesticides cause so much malnutrition as to offset the ecological gains that it brings? What cannot be readily measured can be alleged to be extremely high, or low, by opponents, or supporters, of intervention.

Second, classifying the actual pattern of government intervention as successful or not is partly subjective. Has government safety regulation been (choose one) useful if imperfect, virtually ineffective, or positively adverse? All three views have been advocated.

Third, specifying what constitutes market failure is sometimes difficult. For example, does product differentiation represent market success, by giving consumers the variety they want, or failure, by foisting unwanted variations on them?

Over the last two decades in most of the advanced industrial countries the mix of free-market determination and government ownership and regulation has been shifting towards more market determination. No one believes that government intervention can, or should, be reduced to zero. Do we still have a long way to go in reversing the tide of big intrusive government that flowed through most of the twentieth century? Or perhaps we have gone too far and have given some things to the market that governments could do better? These will be some of the great social debates of the early decades of the twenty-first century.

NOTE

1   Adam Smith, *The Wealth of Nations* (1776; New York: Random House, 1937 edn., pp. 653, 669).

SECTION 5: THE GLOBAL MARKET

INTRODUCTION

In this section, we take a look at the international dimension of economic activity, in both current and historical context.

Chapter 8, *International trade* by Lipsey and Chrystal examines why nations may trade with each other and the potential benefits and costs of international trading activity. It explores why the impact of these costs and benefits may be uneven upon different trading nations, and how a country may lose as a consequence of international trading rather than gaining from it. Lipsey and Chrystal examine why and how countries (especially the developing nations) may restrict or regulate international trade, while pointing out the risks inherent in the policy of protectionism.

Chapter 9, *Protectionism and industrialisation: a historical perspective* situates the arguments for and against free trade in a historical context. Bairoch documents how many of today's industrialized nations protected their industries from the forces of international competition during their initial phases of industrialization. The United States of America was amongst the first nations to do so. The historical evidence cited here is pertinent in the context of the contemporary debate about the degree of protectionism that today's developing nations should be permitted to employ to promote indigenous industrialization in their economies.

Chapter 10, *Multinational corporations* by Sodersten and Reed looks at the (direct) investment dimension of international economic activity and the operation of multinational firms. Firms may go multinational for a variety of motives such as the exploitation of superior technological or managerial expertise, growth opportunities in foreign markets or the possibilities for cost reductions. Sodersten and Reed investigate the potential benefits and costs of multinational activity. The chapter concludes by investigating how national governments may try and use economic policy instruments to regulate the activity of multinationals in their economies.

Chapter 11, *Globalisation in the age of empire* by Hobsbawm raises a number of questions in relation to the nature of globalisation that occurred during the era 1875 to 1914, which Hobsbawm calls the Age of Empire. Scholars may disagree with some of the answers that Hobsbawm provides, but the questions themselves remain interesting and engaging. Can the study of this period teach us any lessons about how to fashion globalization in contemporary times?

8

INTERNATIONAL TRADE

Richard G. Lipsey and K. Alec Chrystal

Economic growth and development [. . .] would be very hard to achieve if residents of an economy could not buy some goods from abroad and export other goods to generate revenue to pay for the imports. *International trade* refers to exchanges of goods and services that take place across international boundaries. The British, for example, buy BMWs made in Germany, Germans take holidays in Italy, Italians buy spices from Tanzania, Belgians import oil from Kuwait, Egyptians buy Japanese cameras, and the Japanese depend heavily on American soybeans as a source of food. Indeed, there is substantial evidence to show that international trade and economic growth are positively linked.

In this chapter we explain why trade increases output and incomes. We then ask why, if trade is generally beneficial, governments have often attempted to restrict the freedom to trade. Finally, we discuss some of the institutional arrangements that affect world trade.

SOURCES OF THE GAINS FROM TRADE

An economy that engages in international trade is called an **open economy**. One that does not is called a **closed economy**. A situation in which a country does no foreign trade is called **autarky**. The advantages realized as a result of trade are called the **gains from trade**. Although politicians often regard foreign trade as being different from domestic trade, economists from Adam Smith on have argued that the causes and consequences of international trade are simply an extension of the principles governing domestic trade. What is the benefit from trade among individuals, among groups, among regions, or among countries?

Interpersonal, interregional, and international trade

Consider trade among individuals. Without trade, each person would have to be self-sufficient; each would have to produce all the food, clothing, shelter, medical services, entertainment, and luxuries that he or she consumed. A world of individual self-sufficiency would be a world with extremely low living standards.

Trade among individuals allows people to specialize in those activities they can do well and to buy from others the goods and services they themselves cannot easily produce. A good doctor who is a bad carpenter can provide medical services not only for his or her own family, but also for an excellent carpenter who lacks the training or the ability to practise medicine. Thus trade and specialization are intimately connected. Without trade, everyone must be self-sufficient. With trade, everyone can specialize in what he or she does well and satisfy other needs by trading.

The same principles apply to regions. Without inter-regional trade, each region would be forced to be self-sufficient. With trade, each region can specialize in producing goods or services for which it has some natural or acquired advantage. Plains regions can specialize in growing grain, mountain regions can specialize in mining and forest products, and regions with abundant power can specialize in manufacturing. Cool regions can produce wheat and other crops that thrive in temperate climates, and hot regions can grow such tropical crops as bananas, sugar, and coffee. Places with lots of sunshine and sandy beaches can specialize in the tourist trade. The living standards of the inhabitants of all regions will be higher when each region specializes in products in which it has some natural or acquired advantage and obtains other products by trade than when all regions seek to be self-sufficient.

The same principle also applies to nations. Nations, like regions or persons, can gain from specialization. More of the goods in which production is specialized are produced than residents wish to consume, while less domestic production of other goods that residents desire is available.

International trade is necessary to achieve the gains that international specialization makes possible. Trade allows each individual, region, or nation to concentrate on producing those goods and services that it produces efficiently while trading to obtain goods and services that it does not produce efficiently.

Specialization and trade go hand in hand, because there is no motivation to achieve the gains from specialization without being able to trade the goods produced for the different goods desired. Economists use the term 'gains from trade' to embrace the results of both. [. . .]

We will examine two sources of the gains from trade. The first is differences among regions of the world in climate and resource endowment that lead to advantages in producing certain goods and disadvantages in producing others. These gains occur even though each country's costs of production are unchanged by the existence of trade. The second source is the reduction in each country's costs of production that results from the greater production that specialization brings.

The gains from specialization with given costs

In order to focus on differences in countries' conditions of production, suppose that each country's average costs of production are constant. We will use an example below involving only two countries and two products, but the general principles apply as well to the real-world case of many countries and many products.

Absolute advantage

One [country] is said to have an **absolute advantage** over another in the production of good X when an equal quantity of resources can produce more X in the first [country] than in the second. [. . .] Total production can be increased if each country specializes in producing the product for which it has an absolute advantage.

These gains from specialization make the gains from trade possible. If consumers in both countries are to get the goods they desire in the required proportions, each must export some of the commodity in which it specializes and import commodities in which other countries are specialized.

Comparative advantage

When each country has an absolute advantage over others in a product, the gains from trade are obvious. But what if one country can produce all commodities more efficiently than other countries? In essence this was the question English economist David Ricardo (1772–1823) posed nearly 200 years ago. His answer underlies the *theory of comparative advantage* and is still accepted by economists today as a valid statement of the potential gains from trade.

The gains from specialization and trade depend on the pattern of comparative, not absolute, advantage. [For example, let] us assume that there are two countries, the United States and the European Union. Both countries produce the same two goods, wheat and cloth, but the opportunity costs of producing these two products differ between countries. The *opportunity cost* in production [. . .] tells us how much of one good we have to give up in order to produce one more unit of the other. [. . .]

For the purposes of our example we assume that the opportunity cost of producing 1 kilogram of wheat is 0.60 metres of cloth in the United States, while in the European Union it is 2 metres of cloth. These data are summarized in Table 8.1. The second column of this table gives the same information again but expressed as the opportunity cost of 1 metre of cloth (so the numbers there are the reciprocals of the numbers in the first column).

The sacrifice of cloth involved in producing wheat is much lower in the USA than it is in the EU. World wheat production can be increased if the USA rather than the EU produces it. Looking at cloth production, we can see that the loss of wheat involved in producing one unit of cloth is lower in the EU than in the USA. World cloth production can be increased if the EU rather than the USA produces it. The gains from a US shift towards wheat production and an EU shift towards cloth production are shown in Table 8.2.

Table 8.1 Opportunity cost of wheat and cloth in the USA and the EU

	Wheat (kg)	Cloth (metres)
USA	0.60m cloth	1.67kg wheat
EU	2.00m cloth	0.50kg wheat

Comparative advantages reflect opportunity costs that differ between countries. Column (1) expresses opportunity cost per kilogram of wheat. Column (2) expresses the same information in terms of metres of cloth. The USA has a comparative advantage in wheat production, the EU in cloth.

Table 8.2 Gains from specialization with differing opportunity costs

	Changes from each producing one more unit of the product in which it has the lower opportunity cost	
	Wheat (kg)	Cloth (metres)
USA	+1.0	−0.6
EU	−0.5	+1.0
Total	+0.5	+0.4

Whenever opportunity costs differ between countries, specialization can increase the production of both products. These calculations show that there are gains from specialization given the opportunity costs of Table 8.1. To produce one more kilogram of wheat, the USA must sacrifice 0.6m of cloth. To produce one more metre of cloth, the EU must sacrifice 0.5kg of wheat. Making both changes raises world production of both wheat and cloth.

1. Country A has a *comparative advantage* over country B in producing a product when the opportunity cost (in terms of some other product) of production in country A is lower. This implies, however, that it has a comparative disadvantage in the other product.
2. Opportunity costs depend on the relative costs of producing two products, not on absolute costs.
3. When opportunity costs are the same in all countries, there is no comparative advantage and there is no possibility of gains from specialization and trade.
4. When opportunity costs differ in any two countries, and both countries are producing both products, it is always possible to increase production of both products by a suitable reallocation of resources within each country.

Gains from specialization with variable costs

So far, [. . .] we have assumed that unit costs are the same whatever the scale of output, and we have seen that there are gains from specialization and trade as long as there are interregional differences in opportunity costs. If costs vary with the level of output, or as experience is acquired via specialization, *additional* sources of gain are possible.

Scale and imperfect competition

Real production costs, measured in terms of resources used, often fall as the scale of output increases. The larger the scale of operations, the more efficiently large-scale machinery can be used and the more efficient the division of labour that is possible. Smaller countries such as Switzerland, Belgium, and Israel whose domestic markets are not large enough to exploit economies of scale would find it prohibitively expensive to become self-sufficient by producing a little bit of everything at very great cost.

Trade allows smaller countries to specialize and produce a few products at high enough levels of output to reap the available economies of scale.

One of the important lessons learned from patterns of world trade since the Second World War results from imperfect competition [markets which are not 'perfectly competitive'] and product differentiation. Virtually all of today's manufactured consumer goods are produced in multiple differentiated product lines. In some industries many firms produce this range; in others only a few firms produce the entire product range. In both cases firms are not price-takers, and they do not exhaust all available economies of scale as a perfectly competitive firm would do. This means that an increase in the size of the market, even in an economy as large as the USA or EU, may allow the exploitation of some previously unexploited scale economies in individual product lines.

These possibilities were first dramatically illustrated when the European Common Market (now called the European Union, the EU) was set up in the late 1950s. Economists had expected that specialization would occur according to the classical theory of comparative advantage, with one country specializing in cars, another in refrigerators, another in fashion clothes, another in shoes, and so on. This is not the way it worked out. Instead, much of the vast growth of trade was in intra-industry trade. Today one can buy French, English, Italian, and German fashion goods, cars, shoes, appliances, and a host of other goods in the shops of London, Paris, Bonn, and Rome. Ships loaded with Swedish furniture bound for London pass ships loaded with English furniture bound for Stockholm; and so on.

What free European trade did was to allow a proliferation of differentiated products, with different countries each specializing in differentiated subproduct lines. Consumers have shown by their expenditures that they value this enormous increase in the range of choice among differentiated products. As Asian countries have expanded into European and American markets with textiles, cars, and electronic goods, European and American manufacturers have increasingly specialized their production, and they now export textiles, cars, and electronic equipment to Japan even while importing similar but differentiated products from Japan.

Learning by doing

The discussion so far has assumed that costs vary only with the level of output. They may also vary with the experience accumulated in producing a good over time.

Some economists place great importance on a factor that we now call *learning by doing*. They argue that as countries gain experience in particular tasks, workers and managers become more efficient in performing them. As people acquire expertise, costs tend to fall. There is substantial evidence that such learning by doing does occur.

[. . .]

Recognition of the opportunities for learning by doing leads to an important implication: policymakers need not accept *current* comparative advantages as given. Through such means as training and tax incentives, they can seek to develop new comparative advantages. Moreover, countries cannot complacently assume that their existing comparative advantages will persist. Misguided tax incentives and subsidies, or policies that discourage risk-taking, can lead to the rapid erosion of a country's comparative advantage in particular products. So, too, can developments in other countries.

THE TERMS OF TRADE

So far we have seen that world production can be increased when countries specialize in the production of the goods and services in which they have a comparative advantage, and then trade with one another. We now ask how these gains from specialization and trade will be shared among countries. The division of the gain depends on what is called the **terms of trade**, which measure the quantity of imported goods that can be obtained per unit of goods exported.

A rise in the price of imported goods, with the price of exports unchanged, indicates a fall in the terms of trade; it will now take more exports to buy the same quantity of imports. Similarly, a rise in the price of exported goods, with the price of imports unchanged, indicates a rise in terms of trade; it will now take fewer exports to buy the same quantity of imports. Thus the ratio of these prices measures the amount of imports that can be obtained per unit of goods exported.

Because actual international trade involves many countries and many products, a country's terms of trade are computed as an index number:

$$\text{Terms of trade} = \frac{\text{Index of export prices}}{\text{Index of import prices}} \times 100.$$

A rise in the index is referred to as a *favourable* change in a country's terms of trade. A favourable change means that more can be imported per unit of goods exported than previously. For example, if the export price index rises from 100 to 120 while the import price index rises from 100 to 110, the terms of trade index rises from 100 to 109. At the new terms of trade, a unit of exports will buy 9 per cent more imports than at the old terms.

A decrease in the index of the terms of trade, called an *unfavourable* change, means that the country can import less in return for any given amount of exports or, equivalently, that it must export more to pay for any given amount of imports. For example, the sharp rise in oil prices in the 1970s led to large unfavourable shifts in the terms of trade of oil-importing countries. When oil prices fell sharply in the mid-1980s, the terms of trade of oil-importing countries changed favourably. The converse was true for oil-exporting countries.

[. . .]

We now turn to a discussion of the arguments for and against government intervention in international trade.

THE THEORY OF COMMERCIAL POLICY

Government policy towards international trade is known as **commercial policy**. Complete freedom from interference with trade is known as a **free trade** policy. Any departure from free trade designed to give some protection to domestic industries from foreign competition is called **protectionism**.

Today debates over commercial policy are as heated as they were 200 years ago when the theory of the gains from trade that we presented above was still being worked out. Should a country permit the free flow of international trade, or should it seek to protect its local producers from foreign competition? Such protection may be achieved either by **tariffs**, which are taxes designed to raise the price of foreign goods, or by **non-tariff barriers**, which are devices other than tariffs that are designed to reduce the flow of imports; examples of the latter include quotas and customs procedures deliberately made more cumbersome than is necessary.

The case for free trade

The case for free trade is based on the analysis presented above. We saw that whenever opportunity costs differ among countries, specialization and trade will raise world living standards. Free trade allows all countries to specialize in producing products in which they have a comparative advantage.

> Free trade allows the maximization of world production, thus making it possible for each consumer in the world to consume more goods than he or she could without free trade.

This does not necessarily mean that everyone will be better off with free trade than without it. Protectionism could allow some people to obtain a larger share of a smaller world output so that they would benefit even though the average person would lose. If we ask whether it is possible for free trade to improve everyone's living standards, the answer is 'yes'. But if we ask whether free trade does in fact always do so, the answer is 'not necessarily'.

There is abundant evidence that significant differences in opportunity costs exist and that large gains are realized from international trade because of these differences. What needs explanation is the fact that trade is not wholly free. Why do tariffs and non-tariff barriers to trade continue to exist two centuries after Adam Smith and David Ricardo stated the case for free trade? Is there a valid case for protectionism?

The case for protectionism

Two kinds of arguments for protection are commonly offered. The first concerns national objectives other than total income; the second concerns the desire to increase one country's national income, possibly at the expense of world national income.

Objectives other than maximizing national income as reasons for protectionism

It is possible to accept the proposition that national income is higher with free trade, and yet rationally to oppose free trade, because of a concern with policy objectives other than maximizing income.

Non-economic advantages of diversification Comparative advantage might dictate that a country should specialize in producing a narrow range of products. The government might decide, however, that there are distinct social advantages in encouraging a more diverse economy. Citizens would be given a wider range of occupations, and the social and psychological advantages of diversification would more than compensate for a reduction in living standards to, say, 5 per cent below what they could be with complete specialization of production according to comparative advantage.

Risks of specialization For a very small country, specializing in the production of only a few products – though dictated by comparative advantage – may involve risks that the country does not wish to take. One such risk is that technological advances may render its major product obsolete. Everyone understands this risk, but there is debate over what governments can do about it. The pro-tariff argument is that the government can encourage a more diversified economy by protecting industries that otherwise could not compete. Opponents argue that governments, being naturally influenced by political motives, are in the final analysis poor judges of which industries can be protected in order to produce diversification at a reasonable cost.

National defence Another non-economic reason for protectionism concerns national defence. It used to be argued, for example, that the United Kingdom needed an experienced merchant navy in case of war, and that this industry should be fostered by protectionist policies even though it was less efficient than the foreign competition. The same argument is sometimes made for the aircraft industry.

Protection of specific groups Although free trade will maximize per capita GDP over the whole economy, some specific groups may have higher incomes under protection than under free trade. An obvious example is a firm or industry that is given monopoly power when tariffs are used to restrict foreign competition. If a small group of firms, and possibly their employees, find their incomes increased by, say, 25 per cent when they get tariff protection, they may not be concerned that everyone else's incomes fall by, say, 2 per cent. They get a much larger share of a slightly smaller total income and end up better off. If they gain from the tariff, they will lose from free trade.

> Tariffs tend to raise the relative income of a group of people who are in short supply domestically and to lower the relative income of a group of people who are in plentiful supply domestically. Free trade does the opposite.

Conclusion Other things being equal, most people prefer more income to less. Economists cannot say that it is irrational for a society to sacrifice some income in order to achieve other goals. Economists can, however, do three things when faced with such reasons for adopting protectionist measures. First, they can ask if the proposed measures really do achieve the ends suggested. Second, they can calculate the cost of the measures in terms of lowered living standards. Third, they can see if there are alternative means of achieving the stated goals at lower cost in terms of lost output.

Maximizing national income as a reason for protectionism

Next we consider five important arguments for the use of tariffs when the objective is to make national income as large as possible.

To alter the terms of trade Trade restrictions can be used to turn the terms of trade in favour of countries that produce, and export, a large fraction of the world's supply of some product. They can also be used to turn the terms of trade in favour of countries that constitute a large fraction of the world demand for some product that they import.

When the OPEC countries restricted their output of oil in the 1970s, they were able to drive up the price of oil relative to the prices of other traded goods. This turned the terms of trade in their favour; for every barrel of oil exported, they were able to obtain a larger quantity of imports. When the output of oil grew greatly in the mid-1980s, the relative price of oil fell dramatically, and the terms of trade turned unfavourably for the oil-exploring companies. These are illustrations of how changes in the quantities of exports can affect the terms of trade.

Now consider a country that provides a large fraction of the total demand for some product that it imports. By restricting its demand for that product through tariffs, it can force the price of that product down. This turns the terms of trade in its favour because it can now get more units of imports per unit of exports.

Both of these techniques lower world output. They can, however, make it possible for a small group of countries to gain because they get a sufficiently larger share of the smaller world output. However, if foreign countries retaliate by raising their tariffs, the ensuing tariff war can easily leave every country with a lowered income.

To protect against 'unfair' actions by foreign firms and governments Tariffs may be used to prevent foreign industries from gaining an advantage over domestic industries by use of predatory practices that will harm domestic industries and hence lower national income. Two common practices are subsidies paid by foreign governments to their exporters and price discrimination by foreign firms, which is called *dumping* when it is done across international borders. These practices are typically countered by levying tariffs called countervailing and anti-dumping duties.

To protect infant industries The oldest valid argument for protectionism as a means of raising living standards concerns economies of scale. It is usually called the **infant industry argument**. If an industry has large economies of scale, costs will be high when the industry is small, but will fall as the industry grows. In such industries the country first in the field has a tremendous advantage. A newly developing country may find that in the early stages of development its industries are unable to compete with established foreign rivals. A trade restriction may protect these industries from foreign competition while they grow up. When they are large enough, they will be able to produce as cheaply as foreign rivals and thus will be able to compete without protection.

To encourage learning by doing Learning by doing suggests that the pattern of comparative advantage can be changed. If a country learns enough through producing products in which it currently is at a comparative disadvantage, it may gain in the long run by specializing in those products, and could develop a comparative advantage as the learning process lowers their costs.

The successes of such newly industrializing countries (NICs) as Brazil, Hong Kong, South Korea, Singapore, and Taiwan seemed to many observers to be based on acquired skills and government policies that created favourable business conditions. This gave rise to the theory that comparative advantages can change, and that they can be developed by suitable government policies.

Protecting a domestic industry from foreign competition may give its management time to learn to be efficient, and its labour force time to acquire the needed skills.

If this is so, it may pay in the very long run to protect the industry against foreign competition while a dynamic comparative advantage is being developed.

Some countries have succeeded in developing strong comparative advantages in targeted industries, but others have failed. One reason such policies sometimes fail is that protecting local industries from foreign competition may make the industries unadaptive and complacent. Another reason is the difficulty of identifying the industries that will be able to succeed in the long run. All too often the protected infant grows up to be a weakling requiring permanent tariff protection for its continued existence; or else the rate of learning is slower than for similar industries in countries that do not provide protection from the chill winds of international competition. In these instances the anticipated comparative advantage never materializes.

To create or to exploit a strategic trade advantage An important recent argument for tariffs or other trade restrictions is to create a strategic advantage in producing or marketing some new product that is expected to generate profits. To the extent that all lines of production earn normal profits, there is no reason to produce goods other than ones for which a country has a comparative advantage. Some goods, however, are produced in industries containing a few large firms where large-scale economies provide a natural barrier to further entry. Firms in these industries can earn extra-high profits over long periods of time. Where such industries are already well established, there is little chance that a new firm will replace one of the existing giants.

The situation is, however, more fluid with new products. The first firm to develop and market a new product successfully may earn a substantial pure profit over all of its opportunity costs and become one of the few established firms in the industry. If protection of the domestic market can increase the chance that one of the protected domestic firms will become one of the established firms in the international market, the protection may pay off.

Many of today's high-tech industries have falling average total cost curves because of their large fixed costs of product development. For a new generation of civilian aircraft, silicon chips, computers, artificial-intelligence machines, and pharmaceuticals, a very high proportion of each producer's total costs goes to product development. These are fixed costs of entering the market, and they must be incurred before a single unit of output can be sold. In such industries there may be room for only a few firms.

The production of full-sized commercial jet aeroplanes provides an example of an industry that possesses many of these characteristics. The development costs of a new generation of jet aircraft have risen with each new generation. If the aircraft manufacturers are to recover these costs, each of them must have large sales. Thus the number of firms that the market can support has diminished steadily, until today there is room in the world aircraft industry for only two or three firms producing a full range of commercial jets.

The characteristics just described are sometimes used to provide arguments for subsidizing the development of such industries and/or protecting their home markets with a tariff. Suppose, for example, that there is room in the aircraft industry for only three major producers of the next round of passenger jets. If a government assists a domestic firm, this firm may become one of the three that succeed, and the profits that are subsequently earned may more than repay the cost of the subsidy. Furthermore, another country's firm, which was not subsidized, may have been just as good as the three that succeeded. Without the subsidy, however, this firm may lose out in the battle to establish itself as one of the three surviving firms in the market.

This example is not unlike the story of the European Airbus. The European producers received many direct subsidies (and they charge that their main competitor, the Boeing 767, received many indirect ones). Whatever the merits of the argument, several things are clear: the civilian jet aircraft industry remains profitable; there is room for only two or three major producers; and one of these would not have been the European consortium if it had not been for substantial government assistance.

Generalizing from this and similar cases, some economists advocate that their governments should adopt *strategic trade policies* more broadly than they now do. This means, for high-tech industries, government protection of the home market and government subsidization (either openly or by more subtle back-door methods) of the product development stage. These economists say that if their country does not follow their advice, it will lose out in industry after industry to the more aggressive Japanese and North American competition – a competition that is adept at combining private innovative activity with government assistance.

Opponents argue that once all countries try to be strategic, they will all waste vast sums trying to break into industries in which there is no room for most of them. Advocates of strategic trade policy reply that a country cannot afford to stand by while others play the strategic game.

Advocates also argue that there are key industries that have major 'spillovers' into the rest of the economy. If a country wants to have a high living standard, it must, they argue, compete with the best. If a country lets all of its key industries migrate to other countries, many of the others will follow. The country then risks being reduced to the status of a less developed nation.

Opponents argue that strategic trade policy is just the modern version of mercantilism, a policy of trying to enrich oneself at the expense of one's neighbours rather than looking for mutually beneficial gains from trade. They point to the rising world prosperity of the entire period following the Second World War, which has been built largely on a rising volume of relatively free international trade. There are real doubts that such prosperity could be maintained if the volume of trade were to shrink steadily because of growing trade barriers.

[. . .]

Methods of protection

We have now studied some of the many reasons why governments may wish to provide some protection for some of their domestic industries. Our next task is to see how they do it. What are the tools that provide protection?

[There are] two main types of protectionist policy. [. . .] Both cause the price of the imported good to rise and its quantity to fall. They differ, however, in how they achieve these results. [. . .]

Policies that directly raise prices

The first type of protectionist policy directly raises the *price* of the imported product. A tariff, also often called an *import duty*, is the most common policy of this type. Other such policies include any rules or regulations that fulfil three conditions: they are costly to comply with; they do not apply to competing, domestically produced products; and they are more than is required to meet any purpose other than restricting trade.

[Tariffs] affect both foreign and domestic producers, as well as domestic consumers. The initial effect is to raise the domestic price of the imported product above its world price by the amount of the tariff. Imports fall, and as a result foreign producers sell less and so must transfer resources to other lines of production. The price received on domestically produced units rises, as does the quantity produced domestically. On both counts domestic producers earn more. However, the cost of producing the extra output at home exceeds the price at which it could be purchased on the world market. Thus the benefit to domestic producers comes at the expense of domestic consumers. Indeed, domestic consumers lose on two counts: first, they consume less of the product because its price rises; and second, they pay a higher price for the amount that they do consume. This extra spending ends up in two places: the extra that is paid on all units produced at home goes to domestic producers (partly in the resource costs of extra production and partly in profit), and the extra that is paid on units still imported goes to the government as tariff revenue.

Policies that directly lower quantities

The second type of protectionist policy directly restricts the quantity of an imported product. Any implicit or explicit restriction on trade that does not involve a tariff is known as a **non-tariff barrier**. These can take various subtle forms including quality standards that are complicated to interpret or customs forms that take weeks to get approved. But many non-tariff barriers are more obvious and easy to understand. A common example is the **import quota**, by which the importing country sets a maximum on the quantity of some product that may be imported each year. Increasingly popular in the recent past, however, has been the **voluntary export restriction** (VER), an agreement by an exporting country to limit the amount of a good that it sells to the importing country.

The European Union and the United States have used VERS extensively, and the European Union also makes frequent use of import quotas. Japan has been pressured into negotiating several VERs with the European Union and the United States in order to limit sales of some of the Japanese goods that have had the most success in international competition. For example, in 1983 the United States and Canada negotiated VERs whereby the Japanese government agreed to restrict total sales of Japanese cars to these two countries for three years. When the agreements ran out in 1986, the Japanese continued to restrain their car sales by unilateral voluntary action.

GLOBAL COMMERCIAL POLICY

We now discuss supranational influences on commercial policy in the world today. We start with the many international agreements that govern current commercial policies and then look in a little more detail at the European Union.

Before 1947 any country was free to impose any tariffs on its imports. However, when one country increased its tariffs, the action often triggered retaliatory actions by its trading partners. The Great Depression of the 1930s saw a high-water mark of world protectionism, as each country sought to raise its employment by raising its tariffs. The end result was lowered efficiency, less trade – but no increase in employment. Since that time, much effort has been devoted to reducing tariff barriers, on both a multilateral and a regional basis.

GATT and the WTO

One of the most notable achievements of the post-war era was the creation of the General Agreement on Tariffs and Trade (GATT). The principle of GATT is that each member country agrees not to make unilateral tariff increases. This prevents the outbreak of tariff wars in which countries raise tariffs to protect particular domestic industries and to retaliate against other countries' tariff increases. Such wars usually harm all countries as mutually beneficial trade shrinks under the impact of escalating tariff barriers.

There have been eight 'rounds' of global trade talks since 1948. The three most recently completed rounds of GATT agreements, the Kennedy round (completed 1967), the Tokyo round (completed 1979), and the Uruguay round (completed 1993), have each agreed to reduce world tariffs substantially, the first two by about one-third each, and the last by about 40 per cent.

The Uruguay round created a new body, the World Trade Organization (WTO), that superseded the GATT in 1995. It also created a new legal structure for multilateral trading. Under this new structure all members have equal mutual rights and obligations. Until the WTO was formed, developing countries who were in GATT enjoyed all the GATT rights but were exempt from most of its obligations to liberalize trade – obligations that applied only to the developed countries. Now, however, all such special treatments are being phased out over seven years from 1995. There is also a new dispute-settlement mechanism with much more power to enforce rulings over non-tariff barriers than existed in the past. In its first three years the WTO dealt with 132 complaints; while the GATT only heard 300 in forty-seven years!

In 1997 three strands of negotiation that had been left incomplete in the Uruguay round were completed, involving agreements to lower trade barriers in telecommunications, financial services, and information technology. These agreements were important because they greatly increase the amount of trade covered by WTO rules and dispute-settlement procedures, they may lead to larger trade volume gains than the entire Uruguay round, and they complete most of the unfinished business from Uruguay, clearing the way for a new global trade round.

By 1998 the WTO had 132 member countries, with a further 30 including Russia and China hoping to join.[1] It is thus growing into a truly global forum for the regulation of government involvement in world trade. [. . .]

Types of regional agreement

Regional agreements seek to liberalize trade over a much smaller set of countries than the WTO membership. Three standard forms of regional trade-liberalizing agreement are free-trade areas, customs unions, and common markets.

A free-trade area (FTA) is the least comprehensive of the three. It allows for tariff-free trade among the member countries, but it leaves each member free to impose its own trade restrictions on imports from other countries. As a result members must maintain customs points at their common borders to make sure that imports into the free-trade area do not all enter through the member that is levying the lowest tariff on each item. They must also agree on rules of origin to establish when a good is made in a member country, and hence is able to pass duty-free across their borders, and when it is imported from outside the free-trade area, and hence is liable to pay duties when it crosses borders within the free-trade area.

A **customs union** is a free-trade area plus an agreement to establish common barriers to trade with the rest of the world. Because they have a common tariff against the outside world, the members need neither customs controls on goods moving among themselves nor rules of origin.

A **common market** is a customs union that also has free movement of labour and capital among its members.

EFTA, NAFTA, and other FTAs

The first important free-trade area in the modern era was the European Free Trade Association (EFTA). It was formed in 1960 by a group of European countries that were unwilling to join the European Economic Community as the EU was then called because of its all-embracing character. Not wanting to be left out of the gains from trade, they formed an association whose sole purpose was tariff removal. First, they removed all tariffs on trade among themselves. Then each country signed a free-trade-area agreement with the EEC. This made the EEC–EFTA market the largest tariff-free market in the world (over 300 million people). Three of the EFTA countries switched to full membership of the EU in 1995.

In 1988 a sweeping agreement was signed between Canada and the United States, instituting free trade on all goods and most non-government services, and covering what is the world's largest flow of international trade between any two countries. In 1993 this agreement was extended into the North American Free Trade Agreement (NAFTA) by renegotiation of the Canada–USA agreement to include Mexico. Australia and New Zealand have also entered into an association that removes restrictions on trade in goods and services between their two countries, and a group of countries in Southeast Asia have formed the ASEAN trade group.

The countries of Latin America have been experimenting with free-trade areas for many decades. Most earlier attempts failed, but in the last few years a more durable free-trade area has been formed, known as Mercosur. In April 1998 an initiative was taken to put in place a free-trade area for the whole of the Americas by 2005 which would in effect be based upon a merger of NAFTA and Mercosur. It remains to be seen if this will come to fruition. Currently the US legislature is blocking all efforts to extend NAFTA to other countries, beginning with Chile.

Common markets: the European Union

By far the most successful common market, which is now referred to as a single market, is the European Union. Its origins go back to the period immediately following the Second World War in 1945. After the war there was a strong belief throughout Europe that the way to avoid future military conflict was to create a high level of economic integration between the existing nation-states. Later the motivation switched to creating a powerful economic bloc which could be competitive with Japan and the USA.

In 1952, as a first step towards economic union, France, Belgium, West Germany, Italy, Luxembourg, and Holland formed the European Coal and Steel Community. This removed trade restrictions on coal, steel, and iron ore among these six countries. In 1957 the same six countries signed the Treaty of Rome. This created the European Economic Community (EEC), which later became the European Community (EC), and after 1993 the European Union (EU). In 1973 the United Kingdom, Denmark, and Ireland joined, and they were followed in 1981 by Greece and in 1986 by Spain and Portugal. Austria, Sweden, and Finland entered in 1995. Several other countries, such as Poland, Hungary, the Czech Republic, and Cyprus are hoping to join in the early twenty-first century.

In the first two decades of its existence the main economic achievements of the EEC were the elimination of internal tariff barriers and the establishment of common external tariffs (in other words the establishment of a customs union), and the establishment of the Common Agricultural Policy, which, for better or for worse, guarantees farm prices by means of intervention and an import levy [. . .]. There were other significant EEC policies, such as regional aid and protection of competition, but they did not have great economic impacts early on.

By the mid-1980s it was clear that the intended 'Common Market' had not been achieved. There remained many non-tariff barriers to trade and to the mobility of labour. These included quality standards, licensing requirements, and a lack of recognition of qualifications. In financial services there were explicit exchange controls and other regulatory restrictions on cross-border trade. In response a new push to turn the customs union into a genuine common market began in 1985.

The Single Market Programme

The Single Market Act was signed in 1986. Its intention was to remove all remaining barriers to the creation of a fully integrated single market by the end of 1992. The Single Market Act did not in itself create the single market. Rather, it was a statement (or treaty) of intent which instituted a simplified administrative procedure whereby most of the single market legislation needed only 'weighted majority' support, rather than unanimity. The single market itself was to be created by a large number of Directives, which are drafted by the European Commission, the EU's civil service. These become Community law after they have been 'adopted' by the European Council (a committee of the heads of state or other ministers of member states). They then have to be ratified in the law of each member state. Once in force, they have precedence over the domestic laws of member states if there is a conflict.

Eliminating non-tariff barriers has been approached on a product-by-product basis. Only in this way could minimum quality standards be created which would permit cross-border trade without the threat of quality checks as a prerequisite to entry (a problem that plagues some branches of Canada–USA trade). This has required a complicated set of negotiations on quality standards relating to everything from condoms to sausages and from toys to telecommunications. There is even a quality standard for the bacterial content of aqueous toys – transparent plastic souvenirs containing, perhaps, a model of Big Ben or the Eiffel Tower, which, when shaken, create a snow scene.

All countries have such safety or quality standards for their products, and what has been happening is the harmonization of these standards, which is something that Canada and the United States have been trying to do since their Agreement was put into force in 1989.

The Single Market Programme is an ongoing process, not a discrete jump. Some of the intended measures have been implemented, but many are still in the pipeline. The process will continue well into the twenty-first century.

Many important steps were achieved by the end of 1992, including the removal of some border checks. (At UK ports and airports, this means a blue channel through which EU citizens are permitted to carry as many goods as they like, if bought in other EU countries, so long as they are for personal use.) But the process of increasing economic integration continued well after 1992.

The Maastricht Treaty

Signed in 1992, the Maastricht Treaty pushed the process of EU integration further. It included an agreement creating the common currency that came into being in January 1999. It is likely that the introduction of the single currency will do as much as any of the previous tariff reductions to integrate the economies of the European Union, as it makes the price system much more transparent and eliminates exchange rate risk. The implications of the single currency will be unclear until the early years of the twenty-first century.

The Maastricht Treaty also contained a Social Chapter, covering harmonization of policies with respect to labour markets and other social areas. The United Kingdom opted out of this Chapter initially, but opted back in in 1997.

NOTE

1 The latest information about the WTO can be found on the Internet at www.wto.org.

9

PROTECTIONISM AND INDUSTRIALIZATION: A HISTORICAL PERSPECTIVE*

Paul Bairoch

The European commercial expansion resulting from the Industrial Revolution had very different consequences on the trade policies of the rest of the world. In simplified terms, this can be divided into two spheres. In those parts of the world which gradually became part of the developed world, protectionism was the dominant commercial policy. This was especially the case in the United States, which, far from being a liberal country as many think, can be characterized as 'the mother country and bastion of modern protectionism'. In the second sphere, the future Third World (and especially those countries that were colonized), liberalism prevailed, but it was not by choice; it was enforced liberal commercial policy.

[. . .]

THE UNITED STATES: MOTHER COUNTRY AND BASTION OF MODERN PROTECTIONISM (1791–1860)

The long protectionist history of the United States is forgotten more often than that of Continental Europe,[1] even though as early as the nineteenth century the relative economic importance of the United States among the non-European developed countries was very large. To give just one example: in 1860 the US population was 32 million compared to 5 million for the total of the rest of this group (Australia, Canada and New Zealand).

As noted earlier, one should not forget that modern protectionism was born in the United States. In 1791, Alexander Hamilton, the First Secretary of the Treasury (between 1789 and 1795) in the first US government, drew up his famous *Report on Manufactures*, which is considered to be the first formulation of modern protectionist theory. [. . .] The major contribution of Hamilton is the emphasis he put on the idea that industrialization is not possible without tariff protection. He was apparently the first to have introduced the term 'infant industries'. Even if the 'infant industry' argument was already present in mercantilist theories, Hamilton put it to the forefront of economic thinking.

At the end of the nineteenth century, Callender could write, with no exaggeration, that:

> Next to currency problems no purely economic subject has aroused so much interest in the United States, and played so great a part in political discussion both in and out of Congress as the tariff policy of the federal government. From the first measure of 1789 until the present time no generation of the American people has escaped the tariff controversy.[2]

A legislator in the state of Pennsylvania suggested that man should be redefined as 'an animal that makes tariff speeches.'[3] Further, it is no exaggeration to say that the tariff question had been one of the causes of the American Revolution.

The first tariff of 1789 is often described as moderately protectionist; in fact, analysis of the levels of import duties shows it to be a liberal tariff. It is true that, compared with the previous situation, this tariff was a step towards protectionism, and, in addition, the remoteness of the United States from other world economies constituted a natural, protective barrier. This first American tariff, which, according to its preamble, was aimed at protecting local industry, provided duties for manufactured goods averaging about 7.5–10%. After two successive revisions, the tariff of 1792 increased duties on most categories of goods by 50%. On many subsequent occasions various duties were increased, leading to the 1816 tariff, where import duties were about 35% for almost all manufactured goods.

The opposition between the South, which as an exporter of agricultural products (cotton, tobacco) was liberal, and the North, which was industrializing and hence protectionist, emerged during this period. The protectionist movement – supported by economists such as Daniel Raymond and, later, Henry C. Carey – was encouraged by pockets of unemployment and by cyclical crises. From 1819 onwards, associations were formed to press for industrialization to be achieved as a result of protectionism. This movement was also well supported by publications.

From then on it is possible to divide nineteenth-century American commercial history into three relatively distinct periods. The first, which can be called a protectionist phase, lasted from 1816 to 1846. From 1846 to 1861 came a period which is sometimes said to have been liberal, but should more accurately be described as one of very modest protectionism. The final phase, which lasted from 1861 to the end of our period (and in fact to the end of World War II), was one of strict protectionism. Let us examine this in more detail.

After some congressional vicissitudes, a series of modifications adopted between 1824 and 1832 further strengthened the protectionist nature of the 1816 tariff. Import duties on woollen manufactured goods were 40–45% and those for clothing 50%; but import duties on all manufactured goods averaged 40%. Some duties on agricultural products were also increased: on many these amounted to more than 60% of their value. On the basis of the importance of import duties relative to import values – not a perfect indicator – the tariff in force after 1829 showed American protectionism at its height (see Table 9.1).

This development led to a serious crisis because of opposition from the South and certain states declared the federal laws on these matters null and void. The crisis was resolved in 1832 by the adoption of the Compromise Bill, which provided for a progressive reduction in the highest import duties, leading to a relatively unified level of 20% in 1842. This liberalization of trade policy reached its peak with the tariff of 1842, which reduced import duties on manufactured goods to an average of 25% and increased the number of products that could enter freely. However – and this was characteristic of American tariff history – this rather liberal tariff remained in force for only a very short period: two months. The emergence of the Whig Party (which was highly protectionist) and the political crisis of 1841–2 (linked to the death of President William Harrison one month after his inauguration in 1841) led to the tariff of 1842, which more or less restored the high tariff levels of 1832.

The return of the Democrat Party in 1844 resulted in the tariff of 1846, which reduced import duties by about 10–20% and generalized the system of *ad valorem* duties. The average *ad valorem* duty on the 51 most important categories of imported goods was 27%. There were scarcely any major modifications until the tariff of 1861, and this is the phase we have called modest protectionism.

Table 9.1 Ratio of import duties to imports in the United States for significant trade policy periods and recent data, 1823/4–1988/90

| | Ratio of duties calculated to imports (%) | |
	Total imports (free and dutiable)	Dutiable imports
1823/4	43.4	45.8
1829/31	50.8	54.4
1842/6	25.3	31.9
1857/61	16.3	20.6
1867/71	44.3	46.7
1891/4	22.9	48.9
1908/13	20.1	41.3
1914	14.9	37.6
1923/7	14.1	37.7
1931/3	19.0	55.3
1935/8	16.4	39.8
1944/6	9.5	28.3
1968/72	6.5	10.1
1978/82	3.5	5.8
1988/90	3.6	5.4

Sources: US Bureau of Census, *Historical Statistics of the United States, Colonial Times to 1970*, Washington, 1975, p. 888. US Bureau of Census, *Statistical Abstract of the United States*, Washington, various issues.

The year of Napoleon III's liberal *coup d'état*, 1860, is in the United States the year in which Abraham Lincoln was elected and which marked the beginning of the Southern states' secession. The long and bloody American Civil War, which ended in April 1865, signified the victory not only of the abolitionists of the North over the pro-slavery South but also the triumph of the protectionists of the Northern industrial states over the free marketers of the South, whose main export was raw cotton. [Around] 1875, at the height of economic liberalism in Europe, whereas in Continental Europe the average level of duties on manufactured goods was 9–12% the rate in the United States was 40–50%. To these figures one must still remember to add the natural protection resulting from geographical distance of European exporters.

If in 1791 the new-born United States was a very small economic entity, things were very different by 1860. To give some idea of the rapid changes, let us first note that in 1791 the US population had just passed 4 million, which represented 2% of Europe's population (including Russia), and US manufacturing capacity represented probably 1% of that of Europe. In 1860 the US population had reached 32 million which not only represented 11% of that of Europe but put the United States on a level with the greatest European states. At the time France had 37 million inhabitants; Germany, 36 million; Austria–Hungary 35 million; the United Kingdom 29 million: Italy 25 million; and Spain 16 million. Only backward Russia had a much larger population (probably 78–84 million). In 1860 the volume of United States' industrial production represented 13% of that of Europe, and only 20 years later the ratio would rise to 24%. This means that from 1870 to 1880 onwards tariff events in the United States became events of world importance.

THE UNITED STATES: FROM 'INFANT INDUSTRIES' ARGUMENTS TO THE PROTECTION OF AMERICAN WAGES (1861–1914)

As noted earlier, at the beginning of the 1860s the turning points in tariff history in Europe and the United States were very different, and it is during the 1860–90 period that the contrast between European and American trade policies became most marked. The 1861 tariff was the beginning of a policy that was to be followed in the United States until the end of World War II. Import duties were increased again during the American Civil War, and victory by the North brought further protectionism. The tariff in force from 1866 to 1883 provided for import duties averaging 45% for manufactured goods (the lowest rates of duty were about 25% and the highest about 60%).

The way in which the United States caught up with, and even overtook, European industry rendered obsolete the 'infant industries' argument for United States protectionists. The Republican Party therefore based its case for introducing the McKinley Tariff of 1890 on the need to safeguard the wage levels of American workers and to give the agricultural sector more protection. This tariff implied a distinct increase in effective protection, due to a general increase in import duties, a combination of specific and *ad valorem* duties (with sliding scales) and an enlargement of the number of tariff items.

During the 1890–1913 period there was a series of tariff modifications which alternately reduced and increased import duties by small amounts, according to the results of elections. The principle of reciprocity, which was already central to United States' trade policy, was retained. In his message to Congress in 1901, Theodore Roosevelt wrote:

> Reciprocity must be treated as the handmaiden of Protection. Our first duty is to see that the protection granted by the tariff in every case where it is needed is maintained, and that reciprocity be sought for so far as it can be safely done without injury to our home industries.[4]

On 4 October 1913 a serious (but very temporary) break with previous policy occurred. This change in direction was made possible by the victory of the Democratic Party in the 1912 elections. The so-called Underwood Tariff of 4 October 1913 led to a large increase in the categories of goods allowed free entry and to a substantial drop in average import duties. According to calculations by the League of Nations, the average duty on imports fell from 33% to 16% and the average duty on manufactured goods from 44% to 25%.[5] This still remained one of the highest tariff rates in the world (see Table 9.2).

This interlude of moderation in US protectionist policies did not last long. World War I prevented the tariff of October 1913 from having any important role, and following the return to power of the Republican Party in May 1921 new 'emergency' tariff legislation came into force on 22 September 1922. This involved a distinct increase in protectionism compared with the 1913 tariff. Although import duties did not return to the high levels of the tariffs in force in the 1861–1913 period, the percentage effectively paid on manufactured goods rose by 30%. So strong is the idea of the United States as a leader in free trade policies that, despite the fact that the October 1913 tariff had almost no practical meaning, often we find that it is generally accepted as an indicator of the US level of duties for the pre-World War I period.

Table 9.2 Indicators of tariff levels in 1913 in different types of country

	Import duties as % of special total imports (1908/12)	Approximate average level of import duties on manufactures	Level of duties on wheat
Developed countries			
Continental Europe	10.4	19	25
United Kingdom	5.7	0	0
Australia	18.2	16	22
Canada	18.7	26	–
Japan	9.1	25–30	18
New Zealand	16.6	15–20	3
United States	21.4	44	0[a]
Non-developed countries			
Selected independent (in 1913) countries			
Argentina	21.6	28	0
Brazil	37.4	50–70	–
Colombia	49.1[b]	40–60	20
Mexico	33.7[b]	40–50[c]	42
Selected semi-independent (in 1913) countries			
China	3.3	4–5	0
Iran	8.0[b]	3–4	0
Siam	2.7[d]	2–3	3
Turkey	–	5–10	11

[a] With 10% for wheat originating from countries where US wheat is imposed.

[b] To total imports.

[c] 1910.

[d] 1910/13.

Sources: Percentages of import duties: author's computations based on various national sources.

Average level for manufactures:
Ranges: author's estimates on basis of individual tariffs.
Other figures: see Table 2.3 [of Bairoch, P. (1993) *Economics and World History*, Harvester Wheatsheaf, p. 26] and national sources.
Level of duties on wheat: see Table 2.3 [of Bairoch 1993] for method of calculation. Additional sources were used for this table.

BRITISH DOMINIONS: TARIFF INDEPENDENCE BRINGS PROTECTIONISM

The fact that tariffs played an important role in the rejection by the United States of British rule was an important factor in Britain's early decision to grant a large measure of tariff independence to what were later (at the end of the century) to become the self-governing colonies, in other words, essentially those with large European populations (Canada, Australia and New Zealand). In the nineteenth century the trade policies in these countries went through two main phases. The first, which, depending on the country, lasted until 1867–88, was a period of liberal policies justified mainly by the export opportunities for agricultural products favoured until the early 1850s by the British preferential system. During the second phase (between 1867/88 and 1913), all these countries sought, to some degree and with varying amounts of success, to encourage their industrial sectors through protectionist tariff policies. The geographical position of these countries was an important influence on their policies: the isolation of Australia and New Zealand contrasted with the proximity of the United States to Canada.

In Canada, the repeal of the Corn Laws in Britain (in 1846) and the abolition of other preferences on Canadian goods led to the necessity of a drastic reorganization of Canadian trade policy, since from 1840 to 1846 60–70% of Canadian exports went to the United Kingdom. The Canadians naturally turned towards their southern neighbour, and this led to the reciprocity treaty of 1854 with the United States which resulted in free trade in agricultural products between the two countries in exchange for fishing and navigation rights for the Americans.

However, the major turning point came when the Canadian Conservative Party adopted a 'National Policy' based on protectionism as their election platform in October 1878. The new tariff legislation of 1879 protected both agriculture and industry. For agricultural goods, average import duties were between 20% and 50% *ad valorem*, and manufactured goods about 20–30%. This was only the beginning of a series of increases in duties which continued to 1887, raising the degree of effective protection in most sectors of industry. By 1887 the average import duties on manufactured goods were around 25–35%. This protective policy did not exclude the 'motherland', but in 1898 a unilateral preference of 25% for British goods was introduced.

Australia or, more precisely, the colony of Victoria (accounting at the end of the nineteenth century for about 46% of the population of the six separate colonies which formed the Commonwealth of Australia), was the first British colony to introduce a trade policy intended to promote industry by means of a protectionist tariff. This policy, which dates from 1867, can be largely explained by the unemployment in this region at the beginning of the 1860s. The unemployment was itself the result of the extremely rapid influx of population[6] resulting from the discovery of rich gold seams in 1851. After 1856 gold production began to drop, thus creating a large unemployed workforce composed mainly of townspeople.

The first Australian federal tariff in 1902 represented a compromise between the protectionism of Victoria and the liberalism of the other states. This truce did not last long: the 1906 Australian elections returned a protectionist majority. In 1906 the Australian Industries Preservation Act was passed, which was an anti-dumping law. The new tariff of 1908 aimed at protection and provided for a doubling of import duties on most categories of goods, while retaining preferences for British products. On the whole, the degree of protection in 1913 (see Table 9.2) was lower than that prevailing in Canada, and lower even than the average level in Continental Europe. But Australia's extreme remoteness from Europe must be taken into account. Further, the tariff reform of 1914 provided for an increase in import duties on manufactured goods of about 25%. Even though this increase was a war measure, it should be noted that the tariffs adopted after the war reinforced protectionist tendencies.

Throughout the entire nineteenth century New Zealand had a more liberal tariff than either Australia or Canada. This can be explained by the size of the country (fewer than 500,000 inhabitants in 1880, as opposed to 2,500,000 in Australia and 4,300,000 in Canada) and by the dominant importance of agriculture in the New Zealand economy. Except for some processing industries linked to agricultural exports, the local market was too small to permit real industrialization. However, even in New Zealand the depression of the 1880s caused a change in attitude towards the tariff system, which had until then been regarded purely as a means of raising revenue. In much the same way as had happened in Australia, the decrease in gold production resulted in the strengthening of a protectionist trend which was already noticeable in 1873. Again, as in Australia, the workers' parties strongly supported the protectionist movement. This pressure came to a head in 1888, and the tariff adopted in that year involved a policy based in principle on the protection of certain sectors of industry.

Thus, as we have seen, it is no exaggeration to claim that, with the exception of Britain, the developed world was an ocean of protectionism. It was an ocean that did not recede until after World War II (see Table 9.3).

Table 9.3 Average tariff rates on manufactured products in selected developed countries, 1820–1987 (weighted average; in percentages of value)

	1820[a,b]	1875[b]	1913	1925	1931	1950	1980	1990
EUROPE								
Austria[c]	*	15–20	18	16	24	18	14.6	12.7
Belgium[d]	6–8	9–10	9	15	14	11	8.3	5.9
Denmark	25–35	15–20	14	10	–	3	8.3	5.9
France	*	12–15	20	21	30	18	8.3	5.9
Germany[e]	8–12	4–6	13	20	21	26	8.3	5.9
Italy	–	8–10	18	22	46	25	8.3	5.9
Netherlands	6–8	3–5	4	6	–	11	8.3	5.9
Russia	*	15–20	84	*	*	*	*	*
Spain	*	15–20	41	41	63	–	8.3	5.9
Sweden	*	3–5	20	16	21	9	6.2	4.4
Switzerland	8–12	4–6	9	14	19	–	3.3	2.6
United Kingdom	45–55	0	0	5	–	23	8.3	5.9
United States	35–45	40–50	44	37	48	14	7.0	4.8
Japan	*	5	30	–	–	–	9.9	5.3

* Numerous and important restrictions in importation of manufactured products, which make all calculations of average tariff rates not significant.
– Not available.
[a] Very approximate rates.
[b] Range of average rates, not extremes.
[c] Before 1925 Austria–Hungary.
[d] In 1820: the Netherlands.
[e] In 1820: Prussia; after 1931 Federal Republic of Germany.

Note: The data for one period are not strictly comparable to those following it, with the exception of 1820/75, 1913/25 and 1978/87.

Sources:
1820 and 1875: Author's calculations. See Bairoch, P., *Commerce extérieur et développement économique de l'Europe au XIXe siècle*, Paris and The Hague, 1976; except United States and Japan: Bairoch, P., 'European trade policy, 1815–1914', in Mathias, P. and Pollard, S. (eds), *The Cambridge Economic History of Europe* (Volume VIII, *The Industrial Economies: The Development of Economic and Social Policies*), Cambridge, 1989, pp. 1–160.
1913 and 1925: League of Nations, *Tariff Level Indices*, Geneva, 1927; except for Japan: Bairoch, P., 'European trade policy, 1815–1914', *op. cit.*
1931: Liepmann, H., *Tariff Levels and the Economic Unity of Europe*, London, 1938. Except for the United States and Japan: Bairoch, P., 'European trade policy, 1815–1914', *op. cit.*
1950: Woytinsky, W.S. and Woytinsky, E. C., *World Commerce and Governments*, New York, 1955.
1980 and 1990 (or pre and post Tokyo round): GATT's Secretariat.

IN THE FUTURE THIRD WORLD: LIBERALISM ENFORCED

If we move outside the ocean of protectionism that washed the developed world there is no doubt that the future Third World was an ocean of liberalism. But it was compulsory economic liberalism, an economic liberalism of two main types, one for real colonies, and another for nominally independent countries for which certain customs regulations had been suggested (or imposed).

As far as the colonies were concerned, the general rule consisted of free access to all the products of the mother country (occasionally charged with low duties for fiscal reasons). In certain colonies, particularly the British ones, in the second half of the nineteenth century all goods, whatever their place of origin, were freely allowed in but with disguised measures for giving precedence to products from the mother country. These measures consisted mainly of formal or informal pressures on public or semi-public sectors, such as railways, to use the 'motherland's' products.

Furthermore, in some cases when import duties were imposed on manufactured goods for fiscal reasons, they were minimal and often counterbalanced by local fiscal measures. This was notably the case of India when, after 1859, the British government reintroduced modest duties (5%) on textile goods. As the result of a 'legitimate' protest by British manufacturers, local Indian producers of those goods were subject to a tax of the same magnitude in order to put the two types of production on the 'same footing'.

As for the Third World countries which were independent or not real colonies in the nineteenth century, that is, the most important parts of Latin America, China, Thailand and the Middle East as a whole, Western pressure had imposed on most of them treaties that entailed a more or less total elimination of customs duties on imports. Generally, it was the '5% rule' that applied, that is, a tariff regulation under which no duty could rise above 5% of the import value of the goods.

Most of those treaties, rightly called 'unequal treaties', were signed between 1810 and 1850, mainly initiated by British pressure. The political independence of almost all Latin American countries (which took place mainly between 1804 and 1822) had been largely helped by British intervention. This led to numerous trade treaties, one of the earliest of which was with Brazil in 1810. All these treaties opened those countries' markets to British and European manufactured products. Before their independence, it should be remembered that almost all Latin American countries were under Spanish or Portuguese domination; i.e. by the least industrialized countries in Europe.

A tariff treaty with the Ottoman Empire was signed in 1838, opening still further what was already a very open economy [. . .]. The Opium Wars (1839–42), which in fact aimed at making the vast Chinese territory available to British trade, ended with the Treaty of Nanking on 29 August 1842. This was the first step towards China's loss of tariff independence, which went as far as the appointment of a British citizen (R. Hart) as Inspector-General of customs, who remained in office from 1863 to 1908. The most comprehensive treaty with Thailand, leading to a real open economy, was signed in 1855, but this was preceded by others in 1824, 1826 and 1833.

If certain countries, particularly the large ones of Latin America, were able to modify their customs policies from 1880 onwards, we will see [elsewhere] that others had to wait until World War I and even later to free themselves from these restraints. For example, China regained independence in this field only in 1929, and Turkey in 1923.

[Elsewhere I have] described the trade policy of Europe around 1815 as an ocean of protectionism with a few liberal islands. To a very large extent, the same description holds true for the entire world around 1913. In the developed part of this world there were only two islands of liberalism. The most important one was indeed an island in real terms: Britain; and the other country is very open to the sea: the Netherlands. The combined exports of these two countries then represented 21% of those of all the developed countries (this was also the share of Germany and Belgium). In the Third World the independent (or semi-independent such as China) liberal countries' combined exports represented only 22% of Third World exports, and this was enforced liberalism. The rest of the Third World's exports came from colonies which even had more liberal tariffs. Therefore, the Third World was an ocean of liberalism without any island of protectionism. Between 1815 and 1913 only Europe had a short period of real liberalism lasting, on average, no more than a fifth of this time span. Since we must wait until the early 1960s to see the beginning of a new liberal period, the liberal interlude was reduced to a seventh of the time span, not counting the mercantilist centuries that preceded 1815. Therefore, from 1815 to 1960 it is very difficult to speak, as is often done, of a past Golden Era of free trade!

NOTES

*   This chapter has been adapted from, Bairoch, P. (1993) 'Was there Free Trade in the Rest of the World', in Bairoch, P. *Economics and World History*, ch. 3, pp. 30–43, Harvester Wheatsheaf.

1   A few years ago, I listened to a Voice of America programme on American radio in which a debate was held between a 'free trader' and a 'protectionist' on the necessity for a change in United States' trade policy on manufactured goods. One of the major and 'devastating' arguments of the 'free trader' was to ask his opponent the following question (I am quoting from memory): 'What would have happened in the past if this country had adopted a protectionist policy; would the United States have reached such a high level of industrialization?' The most astonishing fact was that, apparently, the 'protectionist' representative was not aware of the United States' long history of protectionism.

2   Callender, G. S., *Selection from the Economic History of the United States, 1765–1860*, Boston, 1909; quoted by Taylor, G. R. in Taylor, G. R. (ed.), *The Great Tariff Debate, 1820–1830*, Boston, 1968, p. v.

3   Eiselen, M. R., *The Rise of Pennsylvania Protectionism*, Philadelphia, 1932, p. 7.

4   Ashley, P., *Modern Tariff History: Germany–United States–France*, 3rd edn, London, 1920, p. 238.

5   League of Nations, *Tariff Level Indices* (International Economic Conference, Geneva, May 1927), Geneva, 1927.

6   In 1850 Victoria had 76,000 inhabitants, but by 1860 there were 538,000 (representing an annual growth rate of 22%).

10

MULTINATIONAL CORPORATIONS

Bo Södersten and Geoffrey Reed

I INTRODUCTION

Foreign direct investment (FDI) is increasing in importance in the world economy. They have always attracted a good deal of attention and given rise to heated controversy. This, perhaps, is not astonishing in a world of nationalism. The Marxists saw them in the beginning of the twentieth century as the natural consequence of a maturing capitalism: the logical fruits of an ever-hardening competition, the last manifestations of a doomed system before its collapse. During recent years they have attracted renewed interest both in underdeveloped and developed countries. Resolutions at UNCTAD conferences have increasingly reflected a growing suspicion of foreign direct investment.

As stated [elsewhere], the main distinction between direct and portfolio investments is that in the former the investor retains control over the invested capital. Direct investments and management go together. With portfolio investments, no such control is exercised. Here the investor lends the capital in order to get a return on it, but has no control over the use of that capital.

The balance between portfolio and direct investments has changed markedly since the First World War. Until then the largest part of foreign investment consisted of portfolio investment. Great Britain provided more than 50 per cent of the total international capital outstanding in 1914, and about 90 per cent of this was of a portfolio type. The other two major lending countries, France and Germany, were also primarily engaged in portfolio investments. The major recipients of foreign capital were other developed countries – Europe, the United States, Canada and Australasia accounted for over 50 per cent of the outstanding debt in 1913–14, and Latin America for over 40 per cent of the remainder. During a period when exchange risks were negligible and the political situation from this angle was stable, international investments were primarily governed by interest-rate differentials. Young expanding economies, which offered high returns on capital invested, could borrow money from the major lending countries. Interestingly, the United States already differed in this respect. American investors seem to have been of a more dynamic type, not content merely to reap a fairly small interest-rate differential. Even before the First World War a dominant share of US capital exports consisted of direct investments.

Between the two World Wars the flow of international investment decreased, with portfolio investment declining to about three-quarters of that reduced total, and the United States emerging as a major foreign lender, primarily in direct investment.

From the ending of the Second World War to the late 1950s, the role of private portfolio investments was negligible. The most important capital flows were official gifts and loans, followed by direct investments. The United States, with consistently large surpluses on its current account, was the major contributor to all forms of capital flows in the 1940s. In the following period however the United States started to run a deficit due to increased military expenditure abroad and the greater competitiveness of European countries.

From the late 1950s foreign investment started to increase: in real terms the total foreign investment in 1956–61 was over 50 per cent higher than in 1951–55. Some two-thirds of that investment came from the United States (with the encouragement of favourable tax regulations), with a large proportion being direct investment.

During the 1960s some governments started to feel disquiet about the level of FDI in their economies, and through the 1970s there was in general less FDI than before (though Britain, with its oil surpluses, became a large net investor again). At the same time, the flow of FDI into the United States started to increase, encouraged by a weaker dollar post-1973 and restrictive US trade policies (the annual average for 1974–78 was over four times that for 1970–72). The 1970s also saw the start of major private international lending to the less-developed countries (LDCs), with portfolio and direct forms being of approximately equal importance.

There were three major elements in international capital flows in the 1980s. First, there was a continued increase in FDI in the United States. Second, Japan became a major source of FDI, principally to the United States but also to the European Community, while at the same time pursuing policies to restrict FDI in Japan. Finally, portfolio lending to the LDCs, which had continued at a high level, faced a crisis in 1982–83 as a consequence of the inability of many borrowing countries to meet interest and repayment obligations.

[. . .]

II DIRECT INVESTMENTS AND MULTINATIONAL ENTERPRISES

As we have emphasised [above], the distinguishing feature of FDI is the exercise of control over decision-making in an enterprise located in one country by investors located in another. Although such investments may be made by individuals or partnerships, most FDI is undertaken by enterprises, and the larger part of that by multinational enterprises (MNEs).[1]

Multinational enterprises are essentially those that own or control production facilities in more than one country. Obviously, a MNE could not come into existence without there having been FDI in the first place. However, their importance nowadays is as major providers of FDI, often using capital which has been raised in the capital markets of the country in which they are investing rather than in the capital market of their home country.

The power (and the need) to exercise control over operations tells us that more is involved in FDI than the mere flow of capital. FDI occurs because the investing enterprise has some advantage, perhaps in technology or management, which it wishes to exploit in foreign markets, or perhaps some disadvantage that it wishes to eliminate. Direct investment is typically industry-specific. Industry-specific investments take two important forms: horizontal and vertical integration. Large corporations wish to integrate horizontally by opening new subsidiaries in various parts of the world. This is often done in a predatory way: one or several existing, competing firms in the host country are simply bought up by a large international rival. In the process, competition is often reduced.

Vertical integration is also a strong motive for direct investment. For instance, there are only a few companies that refine and fabricate copper. It is not surprising that they have sought control over copper mines by vertically integrating backwards in the production process. One obvious reason for vertical integration is a desire to reduce risk.

The investment *per se* may, in the extreme, be seen as a way of facilitating the exploitation of this advantage rather than as an end in itself: capital, it is argued, is only the complementary factor in a direct investment. The central element of FDI is that it consists of a package of capital, knowledge, skills, etc. This of course suggests an explanation of why the majority of FDI is industry-specific, and suggests that we should look for explanations of FDI in the characteristics of those industries.

The immediate problem however is to explain why foreign direct investment occurs (or why MNEs exist) in the first place. There are obvious alternatives to foreign investment. Why does the enterprise possessing the advantages cited above elect to operate in a foreign country rather than expand production at home and increase its exports? Why does it not license foreign firms to produce the goods in question? The simple answer of course is that FDI must be more profitable than the alternatives. That however just begs the basic question: *why* is it more profitable?

III THE THEORY OF DIRECT INVESTMENTS

The product-cycle hypothesis

In his work on the 'product-cycle' hypothesis [. . .] Vernon has emphasised that a firm tends to become multinational at a certain stage in its growth.[2] In the early stages of the product cycle, initial expansion into overseas markets is by means of exports. Because countries are at different stages of economic development, separated by a 'technology gap', new markets are available to receive new products through the *demonstration effect* of richer countries. Prior to the standardisation of the production process, the firm requires close contacts with both its product market and its suppliers.

However, once the product has evolved in a standard form and competing products have been developed, the firm may decide to look overseas for the lower-cost locations and new markets. It is not only that factor inputs may be less expensive abroad but that considerable scale economies from longer production runs may be obtained through the allocation of component production and assembly to different plants. On the demand side, new markets can be established by price reductions, or more typically by the firm operating in an oligopolistic market situation by means of product differentiation.

The product-cycle hypothesis is useful on several counts. It offers an explanation of the concentration of innovations in developed countries, and an integrated theory of trade and FDI. It also provides an explanation of the rapid growth in exports of manufactured goods by the newly industrialised countries. It therefore offers a useful point of departure for a study of the causes of international investment.

Market imperfections and FDI

The product-cycle hypothesis does not resolve the question of why MNEs elect to use FDI rather than to license their technology to foreign firms. This issue has been examined by reference to the theory of the firm, notably by Hymer, Kindleberger and Caves.[3]

Such explanations focus on the advantages which some firms enjoy and on which they may be able to obtain rents in foreign markets. Such advantages include access to patented and generally unavailable technology, team-specific management skills, plant economies of scale, special marketing skills, possession of a brand name, and so on.[4] The potential gains from these advantages must of course outweigh the disadvantages of establishing and operating in a foreign country, such as communication difficulties and ignorance of institutions, customs and tastes, before the firm will invest abroad.

FDI allows the firm to exploit its advantages to the full, so that it can capture all the rents given by that control. The licence fee which foreign companies would be prepared to pay might, on the other hand, be lower than those rents. Selling the technology to a foreign enterprise, another possible alternative, may also yield a return which is lower than the (discounted sum of) rents from FDI. In both cases this may be due to foreign enterprises perceiving possible inefficiencies in their management of these advantages, perhaps because they are inexperienced in the operation of the new technology. Management and technology are often complementary. A further concern to the original enterprise may be that lack of direct control will increase the likelihood of the leaking of the technology to competitors.

Caves argues that such phenomena are due to market failures associated with *arm's-length* transactions in intangible assets. Such assets, especially technical knowledge, are public goods, in the sense that their use does not diminish their stock. They may also be replicated at a marginal cost which is low compared to the average cost of producing them in the first place. Second, the potential purchaser will wish to obtain all the information on using the asset before purchase, whereas the prospective seller knows that if all that information is revealed before the sale then the sale may not be completed. Thirdly, as we suggested earlier, there are uncertainty problems in that neither the buyer nor the seller can be completely sure how the asset will perform when managed by the buyer. Finally, the potential seller may not be able to 'disentangle' particular assets from the rest of his operations.

Hymer's analysis views the firm that undertakes FDI as an oligopolist [one of a small number of sellers] (or perhaps a monopolist) in the goods market which either invests in existing foreign firms in order to control them and so suppress competition and preserve its rents, or establishes a subsidiary in a new market so as to pre-empt the possibility that a rival firm will do so. The latter strategy, termed 'defensive investment', may explain some part of FDI. Examples that have been proposed include Ford and General Motors, each of whom is alleged to have established plants in LDCs in order to keep the other out.

Another explanation of FDI and the role of the MNE that emphasises market imperfections, but this time for intermediate inputs and technology, is due to Buckley and Casson.[5] These markets are imperfect because they are difficult to organise and involve considerable uncertainty.

Faced with imperfect external markets, firms may choose to *internalise* by using backward and forward integration. A particular example is in the development of new processes and products, where there are time-lags, uncertainty, and high investment expenditures, and where success may depend on co-ordination, rapid exchange of information and detailed planning. Internalisation may increase the efficiency with which all of these are done. When internalisation (to the firm) involves operations across national boundaries then there must necessarily be FDI, and a multinational is created.

Barriers to trade and FDI

Transport costs offer one explanation of FDI, as indeed they do for multi-plant operations for a firm within a national market. If transport costs are sufficiently high then they may make the expansion of production in domestic plants and the export of that increased production less profitable than production within the putative importing country. This may be the case even if production in the foreign subsidiary firm is at a higher cost than that in the domestic plants.

Transport costs however are part of the 'nature of things'. In particular, we do not usually think of them as being a policy instrument which the government may use to restrict access to markets.[6] The same is not of course true of such barriers to trade as tariffs, import quotas and so on. The imposition of such import restrictions may have as a consequence an increase in FDI inflows; it is open to debate whether increasing such inflows is a possible explanation for the use of protection.

Import barriers have several effects which may be an encouragement to FDI. First, they raise the price of the good within the protected market, so providing increased profits to those firms who produce within the protected market. This provides an obvious incentive for a foreign firm to enter the protected market, by establishing a new subsidiary, by buying control of an existing firm, or by entering into a partnership agreement with an existing firm. Second, import barriers reduce the exports of firms in other countries, who may be induced to invest in the protected country in order to maintain their market share (another example of 'defensive investment'). It has been argued that the investment by Japanese motor manufacturers in both the United States and in Britain in the 1980s, either in the creation of subsidiary companies or through partnerships with existing domestic producers, is an example of this. [. . .]

Dunning's 'eclectic theory'

It should be apparent from the preceding discussion that there are several explanations for FDI, that many start from similar premises, and that none offers a complete explanation. Dunning has suggested an eclectic theory of FDI, often referred to as the *OLI paradigm*, that attempts to integrate these explanations.[8]

The *O*, *L* and *I* in the paradigm refer to three groups of conditions that determine whether a firm, industry or company will be a source or a host of FDI (or neither, of course). These groups are *Ownership* advantages, *Locational* considerations, and *Internalisation* gains.

Ownership advantages are advantages which are specific to the firm. It may enjoy such advantages over domestic as well as foreign competitors, so that expansion in the domestic market may be an alternative strategy. We have discussed some of them above, for example advantages in technology and in management and organisational skills. Others often cited are size and diversification, access to or control over raw materials, the ability to call on the political support of their government, access to finance on favourable terms, perhaps in foreign as well as domestic markets, and the ease with which the firm can shift production between countries. There is of course an element of feedback here: the fact that an enterprise is multinational may increase some of its ownership advantages, which in turn may allow it to expand its multinational activities.

Locational considerations encompass such things as transport costs facing both finished products and raw materials, import restrictions, the ease with which the firm can operate in another country, the profitability with which the ownership advantages may be combined with factor endowments in other countries, the tax policies in both source and host countries, and political stability in the host country.

Internalisation gains concern those factors which make it more profitable to carry out transactions within the firm than to rely on external markets. As we saw earlier, such gains arise from avoiding market imperfections (uncertainty, economies of scale, problems of control, the undesirability of providing full information to a prospective purchaser, and so on). The existence of internalisation gains obviously depends to some extent on the existence of ownership advantages.

The essential element in the eclectic theory is that all three types of condition must be met before there will be foreign direct investment. That is, all three conditions are necessary, but no one is sufficient. Suppose for example that a firm has an ownership advantage. If locational considerations indicate that production within a foreign market would be more profitable than producing at home and exporting, but there are no internalisation advantages (the product could be made by a foreign firm with equal efficiency and without jeopardising the home firm's ownership advantages), then the most profitable course for the home firm would be to license its ownership advantage to the foreign firm.

If, on the other hand, there were internalisation gains but no locational advantage to be gained by operating in another country then the firm would choose to expand production in its home market and export to the foreign market.

Taxation and the transfer pricing problem

Taxation policies in source and host countries will affect the flow of FDI. Differences in such policies between countries may also encourage multinational enterprises to engage in (unproductive) activities designed to maximise their post-tax profits on a global (rather than country) basis. We shall discuss this latter problem – *transfer pricing* – at the end of this section.[11]

Other things being equal, comparatively high rates of tax on profits will encourage firms to look outside their home country for a base for some or all of their operations in which they will pay lower taxes. Special provisions in policy on profits earned externally, such as those allowing firms to defer tax payments until the profits were repatriated, will offer further encouragement.

Similarly, a country with comparatively low profit taxes will tend to attract FDI inflows. Such a policy may be designed to obtain just such a result, and may be reinforced by other incentives, such as allowing a foreign firm some period in which it does not pay profit taxes (a 'tax holiday') or generous allowances for writing-off investments against taxes.

Taxation policies may also have an effect on flows of goods between the various establishments making up a multinational, and perhaps also on the prices at which those goods are transferred between one establishment and another. As a simple example, suppose that a multinational has a plant in a low-tax country (country A) which makes an intermediate product (say, car engines), and that these engines are then transported to a plant in a high-tax country (country B) where the final product is manufactured. As Table 10.1 shows, the MNE can increase its profits by increasing the 'price' at which the engines are 'sold' to the plant in the high-tax country.

The 'price' at which car engines are sold by the establishment in A to that in B is an 'accounting price' or 'transfer price', set internally by the multinational. By increasing the price from £500 to £900 the multinational can generate a larger proportion of its profit in the low-tax country, and can increase its total post-tax profit.

There are obviously practical limits to the extent to which these transfer prices can be manipulated. In the extreme, it would presumably be unwise for the MNE to arrange to make a zero profit in country B as this would provoke some reaction from the tax authorities in B. On a more realistic level, the MNE in the above example would take care not to charge a transfer price which was very different from the price at which a car engine would be sold on the open market. On the other hand, the ingenuity of accountants in devising ways of exploiting loopholes in the tax laws of different countries should not be underestimated.

Inputs of capital equipment and technology transferred from the parent company can also be priced internally in such a manner that the real rate of profit is reduced. The extent to which transfer pricing can be used would appear to depend critically on the degree to which goods and services are traded within the firm rather than on the open market, at 'arm's length', to use Lall's apt phrase.[12] Consequently, considerable scope for transfer pricing

Table 10.1 An example of transfer pricing

	Pricing policy 1	Pricing policy 2
Price at which engine is sold (£)	500	900
Volume of sales (thousand)	20	20
Revenue of engine plant (£ million)	10	18
Production costs in country A (£ million)	6	6
Pre-tax profit in country A (£ million)	4	12
Tax rate in country A (%)	25	25
Post-tax profit in country A (£ million)	3	9
Revenue from car sales in country B (£ million)	80	80
Costs of engines from country A (£ million)	10	18
Other production costs in country B (£ million)	40	40
Pre-tax profit in country B (£ million)	30	22
Tax rate in country B (%)	50	50
Post-tax profit in country B (£ million)	15	11
Total pre-tax profit to MNE (£ million)	34	34
Total post-tax profit to MNE (£ million)	18	20

exists within the large foreign-owned enterprises which are vertically integrated with the parent company and which are typical of such industries as motor vehicles, chemicals and electrical engineering.

Lall has put forward two forms of explanation for the use of transfer prices. First, there is the kind of transfer pricing which seeks to maximise the present value of total multinational profits in a world characterised by different rates of taxes, tariffs, subsidies, and by multiple exchange rates. However, there is also the need to protect the future level of profits against possible changes in price controls, taxation and, indeed, governments. The role of the multinationals in exacerbating the economic difficulties that confronted the Allende government in Chile between 1970 and 1973 is a case in point.[13]

Quantitative evidence on the actual importance of transfer pricing is limited. It is naturally difficult to assess the extent to which the internal flow of goods and factors are over or under valued. However, Kopitz argues in a survey of the evidence[14] that the hypothesis that transfer pricing is stimulated by tax-rate differentials is not supported. The main incentive for transfer pricing seems to be other policies pursued by host governments, such as ceilings on profit repatriation. There is no doubt that within the context of the LDC, whose economy is heavily dependent on a small number of foreign-owned corporations, particularly of the vertically integrated variety, there is ample scope for the use of transfer pricing.

The cases referred to above will perhaps suffice to illustrate the principle that national economic policy will encounter difficulties in a world where economic integration becomes increasingly important but where the national state is still the dominant political entity. Direct investments certainly give very tangible advantages to firms in the investing countries, but they also lead to policy complications for governments of these countries.

There may of course be competition between potential host countries to set tax rates or offer concessions in order to attract FDI (we shall consider the nature of the gains to host countries later in the chapter). For example, in the 1970s Britain, Belgium and Spain tried to outbid one another in an attempt to persuade Ford to build a proposed new engine plant within their frontiers. The outcome was that Britain, the eventual 'winner', probably paid Ford substantially more than would have been necessary (and which might have been zero) had there been no such competition.

As an example of the possible impact of differences in tax rates on the profits declared by multinationals in different countries, consider the data in Table 10.2. This shows the declared earnings on US direct investments abroad before and after a change in US tax laws, paying particular attention to the role of Switzerland. It illustrates the possible role of taxes which are relatively low on the international scale in attracting FDI, and of concessions in tax laws in encouraging it.

Table 10.2 Earnings on US direct investments abroad* (percentage of book value at the beginning of year)

	1958	*1962*	*1966*
MANUFACTURING			
Europe	16	12	11
EEC	17	14	11
Switzerland	36	11	15
TRADE AND OTHER†			
EEC	20	18	6
Switzerland	42	40	16

*After foreign taxes.
† All direct investments other than mining and smelting, manufacturing, and petroleum.
Source: US Department of Commerce, *Survey of Current Business*, various issues

Switzerland had exceptionally low taxes and favourable treatment of foreign firms in the 1950s. (This seems still to be so even if a certain harmonisation of tax regulations has taken place.) This led to many American firms routing their sales from all over the world through sales offices located in Switzerland. This also led to exceptionally high earnings on investments in Switzerland.

In 1962, the United States changed its tax laws. Earlier, taxes on earnings from subsidiaries abroad were deferred until they were repatriated. In 1962 this provision was changed so that earnings on holding companies and so-called 'tax haven operations' became taxable when earned. This had an immediate effect on the location of service and sales offices: in 1961–62, 40 per cent of these were located in Switzerland; in 1963 this figure fell to 10 per cent.

This is an example of how the source country can try to counteract the undesirable effects of FDI by changes in its legislation. The possibilities for such countervailing measures, however, are limited. Several countries, especially well-developed ones with big taxes and highly developed social services, could find their tax base shrinking as a result of direct investments. Their possibilities of implementing economic policies could also become circumscribed by the operations of multinational firms.

More recently, California and some other American states introduced so-called 'unitary taxation' of the profits of multinationals in an attempt to overcome the transfer pricing problem. The essence of the unitary tax system is that the tax authorities are not prepared to accept a multinational's declaration of where its profits were earned. Rather, they assume that the multinational has earned profits within the state which are in proportion to some other indicator of the relative importance of its activities within the state, such as the proportion of its total assets or of its total labour costs.

It may be argued that, in order to avoid double taxation, the MNE will declare as profits within the state that which the tax authorities consider correct. That is, there is no point in declaring that 40 per cent of profits were earned in the state, and paying tax on the remaining 60 per cent elsewhere, when the state is going to assume that 75 per cent of profits were earned within its boundaries and levy their tax on that basis. What may happen in practice is that the multinationals affected by this policy will use resources in lobbying for a change in the tax laws. In extreme cases MNEs may even elect to leave the state by disinvesting there and reinvesting elsewhere, so reducing the state's tax revenue.

With the increasing internationalisation of firms, the possibility of any single country pursuing its own independent economic policy becomes circumscribed. Corporations could gather in one country to work out pricing and market arrangements for another country. As long as there is no international legislation concerning taxes, restrictive business practices, etc., any single country will have difficulties in efficiently implementing its own laws.

IV THE CONSEQUENCES OF MNE ACTIVITY

Control

An essential aspect of the critique raised against direct investments has been that of *control*. We have already noted that this is an integral part of FDI, distinguishing it from other forms of capital movements. To the host country this means that part of its industry will be controlled by foreigners. Many host countries find this difficult to accept; it has led to counter-measures in many countries.

One obvious aspect of control is that the multinationals may require their subsidiaries to operate policies which are inefficient and/or cause distortions in national markets. Examples of such policies are restrictions on exports, perhaps to avoid competition with other subsidiaries in other countries, and on R&D within the subsidiary. In the latter case, the host countries are deprived of the important stimulus given by research in these industries. Concern over this motivated demands for a Code of Conduct for the transfer of technology at the fourth conference of UNCTAD in 1976.

The fear is that R&D in subsidiary companies is suppressed, so that research becomes concentrated in the home country. The home country started with a comparative advantage in the production of goods which are intensive in research and innovating capacity. By the cumulative effects related to direct investments, this comparative advantage tends to become even more pronounced, and the host countries tend to sink into a position of 'second-rate' economic powers.

Because they are international, multinationals can often circumvent national domestic policies. The example most often cited is their ability to avoid restrictions on credit or on foreign exchange transactions by transferring money internally. In an extreme case a multinational may even be able to make a government policy inoperable, as when Ford (UK) refused to adhere to the British government's pay policy, and the government was unable to enforce compliance.

A multinational may, of course, lobby the government of the host country to persuade it to pursue policies favourable to the MNE's interests. Their ability to transfer operations, in whole or in part, to other countries is a powerful argument in such activities. Part of this lobbying (or pressurising) of the host government may take the form of successful lobbying of the source country government to exert pressure, as was the case with International Telephone and Telegraph in Chile under the Allende government.

External benefits of FDI to the host country

It is often argued that multinationals confer benefits on the host country, such as training the local labour in more sophisticated techniques or demonstrating the gains that may be made by different management practices. Such benefits can be labelled as 'external' if they are costless to those learning them and become available and usable in the rest of the economy. If the workers pay for their training (by accepting a wage that is below that which they could earn elsewhere) then the externality is reduced, and may be eliminated. If the skills learned are inapplicable elsewhere in the economy (perhaps because they can only be used with specific equipment which is not available outside the MNE), then there is no external benefit.

It is widely believed that expenditures on R&D have important external effects. In the process of developing a certain product or improving production techniques, scientists and technicians are stimulated; new applications valuable outside the immediate project will be discovered; encouragement for, and incentives to, research in universities and other organisations outside the industry will be provided; and so on. A rational attitude geared toward experimenting will be fostered, competent scientists will be trained, etc., and all this will have positive effects on the whole intellectual climate of the country.

If foreign firms via direct investments take over control of important parts of a country's industry, they may tend to shift research to their home country. This could be entirely rational from the point of view of the international firm, which is simply taking advantage of the economies of scale connected with the research activity. It can even be argued that this behaviour is rational from the world's standpoint, because it maximises world income. It still can have very detrimental effects on the host country, which is deprived of research activities that are perhaps comparatively inefficient but which, to the country itself, can be of great importance. It may even be the case that would-be researchers will emigrate in order to train, and possibly work, in the source country.

The question of external gains has been the subject of various empirical studies, particularly of LDCs. Some of these suggest that the capital-intensive nature of much of the technology exported limits the scope for external gains. There is a tendency for the MNEs in LDCs to become part of a distinct industrial sector with limited linkages to domestic firms, resulting in a so-called 'dualistic economy'. The external effects of FDI in other developed economies are, on the other hand, more likely to be beneficial, though even here there are *caveats* about the tendency to import higher management rather than train local employees, and the apparent suppression of R&D activity mentioned above.

V POLICY RESPONSES IN HOST COUNTRIES

Policy responses to FDI are far from uniform. Some countries, perceiving the costs as outweighing the benefits, have sought to restrict FDI and/or the operations of multi-nationals, by various means. Others, as in the case of Britain's encouragement of Ford's establishment of a new engine plant, have encouraged FDI. We shall discuss examples of both responses, starting with those intended to restrict and/or control FDI.

The problem of foreign control of domestic industry has probably been most acute in Canada. Here nearly 60 per cent of the total capital in manufacturing is controlled by foreigners (over 80 per cent by Americans). Efforts have been made from time to time to increase Canada's control over FDI. In 1963, for instance, a new tax law was introduced requiring firms of less than 25 per cent Canadian ownership and with less than 25 per cent Canadian representation on the board of directors to be taxed at a somewhat higher rate than Canadian corporations.[16] Further legislation in 1973 required that all new FDI be required to obtain government approval. This policy was however gradually reversed in the 1980s, this more open view culminating in the United States–Canada free trade pact of 1987.

Some developing countries, such as Mexico, [required] 50 per cent of ownership and directorship to be in domestic hands. Although wholly foreign-owned investment [was] permitted in the export processing sector, all foreign investment [was] screened, as is also the case in India, by a Foreign Investment Commission, which lays down criteria (often statutory) for the investment. These requirements usually relate to such matters as the sector and location of the investment, the extent of local participation, the transfer of technology, and disclosure of company information. A number of LDCs have also attempted to increase their control of foreign investments by means of equity participation and joint ventures. The latter can be viewed not only as a means of control over foreign investment but as a training ground for local entrepreneurs, managers and technicians.[17]

[. . .]

'Unbundling the package'

FDI is, as we have seen, a bundle of capital, technology and management skills (the *unambiguous package*) which involves control. It may also, it is argued, be a relatively expensive way of obtaining foreign capital and technology. This offers an explanation of the increasing preference of LDCs for joint ventures between locally-owned and foreign firms (the *ambiguous package*) or for technology-licensing agreements with little or no foreign capital involvement (the *unpackaged* or *unbundling* alternative).[19]

Despite the reluctance of firms to sell or rent their know-how, for reasons which we discussed earlier, licensing arrangements for the sale of technology do exist, for example in India, Brazil and South Korea. This may reflect the ability of the host country government to restrict or deny access for FDI, forcing foreign firms to choose licensing as the second-best alternative (although some, of course, may choose not to license either). Licensing may also be a consequence of the foreign firm having a shortage of managerial skills and/or a lack of knowledge of the host country market, or of a belief that a joint venture will reduce the risks of expropriation.

A final possibility is that foreign firms enter into licensing agreements for technologies which are likely to be overtaken by new developments (in order to maximise their gains during the remaining economic life of the old technology), or for technologies which are relatively unsophisticated. In this case we may presume that licensing is an inefficient way of transferring the most recent technology. The counter-argument, of course, is that the unsophisticated technology may be better suited to the factor endowments of the host country.

The question of course is how these preferred alternatives compare to the unambiguous package. Do they transfer (appropriate) technology and its associated knowledge relatively efficiently, and are they relatively inexpensive? It has been argued that licensing and joint ventures may not be cheaper than the unambiguous package. Joint ventures do not necessarily reduce the outflow of profits to the foreign firm, since there are several ways in which that firm can increase its net profits, such as charging higher royalties and technical fees than they would to wholly-owned subsidiaries, and by using transfer pricing.

The possibility of transfer pricing does not of course exists when there is a licensing arrangement (though royalties, etc. may still be high). If, however, the locally-owned firm has to raise capital on foreign markets then it is possible that it will pay a higher rate of interest than that on foreign capital provided under the FDI alternative.

Export-processing zones

Export-processing zones[20] (EPZs) are designated areas within the host country, intended to attract investment, largely from foreign firms, by offering favoured treatment. The privileges offered typically include the absence of import controls (so that, for example, tariffs are not levied on imported intermediate goods provided that the finished products are re-exported). Other privileges may include exemption from domestic taxation and industrial regulations, and the provision of infrastructure.

Export-processing zones have become a favoured option of many LDCs. Establishment of an EPZ requires substantial public investment by the host country, so it is important to enquire whether they yield a net welfare gain, and whether there are better alternatives.

Warr[21] argues that economic activity within EPZs has been typified by labour-intensive industries (such as electronics assembly and garment manufacture), with a high rate of turnover of firms. That is, EPZs tend to attract 'footloose' firms, which will move readily from the current EPZ base, perhaps to another, in response to changing conditions. Since many countries now have EPZs, there is considerable competition between them to attract foreign firms.

The objectives cited by host-country governments when establishing export processing zones usually fall under three headings: increasing foreign exchange earnings, increasing employment, and encouraging the transfer of technology and management skills. Warr argues that the EPZs have contributed to the attainment of the first two objectives, but that the sought-after technology transfer has not in general occurred. He concludes that the benefits from EPZs are limited and that they are certainly not 'engines of development'. He argues that where they have been successful, greater success could have been achieved by a liberalisation of the domestic economy rather than by the establishment of a liberalised zone within the economy.

Trade-related investment measures

As we have noted before, governments may compete to attract FDI by multinationals through offering different policy packages. Part of such packages may consist of requirements that the MNE's subsidiary contracts to export some specified proportion of its output, and/or purchase a specified proportion of inputs in the host economy, and/or employ some proportion of its management domestically. In many cases, of course, such requirements are disincentives, which the MNE will trade-off against the incentives in the package in making its decision on location of a subsidiary. Such requirements are known generally as *trade-related investment measures*, or TRIMs.

Greenaway[22] makes the point that TRIMs have to be considered in conjunction with FDI and the incentives given to multinationals to invest in the country concerned. [. . .] What is left unanswered at the moment is whether there are feasible policy alternatives which are better than TRIMs. [. . .]

NOTES

1 Also referred to as multinational firms (MNFs), multinational companies (MNCs) or transnational enterprises.
2 Vernon (1966) and (1971 and 1977).
3 Hymer (1976).
 Kindleberger (1969).
 Caves (1982).
4 This discussion, and that later in the chapter of technological transfer, are based on Balasubramanyam (1985).
5 Buckley and Casson (1976).
6 This is not always the case. The infamous 'American Bottoms' legislation, which required imports into the United States to be landed from American ships, had the effect of increasing the costs of exporting to the United States and so protected the American market.
8 Dunning (1977).
11 A warning! Do not confuse the *transfer problem* discussed in Chapter 21, which is essentially a balance-of-payments problem, with *transfer pricing*, which concerns an MNE's reactions to differential taxes.

12 Lall (1973).
13 de Vylder (1974).
14 Kopitz (1976).
16 Safarian (1966).
17 Morton and Tulloch (1977), p. 228.
19 This discussion is based upon Balasubramanyam (1985). The terminology is due to Vernon (1971).
20 For a full discussion of export processing zones, see Warr (1990), on which this brief discussion is based.
21 Warr (1990).
22 Greenaway (1991).

BIBLIOGRAPHY

Balasubramanyam, V. N. (1985) 'Foreign Direct Investment and the International Transfer of Technology', in *CIIT*.
Buckley, P. J. and Casson, M. (1976) *The Future of Multinational Enterprises* (London: Macmillan).
Caves, R. E. (1974) 'The Causes of Direct Investment: Foreign Firms' Shares in Canadian and UK Manufacturing Industry', *Review of Economics and Statistics*, 56, 279–93.
Dunning, J. (1977) 'Trade, Location of Economic Activity and the MNE: A Search for an Eclectic Approach', in Ohlin *et al.* (eds) (1977).
Greenaway, D. (1991) 'Why Are We Negotiating on TRIMS?', in Greenaway *et al.* (eds) (1991).
Hymer, S. H. (1976) *The International Operations of National Firms: A Study of Direct Foreign Investment* (Cambridge, MA.: MIT Press).
Kindleberger, C.P. (1969) *American Business Abroad: Six Lectures on Direct Investment* (New Haven: Yale University Press).
Kopitz, G.F. (1976) 'Taxation and Multinational Firm Behaviour: A Critical Survey', *IMF Staff Papers*, 23, 624–73.
Lall, S. (1973) 'Transfer Pricing by Multi-national Manufacturing Firms', *Oxford Bulletin of Economics and Statistics*, 35, 173–95.
Morton, K. and Tulloch, P. (1977) *Trade and Developing Countries* (London: Croom Helm).
Safarian, A.E. (1966) *Foreign Ownership of Canadian Industry* (Toronto: Toronto University Press).
Vernon, R. (1966) 'International Investment and International Trade in the Product Cycle', *Quarterly Journal of Economics*, 80, 190–207.
Vernon, R. (1971) *Sovereignty at Bay: The Multinational Spread of U.S. Enterprises* (London: Basic Books).
Vernon, R. (1977) *Storm Over Multinationals: The Real Issues* (Cambridge, MA.: Harvard University Press).
Vylder, S. de (1974) *Chile 1970–73: The political Economy of the Rise and Fall of the Unidad Popular* (Stockholm: 'Unga Filosofers Forlag).
Warr, P. (1990) 'Exporting Processing Zones', in Milner (ed.) (1990).

ACKNOWLEDGEMENT

The authors and publishers are grateful to the following for permission to use copyright material:

The United States Department of Commerce for table 10.2 from *The Survey of Current Business*.

11

GLOBALIZATION IN THE AGE OF EMPIRE*

Eric Hobsbawm

Only complete political confusion and naive optimism can prevent the recognition that the unavoidable efforts at trade expansion by all civilized bourgeois-controlled nations, after a transitional period of seemingly peaceful competition, are clearly approaching the point where *power alone* will decide each nation's share in the economic control of the earth, and hence its people's sphere of activity, and especially its workers' earning potential.

Max Weber, 1894[1]

'Whin ye get among th'Chinee' . . . says [the Emperor of Germany], 'raymimber that ye ar-re the van guard iv Christyanity' he says, 'an' stick ye'er baynet through ivry hated infidel you see' he says. 'Lave him understand what our westhern civilisation means. . . . An' if be chance ye shud pick up a little land be th' way, don't lave e'er a Frinchman or Roosshan take it from ye.'

Mr Dooley's Philosophy, 1900[2]

I

A world economy whose pace was set by its developed or developing capitalist core was extremely likely to turn into a world in which the 'advanced' dominated the 'backward'; in short into a world of empire. But, paradoxically, the era from 1875 to 1914 may be called the Age of Empire not only because it developed a new kind of imperialism, but also for a much more old-fashioned reason. It was probably the period of modern world history in which the number of rulers officially calling themselves, or regarded by western diplomats as deserving the title of, 'emperors' was at its maximum.

In Europe the rulers of Germany, Austria, Russia, Turkey and (in their capacity as lords of India) Britain claimed this title. Two of these (Germany and Britain/India) were innovations of the 1870s. They more than offset the disappearance of the 'Second Empire' of Napoleon III in France. Outside Europe, the rulers of China, Japan, Persia and – perhaps with a larger element of international diplomatic courtesy – Ethiopia and Morocco were habitually allowed this title, while until 1889 an American emperor survived in Brazil. One or two even more shadowy 'emperors' might be added to the list. In 1918 five of these had disappeared. Today (1987) the only titular survivor of this select company of super-monarchs is the ruler of Japan, whose political profile is low and whose political influence is negligible.[3]

In a less trivial sense, our period is obviously the era of a new type of empire, the colonial. The economic and military supremacy of the capitalist countries had long been beyond serious challenge, but no systematic attempt to translate it into formal conquest, annexation and administration had been made between the end of the eighteenth and the last quarter of the nineteenth century. Between 1880 and 1914 it was made, and most of the world outside Europe and the Americas was formally partitioned into territories under the formal rule or informal political domination of one or other of a handful of states: mainly Great Britain, France, Germany, Italy, the Netherlands, Belgium, the USA and Japan. The victims of this process were to some extent the ancient surviving pre-industrial European empires of Spain and Portugal, the former – in spite of attempts to extend the territory under its control in North-west Africa – more than the latter. However, the survival of the major Portuguese territories in Africa (Angola and Mozambique), which were to outlast other imperialist colonies, was due primarily to the inability of their modern rivals to agree on the exact manner of dividing them among themselves. No similar rivalries saved the relics of the Spanish Empire in the Americas (Cuba, Puerto Rico) and in the Pacific (the Philippines) from the USA in 1898. Nominally most of the great traditional empires of Asia remained independent, though the western powers carved out 'zones of influence' or even direct administration in them which could (as in the Anglo-Russian agreement over Persia in 1907) cover their entire territory. In fact, their military and political helplessness was taken for granted. Their independence rested either on their convenience as buffer-states (as in Siam – now Thailand – which divided the British and French zones in South-east Asia, or Afghanistan, which separated Britain and Russia), on the inability of rival imperial powers to agree on a formula for division, or on their sheer size. The only non-European state which successfully resisted formal colonial conquest when this was attempted was Ethiopia, which held Italy at bay, the weakest of the imperial states.

Two major regions of the world were, for practical purposes, entirely divided up: Africa and the Pacific. No independent states were left at all in the Pacific, now totally distributed among the British, French, Germans, Dutch, USA and – still on a modest scale – Japan. By 1914, except for Ethiopia, the insignificant West African republic of Liberia and that part of Morocco which still resisted complete conquest, Africa belonged entirely to the British, French, German, Belgian, Portuguese and, marginally, Spanish empires. Asia, as we have seen, retained a large and nominally independent area, though the older European empires extended and rounded off their large holdings – Britain by annexing Burma to its Indian empire and establishing or strengthening the zone of influence in Tibet, Persia and the Persian Gulf area, Russia by moving further into Central Asia and (less successfully) Pacific Siberia and Manchuria, the Dutch by establishing firmer control in outlying regions of Indonesia. Two virtually new empires were established by the French conquest of Indochina, initiated in the period of Napoleon III, and by the Japanese at China's expense in Korea and Taiwan (1895) and later more modestly at Russia's expense (1905). Only one major region of the globe remained substantially unaffected by this process of partition. The Americas in 1914 were what they had been in 1875, or for that matter in the 1820s, a unique collection of sovereign republics, with the exception of Canada, the Caribbean islands and parts of the Caribbean littoral. Except for the USA, their political status rarely impressed anyone but their neighbours. It was perfectly understood that economically they were dependencies of the developed world. Yet even the USA, which increasingly asserted its political and military hegemony in this vast area, did not seriously try to conquer and administer it. Its only direct annexations were limited to Puerto Rico (Cuba was allowed an admittedly nominal independence) and a narrow strip along the new Panama Canal, which formed part of another small and nominally independent republic detached from the rather larger Colombia for this purpose by a convenient local revolution. In Latin America economic domination and such political arm-twisting as was necessary was conducted without formal conquest. The Americas, of course, were the only major region of the globe in which there was no serious rivalry between great powers. Except for the British, no European state possessed more than the scattered relics of (mainly Caribbean) eighteenth-century colonial empire, which were of no great economic or other significance. Neither the British nor anyone else saw a good reason for antagonizing the USA by challenging the Monroe Doctrine.[4]

This partition of the world among a handful of states, [. . .] was the most spectacular expression of that growing division of the globe into the strong and the weak, the 'advanced' and the 'backward', which we have already noted. It was also strikingly new. Between 1876 and 1915 about one-quarter of the globe's land surface was distributed or redistributed as colonies among a half-dozen states. Britain increased its territories by some 4 million square miles, France by some 3.5 millions, Germany acquired more than 1 million, Belgium and Italy just under 1 million each. The USA acquired some 100,000, mainly from Spain, Japan something like the same amount from China, Russia and Korea. Portugal's ancient African colonies expanded by about 300,000 square miles; Spain, while a net loser (to the USA), still managed to pick up some stony territory in Morocco and the Western Sahara. Russian imperial growth is more difficult to measure, since all of it was into adjoining territories and continued some centuries of secular territorial expansion of the tsarist state; moreover, as we shall see, Russia lost some territory to Japan. Of the major colonial empires only the Dutch failed, or refused, to acquire new territory, except by extending their actual control over Indonesian islands which they had long formally 'owned'. Of the minor ones, Sweden liquidated its only remaining colony, a West Indian island, by selling it to France, and Denmark was about to do the same – retaining only Iceland and Greenland as dependencies.

What is most spectacular is not necessarily most important. When observers of the world scene in the later 1890s began to analyse what obviously seemed a new phase in the general pattern of national and international development, notably different from the free-trading and freely competing liberal world of the mid-century, they saw the creation of colonial empires merely as one of its aspects. Orthodox observers thought they discerned, in general terms, a new era of national expansion in which (as we have suggested) political and economic elements were no longer clearly separable and the state played an increasingly active and crucial role both at home and abroad. Heterodox observers analysed it more specifically as a new phase of capitalist development, arising out of various tendencies which they discerned in this development. The most influential among these analyses of what was soon called 'imperialism', Lenin's little book of 1916, actually did not consider 'the division of the world among the great powers' until the sixth of his ten chapters.[5]

Nevertheless, if colonialism was merely one aspect of a more general change in world affairs, it was plainly the most immediately striking. It formed the point of departure for wider analyses, for there is no doubt that the word 'imperialism' first became part of the political and journalistic vocabulary during the 1890s in the course of the arguments about colonial conquest. Moreover that is when it acquired the economic dimension which, as a concept, it has never since lost. That is why references to the ancient forms of political and military aggrandizement on which the term is based are pointless. Emperors and empires were old, but imperialism was quite new. The word (which does not occur in the writings of Karl Marx, who died in 1883) first entered politics in Britain in the 1870s, and was still regarded as a neologism at the end of that decade. It exploded into general use in the 1890s. By 1900, when the intellectuals began to write books about it, it was, to quote one of the first of them, the British Liberal J. A. Hobson, 'on everybody's lips . . . and used to denote the most powerful movement in the current politics of the western world'.[6] In short, it was a novel term devised to describe a novel phenomenon. This evident fact is enough to dismiss one of the many schools in the tense and highly charged ideological debate about 'imperialism', namely the one which argues that it was nothing new, perhaps indeed that it was a mere pre-capitalist survival. It was, at any rate, felt to be new and was discussed as a novelty.

The arguments which surround this touchy subject are so impassioned, dense and confused that the first task of the historian is to disentangle them so that the actual phenomenon can be seen for itself. For most of the arguments have not been about what happened in the world of 1875–1914 but about Marxism, a subject which is apt to raise strong feelings; for, as it happens, the (highly critical) analysis of imperialism in Lenin's version was to become central to the revolutionary Marxism of the communist movements after 1917 and to the revolutionary movements of the 'third world'. What has given the debate a special edge is that one side in it appears to have had a slight built-in advantage, for those supporters and opponents of imperialism have been at each other's throats since the 1890s, the word itself has gradually acquired, and is now unlikely to lose, a pejorative colouring. Unlike 'democracy', which even its enemies like to claim because of its favourable connotations, 'imperialism' is commonly something to be disapproved of, and therefore done by others. In 1914 plenty of politicians were proud to call themselves imperialists, but in the course of our century they have virtually disappeared from sight.

The crux of the Leninist analysis (which frankly based itself on a variety of contemporary writers, both Marxian and non-Marxian) was that the new imperialism had economic roots in a specific new phase of capitalism, which, among other things, led to 'the territorial division of the world among the great capitalist powers' into a set of formal and informal colonies and spheres of influence. The rivalries between the capitalist powers which led to this division also engendered the First World War. We need not here discuss the specific mechanisms by which 'monopoly capitalism' led to colonialism – opinions differed on this, even among Marxists – or the more recent extension of such analyses into a more sweeping 'dependency theory' in the later twentieth century. All assume in one way or another that overseas economic expansion and the exploitation of the overseas world were crucial for capitalist countries.

To criticize these theories would not be particularly interesting, and would be irrelevant in the present context. The point to note is simply that non-Marxist analysts of imperialism have tended to argue the opposite of what the Marxists said, and in doing so have obscured the subject. They tended to deny any specific connection between the imperialism of the late nineteenth and twentieth centuries with capitalism in general, or with the particular phase of it which, as we have seen, appeared to emerge in the late nineteenth century. They denied that imperialism had any important economic roots, that it benefited the imperial countries economically, let alone that the exploitation of backward zones was in any sense essential to capitalism, and that it had negative effects on colonial economies. They argued that imperialism did not lead to unmanageable rivalries between the imperial powers, and had no serious bearings on the origin of the First World War. Rejecting economic explanations, they concentrated on psychological, ideological, cultural and political explanations, though usually careful to avoid the dangerous territory of domestic politics, since Marxists also tended to stress the advantages to metropolitan ruling classes of imperialist policies and propaganda which, among other things, counteracted the growing appeal to the working classes of mass labour movements. Some of these counter-attacks have proved powerful and effective, though several of such lines of argument were mutually incompatible. In fact, much of the pioneer theoretical literature of anti-imperialism is not tenable. But the disadvantage of the anti-anti-imperialist literature is that it does not actually explain that conjunction of economic and political, national and international, developments, which contemporaries around 1900 found so striking that they sought a comprehensive explanation for them. It does not explain why contemporaries felt that 'imperialism' at the time was both a novel and historically *central* development. In short, much of this literature amounts to denying facts which were obvious enough at the time and still are.

Leaving Leninism and anti-Leninism aside, the first thing for the historian to re-establish is the obvious fact, which nobody in the 1890s would have denied, that the division of the globe had an economic dimension. To demonstrate this is not to explain everything about the imperialism of the period. Economic development is not a sort of ventriloquist with the rest of history as its dummy. For that matter, even the most single-minded businessman pursuing profit into, say, the South African gold- and diamond-mines, can never be treated exclusively as a money-making machine. He was not immune to the political, emotional, ideological, patriotic or even racial appeals which were so patently associated with imperial expansion. Nevertheless, if an economic connection can be established between the tendencies of economic development in the capitalist core of the globe at this time and its expansion into the periphery, it becomes much less plausible to put the full weight of explanation on motives for imperialism which have no intrinsic connection with the penetration and conquest of the non-western world. And even those which appear to have, such as the strategic calculations of rival powers, must be analysed while bearing the economic dimension in mind. Even today politics in the Middle East, which are far from explicable on simple economic grounds, cannot be realistically discussed without considering oil.

Now the major fact about the nineteenth century is the creation of a single global economy, progressively reaching into the most remote corners of the world, an increasingly dense web of economic transactions, communications and movements of goods, money and people linking the developed countries with each other and with the undeveloped world. [. . .] Without this there was no particular reason why European states should have taken more than the most fleeting interest in the affairs of, say, the Congo basin or engaged in diplomatic disputes about some Pacific atoll. This globalization of the economy was not new, though it had accelerated considerably in the middle decades of the century. It continued to grow – less strikingly in relative terms, but more massively in terms of volume and numbers – between 1875 and 1914. European exports had indeed grown more than four-fold between 1848 and 1875, while they only doubled from then until 1915. But the world's merchant shipping had only risen, between 1840 and 1870, from 10 to 16 million tons, whereas it doubled in the next forty years, as the world's railway network expanded from a little over 200,000 kilometres (1870) to over 1 million kilometres just before the First World War.

This tightening web of transport drew even the backward and previously marginal into the world economy, and created a new interest among the old centres of wealth and development in these remote areas. Indeed, now that they were accessible many of these regions seemed at first sight to be simply potential extensions of the developed word, which were already being settled and developed by men and women of European stock, extirpating or pushing back the native inhabitants, generating cities and doubtless, in due course, industrial civilization: the USA west of the Mississippi, Canada, Australia, New Zealand, South Africa, Algeria, the southern cone of South America. The prediction, as we shall see, was off the mark. Nevertheless, though often remote, such areas were in contemporary minds distinct from those other regions where, for climatic reasons, white settlement was unattractive, but where – to quote a leading imperial administrator of the time – 'the European may come, in small numbers, with his capital, his energy and his knowledge to develop a most lucrative commerce, and obtain products necessary to the use of his advanced civilisation'.[7]

For that civilization now had need of the exotic. Technological development now relied on raw materials which, for reasons of climate or the hazards of geology, were to be found exclusively or profusely in remote places. The internal-combustion engine, that typical child of our period, relied on oil and rubber. Oil still came overwhelmingly from the USA and Europe (Russia and, a long way behind, Rumania) but already the oilfields of the Middle East were the subject of intensive diplomatic confrontation and horse-trading. Rubber was exclusively a tropical product, extracted by the atrocious exploitation of natives in the rainforests of the Congo and the Amazon, the target of early and justified anti-imperialist protest. In due course it was extensively cultivated in Malaya. Tin came from Asia and South America. Non-ferrous metals of previously negligible importance became essential for the steel alloys required by high-speed technology. Some of these were freely available in the developed world, notably the USA, but others were not. The new electrical and motor industries hungered for one of the most ancient metals, copper. Its major reserves, and eventually producers, were in what the late twentieth century called the Third World: Chile, Peru, Zaire, Zambia. And, of course, there was the constant and never satisfied demand for the precious metals which, in this period, turned South Africa into by far the greatest gold-producer in the world, not to mention its wealth of diamonds. Mines were the major pioneers in opening up the world to imperialism, and all the more effective because their profits were sensational enough to justify also the construction of feeder-railways.

Quite apart from the demands of a new technology, the growth of mass consumption in the metropolitan countries produced a rapidly expanding market for foodstuffs. In sheer volume this was dominated by the basic foodstuffs of the temperate zone, grain and meat, now produced cheaply and in vast quantities in several zones of European settlement – in North and South America, Russia and Australasia. But it also transformed the market for the products long and characteristically known (at least in German) as 'colonial goods' and sold by the grocers of the developed worlds: sugar, tea, coffee, cocoa and its derivatives. With rapid transport and conservation, tropical and sub-tropical fruits became available: they made possible the 'banana republic'.

Britons, who had consumed 1.5 lb of tea per head in the 1840s and 3.26 lb in the 1860s, were consuming 5.7 lb in the 1890s – but this represented an average annual import of 224 million lb compared with less than 98 millions in the 1860s and about 40 millions in the 1840s. While the British abandoned what few cups of coffee they had drunk to fill their teapots from India and Ceylon (Sri Lanka), Americans and Germans imported coffee in ever more spectacular quantities, notably from Latin America. In the early 1900s New York families consumed 1 lb of coffee per week. The Quaker beverage and chocolate manu-facturers of Britain, happy in dispensing non-alcoholic refreshment, got their raw material from West Africa and South America. The canny Boston businessmen who founded the United Fruit Company in 1885 created private empires in the Caribbean to supply America with the previously insignificant banana. The soap manufacturers, exploiting the market which first demonstrated to the full the capacities of the new advertising industry, looked to the vegetable oils of Africa. Plantations, estates and farms were the second pillar of imperial economies. Metropolitan traders and financiers were the third.

These developments did not change the shape and character of the industrialized or industrializing countries, though they created new branches of big business whose fortunes were closely tied to those of particular parts of the globe, such as the oil companies. But they transformed the rest of the world, inasmuch as they turned it into a complex of colonial and semi-colonial territories which increasingly evolved into specialized producers of one or two primary products for export to the world market, on whose vagaries they were entirely dependent. Malaya increasingly meant rubber and tin, Brazil coffee, Chile nitrates, Uruguay meat, Cuba sugar and cigars. In fact, with the exception of the USA, even the white-settler colonies failed to industrialize (at this stage) because they too were caught in this cage of international specialization. They could become exceedingly prosperous, even by European standards, especially when inhabited by free and, in general, militant European immigrants with political muscle in elected assemblies, whose democratic radicalism could be formidable, though it usually stopped short of including the natives.[8] A European wishing to emigrate in the Age of Empire would probably have done better to move to Australia, New Zealand, Argentina or Uruguay than anywhere else, including the USA. All these countries developed labour and radical–democratic parties, or even governments, and ambitious systems of public social welfare and security (New Zealand, Uruguay) long before European states did. But they did so as complements to the European (i.e. essentially British) industrial economy, and hence it did not pay them – or at any rate the interests committed to exporting primary products – to industrialize. Not that the metropoles would have welcomed their industrialization. Whatever the official rhetoric, the function of colonies and informal dependencies was to complement metropolitan economies and not to compete with them.

The dependent territories which did not belong to what has been called (white) 'settler capitalism' did not do so well. Their economic interest lay in the combination of resources with a labour force which, consisting of 'natives', cost little and could be kept cheap. Nevertheless the oligarchies of landowners and compradore traders – local, imported from Europe or both – and, where they had them, their governments, benefited from the sheer length of the period of secular expansion for their region's export staples, interrupted only by short-lived, though sometimes (as in Argentina in 1890) dramatic crises generated by trade cycle, overspeculation, war and peace. However, while the First World War disrupted some of their markets, the dependent producers were remote from it. From their point of view the era of empire, which began in the late nineteenth century, lasted until the Great Slump of 1929–33. All the same, in the course of this period they were to become increasingly vulnerable, as their fortunes were increasingly a function of the price of coffee (which by 1914 already produced 58 per cent of the value of Brazilian and 53 per cent of Colombian exports), of rubber and tin, of cocoa, beef or wool. But until the vertical fall in the price of primary commodities during the 1929 slump, this vulnerability did not seem of much long-term significance compared to the apparently unlimited expansion of exports and credits. On the contrary, as we have seen, before the terms of trade appeared to be, if anything, running in favour of the primary producers.

Nevertheless, the growing economic significance of such areas for the world economy does not explain why, among other things, there should have been a rush by the leading industrial states to carve up the globe into colonies and spheres of influence. The anti-imperialist analysis of imperialism has suggested various reasons why this should have been so. The most familiar of these, the pressure of capital for more profitable investment than could be ensured at home, investment secure from the rivalry of foreign capital, is the least convincing. Since British capital exports expanded enormously in the last third of the century, and indeed, the income from such investments became essential for the British balance of payments, it was natural enough to connect the 'new imperialism' with capital exports, as J. A. Hobson did. But there is no denying that very little indeed of this massive flow went to the new colonial empires: most of British foreign investment went to the rapidly developing and generally old white-settler colonies, soon to be recognized as virtually independent 'dominions' (Canada, Australia, New Zealand, South Africa), and to what might be called 'honorary' dominions such as Argentina and Uruguay, not to mention the USA. Moreover, the bulk of such investment (76 per cent in 1913) took the form of public loans to railways and public utilities which certainly paid better than investment in the British government debt – an average of 5 per cent as against an average of 3 per cent – but were equally certainly less lucrative than the profits of industrial capital at home, except no doubt for the bankers organizing them. They were supposed to be secure rather than high-yield investments. None of this means that colonies were not acquired because some group of investors did not expect to make a killing, or in defence of investments already made.[9] Whatever the ideology, the motive for the Boer War was gold.

A more convincing general motive for colonial expansion was the search for markets. The fact that this was often disappointed is irrelevant. The belief that the 'overproduction' of the Great Depression could be solved by a vast export drive was widespread. Businessmen, always inclined to fill the blank spaces on the map of world trade with vast numbers of potential customers, would naturally look for such unexploited areas: China was one which haunted the imagination of salesmen – what if every one of those 300 million bought only one box of tin-tacks? – and Africa, the unknown continent, was another. The Chambers of Commerce of British cities in the depressed early 1880s were outraged by the thought that diplomatic negotiations might exclude their traders from access to the Congo basin, which was believed to offer untold sales prospects, all the more so as it was being developed as a paying proposition by that crowned businessman, King Leopold II of the Belgians.[10] (As it happened, his favourite method of exploitation by forced labour was not designed to encourage high *per capita* purchases, even when it did not actually diminish the number of customers by torture and massacre.)

But the crux of the global economic situation was that a number of developed economies simultaneously felt the same need for new markets. If they were sufficiently strong their ideal was 'the open door' on the markets of the underdeveloped world; but if not strong enough, they hoped to carve out for themselves territories which, by virtue of ownership, would give national business a monopoly position or at least a substantial advantage. Partition of the unoccupied parts of the Third World was the logical consequence. In a sense, this was an extension of the protectionism which gained ground almost everywhere after 1879 (see previous chapter). 'If you were not such persistent protectionists,' the British premier told the French ambassador in 1897, 'you would not find us so keen to annex territories.'[11] To this extent the 'new imperialism' was the natural by-product of an international economy based on the rivalry of several competing industrial economies, intensified by the economic pressures of the 1880s. It does not follow that any particular colony was expected to turn into Eldorado by itself, though this is what actually happened in South Africa, which became the world's greatest gold-producer. Colonies might simply provide suitable bases or jumping-off points for regional business penetration. That was clearly stated by an official of the US State Department round the turn of the century, when the USA followed international fashion by making a brief drive for a colonial empire of its own.

At this point the economic motive for acquiring some colonial territory becomes difficult to disentangle from the political action required for the purpose, for protectionism of whatever kind is economy operating with the aid of politics. The strategic motive for colonization was evidently strongest in Britain, which had long-established colonies which were crucially placed to control access to various zones of land and sea believed to be vital to Britain's worldwide commercial and maritime interests or, with the rise of the steamship, which could function as coaling stations. (Gibraltar and Malta were old examples of the first, Bermuda and Aden turned out to be useful examples of the second.) There was also the symbolic or real significance for robbers of getting an appropriate share of loot. Once rival powers began to carve up the map of Africa or Oceania, each naturally tried to safeguard against an excessive portion (or a particularly attractive morsel) going to the others. Once the status of a great power thus became associated with raising its flag over some palm-fringed beach (or, more likely, over stretches of dry scrub), the acquisition of colonies itself became a status symbol irrespective of their value. Around 1900 even the USA, whose kind of imperialism has never before or since been particularly associated with the possession of formal colonies, felt obliged to follow the fashion. Germany deeply resented the fact that so powerful and dynamic a nation as herself should own so notably smaller a share of colonial territory than the British and the French, though her colonies were of little economic and less strategic interest. Italy insisted on capturing notably unattractive stretches of African desert and mountain in order to back her standing as a great power; and her failure to conquer Ethiopia in 1896 undoubtedly lowered that standing.

For if great powers were states which acquired colonies, small powers had, as it were, 'no right' to them. Spain lost most of what remained of her colonial empire as a consequence of the Spanish–American War of 1898. As we have seen, plans to partition the remainder of Portugal's African empire between the new colonialists were seriously discussed. Only the Dutch quietly kept their rich and ancient colonies (mainly in South-east Asia), and the King of the Belgians, as we have also seen, was permitted to carve out his private domain in Africa on condition that he allowed it to be accessible to all, because no great power was willing to give others a significant share of the great basin of the Congo river. One ought, of course, to add that there were large tracts of Asia and the Americas where, for political reasons, massive share-outs of territory by European powers were out of the question. In the Americas the situation of the surviving European colonies was frozen by the Monroe Doctrine: only the USA had freedom of action. In most of Asia, the struggle was for spheres of influence in nominally independent states, notably China, Persia and the Ottoman Empire. Exceptions to this were the Russians and the Japanese – the former successful in extending their area in Central Asia but unsuccessful in acquiring chunks of north China, the latter acquiring Korea and Formosa (Taiwan) as a result of a war with China in 1894–5. The main zones of competitive land-grabbing were thus, in practice, in Africa and Oceania.

Essentially strategic explanations of imperialism have thus attracted some historians, who have tried to account for the British expansion in Africa in terms of the need to defend the routes to, and the maritime and terrestrial glacis of, India against potential threats. It is indeed important to recall that, speaking globally, India was the core of British strategy, and that this strategy required control not only over the short sea-routes to the subcontinent (Egypt, the Middle East, the Red Sea, Persian Gulf and South Arabia) and the long sea-routes (the Cape of Good Hope and Singapore), but over the entire Indian Ocean, including crucial sectors of the African coast and its hinterland. British governments were keenly aware of this. It is also true that the disintegration of local power in some areas crucial for this purpose, such as Egypt (including the Sudan), drew the British into establishing a much greater direct political presence than originally intended, and even into actual rule. Yet these arguments do not invalidate an economic analysis of imperialism. In the first place, they underestimate the directly economic incentive to acquire some African territories, of which Southern Africa is the most obvious. In any case the scramble for West Africa and the Congo was primarily economic. In second place they overlook the fact that India was the 'brightest jewel in the imperial crown' and the core of British global strategic thinking precisely because of her very real importance to the British economy. This was never greater than at this time, when anything up to 60 per cent of British cotton exports went to India and the Far East, to which India was the key – 40–45 per cent went to India alone – and when the international balance of payments of Britain hinged on the payments surplus which India provided. In the third place, the disintegration of indigenous local governments, which sometimes entailed the establishment of European rule over areas Europeans had not previously bothered to administer, was itself due to the undermining of local structures by economic penetration. And, finally, the attempt to prove that nothing in the internal development of western capitalism in the 1880s explains the territorial redivision of the world fails, since world capitalism in this period clearly was different from what it had been in the 1860s. It now consisted of a plurality of rival 'national economies' 'protecting' themselves against each other. In short, politics and economics cannot be separated in a capitalist society, any more than religion and society in an Islamic one. The attempt to devise a purely non-economic explanation of the 'new imperialism' is as unrealistic as the attempt to devise a purely non-economic explanation of the rise of working-class parties.

In fact, the rise of labour movements or more generally of democratic politics [. . .] had a distinct bearing on the rise of the 'new imperialism'. Ever since the great imperialist Cecil Rhodes observed in 1895 that if one wanted to avoid civil war one must become imperialist,[12] most observers have been aware of so-called 'social imperialism', i.e. of the attempt to use imperial expansion to diminish domestic discontent by economic improvements or social reform in other ways. There is no doubt at all that politicians were perfectly aware of the potential benefits. In some cases – notably Germany – the rise of imperialism has been explained primarily in terms of 'the primacy of domestic politics'. Probably Cecil Rhodes' version of social imperialism, which thought primarily of the economic benefits that empire might bring, directly or indirectly, to the discontented masses, was the least relevant. There is no good evidence that colonial conquest as such had much bearing on the employment or real incomes of most workers in the metropolitan countries,[13] and the idea that emigration to colonies would provide a safety-valve for overpopulated countries was little more than a demagogic fantasy. (In fact, never was it easier to find somewhere to emigrate to than between 1880 and 1914, and only a tiny minority of emigrants went to anyone's colonies – or needed to.)

Much more relevant was the familiar practice of offering the voters glory rather than more costly reforms: and what was more glorious than conquests of exotic territories and dusky races, especially as these were usually cheaply won? More generally, imperialism encouraged the masses, and especially the potentially discontented to identify themselves with the imperial state and nation, and thus unconsciously to endow the social and political system represented by that state with justification and legitimacy. And in an era of mass politics [. . .] even old systems required new legitimacy. Here again, contemporaries were quite clear about this. The British coronation ceremony of 1902, carefully restyled, was praised because it was designed to express 'the recognition, by a free democracy, of a hereditary crown, *as a symbol of the world-wide dominion of their race*' (my emphasis).[14] In short, empire made good ideological cement.

How effective this specific variant of patriotic flag-waving was is not quite clear, especially in countries where liberalism and the more radical left had acquired strong anti-imperial, anti-military, anti-colonial or more generally anti-aristocratic traditions. There is little doubt that in several countries imperialism was extremely popular among the new middle and white-collar strata, whose social identity largely rested on a claim to be the chosen vehicles of patriotism [. . .]. There is much less evidence of any spontaneous enthusiasm of the workers for colonial conquests, let alone wars, or indeed of any great interest in the colonies, new or old (except those of white settlement). Attempts to institutionalize pride in imperialism, as by establishing an 'Empire Day' in Britain (1902), largely relied for their success on mobilizing the captive audiences of school-children. (The appeal of patriotism in a more general sense will be considered below.)

Nevertheless, it is impossible to deny that the idea of superiority to, and domination over, a world of dark skins in remote places was genuinely popular, and thus benefited the politics of imperialism. In its great International Expositions [. . .] bourgeois civilization had always gloried in the triple triumphs of science, technology and manufactures. In the era of empires it also gloried in its colonies. At the end of the century 'colonial pavilions', hitherto virtually unknown, multiplied: eighteen complemented the Eiffel Tower in 1889, fourteen attracted the tourists in Paris in 1900.[15] No doubt this was planned publicity, but like all really successful propaganda, commercial or political, it succeeded because it touched a public nerve. Colonial exhibits were a hit. British jubilees, royal funerals and coronations were all the more impressive because, like ancient Roman triumphs, they displayed submissive maharajahs in jewelled robes – freely loyal rather than captive. Military parades were all the more colourful because they contained turbaned Sikhs, moustached Rajputs, smiling and implacable Gurkhas, Spahis and tall black Senegalese: the world of what was considered barbarism at the service of civilization. Even in Habsburg Vienna, uninterested in overseas colonies, an Ashanti village magnetized the sightseers. The Douanier Rousseau was not the only man to dream of the tropics.

The sense of superiority which thus united the western whites, rich, middle-class and poor, did so not only because all of them enjoyed the privileges of the ruler, especially when actually in the colonies. In Dakar or Mombasa the most modest clerk was a master, and accepted as a 'gentleman' by people who would not even have noticed his existence in Paris or London; the white worker was a commander of blacks. But even where ideology insisted on at least potential equality, it was dissolved into domination. France believed in transforming its subjects in Frenchmen, notional descendants (as school textbooks insisted, in Timbuctoo and Martinique as in Bordeaux) of 'nos ancêtres les gaulois' (our ancestors the Gauls), unlike the British, convinced of the essential and permanent non-Englishness of Bengalis and Yoruba. Yet the very existence of these strata of native *évolués* underlined the lack of 'evolution' of the great majority. The Churches set out to convert the heathen to various versions of the true Christian faith, except where actively discouraged by colonial governments (as in India) or where the task was clearly impossible (as in Islamic regions).

This was the classic age of massive missionary endeavour.[16] Missionary effort was by no means an agency of imperialist politics. Often it was opposed to the colonial authorities; pretty well always it put the interests of its converts first. Yet the success of the Lord was a function of imperialist advance. Whether trade followed the flag may still be debated, but there is no doubt at all that colonial conquest opened the way for effective missionary action – as in Uganda, Rhodesia (Zambia and Zimbabwe) and Nyasaland (Malawi). And if Christianity insisted on the equality of souls, it underlined the inequality of bodies – even of clerical bodies. It was something done by whites for natives, and paid for by whites. And though it multiplied native believers, at least half the clergy remained white. As for a coloured bishop, it would require a powerful microscope to detect one anywhere between 1880 and 1914. The Catholic Church did not consecrate its first Asian bishops until the 1920s, eighty years after observing how desirable such a development would be.[17]

As for the movement most passionately devoted to the equality of all men, it spoke with two voices. The secular left was anti-imperialist in principle and often in practice. Freedom for India, like freedom for Egypt and Ireland, was the objective of the British labour movement. The left never wavered in its condemnation of colonial wars and conquests, often – as in the British opposition to the Boer War – at considerable risk of temporary unpopularity. Radicals revealed the horrors of the Congo, in metropolitan cocoa plantations on African islands, in Egypt. The campaign which led to the great electoral triumph of the British Liberal Party in 1906 was largely waged by public denunciations of 'Chinese slavery' in the South African mines. Yet, with the rarest exceptions (such as Dutch Indonesia), western socialists did little actually to organize the resistance of colonial peoples to their rulers, until the era of the Communist International. Within the socialist and labour movement those who frankly accepted imperialism as desirable, or at least an essential stage in the history of peoples not yet 'ready for self-government', were a minority on the revisionist and Fabian right wing, though many trade union leaders probably thought discussions about colonies were irrelevant, or considered coloured peoples primarily as cheap labour threatening sturdy white workers. Certainly the pressure to ban coloured immigrants, which established the 'White California' and 'White Australia' policies between the 1880s and 1914, came primarily from the working class, and Lancashire unions joined with Lancashire cotton-masters to insist that India must remain deindustrialized. Internationally, socialism before 1914 remained overwhelmingly a movement of Europeans and white emigrants or their descendants [. . .]. Colonialism remained marginal to their interests. Indeed, their analysis and definition of the new 'imperialist' phase of capitalism, which they detected from the later 1890s, rightly saw colonial annexation and exploitation simply as one symptom and characteristic of that new phase: undesirable, like all its characteristics, but not in itself central. Few were the socialists who, like Lenin, already had their eye fixed on the 'inflammable material' on the periphery of world capitalism.

Insofar as the socialist (i.e. mainly Marxist) analysis of imperialism integrated colonialism into a much wider concept of a 'new phase' of capitalism, it was undoubtedly right in principle, though not necessarily in the details of its theoretical model. It was also sometimes too inclined, as indeed were contemporary capitalists, to exaggerate the economic significance of colonial expansion for metropolitan countries. The imperialism of the late nineteenth century was undoubtedly 'new'. It was the child of an era of competition between rival industrial–capitalist national economies which was new and which was intensified by the pressure to secure and safeguard markets in a period of business uncertainty [. . .]; in short, it was an era when 'tariff and expansion become the common demand of the ruling class'.[19] It was part of a process of turning away from a capitalism of the private and public policies of *laissez-faire*, which was also new, and implied the rise of large corporations and oligopolies as well as the increased intervention of the state in economic affairs. It belonged to a period when the peripheral part of the global economy became increasingly significant. It was a phenomenon that seemed as 'natural' in 1900 as it would have appeared implausible in 1860. But for this link between the post-1873 capitalism and expansion into the unindustrialized world, it is doubtful whether even 'social imperialism' would have played such part as it did in the domestic politics of states adapting themselves to mass electoral politics. All attempts to divorce the explanation of imperialism from the specific developments of capitalism in the late nineteenth century must be regarded as ideological exercises, though often learned and sometimes acute.

II

This still leaves us with the questions about the impact of western (and from the 1890s Japanese) expansion on the rest of the world, and about the significance of the 'imperial' aspects of imperialism for the metropolitan countries.

The first of these questions can be answered more quickly than the second. The economic impact of imperialism was significant, but, of course, the most significant thing about it was that it was profoundly unequal, for the relationship between metropoles and dependencies was highly asymmetrical. The impact of the first on the second was dramatic and decisive, even without actual occupation, whereas the impact of the second on the first might be negligible, and was hardly ever a matter of life or death. Cuba stood or fell by the price of sugar and the willingness of the USA to import it, but even quite small 'developed' countries – say Sweden – would not have been seriously inconvenienced if all Caribbean sugar had suddenly disappeared from the market, because they did not depend exclusively on that area for sugar. Virtually all the imports and exports of any region in sub-Saharan Africa came from or went to a handful of western metropoles, but metropolitan trade with Africa, Asia and Oceania, while increasing modestly between 1870 and 1914, remained quite marginal. About 80 per cent of European trade throughout the nineteenth century, both exports and imports, was with other developed countries, and the same is true of European foreign investments.[20] Insofar as these were directed overseas, they went mostly to a handful of rapidly developing economies mainly populated by settlers of European descent – Canada, Australia, South Africa, Argentina, etc. – as well as, of course, to the USA. In this sense the age of imperialism looks very different when seen from Nicaragua or Malaya than it does from the point of view of Germany or France.

Among the metropolitan countries imperialism was obviously of greatest importance to Britain, since the economic supremacy of that country had always hinged on her special relationship with the overseas markets and sources of primary products. In fact it is arguable that at no time since the industrial revolution had the manufactures of the United Kingdom been particularly competitive on the markets of industrializing economies, except perhaps during the golden decades of 1850–70. To preserve as much as possible of its privileged access to the non-European world was therefore a matter of life and death for the British economy.[21] In the late nineteenth century it was remarkably successful in doing so, incidentally expanding the area officially or actually under the British monarchy to a quarter of the surface of the globe (which British atlases proudly coloured red). If we include the so-called 'informal empire' of independent states which were in effect satellite economies of Britain, perhaps one-third of the globe was British in an economic, and indeed cultural, sense. For Britain exported even the peculiar shape of her post-boxes to Portugal, and so quintessentially British an institution as Harrods department store to Buenos Aires. But by 1914 much of this zone of indirect influence, especially in Latin America, was already being infiltrated by other powers.

However, not a great deal of this successful defensive operation had much to do with the 'new' imperialist expansion, except that biggest of bonanzas, the diamonds and gold of South Africa. This generated a crop of (largely German) instant millionaires – the Wernhers, Beits, Ecksteins, *et al.* – most of whom were equally instantly incorporated into British high society, never more receptive to first-generation money if it was splashed around in sufficiently large quantities. It also led to the greatest of colonial conflicts, the South African War of 1899–1902, which eliminated the resistance of two small local republics of white peasant settlers.

Most of Britain's overseas success was due to the more systematic exploitation of Britain's already existing possessions or of the country's special position as the major importer from, and investor in, such areas as South America. Except for India, Egypt and South Africa, most British economic activity was in countries which were virtually independent, like the white 'dominions', or areas like the USA and Latin America, where British state action was not, or could not be, effectively deployed. For in spite of the cries of pain emanating from the Corporation of Foreign Bondholders (established during the Great Depression) when faced with the well-known Latin practice of suspending debt-payment or paying in devalued currency, the government did not effectively back its investors in Latin America, because it could not. The Great Depression was a crucial test in this respect, because, like later world depressions (including the one of the 1970s and 1980s) it led to a major international debt crisis, which put the banks of the metropolis at serious risk. The most the British government could do was to arrange for the great house of Baring to be saved from insolvency in the 'Baring crisis' of 1890, when that bank had, as banks will, ventured too freely into the whirlpools of defaulting Argentinian finance. If it backed investors with diplomacy of force, as it increasingly did after 1905, it was to support them against entrepreneurs of other countries backed by their own governments, rather than against the larger governments of the dependent world.[22]

In fact, taking the good years with the bad, British capitalists did rather well out of their informal or 'free' empire. Almost half of all Britain's long-term publicly issued capital in 1914 was in Canada, Australia and Latin America. More than half of all British savings were invested abroad after 1900.

Of course Britain took her share of the newly colonialized regions of the world, and, given British strength and experience, it was a larger and probably more valuable share than that of anyone else. If France occupied most of West Africa, the four British colonies in this area controlled 'the denser African populations, the larger productive capacities, and the preponderance of trade'.[23] Yet the British object was not expansion but defence against others encroaching upon territories hitherto, like most of the overseas world, dominated by British trade and British capital.

Did other powers benefit proportionately from their colonial expansion? It is impossible to say, since formal colonization was only one aspect of global economic expansion and competition, and, in the case of the two major industrial powers, Germany and the USA, not a major aspect of it. Moreover, as we have already seen, for no country other than

Britain (with the possible exception of the Netherlands) was a special relationship with the non-industrial world economically crucial. All we can say with fair confidence is this. First, the drive for colonies seems to have been proportionately stronger in economically less dynamic metropolitan countries, where it served to some extent as a potential compensation for their economic and political inferiority to their rivals – and, in the case of France, her demographic and military inferiority. Second, in all cases there were particular economic groups – notably those associated with overseas trade and industries using overseas raw materials – pressing strongly for colonial expansion, which they naturally justified by the prospects of national advantage. Third, while some of these groups did rather well out of such expansion – the Compagnie Française de l'Afrique Occidentale paid dividends of 26 per cent in 1913[24] – most of the actual new colonies attracted little capital and their economic results were disappointing.[25] In short, the new colonialism was a by-product of an era of economic-political rivalry between competing national economies, intensified by protectionism. However, insofar as the metropolitan trade with the colonies almost invariably increased as a percentage of its total trade, that protectionism was modestly successful.

Yet the Age of Empire was not only an economic and political but cultural phenomenon. The conquest of the globe by its 'developed' minority transformed images, ideas and aspirations, both by force and institutions, by example and by social transformation. In the dependent countries this hardly affected anyone except the indigenous elites, though of course it must be remembered that in some regions, such as sub-Saharan Africa, it was imperialism itself, or the associated phenomenon of Christian missions, which created the possibility of new social elites based on education in the western manner. The division between 'francophone' and African states today exactly mirrors the distribution of the French and British colonial empires.[26] Except in Africa and Oceania, where Christian missions sometimes secured mass conversions to the western religion, the great mass of the colonial populations hardly changed their ways of life if they could help it. And, to the chagrin of the more unbending missionaries, what indigenous peoples adopted was not so much the faith imported from the west as those elements in it which made sense to them in terms of their own system of beliefs and institutions, or demands. Just like the sports brought to Pacific islanders by enthusiastic British colonial administrators (so often selected from among the more muscular products of the middle class), colonial religion often looked as unexpected to the western observer as Samoan cricket. This was so even where the faithful nominally followed the orthodoxies of their denomination. But they were also apt to develop their own versions of the faith, notably in South Africa – the one region in Africa where really massive conversions took place – where an 'Ethiopian movement' seceded from the missions as early as 1892 in order to establish a form of Christianity less identified with the whites.

What imperialism brought to the elites or potential elites of the dependent world was therefore essentially 'westernization'. It had, of course, begun to do so long before then. For all governments and elites of countries faced with dependency or conquest it had been clear for several decades that they had to westernize or go under [. . .]. And, indeed, the ideologies which inspired such elites in the era of imperialism dated back to the years between the French Revolution and the mid-nineteenth century, as when they took the form of the positivism of August Comte (1798–1857), a modernizing doctrine which inspired the governments of Brazil, Mexico and the early Turkish Revolution [. . .] Elite resistance to the west remained westernizing even when it opposed wholesale westernization on grounds of religion, morality, ideology or political pragmatism. The saintly Mahatma Gandhi, wearing loincloth and bearing a spindle (to discourage industrialization), was not only supported and financed by the owners of mechanized cotton-factories in Ahmedabad[27] but was himself a western-educated lawyer visibly influenced by western-derived ideology. He is quite incomprehensible if we see in him only a Hindu traditionalist.

In fact, Gandhi illustrates the specific impact of the era of imperialism rather well. Born into a relatively modest caste of traders and money-lenders not previously much associated with the westernized elite which administered India under British superiors, he nevertheless acquired a professional and political education in England. By the late 1880s this was so accepted an option for ambitious young men from his country that Gandhi himself began to write a guide-book to English life for prospective students of modest circumstances such as himself. Written in superb English, it advised them on everything from the journey by P & O steamer to London and how to find lodgings, to ways of meeting the diet requirements of the pious Hindu and how to get used to the surprising western habit of shaving oneself rather than having it done by a barber.[28] Gandhi clearly saw himself neither as an unconditional assimilator nor as an unconditional opponent of things British. As many pioneers of colonial liberation have done since, during their temporary stay in the metropole, he chose to move in western circles which were ideologically congenial – in his case those of British vegetarians, who may safely be taken as being in favour of other 'progressive' causes also.

Gandhi learned his characteristic technique of mobilizing traditionalist masses for non-traditionalist purposes by means of passive resistance, in an environment created by the 'new imperialism'. It was, as one might expect, a fusion of western and eastern elements for he made no secret of his intellectual debt to John Ruskin and Tolstoi. (Before the 1880s the fertilization of Indian political flowers by pollen carried from Russia would have been inconceivable, but by the first decade of the new century it was already common among Indian, as it was to be among Chinese and Japanese radicals.) South Africa, the boom country of diamonds and gold, attracted a large community of modest immigrants from India, and racial discrimination in this novel setting created one of the few situations in which the non-elite Indians were ready for modern political mobilization. Gandhi gained his political experience and won his political spurs as the champion of Indian rights in South Africa. He could hardly as yet have done the same in India itself, where he eventually returned – but only after the outbreak of the 1914 war – to become the key figure in the Indian national movement.

In short, the Age of Empire created both the conditions which formed anti-imperialist leaders and the conditions which, as we shall see, began to give their voices resonance. But, of course, it is an anachronism and a misunderstanding to present the history of the peoples and regions brought under the domination and influence of the western metropoles primarily in terms of resistance to the west. It is an anachronism because, with exceptions to be noted below, the era of significant anti-imperial movements begins for most regions at the earliest with the First World War and the Russian Revolution, and a misunderstanding, because it reads the text of modern nationalism – independence, the self-determination of peoples, the formation of territorial states, etc. [. . .] into a historical record which did not yet, and could not yet, contain it. In fact, it was the westernized elites which first made contact with such ideas through their visits to the west and through the educational institutions formed by the west, for that is where they came from. Young Indian students returning from Britain might bring with them the slogans of Mazzini and Garibaldi, but as yet few of the inhabitants of the Pandjab, let alone of regions like the Sudan, would have the slightest idea of what they could mean.

The most powerful cultural legacy of imperialism was, therefore, an education in western ways for minorities of various kinds: for the favoured few who became literate and therefore discovered, with or without the assistance of Christian conversion, the high road of ambition which wore the white collar of the clergyman, teacher, bureaucrat or office worker. In some regions it also included those who acquired new ways as soldiers and policemen of the new rulers, wearing their clothes, adopting their peculiar ideas of time, place and domestic arrangement. These, of course, were the minorities of potential movers and shakers, which is why the era of colonialism, brief even by the measure of a single human life, has left such lasting effects. For it is a surprising fact that in most parts of Africa the entire experience of colonialism from original occupation to the formation of independent states, fits within a single lifetime – say that of Sir Winston Churchill (1874–1965).

What of the opposite effect of the dependent world on the dominant? Exoticism had been a by-product of European expansion since the sixteenth century, though philosophical observers in the age of Enlightenment had more often than not treated the strange countries beyond Europe and European settlers as a sort of moral barometer of European civilization. Where they were plainly civilized, they could illustrate the institutional deficiencies of the west, as in Montesquieu's *Persian Letters*; where they were not, they were apt to be treated as noble savages whose natural and admirable comportment illustrated the corruption of civilized society. The novelty of the nineteenth century was that non-Europeans and their societies were increasingly, and generally, treated as inferior, undesirable, feeble and backward, even infantile. They were fit subjects for conquest, or at least for conversion to the values of the only *real* civilization, that represented by traders, missionaries and bodies of armed men full of firearms and fire-water. And in a sense the values of traditional non-western societies increasingly became irrelevant to their survival in an age when force and military technology alone counted. Did the sophistication of imperial Peking prevent the western barbarians from burning and looting the Summer Palace more than once? Did the elegance of elite culture in the declining Mughal capital, so beautifully portrayed in Satyajit Ray's *The Chessplayers*, hold up the advancing British? For the average European, such people became objects of contempt. The only non-Europeans they took to were fighters, preferably those who could be recruited into their own colonial armies (Sikhs, Gurkhas, Berber mountaineers, Afghans, Beduin). The Ottoman Empire earned a grudging respect, because even in decline it had an infantry which could resist European armies. Japan came to be treated as an equal when it began to win wars.

And yet the very density of the network of global communication, the very accessibility of foreign lands, directly or indirectly, intensified the confrontation and the intermingling of the western and the exotic worlds. Those who knew and reflected on both were few, though in the imperialist period their number was increased by writers who deliberately chose to make themselves intermediaries between them: writers or intellectuals by vocation and by profession mariners (like Pierre Loti and, greatest of them, Joseph Conrad), soldiers and administrators (like the orientalist Louis Massignon) or colonial journalists (like Rudyard Kipling). But increasingly the exotic became part of everyday education, as in the enormously successful boys' novels of Karl May (1842–1912), whose imaginary German hero ranged through the Wild West and the Islamic east, with excursions into black Africa and Latin America; in the thrillers, whose villains now included inscrutable and all-powerful orientals like Sax Rohmer's Dr Fu Manchu; in the pulp-magazine school stories for British boys, which now included a rich Hindu speaking the baroque Babu–English of the expected stereotype. It could even become an occasional but expected part of everyday experience, as in Buffalo Bill's Wild West show, with its equally exotic cowboys and Indians, which conquered Europe from 1887 on, or in the increasingly elaborate 'colonial villages' or exhibits in the great International Expositions. These glimpses of strange worlds were not documentary, whatever their intention. They were ideological, generally reinforcing the sense of superiority of the 'civilized' over the 'primitive'. They were imperialist only because, as the novels of Joseph Conrad show, the central link between the worlds of the exotic and the everyday was the formal or informal penetration of the Third World by the west. When colloquial language, mainly via various forms of slang, notably that of colonial armies, absorbed words from the actual imperial experience, they often reflected a negative view of its subjects. Italian workers called strike-breakers *crumiri* (after a North African tribe) and Italian politicians called the regiments of docile southern voters marched into elections by local patrons *ascari* (colonial native troops). *Caciques*, the Indian chieftains of

Spain's American empire, had become a synonym for any political boss; *caids* (North African indigenous chiefs) provided the term for leaders of criminal gangs in France.

Yet there was a more positive side to this exoticism. Intellectually minded administrators and soldiers – businessmen were less interested in such matters – pondered deeply on the differences between their own societies and those they ruled. They produced both bodies of impressive scholarship about them, especially in the Indian empire, and theoretical reflections which transformed western social sciences. Much of this work was the by-product of colonial rule or intended to assist it, and most of it unquestionably rested on a firm and confident sense of the superiority of western knowledge to any other, except perhaps in the realm of religion, where the superiority of e.g. Methodism to Buddhism was not obvious to impartial observers. Imperialism brought a notable rise in the western interest in, and sometimes the western conversion to, forms of spirituality derived from the orient, or claiming to be so derived.[29] Yet, in spite of post-colonial criticism, this body of western scholarship cannot be dismissed simply as a supercilious depreciation of non-European cultures. At the very least the best of it took them seriously, as something to be respected and from which to derive instruction. In the field of art, and especially the visual arts, western *avant gardes* treated non-western cultures entirely as equals. They were indeed largely inspired by them in this period. This is true not only of arts believed to represent sophisticated civilizations, however exotic (like the Japanese, whose influence on French painters was marked), but of those regarded as 'primitive', and notably those of Africa and Oceania. No doubt their 'primitivism' was their main attraction, but it is undeniable that the *avant-garde* generations of the early twentieth century taught Europeans to see such works as art – often as great art – in its own right, irrespective of its origin.

One final aspect of imperialism must be briefly mentioned: its impact on the ruling and middle classes of the metropolitan countries themselves. In one sense imperialism dramatized the triumph of these classes and the societies created in their image as nothing else could possibly have done. A handful of countries, mainly in north-western Europe, dominated the globe. Some imperialists, to the resentment of the Latins not to mention the Slavs, even liked to stress the peculiar conquering merits of those of Teutonic and especially Anglo-Saxon origins who, whatever their rivalries, were said to have an affinity to each other which still echoes through Hitler's grudging respect for Britain. A handful of men of the upper and middle class within these countries – officers, administrators, businessmen, engineers – exercised that domination effectively. Around 1890 a little over 6000 British officials governed almost 300 million Indians with the help of a little over 70,000 European soldiers, the rank-and-file of whom were, like the much more numerous indigenous troops, mercenaries who took orders, and who indeed were disproportionately drawn from that older reservoir of native colonial fighters, the Irish. The case is extreme, but by no means untypical. Could there be a more extraordinary proof of absolute superiority?

The number of people directly involved in empire was thus relatively small – but their symbolic significance was enormous. When the writer Rudyard Kipling, the bard of the Indian empire, was believed to be dying of pneumonia in 1899, not only the British and the Americans grieved – Kipling had just addressed a poem on 'The White Man's Burden' to the USA on its responsibilities in the Philippines – but the Emperor of Germany sent a telegram.[30]

Yet imperial triumph raised both problems and uncertainties. It raised problems insofar as the contradiction between the rule of metropolitan ruling classes over their empires and their own peoples became increasingly insoluble. Within the metropoles, as we shall see, the politics of democratic electoralism increasingly, and as it seemed inevitably, prevailed or were destined to prevail. Within the colonial empires autocracy ruled, based on the combination of physical coercion and passive submission to a superiority so great as to appear unchallengeable and therefore legitimate. Soldiers and self-disciplined 'proconsuls', isolated men with absolute powers over territories the size of kingdoms, ruled over continents, while at home the ignorant and inferior masses were rampant. Was there not a lesson – a lesson in the sense of Nietzsche's *Will to Power* – to be learned here?

Imperialism also raised uncertainties. In the first place it confronted a small minority of whites – for even the majority of that race belonged to those destined to inferiority, as the new discipline of eugenics unceasingly warned [. . .] – with the masses of the black, the brown, perhaps above all the yellow, that 'yellow peril' against which the Emperor William II called for the union and defence of the west.[31] Could world empires, so easily won, so narrowly based, so absurdly easily ruled thanks to the devotion of a few and the passivity of the many, could they last? Kipling, the greatest – perhaps the only – poet of imperialism welcomed the great moment of demagogic imperial pride, Queen Victoria's Diamond Jubilee in 1897, with a prophetic reminder of the impermanence of empires:

> Far-called, our navies melt away;
> On dune and headland sinks the fire:
> Lo, all our pomp of yesterday
> Is one with Nineveh and Tyre!
> Judge of the Nations, spare us yet,
> Lest we forget, lest we forget.[32]

Pomp planned the building of an enormous new imperial capital for India in New Delhi. Was Clemenceau the only sceptical observer who would foresee that it would be the latest of a long series of ruins of imperial capitals? And was the vulnerability of global rule so much greater than the vulnerability of domestic rule over the white masses?

The uncertainty was double-edged. For if empire (and the rule of the ruling classes) was vulnerable to its subjects, though perhaps not yet, not immediately, was it not more immediately vulnerable to the erosion from within of the will to rule, the willingness to wage the Darwinian struggle for the survival of the fittest? Would not the very wealth and luxury which power and enterprise had brought weaken the fibres of those muscles whose constant efforts were necessary to maintain it? Did not empire lead to parasitism at the centre and to the eventual triumph of the barbarians?

Nowhere did such questions sound a more doom-laden echo than in the greatest and most vulnerable of all empires, the one which in size and glory surpassed all empires of the past, and yet in other respects was on the verge of decline. But even the hard-working and energetic Germans saw imperialism as going hand in hand with that 'rentier state' which could not but lead to decay. Let J. A. Hobson give word to these fears: if China were to be partitioned,

> the greater part of Western Europe might then assume the appearance and character already exhibited by tracts of country in the South of England, in the Riviera, and in the tourist-ridden or residential parts of Italy and Switzerland, little clusters of wealthy aristocrats drawing dividends and pensions from the Far East, with a somewhat larger group of professional retainers and tradesmen and a large body of personal servants and workers in the transport trade and in the final stages of production of the more perishable goods: all the main arterial industries would have disappeared, the staple foods and manufacturers flowing in as tribute from Africa and Asia.[33]

The bourgeoisie's *belle époque* would thus disarm it. The charming, harmless Eloi of H. G. Wells' novel, living lives of play in the sun, would be at the mercy of the dark Morlocks on whom they depended, and against whom they were helpless.[34] 'Europe', wrote the German economist Schulze-Gaevernitz, '. . . will shift the burden of physical toil, first agriculture and mining, then the more arduous toil in industry – on to the coloured races, and itself be content with the role of rentier, and in this way, perhaps, pave the way for the economic and later, the political emancipation of the coloured races.'[35]

Such were the bad dreams which disturbed the sleep of the *belle époque*. In them the nightmares of empire merged with the fears of democracy.

Table 11.1 British investments abroad: % share

	1860–70	1911–13
British Empire	36	46
Latin America	10.5	22
USA	27	19
Europe	25	6
Other	3.5	7

Source: C. Feinstein cited in M. Barratt Brown, *After Imperialism* (London 1963), p. 110.

Table 11.2 World output of principal tropical commodities, 1880–1910 (in 000 tons)

	1880	1900	1910
Bananas	30	300	1,800
Cocoa	60	102	227
Coffee	550	970	1,090
Rubber	11	53	87
Cotton fibre	950	1,200	1,770
Jute	600	1,220	1,560
Oil Seeds	–	–	2,700
Raw sugar cane	1,850	3,340	6,320
Tea	175	290	360

Source: P. Bairoch, *The Economic Development of the Third World Since 1900* (London, 1975), p. 15.

Table 11.3 Shipping: tonnage (vessels over 100 tons only) (in 000 tons)

	1881	1913
World total	18,325	46,970
Great Britain	7,010	18,696
USA	2,370	5,429
Norway	1,460	2,458
Germany	1,150	5,082
Italy	1,070	1,522
Canada	1,140	1,735*
France	840	2,201
Sweden	470	1,047
Spain	450	841
Netherlands	420	1,310
Greece	330	723
Denmark	230	762
Austria–Hungary	290	1,011
Russia	740	974

* British dominions

Source: Mulhall, *Dictionary of Statistics* (London, 1881) and League of Nations, *International Statistics Yearbook 1913*, Table 76.

Military expenditure by the great powers (Germany, Austria–Hungary, Great Britain, Russia, Italy and France) 1880–1914

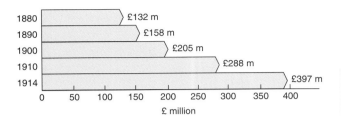

Figure 11.1 The armaments race
Source: The Times Atlas of World History (London, 1978), p. 250

Table 11.4 **Armies (in 000s)**

	1879		1913	
	Peacetime	*Mobilized*	*Peacetime*	*Mobilized*
Great Britain	136	*c.*600	160	700
India	*c.*200	–	249	
Austria–Hungary	267	772	800	3,000
France	503	1,000	1,200	3,500
Germany	419	1,300	2,200	3,800
Russia	766	1,213	1,400	4,400

Table 11.5 **Navies (in number of battleships)**

	1900	1914
Great Britain	49	64
Germany	14	40
France	23	28
Austria–Hungary	6	16
Russia	16	23

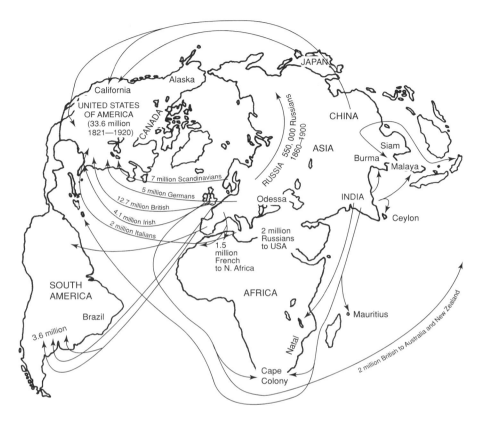

Figure 11.2 International migrations, 1820–1910
Source: The Times Atlas of World History

NOTES

* This chapter has been adapted from, Hobsbawm, E. (1987) 'The Age of Empire', in Hobsbawm, E. *The Age of Empire*, ch. 3, pp. 56–83, London, Abacus Books.

1 Cited in Wolfgang J. Mommsen, *Max Weber and German Politics 1890–1920* (Chicago 1984), p. 77.

2 Finlay Peter Dunne, *Mr Dooley's Philosophy* (New York 1900), pp. 93–4.

3 The Sultan of Morocco prefers the title of 'king'. None of the other surviving mini-sultans in the Islamic world would or could be regarded as 'kings of kings'.

4 This doctrine, first stated in 1823 and subsequently repeated and elaborated by US governments, expressed hostility to any further colonization or political intervention by European powers in the western hemisphere. This was later taken to mean that the USA was the only power with a right to interfere anywhere in that hemisphere. As the USA grew more powerful, the Monroe Doctrine was taken more seriously by European states.

5 V. I. Lenin, 'Imperialism, the Latest Stage of Capitalism', originally published in mid-1917. The later (posthumous) editions of the work use the word 'highest' instead of 'latest'.

6 J. A. Hobson, *Imperialism* (London 1902), preface; (1938 edn), p. xxvii.

7 Sir Harry Johnston, *A History of Colonization of Africa by Alien Races* (Cambridge 1930; first edn 1913), p. 445.

8 In fact, white democracy usually excluded them from the benefits won for white skins, or even refused to consider them as fully human.

9 Michael Barratt Brown, *The Economics of Imperialism* (Harmondsworth 1974), p. 175; for the vast and, for our purposes, oversophisticated debate on this subject, see Pollard, 'Capital Exports 1870–1914', *loc cit.*

10 W. G. Hynes, *The Economics of Empire: Britain, Africa and the New Imperialism, 1870–1895* (London 1979), *passim.*

11 Cited in D. C. M. Platt, *Finance, Trade and Politics: British Foreign Policy 1815–1914* (Oxford 1968), pp. 365–6.

12 Max Beer, "Der neue englische Imperialismus', *Neue Zeit*, XVI (1898), p. 304. More generally, B. Semmel, *Imperialism and Social Reform: English Social–Imperial Thought 1895–1914* (London 1960).

13 In individual cases empire might be useful. The Cornish miners left the declining tin-mines of their peninsula *en masse* for the goldfields of South Africa, where they earned a great deal of money and died even earlier than usual from lung disease. The Cornish mine-owners, at less risk to their lives, bought themselves into the new tin-mines of Malaya.

14 J. E. C. Bodley, *The Coronation of Edward VII: A Chapter of European and Imperial History* (London 1903), pp. 153 and 201.

15 Burton Benedict *et al.*, *The Anthropology of World's Fairs: San Francisco's Panama Pacific International Exposition of 1915* (London and Berkeley 1983), p. 23.

16 Between 1876 and 1902 there were 119 translations of the Bible, compared to 74 in the previous thirty years and 40 in the years of 1816–45. The number of new Protestant missions in Africa during the period 1886–95 was twenty-three or about three times as many as in any previous decade.[17]

17 *Encyclopedia of Missions* (2nd edn New York and London 1904), appendix IV, pp. 838–9.

18 *Dictionnaire de spiritualité* (Paris 1979), X, 'Mission', pp. 1398–9.

19 Rudolf Hilferding, *Das Finanzkapital* (Vienna 1909; 1923 edn), p. 470.

20 P. Bairoch, 'Geographical Structure and Trade Balance of European Foreign Trade from 1800 to 1970', *Journal of European Economic History*, 3 (1974), pp. 557–608; *Commerce extérieur et développement économique de l'Europe au XIXe siècle, p. 81.*

21 *P. J. Cain and A. G. Hopkins, 'The Political Economy of British Expansions Overseas, 1750–1914',* Economic History Review, XXXIII (1980), pp. 463–90.

22 There were a few instances of gunboat economics – as in Venezuela, Guatemala, Haiti, Honduras and Mexico – but they do not seriously modify this picture. Of course British governments and capitalists, faced with the choice between local parties or states favouring British economic interests and those hostile to them, would not refrain from backing the side helpful to British profits: Chile against Peru in the 'War of the Pacific' (1879–82), the enemies of President Balmaceda in Chile in 1891. The issue was nitrates.

23 J. E. Flint, 'Britain and the Partition of West Africa' in J. E. Flint and G. Williams (eds.), *Perspectives of Empire* (London 1973), p. 111.

24 C. Southworth, *The French Colonial Venture* (London 1931), appendix table 7. However, the average dividend for companies operating in French colonies in that year was 4.6 per cent.

25 France did not even succeed in integrating her new colonies fully into a protectionist system, though in 1913 55 per cent of the French Empire's trade was with the home country. Unable to break the already established economic links of these areas to other regions and metropoles, France had to buy a large share of her needs in colonial products – rubber, skins and leather, tropical timber – via Hamburg, Antwerp and Liverpool.

26 Which, after 1918, divided the former German colonies between them.

27 'Ah,' one such patroness is supposed to have exclaimed, 'if Bapuji only knew what it costs to keep him in poverty!'

28 M. K. Gandhi, *Collected Works*, I: 1884–96 (New Delhi 1958).

29 For the unusually successful, for a while, incursion of Buddhism into western milieux, see Jan Romein, *The Watershed of Two Eras* (Middletown, Conn. 1978), pp. 501–3, and the export of Indian holy men abroad, largely via champions drawn from among Theosophists. Among them Vivekananda (1863–1902) of 'Vedanta' can claim to be the first of the commercial gurus of the modern West.

30 R. H. Gretton, *A Modern History of the English People*, II: 1899–1910 (London 1913), p. 25.

31 W. L. Langer, *The Diplomacy of Imperialism, 1890–1902* (New York 1968 edn), pp. 387 and 448. More generally, H. Gollwitzer, *Die gelbe Gefahr: Geschichte eines Schlagworts: Studien zum imperialistischen Denken* (Göttingen 1962).

32 Rudyard Kipling, 'Recessional' in *R. Kipling's Verse, Inclusive Edition 1885–1918* (London n.d.), p. 377.

33 Hobson, *op. cit* (1938 edn), p. 314.

34 See H. G. Wells, *The Time Machine* (London 1895).

35 H. G. v. Schulze-Gaevernitz, *Britischer Imperialismus und englischer Freihandel zu Beginn des 20. Fahrhunderts* (Leipzig 1906).

SECTION 6: MARKETS: GOOD SERVANTS, BAD MASTERS?

INTRODUCTION

This final section is about how societies can try to harness and govern markets so that they serve the needs of society rather than society having to serve every dictate of the market.

Chapter 12, *The diversity of capitalisms* by Hutton discusses the different forms of capitalism by comparing and contrasting three of its variants, namely Anglo-American, Rhineland and Japanese capitalisms. All successful market economies need to create economic, political and social institutions that enable economic agents to combine gains derived from co-operation with gains derived from competition. Moreover, to be fully effective, these institutions as well as societal norms, values and culture need to work together in a complementary fashion, as part of an interdependent 'system'. There is no one or unique way in which this can be achieved. Consequently, in endeavouring to cope with the fundamental competition—co-operation dilemma, societies have evolved distinctive institutional systems, each system possessing its specific mix of strengths and weaknesses. Hutton details some of the distinctive features of the Anglo-American, Rhineland and Japanese capitalisms, which he characterises respectively as the 'individualistic', 'social market' and 'peoplism' capitalisms, and discusses what he thinks are major strengths and drawbacks of each system. One may consider Hutton as being unduly pessimistic and critical about British capitalism, but perhaps that's not so surprising given that Hutton is British!

Chapter 13, *Capitalism and global free markets* by Gray explores whether the liberalisation in world markets in commodities and capital threatens to eliminate the diversity in world capitalist systems. He argues that unregulated global markets in commodities and capital enable business to escape the social costs of its operations. Consequently, businesses operating in economies that oblige them to discharge their social responsibilities cannot compete with businesses that operate in economies where no such pressure exists, unless there is a downward harmonisation of regulatory standards throughout the world. Gray reasons that the 'free' global market weakens the bargaining position of labour vis-à-vis capital and consequently leads to greater income inequality both within developed economies and between the developed and developing world.

Chapter 14, *Why did East Asia grow so fast?* by Singh examines two central policy issues facing all developing nations: what is the optimum degree and kind of openness to the world economy a developing country should seek and what role should the state play in promoting economic development. The World Bank and the IMF claim that the best path for developing countries is to seek close integration with the world economy and to limit the role of the state in their economies. Singh disagrees on both counts. In addition to theoretical arguments, he presents empirical evidence to support his case, pertaining to the highly successful development experience of Japan and South Korea. If Singh is right, then the policies that the World Bank and the IMF recommend to the developing world (and which they frequently impose on them as preconditions for granting debt-relief or developmental assistance) need considerable revision.

12

THE DIVERSITY OF CAPITALISMS*

Will Hutton

After 1945 American capitalism was the envy of the world. In five years the US had transformed itself into a war economy and had outproduced the Soviet Union, Germany, Japan and Britain combined – and not just in planes and tanks, for it increased production across a range of civilian industries too. Its productivity was legendary, its industrial riches apparently beyond peer; its technological lead seemed unassailable.

Yet since the 1950s the US's position has been challenged in two successive waves of industrialisation. First there was the rise of European capitalism; and then Japan, steadily growing throughout this period, became the forerunner of the remarkable rise of East Asian capitalism. The US, which accounted for some half of world manufacturing output in 1945, now accounts for only a fifth. But despite the doom-laden predictions of its decline theorists, the US is not regressing absolutely – its average productivity across the whole of its economy still remains higher than Japan's. In a range of high technology industries it retains and is even increasing its world market share; by any standards it remains a formidable capitalist power.

European, American and Japanese capitalism each have distinctive characteristics. They are all, of course, based on private property and the legal right to make private profits by production and exchange in markets; and they all possess stock markets, income tax and social security systems that make them seem part of the same generic type of society. These features have persuaded some to argue that Western capitalism is converging towards an Anglo-American norm – but that is gravely to misread the depth of the institutional and cultural differences between capitalisms.

For the similarities disguise vast differences between the social and economic purpose of apparently similar institutions, so that each capitalist structure ends up with very different specific capacities and cultures which are very hard to change. But what all do have – even, paradoxically, the US – are strong institutions that allow their firms to enjoy some of the gains from co-operation as well as from competition, and these institutions are created and legitimised by some broad notion of public or national purpose.

The industrial strength of the world's great powers originated not because they followed the injunctions of purist free market economists, but because they succeeded in combining vigorous rivalry between entrepreneurs with a measure of co-operation. When their systems are seen as a whole it is the interlocking of the political, economic and social that is striking, and the varying ways in which they intersect is the key to the puzzle of their societies. The British tragedy is that its system locks together to form the least fecund of all capitalist models – as the following survey of capitalisms will show.

THE US MODEL

American capitalism is commonly regarded as the most individualistic and libertarian of all. Its financial system is highly market based; the returns it requires are very high; and it is therefore important that US corporations can hire and fire their workforces freely to produce the profits their shareholders demand. Unions are weak, employment regulation is minimal and the turnover of workers is high as companies trim their staff to market demands. One worker in five expects to lose his or her job within the next year, according to a 1993 survey, and another 20 per cent expected a spell of temporary unemployment.[1]

There is little spending on social welfare and levels of corporate and personal taxation are low. Welfare entitlements are tightly monitored and means-tested; social security contributions are at the lower end of the international scale. However the US has proved an effective generator of jobs – although by European standards they are astonishingly poorly-paid, with the bottom tenth of the workforce earning 38 per cent of median earnings (compared with the European average of 67 per cent of median earnings).[2] Workers are assumed to be willing to move home in order to work, and to accept low wages with social security acting only as a safety-net of last resort. Unemployment insurance lasts for a mere six months and replaces only 36 per cent of average earnings.

There are few co-operative industrial combines along Japanese and East Asian lines. There is tough anti-monopoly legislation, and the typical firm is owned by stock-holders, a majority of them financial institutions like pension funds, who trade their shares on the stock market while the company operates in a highly competitive arena for its sales. All companies can expect to be taken over or merged when predatory companies buy their shares on the stock market, and this puts a high premium on maintaining the growth of short-term profits and dividend pay-outs to sustain the share price at all costs. Firms' relations with their suppliers are strictly market-driven, with contracts put out to tender and allocated to the lowest bidder. There is little or no public ownership; whatever social objectives are deemed essential are prosecuted through federal and state regulatory authorities. The system is outwardly almost purely capitalist, its apologists celebrating its job-creating and innovative qualities and critics inveighing against its promotion of consumption over longterm investment, its systemic inequality and lack of social provision.

The US has, in fact, retained important institutional shelters against the full blast of competition and these have become ways of expressing co-operative common purpose. At the federal level many of these institutions were inaugurated during President Roosevelt's New Deal which, along with a security safety net and creative make-work programmes, put in place a system of financial regulation, innovative government financial institutions and a system of deposit insurance that has helped mitigate the worst proclivities of the US financial system to this day. The Reconstruction Finance Corporation, the long term investment credit bank whose role was revolutionised by Roosevelt, played an important role in financing the US war effort before being abolished in the 1950s. The range of state-run bodies created to manage the system of housing finance managed to survive into the 1990s, and these have consistently supported housing construction and home ownership. The separation of banking and the securities business by the Glass-Steagall Act forced banks, especially at state level, to become less market-based and so develop longterm relationships with their customers.

Indeed the existence of powerful state banks, entrenched under the New Deal legislation, has been one of the most important buffers between medium-sized companies and the full blast of the US financial system. Texas, California, Pennsylvania, Connecticut, Chicago, Detroit, Minneapolis and Seattle are all important centres of finance and industrial headquarters around which clusters of small and medium-sized firms have formed.[3] Individual states have been able, if they choose, to use procurement policy and subsidies to develop local industries, together with supportive local banks interested in longterm investment. North Carolina, for example, was one of the US pioneers in linking university research, soft loans and new technology in its famous high-tech 'triangle'.

At Federal level a variety of initiatives gives another layer of support to these efforts. Federal spending on research and development, especially on defence, is an important source of funding for high technology industry. Spin-offs from the space programme were crucial in encouraging the US electronics industry's capacity to make miniaturised components. The military-industrial complex built during the Cold War and sustained by the Pentagon was a kind of national industrial policy, using its enormous purchasing power in the late 1980s, for example, to support the US semiconductor industry.[4] The Buy America Act ensures that public procurement is focused on US suppliers, while the US has not been afraid to use trade measures openly to support its own industrial interests. The 'Super 301' trade legislation empowers the US government to take unilateral retaliatory action against countries it considers to be either unfairly blocking imports from the US or subsidising exports.

The best US universities remain world-beating centres of excellence, and skill levels for middle management and craft workers are supplied by a dense network of higher educational establishments. However, public education for the masses remains weak, made even worse because many poor US families are desperately deprived, in a market society that has gone even further than the British. Many children are reared badly and are incapable of learning without considerably more resources than the public authorities are prepared to offer. While skill levels in the middle and upper parts of the labour force are high, US society is crippled by growing numbers of barely literate and numerate workers.

In partial compensation there is a strong culture of participation and engagement and a willingness to use the full array of public institutions to provoke common responses – and this spills over into the private domain. Pension funds, for example, have been obliged to intervene constructively in company affairs, under the pressure of members insisting that their ownership be exercised positively. Individual states have used the provisions of the 1977 Community Reinvestment Act to insist that banks support community developments and minimum wage legislation is a feature of many states.[5]

The democracy of the public realm becomes in this way the yardstick for private action as well. A network of intermediate public institutions at state level intercedes between the individual, the firm and the market. The dominant factor of production in the US remains private capital in a highly market-oriented financial system, and there is little doubt that its search for ever higher financial returns and its short-termism has been an important reason for the hollowing-out of US industry. But with a strong tradition of public citizenship and system of decentralised government there are ways of constraining and regulating the market, and even on occasion turning it to economic and social advantage. Stock market imperatives may loom too large in the strategies of US companies, but by the same token there are demanding standards for transparency and provision of information to share-holders and the wider public – demands that are modelled on the injunctions of the US constitution. Although the value system formally celebrates individual rights, competition and the primacy of markets, there is also a powerful impulse towards charity and solidarity in US culture, signalling the co-existence of a more altruistic co-operative tradition. As De

Tocqueville put it, 'The Anglo-Americans acknowledge the moral authority of the reason of the community as they acknowledge the political authority of the mass of citizens.'[6]

The US may be the home of pristine capitalism but it is qualified by a vigorous public and private morality. This is the home of the most aggressive venture capital industry on earth; but also of the largest private charitable foundations. Bill Gates, chairman of computer giant, Microsoft, followed Ford, Rockefeller and others in giving up almost all of his fortune to a private foundation. The Protestant ethic, although weakening, remains an important underpinning of the US value system and a source of co-operative economic strength.

SOCIAL MARKET EUROPE

The second distinctive species of capitalism is that of Germany, its neighbours in the European Union and of Scandinavia. This is broadly the world of the social market, and once again the political, economic and social institutions hang together to form an interdependent web. Capital and labour operate in partnership; the financial system is less market-based than in the US and thus more committed to the enterprises it finances; the welfare structure is more all-encompassing and inclusive and the political system has a high degree of formal power sharing. Yet this social web still vibrates to the signals sent by the price mechanism; it may be regulated, but it conforms to market imperatives. It is a social *market*.

The great benefit of the system is that its institutional structures favour co-operation, high productivity and investment. The disadvantage is that when the external environment becomes more uncertain, the system finds restructuring more difficult because the centres of power are more diffuse and the bureaucratic regulatory network can slow down firms' responses. None the less restructuring is achievable eventually. In the recent German recession Volkswagen was able to negotiate wage cuts and reduce working hours in agreement with its unions, and Daimler Benz slashed its labour costs by over DM1.5 billion within a year.[7]

At the heart of the European model is the notion of a rule-governed, competitive marker whose power to generate wealth is intimately linked with social cohesion. The partnership between capital and labour embodied in *mitbestimmung* (or co-decision making) at both board and works council level in Germany represents a bargain between manager and unions. Unions forego the right to strike and to pursue their self-interest regardless of the firm's plight; but management eschews the right to run the business autocratically in favour of the shareholders' narrow interests. Instead there is a compromise in favour of concerted and co-operative behaviour aimed at boosting production and investment.

Labour has to recognise the legitimacy of capital; and capital the rights of labour. Seventy-five per cent of German workers are covered by union-negotiated industry-wide wage agreements – which is a major concession by management; on the other hand the agreements are legally binding and a strike can only be called once the contract has expired – a major concession by labour. If the big unions represent a majority of workers, so the employers' organisations represent most of German industry. Both capital and labour are represented by all-encompassing self-governing organisations which are allowed to manage wages and industrial relations. As a result labour turnover rates are lower than in the US and wages considerably higher.

This collaboration is interdependent with the rest of the economic, social and political system. In order for managers and workers to run enterprises collaboratively, financial stakeholders have to concede that they cannot maximise their returns in the short run. Thus the pivot on which the German system turns, as Michel Albert argues, is the patience of the banks – 'the principal guardians of Rhine–Alpine capitalism'. The Frankfurt, Zurich,

Stockholm, Vienna and Amsterdam stock exchanges are modest in size compared with those in London and New York; it is not in the stock market that companies are valued and raise money but through their respective banking systems. Contested takeovers organised through the Stock Exchange, so common in the US and Britain, are almost unknown in Germany, Switzerland and Holland.

The German banks are uniquely powerful, holding shares themselves and on behalf of others in the major German companies, making longterm loans, acting as information clearing houses and assessing industrial and commercial prospects in partnership with their borrowers. They are the stable backers of German industry and loyal longterm shareholders. They know the companies they finance, sit on their boards and can more accurately assess their risks. The system is orderly because its financial components give it the time and space it needs – and the situation is very similar in Austria, Switzerland and Holland.

This stability of ownership and financial support is matched by a welfare system – the *sozialstaat* – which offers a high degree of social protection, the visible expression of social solidarity. Pensions and unemployment benefit are high in relation to average earnings, and the universal health and education systems underwrite Germany's famous sense of social well-being. Education and training are enmeshed, and the 'dual vocational system' combines academic education with workplace experience, providing Germany with among the highest numbers of trained apprentices per head of population in the world. School leavers are educated to a high standard. Over 70 per cent of German employees are technically qualified compared with 30 per cent in the UK[8] and the status of the *handwerke* (craftsman) and *meister* (craftmaster) is deeply etched into German culture.

One of the inevitable consequences of the system is high social overheads for both employers and employees. Health, pension, and unemployment insurance together with taxation make up one of the highest tax burdens in the industrialised world; but, as Wolfgang Streeck argues, the 'social production' of skilled workers, powerful unions and the strong welfare system help to raise the general strength of the economy. The welfare structure, for example, is designed so that firms can hang on to workers during a recession with part of their wages paid by social insurance, keeping their workforces intact, while the constant supply of skilled workers has made German productivity levels the highest in Europe. Powerful unions have been important agents in restructuring German industry, using their dominant position in works councils and their role on supervisory boards to legitimise often painful programmes of job cuts and wage reductions.[9]

The partnership and solidarity of Rhine–Alpine social market institutions has not been built in a political vacuum. It is supported by a particular kind of state. Regional government is strong and culturally entrenched, with a strong tradition of autonomy and a vigorous regional media. Voting is by proportional representation, and the state is seen as part of civil society, rather than ruling from above it. Unlike the British system, where the state is coterminous with whichever party controls the government, the social market state represents a common or public interest in which parties are expected to share power; and this fosters the network of independent government agencies of which the most famous is the German central bank, the Bundesbank.

Many public agencies, even the state television networks, incorporate a similar conception of their responsibility. They are social partners as much as organs of the state; their constitutions allow them to govern themselves but within a mandate set by the state, which by obliging each institution to consider wider interests allows it to become a forum for building consensus within its own particular area of competence. The governing council of the Bundesbank, for example, consists of the presidents of the regional state banks, who are in turn appointed by regional governments. They reflect the broad range of political opinion within the country, allowing a consensus to develop over the direction and execution of German monetary policy.

As the great social market theorist Alfred Muller-Armack argued, a free market order is not a state of nature; it must be produced and regulated. Governance works best when it is as close to its area of competence as possible; hence the case for decentralisation and for independent public agencies like a central bank, or a regulator of competition. It is not only that price stability, a market that respects local custom and practice and real competition are central to an effective market-place; the markets' institutions earn legitimacy by being 'owned' by the wider citizenry, who trust that the fruits of prosperity will be shared fairly.

Wider economic policy is the outcome of negotiation between the various social partners – what is known as concerted action. The government proposes, unions and employers' organisations negotiate, while the Bundesbank acts as a guarantor of price stability – but it is also mindful, as a social partner in its own right, of larger economic and social objectives. The regional governments or opposition parties are not excluded; their participation is assured by their formal membership of the upper house of the parliament (*Bundesrat*) which they may succeed in controlling even if they do not hold a majority in the *Bundestag*. The German Chancellor is thus the conductor of a political concert, relying on power, persuasion and the force of argument to move policy in the direction he wants. To critics used to states where political authority is more clearly delineated, as in Britain, the system seems a glutinous corporatist mess; to its devotees it is a highly effective means of achieving consensus and cohesion.

The usefulness of Germany's system of decentralised power is revealed in the strength of the famous *Mittelstand* – the medium-sized business sector that is proportionally nearly twice the size of its counterpart in Britain. These family-owned companies are the backbone of German industry, but they owe their strength as much to the institutional support around them as to the dynamism of their flexible and innovative owners. At one level they are the quintessential independent capitalist owner-managers – relying on their wit, ingenuity and entrepreneurial light-footedness to win the Darwinian struggle in markets; at another they are the beneficiaries of Germany's unique institutional structure.

They enjoy longterm, committed finance from the regional state banks. They can fish from a stream of skilled workers. As smaller sub-contractors they can build their business around reliable contracts from larger firms who understand the gains from co-operative, longterm relationships – and are themselves financially secure enough to offer such relationships. They can group together in cities and towns in clusters and so reinforce their position, allowing them to share information, because German cities and regions have the autonomy to tailor an industrial policy to suit their companies' particular needs. The independent scientific research and technology institutions, like the Steinbeis Foundation or Fraunhofer Institutes for example, have a strong regional bias and regional governments have the financial power to support them by channelling technology and ideas to the *Mittelstand*. In short, the social and political system is itself a major source of competitive advantage, allowing Germany to develop comparative economic strength. The tariff walls of Friedrich List, father of German protectionism, may no longer exist but Germany's network of institutions offers a modernised form of shelter from unfettered market forces.

Under the pressure of globalisation and intense cost competition the *Mittelstand* has begun to lose ground, and there are fears that large German firms are being compelled to get their supplies in low-cost countries while overseas producers – notably the Japanese – are winning business in the *Mittelstand*'s heartland. German banks, under the same pressures, are allegedly becoming more short-term in their time horizons. Even more threatening is the rise of so-called lean production in which large firms, determined to emulate the Japanese and contain costs by sub-contracting out work and insisting on 'just-in-time' delivery to cut inventories, are asking suppliers to be ever more flexible. This requires heavy new investment even as prices are being pared to the bone, and many companies lack the financial muscle to adopt a more hard-nosed relationship with major buyers. Yet in front of these challenges the German instinct is not to abandon but to update and renew its institutional network – intensifying its training effort, improving systems of technology transfer and developing new networks to share market information. Above all the banks intend to stand by their industrial companies.

Underpinning the notion of the social market is a complex value system that emphasises both the values of order and solidarity. From the Prussian tradition comes a sense of the need for discipline and for a regulated order in human affairs; from Catholicism the tradition of social solidarity and 'subsidiarity' – the location of decision making as close as possible to those who are affected by it. These twin streams in German thinking unite with a third: an accent on the real values of production over those of finance. The rentier tradition is extremely weak in Germany – this is a country which industrialised late and had to marshal its financial resources consciously to achieve it. The country could not afford a large class of rentiers living off unearned income, and company law has never given priority to shareholders' financial interests over those of other stakeholders.

There are inflexibilities in the social market, and the relationship between finance and industry can become incestuous and open to corruption – while strong trade unions don't always behave rationally. In the move to 'lean production' many unions are resolutely opposed to contracting work outside the large firms. The *sozialstaat* is also expensive. Yet in the main the social market's success is testimony to its virtues, and the *schadenfreude* expressed in the Anglo-Saxon world over its difficulties during German reunification is undoubtedly premature.

The social market is a self-conscious way for a capitalist economy to blend the gains from competition with those from co-operation – and the new world of 'lean production', where so much depends on the collaboration between firms and their sub-contractors, will emphasise its strengths. Far from capitulating to the British and American style of capitalism, the social market economy is in the throes of adapting to changed conditions in a unique way. France has set out to copy its main strengths, and Eastern Europe and even the former Soviet Union are looking to this model as their disillusion with the Anglo-Saxon variant grows. It has not failed; the question is how far it can succeed in the new environment.

EAST ASIAN CAPITALISM – 'PEOPLISM'

The third distinctive form of world capitalism, and currently the most dynamic, is that of Japan, the East Asian tigers and the emergent Chinese genre. Although again there are variants within this wider culture, there is enough common ground to attempt a descriptive synthesis under a common label. Here the attempt to capture the gains from co-operation in a competitive environment has been taken to its most extreme. East Asian and particularly Japanese capitalist structures emphasise trust, continuity, reputation and co-operation in economic relationships. Competition is ferocious, but co-operation is extensive; the juxtaposition of apparently inconsistent forms of behaviour may strike those schooled in Anglo-American capitalism as irrational, but for the Japanese the tension actually enhances the strength of each. There is even a widely quoted phrase for it – *kyoryoku shi nagara kyosa* – literally 'co-operating while competing', so that out of the subsequent chaos comes harmony.[10]

As a result human relations and the necessity of nurturing them are centre stage; the dominant factor of production is labour, so that one Japanese analyst has been moved to call the system 'peoplism'.[11] This is probably overstating the humanity of an economy which demands long hours and often demeaning working conditions,[12] but it none the less captures the important stress on personal networks and human relationships. Contracts are even less price mediated than in the European social market economy; wealth creation and productivity are seen to come from co-operative longterm relationships for which the

Japanese are justly famous, and which Alan Blinder calls a 'relational market'. With Japan and East Asia growing explosively, its institutional structure and value system commands increasing respect and even fear; for example, if Japan maintains its current rates of investment as a proportion of national output, nearly a third as high again as the US, then it will be the largest economy in the world by 2005 while East Asia as a whole will become the dominant force in world output and trade by the first decade of the next century.

Given Japan's track record it is unsurprising that the Japanese model has been extensively copied. Its regulated financial system is the least market-based, most traditional, above all most committed to its customers, of all the three principal capitalist variants. Firms' shares are held tightly in a system of cross-holdings with sister firms in other industry groups, the *kigyo shudan* and *keiretsu*, and the required returns are low. Secure financial backing has allowed Japanese firms to cultivate an extraordinary series of innovations in working practices with both shop floor workers and suppliers – and these efficiencies have placed the economy firmly in a virtuous circle in which growth, investment, financial commitment, worker/supplier productivity and continual quality upgrading become mutually reinforcing.

The firm is the core social unit of which individuals are *members* rather than simply workers. Unions are organised around the firm, which promises life-time employment, social protection and a pension, and the firm expects commitment in return. Taxation is at the lower end of the international scale, but so is income inequality; senior managers earn a mere two or three times the average wage. The culture is firmly production-oriented, rooted in Japan's anxiety to catch up with the West which was intensified by the trauma of losing the Second World War.

The state is the architect of these institutional relationships; it seeks to build consensus and then guides firms and the financial system in the direction established by the consensus. In this respect it is nearer to the German social market state, and British notions of parliamentary sovereignty and top-down governance are strikingly at odds with the Japanese conception of government by consent. The boundaries between government, society and economy are remarkably porous, and there is great emphasis on inclusiveness, on respect for various points of view and on the achievement of harmony, while at the same time ensuring that business objectives are at the heart of Japan plc's concerns. On the other hand it means that the country has no hard centre, and fraud and corruption are widespread. Responsibility is diffuse and accountability low.

None the less the leadership – or, as the Japanese would put it, the consensus building – provided after the war by MITI, the Ministry of International Trade and Industry, is justly famous. Even though it now plays a less overtly interventionist role than it did in the 1950s and 1960s it remains a formidable source of 'guidance', leading industrial restructuring and co-ordinating private firms' strategies. The build up of the Japanese ship-building and steel industry, the managed decline of the coal industry and the rise of cars, consumer electronics and information technology are all tributes to MITI's key role. It may no longer be so overtly *dirigiste*, but it remains the ultimate custodian of Japanese industrial and commercial interests.

The system, as with the US and German social market models, locks together as a whole. Without committed finance there can be no parallel commitment to suppliers and workers; but the productivity gains from such commitment justify the financial commitment and vice versa. So while the institutional structure respects the priority of human relations, it incorporates as Masahiko Aoki has brilliantly argued, incentives for economically rational behaviour even though they are not mediated by price signals. Competition, in a sense, is confined to the market where goods and services are offered to the final consumer but in all the intervening stages of production there is an accent on nurturing longterm relationships and capturing the gains from co-operation that game theory and New Keynesian economics promise.

There are four overlapping series of relationships – with finance, employees and subcontractors and, of course, with government. The role of Sumitomo Bank in rescuing Toyo Kogyo has been described already, and this exemplifies the relationship between finance and business. Shares, which in the Anglo-Saxon tradition are titles to a claim on the company's profits in the form of dividends and which are expected to be bought and sold on the stock market, are in Japan tokens of a longterm commitment. The *kigyo shudan* are industrial groups that use shares to cement these relationships. Mitsubishi, Mitsui, Sumitomo, Fuyo, Sanwa, and Daiichi Kanyo Bank are each City banks which, along with a trust bank, life insurance company and trading company, sit at the centre of a constellation of cross-shareholdings. Forty per cent of the equity on the Tokyo stock exchange is held by *kigyo shudan* members. The banks act as presidents of each group, channelling longterm loans, chairing negotiations over joint ventures and generally sharing information and business advice. In cases of financial distress, as with Sumitomo and Toyo Kogyo, they organise the restructuring. Their role is similar to the German banks, but more formally embedded in their clients' business.

The group companies, because of the dense network of cross-shareholdings, in effect own each other and are impregnable to takeover – but the task of monitoring and improving company performance, which [role] takeovers purport to play in the US and British system, is in Japan performed by internal and group pressures. Other features of the Anglo-Saxon system like executive share options are banned while in the event of bankruptcy the banks rank after the employees and subcontractors in having a claim on the company's assets.

Yet, as Aoki shows, the incentives built in to the system lead to rational outcomes. If banks have no prior claim on company assets in the event of bankruptcy then they have a double incentive to ensure that bankruptcy does not happen, which encourages them to establish institutional networks that permit effective monitoring of loans. More to the point, the system allows them to finesse the Keynesian conundrum that the interest rate cannot co-ordinate the demand for financial capital with the supply, so that the higher the interest rate the riskier the project. Intimate access to information means that there is less credit rationing and as Takeo Hoshi[13] shows, the supply of external credit to Japanese companies is made on more favourable terms than to firms outside the industrial groups. Indeed, Japanese banks will lend up to four times more in relation to a firm's assets than British banks. The respective fortunes of the two country's car and consumer electronics industries are a stark illustration of the competitive advantage that such abundant working capital and stability of ownership give to the Japanese.

The role of shares as tokens of relationship also extends into production and to the tiers of sub-contractors who, by allowing great flexibility of production, have allowed the Japanese economy to pioneer the new techniques of lean production. While US manufacturers effectively auction their sub-contract work, Japanese industrialists enmesh themselves in a network of cross-shareholdings with their sub-contractors. These non-financial *kieretsu* cross-shareholdings make up another 30 per cent of the Tokyo stock exchange, complementing the 40 per cent held by the *kigyo shudan*, indicating just how large the 'relational market' in Japan has become.

The cost gains from flexibility and minimal inventory are huge, but so are the co-ordination and design problems. Parts have to be made to pin-point accuracy and production modified with every change in demand, and once a manufacturer has taken a sub-contractor into his confidence over specifications the sub-contractor has every incentive to exploit the privilege by maximising profits because he has his buyer over a barrel. The advantage of the cross-shareholding is that it signifies that the relationship will continue over time and so gives the main contractor a way of responding to any blackmail. He can sell his shares and so tell the wider marketplace that the relationship is not working well – a damning indictment in an economy where such store is set by longterm relationships. But the shareholding commitment also gives the sub-contractor confidence in the continuity of business, and allows him to tie up large amounts of capital in meeting just one customer's requirements – which would otherwise be highly risky.

The other apparent irrationalities in the Japanese-based system turn out to have equal economic value. Lifetime employment and job security means there is little of the labour mobility valued by free market economists, while the compression of pay differentials would seem to offer little in the way of 'incentives' to Japanese workers. Nor are trade unions in thrall to company managements likely to be very effective fighters for individual workers' interests. Yet job security forces employers to develop different kinds of incentive which ultimately prove to be highly economically rational. The counterpart of lifetime employment and low pay differentials is a complex managerial hierarchy that rewards people instead with complex gradations of status, while security of tenure makes middle and lower management less threatened about delegating decision-making downwards. To solve the problem that lifetime workers may be shirkers or prove otherwise inadequate, Japanese firms take great care over recruitment, often talking to schools about the personality, intelligence and general demeanour of specific recruits long before they need to hire. As a result, parents and schools form an alliance to raise educational standards to the highest level to meet the companies' exacting requirements – and high levels of intellectual skills, even on the shop-floor, are the basis of the problem-solving teams that are the key to Japan's famously high levels of productivity.

Lifetime employment also carries a message about those who are unemployed; to lose your job implies that the original firm was in some way unhappy with you as a worker, that you are a 'lemon': an undesirable worker. Workers are under pressure not to lose their jobs, which means that their income in the long run will depend on the welfare of the firm which they will not want to leave. Hence the willingness to co-operate in teams to improve productivity, rather than piggy-backing on others' efforts. The same applies at the top end of the scale: chief executives will have peers who have been in the firm as long as they have so, as Ronald Dore argues, they will be aware of the general opinion that two or three of their contemporaries 'could have done the job just or almost just as well. This knowledge, on the part of CEOs, acts as a useful curb on both greed and megalomania.'

The firm has become the core social unit in Japanese society. It trains and retrains its workers. It offers them a measure of social security. It is the adaptive and creative organisation which constructs networks of finance, teams of workers, and relationships with subcontracting firms that are at the heart of the Japanese system. Paramount above all else is the desire continually to upgrade; Japanese firms could incorporate W. Edward Deming's ideas more easily than their American counterparts because they were in an institutional framework and a cultural value system that allowed them to.

This private institutional network is backed by a public infrastructure that supports economic growth and domestic industry. As in Germany, there is a system of devolved regional government with enough autonomy to draw up industrial policies to meet local needs. Technology transfer happens through the *kohsetsushi*, local centres for the testing of new innovations, similar to the technology transfer network in Germany. And at the level of central government there is the complex system of planning, state funded R&D and investment guidance led by MITI. Telecommunications, transport and construction are all sectors where innovation has been aided and abetted by government action.

Yet this highly innovative, competitive, production machine is an extremely difficult trading partner. With so much internal trade taking place between the *kigyo shudan* and *keiretsu* members as the consequence of protecting rational longterm relationships, it is difficult for foreigners to penetrate Japanese markets even when they have saleable products. They are not part of the relationship network. Japanese companies, pricing their products incrementally off an already low cost base (given the low cost of Japanese capital) are formidable exporters. Consequently there is an inbuilt asymmetry in Japanese trade relations with the entire industrialised West.

The same is true of the emerging East Asian capitalist states, who have all constructed their styles of capitalism around what Ronald Dore calls 'community' firms on the Japanese model. Chinese companies are family-run networks based on ownership by kinsmen as much as on shareholdings across companies, while the South Korean *chaebol* incorporates within one organisation a vast cluster of related enterprises that are given overt state support by the South Korean government and state banks. Similar variants can be seen in Thailand, Taiwan, Indonesia, Singapore, and Malaysia and although Hong Kong is often regarded by neoclassical economists as the paradigm of free market, price-mediated, unallayed capitalism, its successful Chinese companies are based on the same relationship nexus as those in Japan. As James Abbeglen argues, these corporate structures interact with high savings rates and huge state investment in education, and have produced the most dynamic period of capitalist growth in history. There is a real sea change occurring in the world economic system.

In some respects the Asians have been lucky. Confucian conceptions of social harmony have allowed them to build up co-operative firms and networks that are congruent with these deeply held values, while in Japan veneration for age and the wisdom of the elderly can give the young a core of discipline and respect for others around which longterm relationships are easily constructed. Japan is also a profoundly ordered society in which it is understood as a legacy of its feudal past that reputation and the saving of face are important for everybody – another important element in sustaining trust over time.

The astonishing paradox is that Japan did not always have this kind of economic and social structure which we think of as quintessentially Japanese. Between the wars the financial system was more like the Anglo-Saxon model. Companies had large numbers of share-holders, and boards of directors were obsequious to their needs, distributing dividends with an eagerness that would satisfy any British unit trust. As Tetsuji Okazaki[14] demonstrates, the *zaibutsu* combines (parents of today's *kigyo shudan* and *keiretsu*) were comparatively unimportant, representing only ten of the top sixty manufacturing and mining companies. In the non-*zaibutsu* firms quoted on the stock market, R&D and investment took second place to immediate profits, while a multiplicity of banks offered commercial credits and short-term loans, refusing to offer more longterm loans to their borrowers. Senior management insisted on bonus and share option schemes as incentives to further effort, and a 'flexible' labour market was operated in which firms hired and fired workers as demand conditions fluctuated – the lifetime employment system was then very much less important. It all sounds very familiar to anyone who knows Britain and the US today.

But this style of economy failed the Japanese completely. There was widespread despair at the 'degeneration of firm management' and the 'high-handedness and short-sighted selfishness of large stockholders'.[15] In the run-up to the Second World War the government moved to a 'New Economic System' which recast the financial and labour system along broadly contemporary lines. Stockholders' rights were limited, dividends curtailed and firms were to become 'an organic organisation whereby employers and employees are bound together in their respective functions.' Workers' committees were charged with boosting production and the banking system was required to make investment loans, 'not on the certainty of repayment, but on the contribution the project could make to the national purpose'. Responsibility for allocating government and private funds to particular industries was given to specified financial institutions – foreshadowing the role played today by the *kigyo shudan*.

The changes were controversial and widely resisted. There were loud complaints from employers that the initiatives were quasi-socialist. One group opposing the changes cited the British Whiteley Committee as an authority, which rigorously distinguished between the rights of capital and obligations of labour to the firm.[16] There could be no watering down of capital's demands for returns, or advancing of workers' claims to share in management and the design of production processes. This was a corruption of capitalist economic law and would lead to perdition.

Yet the urgency of war and the desperate desire to catch up on the West allowed such complaints to be brushed aside. What mattered was effectiveness, and the contribution that the business sector could make to the war of conquest. After Japan's defeat the US was too distracted by opposing communist trade unions and Japanese socialism to follow through in its attempts to change the system, and the underlying institutional structure survived.

In other words, the constitution of the Japanese firm and its relationship with government, finance and workforce is not a 'natural' evolution. It has developed from a series of experiments about what works best, fired by an overwhelming sense that the country had to catch up – a determination only strengthened by losing the war. Britain, by contrast, was the first country to industrialise. It has never lost a war. The British élite has no sense it needs to catch up, that its system doesn't work and cannot recognise that what passes for timeless economic truth is no more than a particular economic ideology. Britain's chances of reproducing what is happening in East Asia seem negligible.

CAN RIVAL CAPITALISMS CO-OPERATE?

European and Japanese capitalism did not develop in a political and financial vacuum. They benefited from a benign world trade order in which there was open access to the world's largest market – the US – and where until the early 1970s, the US itself was economically powerful enough to anchor a world monetary order which was in essence an extension of its domestic financial system. The first two decades after the war launched the western industrialised countries on the biggest economic boom for a century. And while that growth subsided in Europe after 1973, Japan and East Asia exploited their unique internal advantages, the relative openness of the US market and the increasing volume of credit available on the global capital markets to continue their own industrial boom.

The US did not, of course, establish and manage this system out of altruism. Frightened by the international economic and financial chaos that led to the war, it did not want a repeat performance after the Second World War – and the beneficiary of the political and economic tensions that would arise from any post-war recession was all too obvious. The communist bloc, led by the Soviet Union, was in ideological and economic competition with the US. If liberal capitalism could not flourish in Europe and non-communist Asia, there was a danger that communism could spread from Eastern into Western Europe and from China, Vietnam and North Korea into the whole of Asia. North America might confront a Euro-Asian landmass dominated by communism; a formidable foe in any conflict, operating from a strong enough strategic base to bid for global domination. To prevent this nightmare it was worth making considerable financial and trading sacrifices.

The US was thus prepared to make the dollar the centre of the world's monetary system, and run a defence effort along the whole of the Euro-Asian littoral, and to accept that its market should be open to countries that were developing their economies. There needed to be a successful western and Japanese capitalist community strong enough to act as a bulwark against Stalin and Mao and prosperous enough to beat off the ideological attractions of communism.

So it was that the US played a crucial role in both European and East Asian economic growth. From the Marshall Plan, through to underwriting the Bretton Woods agreement, the US put in place the institutional architecture that allowed Europe to organise its reconstruction. The significance of the collapse of the Bretton Woods system of managed exchange rates in 1972 was that the dollar ceased being overvalued in relation to the German mark, and the imbalance in the strength of the European and US economies was suddenly exposed. Europe had come of age, and the US was no longer willing to accept the same unequal trade and financial relationship, regarding its defence commitment in Europe as enough of an economic burden.

The US and Europe still continued to stand by the rules of international trade as set out in the Gatt, cutting tariffs on manufactured goods and insisting that trade preferences to any one country should be extended to all. At the same time European states, under US pressure, began to liberalise their rules on exports and imports of capital. The foundations of a global capital market were being laid together with the rules that would permit companies to extend their production and distribution internationally, confident that they would be allowed to move goods freely between nation states.

While Europe and the US had come to an accommodation, with Europe accepting a depreciating and volatile dollar as the price for US defence, and which led to a boost in US export volumes and decline in European exports.[16] Japan and Asia were able to use the new open trading rules to their own advantage. Japanese exports grew by 16 per cent per year during the 1960s before settling back to more moderate but still high growth rates in the 1970s, but in the 1980s the East Asian tigers began to follow in Japan's footsteps. Between 1981–86, argues Lester Thurow,[17] 42 per cent of Korea's growth and 74 per cent of Taiwan's growth could be traced to exports to the US market – and in the 1990s China is reproducing the same pattern. While Japan's export growth between 1985–90 had settled down to some 2.7 per cent, China's exports grew at 18.3 per cent – with exports from Indonesia, the Philippines, Thailand, Malaysia, Taiwan, Hong Kong and Singapore all in double figures. South Korea's exports growth had slowed to a mere 8.9 per cent!

The trick has been to use the ultra-competitiveness of Asian capital in the North American and to a lesser extent the European market, which allows Asian firms to build up investment and production runs and launch their economies in to a virtuous circle of growth, balance of payments surpluses, hard currency earnings and low inflation. While the US was able to respond to this threat in the 1970s by allowing the dollar to depreciate against the European currencies and counteract the trends, the same downward movement of the dollar has much less impact in the 1990s. Asian capitalist structures are much more competitive than European ones, and can accommodate their costs more flexibly to changes in exchange rates.

As a result the US is once again running a trade deficit in excess of $100 billion after moving towards balance in the recession years of the early 1990s. Over the 1980s the US ran a cumulative current account deficit of $893 billion financed largely by Japanese and German inward investment in both factories and stocks and shares;[18] but in the 1990s Japan and Germany are proving more unwilling to provide such finance. Germany has to pay for reunification of its state, and is directing funds to Eastern Europe and the former Soviet Union, while Japanese financial institutions, which had to accept substantial losses on their dollar holdings, are less willing to invest in dollar assets. The international financial system is finding it difficult to accommodate the instabilities caused by the relative strength and weakness of the rival capitalisms.

The end of the Cold War frees the US from any obligation to anchor the world trading system by keeping its own markets open, while the flood of cheap imports from East Asia is bidding down the wages of its blue-collar workers. The US has already responded to Japanese exports by imposing quotas and restraints which now extend to 30 per cent of all Japanese exports, and it is plain that other East Asian exports will suffer the same restraints. The political pressure to arrest the decline in living standards of US blue-collar workers is extremely intense.

If the US could increase its exports to Japan and East Asia then there would be an improved chance of keeping both markets open, but as we have seen there is a fundamental asymmetry between them. East Asian 'community firms', embedded in their relationship networks, have an inbuilt protectionist bias and an aggressive attitude to overseas markets – and it is an uphill battle for American and European firms to gain reciprocal access on the same terms. There is no level playing field, and as a result trade tensions are likely to increase. The US is increasingly unable to finance its deficits; open up the vast Asian market; or control its capital outflows. Further US decline, and an ever weaker dollar, now seem unavoidable.

The optimistic view is that East Asia and Japan are maturing as industrial regions and will increasingly trade with each other and with Europe, taking the pressure off the US market. The pessimistic view is that their growth is unstoppable, and that their unbalanced trade relationship with the rest of the world cannot be changed. Regional blocks will form, with the US and Europe protecting themselves from the vigour of Asian capitalism. It is against this uncertain background that British options must be viewed – its structures must be radically overhauled in a world where the power balances are changing fundamentally.

BRITAIN

The contrast between British capitalism and its rivals is marked. The financial system demands the same high returns from companies, with the same lack of commitment, as in the US; but there is not even the saving grace of statutory regulation and strong regional or state banks to moderate the consequences of such pressure: centralisation in London means that the entire economy suffers.

The labour market has many of the worst features of the US – ranging from high turnover to inequality of income – but without the compensating virtues of mobility and managerial dynamism. Nor is there an institutional structure which would allow firms to develop the co-operative, community-based capitalism of Japan and East Asia; examples of such networks are rare and are the exceptions that prove the rule. Arms-length, price-mediated relationships extend all the way from the shop floor to the Stock Exchange. The British medium-sized business sector – the equivalent of the *Mittelstand* – is fragile and small in size.

The accompanying table sets our the principal features of the four capitalist systems. It is not exhaustive and merely attempts to isolate the key features of each variant. Each is an interdependent whole, in which the character of one set of institutions interacts with the others; each shapes and is in turn shaped by the whole system. In Britain, profit-maximising firms that give the building of market share a low priority have to be run autocratically in order to produce the kind of shareholder returns that the financial system demands – and that in turn has consequences for the way the labour market is run: the less committed the financial system, the less firms are able to offer lifetime employment and the less willing they are to undertake training.

Firms whose relations with their workers and suppliers are mediated solely by price have to have low social overheads in order to maintain their competitive position; as a result the welfare system in Britain and America is necessarily less ambitious than it is in social market Europe. The same unwillingness to see the firm as an organic enterprise involving all its stakeholders extends to their attributes to the wider society: British firms resent levies to pay for training, for example, both because they seem to make their operations less competitive and because they are an attempt to impose obligations they do not feel they have. In this kind of market economy everybody looks after themselves.

None the less Britain does have the legacy of the social settlement of 1945. While welfare falls below mainland European levels it is still significantly more universal in scope and generous than in the US. The result is that the country once again gets the worst of both worlds; it has neither low enough taxes nor strong enough institutions of social solidarity and so falls between the American and European stools. The introduction of market

Table 12.1 A comparison of four systems

Characteristic	American capitalism	Japanese capitalism	European social market	British capitalism
Basic principle				
Dominant factor of production	capital	labour	partnership	capital
'Public' tradition	medium	high	high	low
Centralisation	low	medium	medium	high
Reliance on price-mediated markets	high	low	medium	high
Supply relations	arms-length price-driven	close enduring	bureaucracy planned	arms-length price-driven
Industrial groups	partial, defence, etc.	very high	high	low
Extent privatised	high	high	medium	high
Financial system				
Market structure	anonymous securitised	personal committed	bureaucracy committed	uncommitted marketised
Banking system	advanced marketised regional	traditional regulated concentrated	traditional regulated regional	advanced marketised centralised
Stock market	v. important	unimportant	unimportant	v. important
Required returns	high	low	medium	high
Labour market				
Job security	low	high	high	low
Labour mobility	high	low	medium	medium
Labour/ management	adversarial	cooperative	cooperative	adversarial
Pay differential	large	small	medium	large
Turnover	high	low	medium	medium
Skills	medium	high	high	poor
Union structure	sector-based	firm-based	industry-wide	craft
Strength	low	low	high	low
The firm				
Main goal	profits	market share stable jobs	market share fulfilment	profits
Role top manager	boss-king autocratic	consensus	consensus	boss-king hierarchy
Social overheads	low	low	high	medium, down
Welfare system				
Basic principle	liberal	corporatist	corporatist social democracy	mixed
Universal transfers	low	medium	high	medium, down
Means-testing	high	medium	low	medium, up
Degree education tiered by class	high	medium	medium	high
Private welfare	high	medium	low	medium, up
Government policies				
Role of government	limited adversarial	extensive cooperative	encompassing	strong adversarial
Openness to trade	quite open	least open	quite open	open
Industrial policy	little	high	high	non-existent
Top income tax	low	low	high	medium

Source: adapted and extended from Alan Blinder, 1992

principles into education, health, criminal justice, housing, television, pensions and social provision is actively eroding social cohesion, and undermining society.

The tradition of public spirit, common interest and national purpose which variously imbues social market Europe, the US and East Asian capitalism is absent in Britain. The private realm and the market are celebrated as the only efficient and responsive forms of organisation, while notions of public and common interest are dismissed as 'bureaucratic', 'interventionist' or 'socialist'. Nor is it easy to mobilise the country in the name of national purpose when it is not clear what purpose an increasingly divided and atomised society might have. The financial markets have no common cause with the medium-sized business sector, and neither have any sense of solidarity with the growing numbers of the excluded and marginalised. Nor is the parliamentary system a potential source of integration and national leadership.

The failure of this institutional matrix and value system to fit into the rest of Western Europe is clear, but in a world where the risk of trade tensions, financial instability and regional trade controls is growing it is apparent that Britain has no option but to stay a member of the European bloc. If that membership is not going to continue to be a source of tension, the structures of British capitalism will have to change. The élite do not want this to happen, yet change they must. How is change to be brought about? And what are the chances of success?

NOTES

* This chapter has been adapted from, Hutton, W. (1995) 'The Political Economy of the World's Capitalism', in Hutton, W. *The State We're In*, ch. 10, pp. 257–284, London, Jonathan Cape.

1 Richard Freeman, 'Jobs in the USA', *New Economy* (Dryden Press for IPPR), Spring 1994, vol. I, issue I, pp. 20–4.

2 ibid.

3 John Scott, *Capitalist Power and Financial Power*, Harvester Wheatsheaf, 1986, pp. 146–54.

4 The Defence Science Board's memorandum to the Pentagon on Semiconductor Dependency (31 December 1986) is a good example of US industry's expectations of the Pentagon. The response was to organise US manufacturers in a loose coalition to share R&D costs for the next generation of products, which allowed US industry at least to hold the line.

5 Richard Ferlauto, 'Community Capital: Delivering jobs from the bottom-up', delivered to the International Seminar on Growth and Employment, Magdalen College Oxford, 13–15 April 1994.

6 De Tocqueville, *Democracy in America*, p. 393.

7 Cited in David Goodhart's *The Reshaping of the German Model*, IPPR 1994.

8 Quoted in *The Seven Cultures of Capitalism*, by Charles Hampden-Turner and Alfons Trompenaars, p. 229.

9 Wolfgang Streeck, *Industrial Relations in West Germany: a case study of the car industry*, Heinemann, 1984.

10 *The Seven Cultures of Capitalism*, op. cit.

11 Hiroyuki Itami, cited by Weiichi Masuyama in a paper for the National Economic Development Office City and Industry Conference, November 1991.

12 *Japan in the Passing Lane* by Satoshi Kamata (Unwin) gives a very sobering account of life in a Toyota car factory.

13 In Aoki and Dore (eds.), *The Japanese Firm*, Clarendon Press, 1994.

14 ibid.

15 Kamekichi Takahashi, 'The Stock Company: a cause of national decay', quoted in *The Japanese Firm*, op. cit.

16 Guy de Carmoy and Jonathan Storey, *Western Europe in World Affairs*, Praeger, p. 140.

17 Lester Thurow, *Head to Head*, Nicholas Brealey, 1994, p. 62.
18 Andrew Walter, *World Power and World Money*, Harvester Wheatsheaf, pp. 204–8.

REFERENCES

James Abbeglen, *Sea Change*, Free Press, 1994.

Michel Albert, *Capitalism against Capitalism*, Whurr, 1993

Masahiko Aoki and Ronald Dore (eds), *The Japanese Firm*, Clarendon Press, 1994

Alan Blinder, 'Should the Former Socialist Economies look East or West for a model?', presented to the 10th World Congress of the International Economic Association in Moscow, August 1992

Guy de Carmoy and Jonathan Storey, *Western Europe in World Affairs*, Praeger, 1986

Philip Cooke, Kevin Morgan and Adam Price, 'The Future of the Mittelstand', Regional Industrial Research Report no 13, University of Wales

Philip Cooke *et al.*, 'The Challenge of Lean Production in German Industry', Regional Research Report No 12, University of Wales

Colin Crouch and David Marquand, *Ethics and Markets*, Blackwell, 1993

David Goodhart, 'The Reshaping of the German Model', IPPR, 1994

Charles Hampden-Turner and Alfons Trompenaars, *The Seven Cultures of Capitalism*, Piatkus, 1994

Toshihiro Nishiguchi, *Strategic Industrial Sourcing, the Japanese Advantage*, Oxford University Press, New York, 1994

Wolfgang Streeck, *The Social Institutions of Economic Performance*, Sage, 1988

Wolfgang Stutzel *et al.*, *Standard Texts on the Social Market Economy*, Gustav Fischer, 1982

Lester Thurow, *Head to Head*, Nicholas Brealey, 1994

Ezra Vogel, *Comeback*, Simon and Schuster, 1985

Andrew Walter, *World Power and World Money*, Harvester Wheatsheaf, 1993

13

CAPITALISM AND GLOBAL FREE MARKETS*

John Gray

A NEW GRESHAM'S LAW?

> a general law or principle concerning the circulation of money, which Mr Macleod has appropriately named the Law or Theorem of Gresham, after Sir Thomas Gresham, who clearly perceived its truth three centuries ago. This law, briefly expressed, is that bad money drives out good money, but that *good money cannot drive out bad money*.
>
> W. S. Jevons[1]

In the monetary theory, Gresham's Law tells us that bad money drives out good. In a global free market there is a variation on Gresham's Law: bad capitalism tends to drive out good. In any competition that is waged with the rules of global *laissez-faire*, that have been designed to reflect the American free market, the social market economies of Europe and Asia are at a systematic disadvantage. They have no future unless they can modernize themselves by deep and rapid reforms.

Sovereign states are waging a war of competitive deregulation, forced on them by the global free market. A mechanism of downwards harmonization of market economies is already in operation. Every type of currently existing capitalism is thrown into the melting pot. In this contest the socially dislocated American free market possesses powerful advantages.

In economic theory Keynes recognized that the international mobility of financial capital would undercut the full employment policies of national governments. He could not have foreseen that the global mobility of capital would return governments to a world in which national economic management is feasible only at the margin. National governments today can no longer implement the ambitious countercyclical policies that lifted their economies out of recession in the post-war period. Fiscal conservatism – the prudent management of government debt – is forced on them by world markets.

Few in the Keynesian era foresaw that worldwide mobility of capital and production would trigger a competitive downgrading of regulatory and welfare systems by sovereign states. Since the Soviet collapse, competition between central planning and capitalism has been replaced by a rivalry between different sorts of capitalism – American, German, Japanese, Russian, Chinese.

In this new rivalry American free markets work to undercut both European and Asian social market economies. This is despite the fact that the social costs of business are borne in different ways in European and Asian social markets. Both are threatened by the American model because each business bears social obligations that in the United States it has shed. At the same time, Chinese capitalism is emerging as a rival to the American version because it can go further than the American free market in undercutting social markets in Europe and the rest of Asia.

All the familiar models of market institutions are mutating as global competition is played out through the structures of sovereign states. It is a basic error to think that this is a contest that any of the existing models can win. All are being eroded and replaced by new and more volatile types of capitalism. The chief result of this new competition is to make the social market economies of the post-war period unviable while transforming the free-market economies that are its nominal winners.

HOW BAD CAPITALISM DRIVES OUT GOOD

The social costs which businesses carry in social market economies enable them to function as social institutions without undermining the cohesion of the larger societies in which they operate. At the same time these social costs must become burdens in any competition with enterprises operating in free markets. American firms have few such obligations.

The inherent advantages enjoyed by firms operating in free-market economies are neither incidental nor temporary. They are systemic. They cannot be fully compensated for by the superior education and skill levels that social market economies have often achieved, by better infrastructural investment in roads and other public goods and services, or by the social cohesion that such economic systems promote. The superior performance that social markets have displayed in these areas will not enable them to support the levels of welfare provision and the types of management and regulation that distinguished them in the past.

In the long haul of history, Europe's social markets may be as productive as American free markets. In the short run, in terms of rivalry in a global free market, they simply cannot be cost-competitive.

The conditions that confer a strategic advantage to the free market over the social market economies of the post-war period are unregulated global free trade in conjunction with unrestricted global mobility of capital.[2] In a free-trading global market the advantage lies (other things being equal) with firms whose costs are low. This is true whether they are labour costs, regulatory costs or tax costs.

Consider environmental costs. If, in one country, environmental costs are 'internalized' by a tax regime that forces them to be reflected in the costs of enterprises, but those enterprises are forced to compete in a global market with enterprises in other countries that do not carry such environmental costs, the countries that require businesses to be environmentally accountable will be at a systematic disadvantage.

Over time, either the enterprises operating in environmentally accountable regimes will be driven out of business, or the regulatory frameworks of such regimes will drift down to a common denominator in which their competitive disadvantage is reduced. This trade-off is an integral part of the global free market.

A global free market operates to 'externalize' costs that better regimes 'internalized'. In environmentally sensitive economies tax and regulatory policy is designed so that firms are required to pay for the costs their activities impose on society and the natural world. This has long been the case in the countries of continental Europe. Global free markets put heavy pressure on such policies. Goods produced by environmentally accountable firms cost more than similar goods produced by enterprises that are at liberty to pollute.

Global regulation of environmental standards, though an inspiring ideal, is a Utopian prospect. It is not enforceable where it is most needed – for example, there are few effective measures of environmental protection in Russia or China. In both countries, partly as an inheritance from the period of central economic planning and partly as a consequence of market reforms, environmental degradation is cataclysmic. Yet both countries are being induced to enter the global free market where their goods will have to compete with goods produced in environmentally accountable social markets.

Some of the world's advanced industrial economies are rich enough to resist the downward pressure on environmental standards. They may be able to compensate firms who are losing out in competition with businesses based in low-regulation economies. If advanced societies are able to protect their environments in this way it will be partly because they are able to export pollution by moving production to Third World countries where environmental standards are looser. The advanced countries will remain clean at the cost of other parts of the world becoming dirtier.

The overall effect of global free markets on the world environment will be unchanged. It will still work worldwide to unload costs that in an earlier, more accountable species of capitalism were borne by enterprises. More and more of the earth will, as a result, become less and less habitable. At the same time the price will rise for the few societies rich enough to be able to keep their local environments livable, and if, despite this, they persist in imposing the costs of pollution and other environmental social costs on businesses, profits will fall and capital will migrate.

Alternatively societies may adopt policies in which pollution control is paid for directly from public funds. By such measures they may succeed in protecting their local environments from some types of degradation, though they will not insulate themselves from the global impact of local pollution in poorer countries. As Chernobyl demonstrated, some kinds of pollution have a very long reach.

UNREGULATED GLOBAL FREE TRADE AND INTERNATIONAL MOBILITY OF CAPITAL

In the classical theory of free trade capital is immobile. Ricardo's doctrine of comparative advantage – which is still regularly invoked in defence of unregulated global free trade – says that when comparatively inefficient enterprises or industries shrink in any country, others will grow, absorbing the capital and labour released from the declining activities. Within each trading country capital will move to those economic activities in which it is most productive. Ricardian comparative advantage applies *internally* in trading nations, not externally between them. It implies that in a regime of unrestricted free trade the allocation of resources will be maximally productive within each trading nation, and thereby, by inference, throughout the world. Insofar as the world becomes a single market, efficiency and productivity in every country will be maximized.

Ricardo understood that this could be true only so long as capital is not to any significant extent internationally mobile:

the fancied or real insecurity of capital, when not under the immediate control of its owner, together with the natural disinclination which every man has to quit the country of his birth and connections, and intrust himself with all his habits fixed, to a strange government and new laws, checks the emigration of capital. These feelings, which I should be sorry to see weakened, induce most men of property to be satisfied with a low rate of profits in their own country, rather than seek a more advantageous employment for their wealth in foreign nations.[3]

The contrast between this theoretical requirement of unrestricted global free trade and the realities of the late twentieth-century world needs little comment. When capital is mobile it will seek its absolute advantage by migrating to countries where the environmental and social costs of enterprises are lowest and profits are highest. Both in theory and practice the effect of global capital mobility is to nullify the Ricardian doctrine of comparative advantage. Yet it is on that flimsy foundation that the edifice of unregulated global free trade still stands.[4]

The argument against unrestricted global freedom in trade and capital movements is not primarily an economic one. It is, rather, that the economy should serve the needs of society, not society the imperatives of the market. In terms that are strictly and narrowly economic it is true that a global free market is incredibly productive. Equally, in the contest between free market economies and social market systems free markets are often superior in productivity. There is not much doubt that the free market is the most *economically efficient* type of capitalism. For most economists that ends the matter. Yet what social market economies do is in no sense irrational. The Japanese practice of employing workers who are not economically productive in a variety of low-skill occupations is neither unreasonable nor inefficient, provided that one of the criteria of efficiency by which such a policy is judged is the maintenance of social cohesion by the avoidance of mass unemployment.

As some economists have always recognized, the pursuit of economic efficiency without regard to social costs is itself unreasonable and in effect ranks the demands of the economy over the needs of society. That is precisely what drives competition in a global free market. The neglect of social costs, which is a professional deformation of economists, has become an imperative of the entire system.

The economic inefficiencies of restrictions on free trade are so nearly self-evident that anyone who is critical of unregulated global free trade is easily convicted of economic ignorance.[5] But the economic argument for unregulated global free trade involves a wild abstraction from social realities. It is true that restraints on global free trade will not enhance productivity; but maximal productivity achieved at the cost of social desolation and human misery is an anomalous and dangerous social ideal.

GLOBAL FREE MARKETS AND FALLING WAGES

When capital is as mobile as it is today, it will tend, other things being equal, to gravitate to countries whose workers have the lowest absolute wages. Of course things are rarely equal, especially the costs which enterprises incur on top of the costs of labour. The quality of infrastructure and services in different countries varies considerably. The costs and risks associated with political instability, the local rule of law and corruption, differ greatly from country to country. The education of the local workforce, location of plant, cost of transportation, political environment and many other factors are important.

Low wages in some countries – those of Central and West Africa, for example – reflect the fact that those countries are unattractive locations for productive capital. High wages in others, such as Singapore, reflect its excellent levels of education in the workforce, an uncorrupt rule of law and political stability.

Labour costs per capita for Osram's, the German-based company and the world's second largest producer of light bulbs, to manufacture light bulbs in China are a fiftieth of their costs in Germany; but it takes 38 times as many people to turn out the same number of light bulbs. Here we see per capita costs of cheap labour being largely cancelled out by lower skill and productivity levels.[6]

Further, wages rates in any economy are determined by its domestic labour market, not by wage rates in other countries. The taxi that I hail in Piccadilly is not in competition with taxis in Lahore. However, a growing range of skills command a price that is set globally. Many services can be exported to wherever the labour needed for them is cheapest – as has occurred when airlines have transferred ticketing and bookkeeping in India. But most wages are still set by domestic markets.

The decline in workers' bargaining power in the countries of the affluent north has not come from global free trade alone. To think that it could do so would be to exaggerate the impact of international trade and capital flows on national economies. Unemployment in the advanced countries is too significant to be attributed solely to trade with low-wage countries.

New technologies and the deskilling of parts of the population by inadequate education are central causes of long-term unemployment in advanced western societies. Growing income inequalities have been magnified by deregulation of the labour market and neo-liberal tax policies, but the root cause of falling wages and rising unemployment is the worldwide spread of new technology.

Newly industrializing economies and late industrial economies do not fall into simple, homogenous, mutually exclusive categories as far as wages are concerned. In some newly industrialized countries (NICs), such as South Korea, Taiwan and Singapore, wages are higher in many occupations than in some advanced countries, notably Britain and the United States. That is why South–North relocations by Asian multinationals to cheap-labour regions in the First World are nowadays not uncommon.

The Korean conglomerate Lucky Goldstar's decision in early 1997 to locate a factory in Newport, Wales, exported jobs from Korea to a hitherto First World European region that has low wages and low non-wage costs of labour. (It received a considerable subsidy from the British government to encourage it to do so.) A year before, Ronson moved its facilities for the production of cigarette lighters from Korea to Wales and saved nearly 20 per cent on its wage costs.[7]

These examples show that the impact of global *laissez-faire* on job security is no longer primarily on First World labour forces. As the mass demonstrations of workers in Seoul in January 1997 testified, the reduction of job security is worldwide.

First World countries are not homogenous as far as labour costs are concerned either. The wages that Siemens pays its German workers are high, but that is partly because, owing to much higher education and training levels in Germany, the productivity of Siemen's German workers is around twice that of its workers in the American plants.[8]

Yet the overall effect of unregulated global free trade is still to drive down the wages of workers – most particularly unskilled manufacturing workers – in advanced countries. If barriers to international trade are lowered, then – in what economists refer to as 'factor-price equalization' – the price of factors of production *including labour* will tend to converge. This is what economists mean when they talk of the prospect that 'your wages will be set in Peking'.[9]

New information technologies allow many goods, including an expanding range of services, to be produced in developing countries at a fraction of the labour costs they incur in more mature industrial societies. As the International Labour Organisation has put it succinctly: 'Location decisions nowadays are very finely tuned to labour costs.'[10] This is an important truth. Ricardo's theory, in which capital was mobile only within its country of origin, and production was internationally practically immobile, is no longer relevant.

Our world differs from Ricardo's in another crucial respect. There are rapid rates of population growth in new industrializing countries. This serves to reinforce the downwards pressure of unregulated global free trade on wages in mature industrial economies. In most of the latter population growth rates are low, and labour – at least skilled labour – is a scarce resource which commands a premium. In many newly industrializing countries where population is growing quickly, labour – including some kinds of skilled labour – is in practically inexhaustible supply.

When population growth is so uneven labour in NICs undercuts labour in mature industrial economies. When capital and production exercise unregulated mobility across the world they will tend to locate where labour is most abundant and least expensive. At present they can do this whether the labour they need is skilled or unskilled. As Michael Lind has put it:

> Within a generation, the burgeoning Third World population will contain not only billions of unskilled workers, but hundreds of millions of scientists, engineers, architects, and other professionals willing and able to do world-class work for a fraction of the payment their American counterparts expect. The free trade liberals hope that a high-wage, high-skill America need fear nothing from a low-wage, low-skill Third World. They have no answer, however, to the prospect – indeed, the probability – of ever-increasing *low-wage, high-skill* competition from abroad. In these circumstances, neither better worker training nor investment in US infrastructure will suffice. . . . It is difficult to resist the conclusion that civilized social market capitalism and unrestricted global free trade are inherently incompatible.[11]

A survey in 1993 of 10,000 medium-sized German companies found that one-third of them were planning to transfer parts of their production to regions of the world, such as post-communist eastern Europe, where wages were lower and social and environmental regulation weaker. Many companies are outsourcing their computer programming needs to India, where programmers earn a fraction (around $3,000) of what they command in European countries or the United States. Many other examples could be quoted.[12]

The effects of a global market in driving down wages to the level they reach in cheap-labour, unregulated economies are enhanced by new information technologies. Many occupations are being decimated by new technologies. If bank tellers are a doomed profession, so are session musicians. In both cases their work can be synthesized or mimicked at low cost. New technologies would exert a downward pressure on incomes in many occupations even in the absence of a global free market. The substitution of technology for human labour creates dilemmas that no society (except, perhaps, Japan) has yet solved.[13]

Ricardo recognized that technological innovation could be jobdestroying. He did not share the modern faith that new employment will always arise automatically from the side-effects of new technologies. As he noted, 'the discovery and use of machinery may be attended with a diminution of gross produce; and whenever that is the case, it will be injurious to the labouring class, as some of their number will be thrown out of employment, and population will become redundant . . . the opinion entertained by the labouring classes, that the employment of machinery is frequently detrimental to their interests, is not founded on prejudice and error but is conformable to the correct principles of political economy.'[14]

As has been noted, capital will migrate to the countries in which goods can be made for the world's consumers in rich countries at lowest labour costs.[15] These will rarely be the countries in which such goods are consumed. As William Pfaff has commented, 'It is obviously no coincidence that Western trade unionism's bargaining power has suffered a dramatic and progressive decline since globalization began. Until the 1970s, investment in general had to confine itself to a national labour pool in order to manufacture for a national market. When it became not only technologically possible but economically advantageous to manufacture goods for rich-country consumers in poor and unregulated Asian, Latin

American or African labour markets, labour in the advanced countries lost its bargaining power.'[16] Several academic studies tend to corroborate this observation.[17]

In countries of the First World it is the unprecedented combination of rapid technological change with global freedom in trade and capital movements, of labour market deregulation in advanced industrial societies with rapid population growth in developing countries, that has eclipsed the power of organized labour.

NOTES

* This book has been adapted from, Gray, J. (1998) 'How Global Free Markets Favour the Worst Kinds of Capitalisms: a New Gresham's Law', in Gray, J. *False Dawn: The Delusions of Global Capitalism*, ch. 4, pp. 78–92, London, Granta Books.

1 W. Stanley Jevons, *Money and the Mechanism of Exchange*, London: Kegan Paul, Trench Trubner, 1910, p. 81.

2 For powerful critiques of global free trade to which I am indebted, see Herman E. Daly, 'From Adjustment to Sustainable Development: The Obstacle of Free Trade', in *The Case Against Free Trade: GATT NAFTA, and the Globalization of Corporate Power*, San Francisco: Earth Island Press, 1993, pp. 121–32. See also Jerry Mander and Edward Goldsmith, *The Case Against the Global Economy and For a Turn Toward the Local*, San Francisco: Sierra Books, 1996.

3 David Ricardo, *On the Principles of Political Economy and Taxation*, Harmondsworth: Penguin, 1971, p. 155.

4 As Michael Porter notes, in his classic, *The Competitive Advantage of Nations*, London: Macmillan, 1990, p. 12, 'The standard theory (of comparative advantage) assumes that there are no economies of scale, that technologies everywhere are identical, that products are undifferentiated, and that the pool of national factors is fixed. The theory also assumes that factors, such as skilled labour and capital, do not move among nations. All these assumptions bear little relation, in most industries, to actual competition.' A seminal recent statement of comparative advantage theory is that of R. Dornbusch, S. Fisher and Paul Samuelson, 'Comparative Advantage, Trade and Payments in a Ricardian Model with a Continuum of Goods', *American Economic Review*, vol. 67, December 1977, pp. 823–39.

5 This is the strategy of argument of two notable contemporary writers who defend unrestricted global free trade; Douglas A. Irwin, *Against the Tide: An Intellectual History of Free Trade*, Princeton, NJ: Princeton University Press, 1996; and Paul Krugman, *Pop Internationalism*, Cambridge, Mass: MIT Press, 1996. For a classic modern version of the theory of comparative advantage, see Betil Ohlin, *Interregional and International Trade*, Cambridge, Mass: Harvard University Press, 1933.

6 For this comparison, see Peter Marsh, 'A shift to flexibility', *Financial Times*, 21 February 1997.

7 'Come to low-wage Wales', *Independent*, 13 January 1997.

8 For this comparison, see Peter Marsh, 'A shift to flexibility', *Financial Times*, 21 February 1997.

9 R. Freeman, 'Are your wages set in Peking?', *Journal of Economic Perspectives*, 9, Summer 1995.

10 *World Labour Report*, Geneva: International Labour Organisation, 1992.

11 Michael Lind, *The Next American Nation: The New Nationalism and the Fourth American Revolution*, New York: The Free Press, 1995, p. 203.

12 I owe these examples to 'Who competes? Changing landscapes of corporate control', *The Ecologist*, vol. 26, No. 4, July/August 1996, p. 135.

13 On this, see Jeremy Rifkin, *The End of Work: The Decline of the Global Labor Force and the Dawn of the Post-Market Era*, New York: G.P. Putnam, 1995.

14 David Ricardo, *Principles of Political Economy and Taxation*, London: J. M. Dent, 1991, pp. 266–7. For a more recent argument that supports Ricardo's, see Paul Samuelson, 'Mathematical vindication of Ricardo on machinery', *Journal of Political Economy*, vol. 96, 1988,

pp. 24–82, and Samuelson's 'Ricardo was right!', in *Scandinavian Journal of Economics*, vol. 91, 1989, pp. 47–62.

15 See Patrick Minford, 'Free trade and long wages – still in the general interest', *Journal des Economistes et des Etudes Humaines*, vol. 7, Number 1, March 1996, pp. 123–9.

16 William Pfaff, 'Job security is disappearing around the world', *International Herald Tribune*, 8 July 1996, p. 8.

17 See Adrian Wood, *North–South Trade, Employment and Inequality–Changing Fortunes in a Skill-Driven World*, Oxford: Clarendon Press, 1994, and 'How trade hurts unskilled workers' in *Journal of Economic Perspectives*, vol. 9, no. 3, pp. 57–80. See also P. Minford *et al.*, 'The Elixir of Growth', in Snower and de La Dehesa, eds, *Unemployment Policy*, London: Centre for Economic Policy Research, 1996. A counter-argument has been advanced stressing the importance of controls on immigration as means whereby nation-states can protect their workers against globalized competition, especially in the non-traded services sector. On this view, globalization of labour was more advanced in the late nineteenth century than it is today. See Vincent Cable, *Daedalus*, vol. 124, no. 2, June 1995.

14

WHY DID EAST ASIA GROW SO FAST?*

Ajit Singh

Summary

Two central policy issues in economic development today are: how open should a developing country be to the world economy, and what should the government do, or not do, to promote rapid growth. This [chapter] examines these questions in relation to the highly successful East Asian countries, and contributes to the debate between World Bank and heterodox economists. The [chapter] suggests that there has been significant convergence between the two schools on analytical and empirical issues, but not on policy. It takes this debate further by analyzing the principal issues still in contention.

INTRODUCTION

Two principal policy issues in economic development today are: (a) the degree and kind of openness to the world economy a developing country should seek; and (b) what should the government do, or not do, in order to promote fast economic and industrial development.

These questions are controversial and have therefore been the subject of an important debate, not least in the pages of this journal. In view of its direct policy involvement in developing countries around the globe, the World Bank has been a major participant in this debate. In a large number of studies and reports,[1] World Bank economists have provided detailed analysis of these questions. Specifically, they have argued that the best way to achieve economic growth for developing countries is to be open to the world economy and to seek close integration with it. On the second issue, they have suggested a relatively limited role for the state, encapsulated in the concept of a "market-friendly" approach to development.

The importance of the World Bank analyses and conclusions on these subjects for economic policy hardly needs any emphasis. These analyses are however, also significant for another reason: since the beginning of this decade, Bank economists have departed significantly from the extreme free market neoclassical perspectives which often characterized their contributions in the 1980s. In that sense, the Bank's views on these questions today probably represent the professional mainstream.

The main purpose of this [chapter] is to carry forward the recent debate[2] between the World Bank and the heterodox economists, which centers around the analysis of the development experience of the economically highly successful East Asian countries. It is suggested here that this debate has already made considerable progress and has led to a degree of convergence between the two schools on a range of analytical and empirical issues, though, as is evident in the discussion below, not yet on policy. This [chapter] aims to carry this process further by identifying and commenting on the most important issues which still remain in contention.

The [chapter], *inter alia*, outlines an alternative framework for examining the question of openness, which leads to a rather different policy conclusion than that above. It will be argued here that, in contrast to the recommendations of the Bretton Wood institutions, developing countries should actively seek "strategic" rather than "close" integration with the international economy. Further, the [chapter] suggests that government needs to have a far bigger role in economic activity than is envisaged in the "market-friendly" approach. It is contended that in mixed economy countries with reasonably effective states, the government should pursue a dynamic industrial policy to bring about the desired structural transformations in the economy as speedily as possible, to achieve rapid economic growth. These, it is argued, are the correct lessons to be learnt from the East Asian economic record.

Taking into account previous contributions to the debate, the paper concentrates on the following specific issues: (a) the question of the effectiveness of industrial policy; (b) the issue of "openness"; (c) the nature of competition in domestic markets; (d) the relationship between technology policy, industrial policy and international competitiveness. Particular attention will be paid here to the theoretical underpinnings of the World Bank analyses of these issues. Specifically, the neglect of the role of "demand" in such analyses will be highlighted. This, it will be shown, leads to incorrect interpretations of the East Asian development record at key stages of the Bank's argument. For space reasons, and also to sharpen the debate, the empirical analysis will be confined here to Japan and South Korea – two of the most important exemplar countries. A proper consideration of the role of the balance of payments constraint and of demand leads to a rather different interpretation of the experience of these economies from that provided by World Bank economists.

THE MARKET-FRIENDLY APPROACH TO DEVELOPMENT: THE BANK'S THESIS

The concept of the "market-friendly" strategy of development was put forward in the World Bank's seminal 1991 *World Development Report: The Challenge of Development* (World Bank, 1991, hereafter referred to as the 1991 Report). Representing the synthesis of what the World Bank economists have learned from 40 years of development experience, the starting point for the 1991 Report was the question: why during the last four decades some developing countries were successful in the narrow but important sense of substantially raising their per capita incomes while others were not? The central analytical argument is that economic growth is determined essentially by the growth of total factor productivity (TFP) of capital and labor. The Report's analysis came to the conclusion that the more open an economy, the greater the degree of competition and the higher its investment in education, the greater would be its growth of TFP and hence its overall economic growth. Although the significance of international economic factors was recognized, a major argument of the Report was that domestic policy matters far more for raising per capita incomes than world economic conditions.

With respect to economic policy, the Report concluded that: "Economic theory and practical experience suggest that (government) interventions are likely to help provided they are market-friendly" (p. 5). In order for "market-friendly" not to be a mere tautology, the Report, to its credit, defined the concept fairly precisely in the following terms:

- *Intervene reluctantly*: Let markets work unless it is demonstrably better to step in. . . . [It] is usually a mistake for the state to carry out physical production, or to protect the domestic production of a good that can be imported more cheaply and whose local production offers few spillover benefits.
- *Apply checks and balances*: Put interventions continually to the discipline of international and domestic markets.
- *Intervene openly*: Make interventions simple, transparent and subject to rules rather than official discretion.

Overall, the state's role in economic development in this "market-friendly" approach is regarded as important but best limited to providing the social, legal and economic infrastructure, to creating a suitable climate for private enterprise, but also, significantly, to ensuring a high level and appropriate composition of human capital formation. Even this limited role for the state is, nevertheless, an advance over the earlier neoclassical thinking which enjoined governments simply to avoid distortions, and to provide a stable macroeconomic environment and a reliable legal framework.

Both the neoclassical and the "market friendly" analyses have encountered serious intellectual difficulties since neither can satisfactorily explain the outstanding success of East Asian economies. Revisionist authors, such as Boltho (1985a), Amsden (1989), Wade (1990), and Singh (1979, 1993 and 1994a) have pointed out that in countries such as Japan, South Korea and Taiwan, the government has played a leading and a heavily interventionist role in the course of their economic development.

This intellectual challenge was taken up by World Bank (1993), the East Asia "Miracle" study (hereafter referred to as the Miracle Study), which has produced a new analysis of the economic development of the high-performing Asian economies (HPAEs) including Japan. This study fully acknowledges the facts of enormous government economic interventions in most spheres in these countries, much as documented by the revisionist school.

The study goes on to suggest, however, that such interventions, particularly in the sphere of industrial policy, had in general a limited effect. Some of these worked for some of the time in a few countries, but overall they were neither necessary nor sufficient for the extraordinary success of these countries. Thus, the study:

> What are the main factors that contributed to the HPAE's superior allocation of physical and human capital to high yielding investments and their ability to catch up technologically? Mainly, the answer lies in fundamentally sound, market oriented policies. Labour markets were allowed to work. Financial markets . . . generally had low distortions and limited subsidies compared with other developing economies. Import substitution was . . . quickly accompanied by the promotion of exports. . . . the result was limited differences between international relative prices and domestic relative prices in the HPAE's. Market forces and competitive pressures guided resources into activities that were consistent with comparative advantage . . .
>
> (p. 325)

In other words, the final policy conclusion is still to reassert the "market-friendly" strategy of development – developing countries are recommended to seek their comparative advantage, to "get their prices right" and to save free markets as far as possible.

THE TOTAL FACTOR PRODUCTIVITY (TFP) APPROACH TO ECONOMIC GROWTH

The theoretical foundation of the World Bank analyses is the TFP approach to economic growth. It is suggested that intercountry and intertemporal variations in growth rates are caused by variations in total factor productivity of capital and labor. Changes in the latter variable are thought to be determined mainly by economic policy – the degree of openness of an economy, the extent of competition in the product and factor markets, and investment in physical and human capital (education), particularly the latter. The underlying chain of causation is that competition and education promote technical progress, and therefore TFP growth and hence economic expansion. "Free mobility of people, capital, and technology" and "free entry and exit of firms" are regarded as being particularly conducive to the spread of knowledge and technical change.

Now at a theoretical level, there are several well-known objections to the causal model underlying the TFP approach to economic growth. The model assumes for example full employment of resources and perfect competition, none of which obtain in the real world. Moreover, it is a wholly supply-side model which ignores altogether the role of demand factors.[3] The latter, as we shall see below, is a critical weakness which creates serious difficulties for the Bank's analyses of the East Asian as well as other economies.

With respect to empirical evidence, even a cursory consideration of the data presented by Bank economists themselves in the 1991 Report (Table 2.2, p. 43) reveals the serious limitations of the TFP approach. The table provides figures for the growth of GDP, capital and labor inputs and TFP, separately for each of the subperiods, 1960–73 and 1973–87, for each of the five developing regions as well as for a group of 68 developing economies; in addition, it provides similar information for each of the four leading industrial economies. These data show that in every region, and for each country or group of countries shown in the table except South Asia (i.e. in nine out of 10 observations), the rate of growth of TFP fell substantially during 1973–87 compared with 1960–73. For example, TFP growth fell in East Asian developing economies from 2.6% p.a. in the first period to 1.3% p.a. in the second period; in Latin America, the corresponding figures were 1.3% p.a. and –0.4% p.a.; for the group of 68 developing economies, the TFP growth fell from 1.3% to –0.2% over the two periods. But, in South Asia – notably the only region which registered a trend increase in its GDP growth between the two periods – TFP growth rose from zero in 1960–73 to 1.2% p.a. during 1973–87.

In terms of the causal model underlying the World Bank analysis, this almost universal decline in TFP growth in the recent period would be due to policy mismanagement – low rates of technical progress caused by distortions, lack of competition, lack of integration with the world economy, etc. The evidence, however, is not compatible with such an analysis, since as Bank economists themselves note elsewhere in the Report there has actually been more competition, greater integration of the world economy, less distortions in most developing countries in the latter period (particularly in the 1980s) than in the former.

These facts are much more in accord with an alternative theoretical model which would suggest that the decline in the world and the national economic growth rates in the post-1973 period was responsible for the decline in the rate of growth of productivity in most regions (Verdoorn's Law).[4] The decline in world economic growth after 1973, in terms of this model, was due to a lower rate of growth of world and national demand caused by a whole range of factors (e.g. the collapse of the Bretton Woods system, the growth of real wages in a number of industrial countries out-stripping productivity growth in the wake of the first oil shock) connected with the fall of the "Golden Age" of development of the OECD economies.[5]

EFFICACY OF INDUSTRIAL POLICY: CONCEPTUAL ISSUES

The TFP approach is prominently used in the World Bank economists' critique of the industrial policy thesis of the revisionist economists. One of their most controversial findings is what may be called, by analogy to Lucas's well-known theorem,[6] the industrial policy ineffectiveness doctrine. Bank economists assert that contrary to popular perceptions, rigorous quantitative analysis shows that these policies were largely ineffective in the East Asian countries. The clear implication is that if industrial policies could not succeed in these countries with their highly efficient bureaucracies, *ipso facto* these would be inappropriate for the rest of the developing world which is not blessed with such high-quality administrative assets.

In examining this "ineffectiveness doctrine," there are two prior conceptual issues which require attention: What is industrial policy? How should the "success" or otherwise of such a policy be assessed?

What is industrial policy?

Governments in almost all market-economy countries intervene to a greater or a smaller degree in the operation of their industries. For example, even the US government, normally regarded as noninterventionist, in fact, intervenes in industry through a variety of measures, such as anti-trust laws, industrial standards, pollution regulations, and labor laws. Most people would agree, however, that despite such extensive interventions, the United States does not have an "industrial policy," while Japan and East Asian countries do.

What makes Japanese interventions into an "industrial policy" is that in Japan, such interventions are generally coordinated and viewed as a coherent whole, and the government has a strategic view of the country's industrial development in relation to the world economy. In this sense South Korea, and other East Asian countries also have an industrial policy. Japan's strategic view in the 1950s and 1960s was eloquently expressed by Vice Minster Ojimi of MITI as follows:

> The MITI decided to establish in Japan industries which require intensive employment of capital and technology, industries that in consideration of comparative cost of production should be the most inappropriate for Japan, industries such as steel, oil-refining, petro-chemicals, automobiles, aircraft, industrial machinery of all sorts, and electronics, including electronic computers. From a short-run, static viewpoint, encouragement of such industries would seem to conflict with economic rationalism. But, from a long-range viewpoint, these are precisely the industries where income elasticity of demand is high, technological progress is rapid, and labour productivity rises fast.
>
> (OECD, 1972)

At the end of WWII, the bulk of Japanese exports consisted of textiles and light manufactured goods. In the view of Ojimi and his colleagues at MITI, although such an economic structure may have conformed to the theory of comparative advantage (Japan being a labor-surplus economy at the time), it was not capable of raising in the long run the Japanese standard of living to European or US levels. One interpretation of Ojimi's argument above would be that the purpose of the Japanese industrial policy was no more than to pursue the country's dynamic comparative advantage, but to do that as quickly as possible. The other non-neoclassical interpretation, which does not necessarily exclude the previous one, is that the purpose of the industrial policy was to guide the market, and to deliberately create a competitive advantage in areas where world demand was likely to rise rapidly and in which it would, therefore, be in Japan's long-term interest to specialize. As Magziner and Hout (1980) note: "On balance, Japan's industrial policy has been anticipating rather than reacting to international competitive evolution."

Support for the non-neoclassical interpretation is provided by the fact that although in the 1950s and 1960s, MITI's structural program could be justified in orthodox terms by the infant-industry argument, these structural policies have continued, albeit in an attenuated form, right up to the present day. MITI continues to provide blueprints and to seek wide business and social agreement toward its future structural visions for the evolution of the Japanese economy, as the world competitive situation and Japan's role as the world economy changes.[7]

Assessment of industrial policy

How does one assess the success of an industrial policy like that of Japan? It is not a straightforward question since one needs a credible counterfactual – what would have happened in the absence of an industrial policy? Would Japanese industrial production still have grown by nearly 13% a year during 1953–73, its GNP by nearly 10% and its share in world exports of manufactures change by a huge 10 percentage points (Boltho, 1985a)?

One way to answer this kind of question in the absence of a controlled experiment would be to compare the performance of countries which were in other relevant ways similar to Japan, but which did not have an industrial policy like that of Japan. This after all is the broad methodology underlying the 1991 Report which compares the experiences of different countries to find out why some were successful and others were not. A closer analogy would be the studies which assess the success of the Bank's structural adjustment program by comparing countries which have such programs with those which did not. There are of course well-recognized problems with such comparisons: to be able to provide satisfactory evidence on the issue the two groups of countries should be as similar as possible in all other ways.

A second way of assessing the success of Japanese industrial policy would be to compare the country's postwar economic record under an industrial policy, with its own performance in the prewar period when it was not pursuing such policies. A third method of assessment would be to examine the policy in terms of the goals which the country may have set for itself. In the Japanese case, during the high-growth period 1950–73, a critical proximate goal of MITI's was to ensure a current account balance at as high a growth rate as possible. In other words, the balance of payments was seen as the main constraint on fast economic growth in this period (Shinohara, 1982; Tsuru, 1993). The government pursued this objective by a wide range of measures including *inter alia* a policy of extensive import controls, together with the promotion of exports of certain key industries, which changed over time.

Boltho (1985a; 1985b) assesses the Japanese industrial policy on these criteria and concludes that the policy was successful. Boltho's analysis is complemented by Magaziner and Hout's (1980) detailed and careful evidence based on case studies of several specific industries. These strongly suggest that the industrial policies were successful in propelling the targeted industries into preeminence in international competition. So how do World Bank economists conclude that industrial policy in countries such as Japan or South Korea was ineffective?

THE INDUSTRIAL POLICY INEFFECTIVENESS DOCTRINE

The first reason for this negative assessment is that Bank economists have a very narrow definition of industrial policy, considering it only as a policy to upgrade industrial structure.[8] Industrial policy is not viewed as a whole in all its various aspects. They also depart, without adequate justification, from the standard methodology above for assessing the effectiveness of industrial policy. Instead, they adopt a so-called functional approach to examine three types of government interventions: (a) directed credit, (b) export promotion, and (c) structural policy, and conclude that whereas (a) and (b) were successful, (c) was not.

These policies, however, cannot properly be judged individually since (a) and (b), as well as other policies such as extensive import protection for the whole economy (and not just the favored sectors), were closely connected with (c). All three, combined with other relevant policies should therefore be assessed together. To recall the analogy with the Bank's own structural adjustment programs, the Bank's procedure in the present case amounts to an assessment of a single component of the structural adjustment programs, such as devaluation, without reference to the interconnections with the rest of the program. This is not to say that it is not an interesting and a legitimate exercise to consider the effectiveness of a single component of a structural adjustment program or of industrial policy. To do that, however, its links with the other components must be explicitly recognized. It also requires a much more elaborate counterfactual exercise, e.g. simulation of a macroeconometric model, first with the structural adjustment program, and then with one in which the component under reference is not considered.

Bank economists have not, however, carried out such research. The interconnections between different aspects of industrial policy in countries such as Japan or Korea have either not been examined at all or, as shown below, not correctly interpreted. Nevertheless, within their own terms, the Bank's industrial policy ineffectiveness doctrine rests on two empirical propositions. First, the industrial structure which emerged in industrial policy economies such as Japan and Korea was not all that different from what it would have been had these countries not pursued an industrial policy (i.e. that the observed industrial structure was *ex-post* market-conforming and accorded with the changing relative factor intensities and prices). Second, the TFP growth of the industrial policy-favored sectors was no different from that of the unfavored sectors.

As tests of the ineffectiveness of industrial policy, even in this narrow sense, these two propositions are inadequate. To illustrate, suppose we take the neoclassical interpretation of Vice-Minster Ojimi's rationale for Japan's industrial policy noted earlier. In this interpretation, MITI was only pursuing Japan's dynamic comparative advantage, helping create an industrial structure to accord with it. It was attempting to do so, however, in as short a time as possible. The resulting industrial structure would of course in equilibrium be market-conforming. So that even if it were true that the market forces, left to themselves, may have generated the same kind of industrial structure, it may have taken much longer to do so and hence resulted in a much lower rate of economic growth. Bank economists do not address this crucial issue of the speed of adjustment at all.

The problem with the second test is that it overlooks the effects of industrial policy on a country's balance of payments and its long-term rate of growth of domestic demand. By confining their attention only to the supply side effects of productivity growth and technical change, as predicated by the TFP approach, Bank economists hypothesize that "spillovers" of these activities will be confined only to the favored sectors or their close subsectors within the two-digit industrial classification which they have analyzed. To the extent that industrial policy helps to relieve the balance of payments constraint, however, most sectors will benefit from higher rates of growth of production and hence productivity (by Verdoorn's Law) and not just the favored sectors. In other words, the spillovers will be almost universal.

Thus the second empirical test cannot discriminate between industrial policy and nonindustrial policy states. To do that, one needs to look also at the costs and benefits of industrial policy interventions in terms of their relaxing the balance-of-payments constraint in the short and the long run. More specifically, it would require *inter alia*, an examination of the contribution of the favored sectors to the growth of exports or to the reduction in the growth of imports over time.

It is the failure to consider such factors which leads Bank economists to conclude that South Korea's Heavy and Chemical Industry (HCI) drive in the 1970s was unsuccessful, while heterodox economists suggest that it was a success. The reason for these conflicting judgements is that Bank economists do not consider its benefits to the long-term trajectory of the balance of payments and hence to overall economic growth. Amsden (1989) points out that the mainstay of Korea's celebrated export success in the 1980s was precisely these HCI industries.[9]

Parenthetically, a related point which is relevant here is that Bank economists ignore the fact that in Korea the industrial policy-favored sectors were not just capital-intense sectors but included textiles (precisely because of its contribution to the balance of payments) for most of the period (see Chang, forthcoming). The Korean government knew, as did the Japanese before them, that however successful a country may be in the export of textiles, to have sustained rapid overall rates of growth of exports over time, it needs to add regularly new export products to the list. It is necessary to continuously upgrade the industrial and export structure of the economy only, albeit, if it pleases the Bank, in accordance with the country's changing dynamic comparative advantage.

It will be appreciated that the factor proportions (Heckscher-Ohlin) theory does not yield any precise predictions as to where a country's dynamic comparative advantage lies as it accumulates capital and skills. The theory predicts a movement toward skill-intensive exports but does not specify which ones. In Japan and Korea, the government selected and nurtured those industries in which it thought the country had, or should have (in the non-neoclassical interpretation) a dynamic comparative advantage.

Bank economists seem to be unaware of an ironic implication of their analysis. If despite heavy government intervention, the Japanese and the Korean industrial structures still conformed to these countries' dynamic comparative advantage, a reasonable inference must be that on average the government was correctly able to "pick the winners"! Hence, at this level of analysis, in Bank economists' own terms, the Japanese or the Korean industrial policies should be regarded as a success.

To sum up, the above discussion indicates that Bank economists arrive at their industrial policy ineffectiveness doctrine by considering industrial policy in a very narrow sense; by ignoring its multifaceted character and the important linkages between its different components; and even within their own terms by using inappropriate tests for assessing the success or otherwise of industrial policy. The first of their tests is not valid because it does not consider the critical issue of the speed of adjustment to a country's dynamic comparative advantage; the second is marred by the fact that it abstracts from the effects of industrial policy on the balance-of-payments constraint and hence on overall demand – issues which are salient in the real world of imperfect or incomplete markets in semi-industrial economies. The TFP model, with its assumptions of full utilization of resources and perfect competition, which Bank economists use is inappropriate for such analysis.

OPENNESS: "CLOSE" VERSUS "STRATEGIC" INTEGRATION WITH THE WORLD ECONOMY

Degrees of openness of the East Asian economies

The virtues of openness, international competition, and close integration with the world economy, are stressed in several Bank publications (see in particular the 1991 Report). Evidence suggests, however, that these virtues were not in fact practiced by either Japan or Korea.

To illustrate, the Japanese economy operated under rigorous import controls, whether formal or informal, throughout the 1950s and 1960s. As late as 1978, the total imports of manufactured goods into Japan was only 2.4% of GDP. The corresponding figures for manufactured imports for the United Kingdom and other leading European countries were at that time of the order of 14 or 15% of GDP. During 1950–70, the Japanese domestic capital markets were highly regulated and completely shut off from the world capital markets. Only the government and its agencies were able to borrow from or lend abroad. Foreign direct investment was strictly controlled. Foreign firms were prohibited either by legal or administrative means from acquiring a majority ownership in Japanese corporations.

With respect to the questions of exchange rates and distortions, the Japanese Government maintained exchange controls and kept a steady nominal exchange rate with respect to the US dollar over almost the whole of the period of that country's most rapid growth (1950–73). Purchasing power parity calculations by Sachs (1987), using Japanese and US price indices, show a 60% real appreciation of the exchange rate during 1950–70.

Thus, despite the strong export orientation of the Japanese economy, it was far from being open or closely integrated with the world economy. The stories of Taiwan and South Korea, subject to certain modifications, also point in the same general direction (see Amsden, 1989 and Wade, 1990).

Protection and export promotion: alternative interpretations

What was the role of this high degree of protection in the East Asian economies? The Bank economists acknowledge the facts of this protective regime but essentially argue that this was generally a negative influence which was kept in bounds only by the government pursuit of export targets and export "contests."

This interpretation has serious shortcomings. First, as noted earlier, generalized protection was one of the mechanisms used by the Japanese and the Korean governments to alleviate the constraint. Second, and equally significantly, there are both analytical and empirical reasons for the view that protection played an important, positive role in promoting technical change, productivity growth and exports in these countries. To appreciate how protection worked at a microeconomic level, consider the specific case of the celebrated Japanese car industry. Magaziner and Hout (1980) point out that

> government intervention in this industry was characterized by three major goals: discouragement of foreign capital in the Japanese industry and protection against car imports, attempts to bring about rationalization of production, and assistance with overseas marketing and distribution expenditure

(p. 55)

The government imposed comprehensive import controls and adopted a variety of measures to discourage foreign investment in the car industry. Quotas and tariffs were used to protect the industry; the former were applied throughout the mid-1960s, and prohibitively high tariffs until the mid-1970s. Moreover,

> the government controlled all foreign licensing agreements. To make technology agreements more attractive to the licensor, it guaranteed the remittance of royalties from Japan. The policy stipulated, however, that continued remittances would be guaranteed only if 90 percent of the licensed parts were produced in Japan within five years.

This is about as powerful a domestic content arrangement as one can get.

More generally, protection provided the Japanese companies with a captive home market leading to high profits which enabled the firms to undertake higher rates of investment, to learn by doing and to improve the quality of their products. These profits in the protected internal market, which were further enhanced by restrictions on domestic competition not only made possible higher rates of investment but also greatly aided exports. Yamamura (1988) shows how these protective policies gave the Japanese firm "a strategic as well as a cost advantage" over foreign competitors. In other words protection, export promotion and performance standards were complementary policies.

Foreign direct investment

An important feature of both the Japanese and the Korean industrial policy has been the discouragement of foreign direct investment (FDI). Available statistics indicate that among developing countries, Korea was second only to India in its low reliance on FDI inflows. Foreign capital stocks totalled just 2.3% of GNP in 1987 in Korea, above the 0.5% estimate for India, but far below the levels of 5.3% for Taiwan, 17% for Hong Kong, a massive 87% for Singapore, 10% for Brazil and 14% for Mexico (UN, 1993). In the view of the World Bank economists, this discouragement was a self-imposed handicap which was compensated for only by the fact that both Japan and Korea remained open to foreign technology through licensing and other means. This raises the question that if the Japanese and the Korean governments were as efficient and flexible in their economic policy as the Bank economists themselves suggest (to account for their long-term overall economic success), how is it they have persisted with this apparently wrong-headed approach for so long?

An alternative interpretation is that the approach was perhaps not so wrong-headed. It was "functional" within the context of the overall industrial policies which the two countries were pursuing. First, it would have been difficult for MITI or for the Korean authorities to use "administrative guidance" to the same degree with the foreign firms as they were able to do with the domestic ones. Second, as UN (1993) emphasizes, there is a link between the national ownership of the large Korean firms (*Chaebols*) and their levels of investment in research and development. Korea has, in relative terms, by far the largest expenditure on research and development (R&D) among developing countries: 1.9% of GNP in 1988, compared with 1.2% in Taiwan (1988), 0.9% for India (1986) and Singapore (1987), 0.5% for Argentina (1988), 0.6% in Mexico (1984) and 0.4% in Brazil (1985). The country's performance in this area outstrips that of many developed countries (e.g., Belgium, 1.7% in 1987), but is of course still below that of industrial superpowers, Japan and Germany, each at 2.8% in 1987.

Third, Freeman (1989) stresses another important advantage of the policy of mainly rejecting foreign investment as a means of technology transfer. This, he argues, automatically places on the enterprise the full responsibility for assimilating imported technology. This is far more likely to lead to "total system improvements than the 'turn-key plant' mode of import or the foreign subsidiary mode."

Price distortions

Bank economists in their econometric analyses in recent publications use a quantitative measure of openness – the degree to which the relative domestic prices in an economy differ from international relative prices. On that measure, it turns out that both Japan and Korea were among the least open economies (Miracle Study, p. 301). Relative prices in these countries were more distorted than in Brazil, India, Mexico, Pakistan and Venezuela, often held up by the Bretton Woods institutions as prime examples of countries which do not "get the prices right."

The optimal degree of openness and strategic integration with the world economy

To sum up, the experience of Japan and Korea comprehensively contradicts the central theses of many World Bank Reports that, the more open the economy, the closer its integration with the global economy, the faster would be its rate of growth. During their periods of rapid growth, instead of a deep or unconditional integration with the world economy, these countries evidently sought what might be called strategic integration, i.e. they integrated up to the point that it was in their interest to do so as to promote national economic growth. If (as stated in the 1991 Report) the purpose of Bank economists was to find out why countries such as Japan have been so successful in economic development during the last 40 years, they have clearly been using the wrong paradigm for examining Japanese economic history. The basic problem is that the underlying assumptions of this paradigm are greatly at variance with the real world of static and dynamic economies of scale, learning by doing, and imperfect competition. In such a world, even neoclassical analysis now accepts that the optimal degree of openness for a country is not "close" integration with the global economy through free trade.[10] In that case, what is the optimal degree of openness for the economy? This extremely important policy question however, is not seriously addressed by the orthodox theory.[11]

Chakravarty and Singh (1988) provide an alternative theoretical perspective for considering this issue. To put it briefly, they argue that "openness" is a multi-dimensional concept; apart from trade, a country can be "open" or not so open with respect to financial and capital markets, in relation to technology, science, culture, education, inward and outward migration. Moreover a country can choose to be open in some directions (say, trade) but not so open in others such as foreign direct investment or financial markets. Their analysis suggests that there is no unique optimum form or degree of openness which holds true for all countries at all times. A number of factors affect the desirable nature of openness: the world configuration, the past history of the economy, its state of development, among others. The timing and sequence of opening are also critical. They point out that there may be serious irreversible losses if the wrong kind of openness is attempted or the timing and sequence are incorrect. The East Asian experience of "strategic" rather than "close" integration with the world economy is fully comprehensible within this kind of theoretical framework.

Such a framework can also explain why for the second tier of South East Asian newly industrialized countries (NICs) – Malaysia, Thailand, Indonesia – the optimal degree of openness is different from that of the East Asian counties. As noted earlier, in the South-East Asian economies, foreign direct investment has played a far more important role than it did in Japan or South Korea. As a consequence of the rapid development of the East Asian countries, the second tier NICs and faced with a different historical situation. This makes it advantageous for them to attract industries which are no longer economic in the first-tier countries because of the growth of their real wages – as suggested by the so called "flying geese" model of Asian economic development.

It should be emphasized that this model and the associated intraregional pattern of trade and investment in Asia is itself in part a product of the industrial policy in Japan, Korea and other countries. Unlike many other advanced countries which try to protect declining industries, the Japanese practice a "positive" industrial policy of encouraging structural change by assisting the replacement of old industries by the new. This, however, involves an orderly rundown of the older industries, including *inter alia* their transfer to less-developed countries in the region (Okimoto, 1989).

Consequently, Felix (1994) suggests that East Asian foreign direct investment in the region has been structurally more conducive to sustaining backward linkage development in the participant economies than has been the case of foreign direct investment in Latin America. He ascribes this to the fact that the East Asian intraregional pattern has evolved along a dynamic comparative advantage path dominated by cost-minimizing trade and investment. The Latin American pattern, he suggests, has been shaped largely by mercantilist market access rather than by cost-minimizing objectives. As a result, it is more vulnerable to disruptive shifts of trading advantages deriving from changes in the marketing and financial strategies of foreign firms.

COMPETITION IN THE DOMESTIC MARKETS

World Bank economists have traditionally stressed the merits of competition in the domestic product, capital and labor markets. The practice of the successful East Asian countries in this respect, however, has also been rather different. As in relation to the question of integration with the world economy, Japan and Korea appear to have taken the view that from the dynamic perspective of promoting investment and technical change, the optimal degree of competition is not perfect or maximum competition. The governments in these countries have therefore managed or guided competition in a purposeful manner: it has both been encouraged, but also notably restricted in a number of ways.

Collusion and competition in Japan

To illustrate, it is useful to reflect on some of the blatant restrictions which were imposed by the Japanese Government in the 1950s and 1960s on domestic product market competition. To meet its myriad goals which continually changed in the light of economic circumstances facing the country, MITI encouraged a variety of cartel arrangements in a wide range of industries – export and import cartels, cartels to combat depression or excessive competition, rationalization cartels, etc. According to Caves and Uekusa (1976), in the 1960s, cartels accounted for 78.1% of the value of shipments in textiles; 64.8% in clothing; 50% in nonferrous metals; 47% in printing and publishing; 41.2% in stone, clay and glass; 34.5% in steel products, and 37.2% in food products. Although these cartels functioned for only limited periods of time and there was wide variation in their effectiveness, Caves and Uekusa observed that "their mere presence in such broad stretches of the manufacturing sector attests to their importance" (1976, p. 147).

These restraints on competition, however, are only a part of the story. An equally significant part is MITI's strong encouragement of vigorous domestic oligopolistic rivalry and international competitiveness. In general, whether competition was promoted or restricted depended on the industry and its life-cycle: in young industries, during the developmental phase, the government discouraged competition; when these industries became technologically mature, competition was allowed to flourish. Later, when industries were in competitive decline, the government again discouraged competition and, as noted earlier, attempted to bring about an orderly rationalization of the industry (Okimoto, 1989).

Yamamura (1988) provides a useful dynamic model to show how the Japanese competition policy was an integral part of the country's industrial policy. During the rapid growth phase of Japanese development in the 1950s and 1960s, in the key industries which were receiving its attention, MITI essentially organized an "investment race" among large oligopolistic firms in which exports and international market share were significant performance goals. In the real world, markets are always incomplete, and such a race without a coordinator could lead to ruinous competition, price wars and excess capacity, inhibiting the inducement to invest. In the Japanese economic miracle, MITI provided this crucial coordinating role and orchestrated the dynamic combination of collusion and competition which characterizes Japanese industrial policy. Yamamura notes that MITI "guided" the firms to invest in such a way that each large firm in a market expanded its productive capacity roughly in proportion to its current market share – no firm was allowed to make an investment so large that it would destabilize the market. The policy was effective in encouraging competition for the market share (thus preserving the essential competitiveness of the industrial markets) while reducing the risk of losses due to excessive investment. Thus, it promoted the aggressive expansion of capacity necessary to increase productive efficiency.

Large firms and domestic competition in Korea

Turning to Korea, that country also did not follow a policy of maximum domestic competition or unfettered market-determined entry or exit of firms. The Korean government, if anything, went one step further than the Japanese in actively helping create large conglomerates, promoting mergers, and directing entry and exit of firms according to the requirements of technological scale economies and world demand conditions. The result is that Korea's manufacturing industry displays one of the highest level of market concentration anywhere. The top 50 *chaebols* accounted for 15% of the country's GDP in 1990. Among the largest 500 industrial companies in the world in 1990, there were 11 Korean firms, the same number as Switzerland, UN (1993) observes in relation to the Korean industrial structure:

> Such a structure is the deliberate creation of the Government, which utilised a highly interventionist strategy to push industry into large-scale, complex technologically demanding activities while simultaneously restricting FDI inflows tightly to promote national ownership. It was deemed necessary to create enterprises of large size and diversity to undertake the risk inherent in launching in high-technology, high-skill activities that would remain competitive in world markets.

Nevertheless, there is ample evidence to suggest that the big business groups still exhibited highly rivalrous behaviors (Kim, 1992). This was because under rapid growth conditions, as well as the rules of the game which the state had established, there was neither the incentive nor the ability for big business to collude. The Korean government went out of its way to insure that big business did not collude, by allocating subsidies only in exchange for strict performance standards (Amsden, 1989). After 1975 intergroup competition in Korea heated up as each *chaebol*, or diversified business group, tried to qualify for generous subsidies to establish a general trading company by meeting government performance standards regarding minimum export volume and the number of export products (Cho, 1987).

An assessment

There has been a major advance in the World Bank's thinking about the role of free markets and competition in economic development. Implicitly rejecting the view embodied in many previous documents and specifically in the 1991 Report that, "Competitive markets are the best way yet found for efficiently organising the production and distribution of goods and services," the Bank's recent seminal publication (the Miracle Study) accepts the need for cooperation as well as competition to achieve fast economic growth. Specifically in relation to Japan, South Korea and Taiwan, Bank economists acknowledge the positive role of cooperation (or restrictions on competition) in order to correct what they call "the coordination failures," which particularly characterize industrializing country product and capital markets. In this analysis, a much larger role of the government as a referee to mediate these cooperative arrangements is explicitly recognized. Thus intellectually Bank economists accept the heterodox argument that the governments in these East Asian countries guided the market and controlled the competitive process, and that this guidance was conducive to their fast growth. Nevertheless, after this giant conceptual step forward for the Bank economists, in their policy recommendations to other developing countries, they retreat to their earlier perspective of free and competitive markets. The main argument made for this reversal is that other countries do not have the institutional capacity to successfully implement the required combination of competition and cooperation.

INDUSTRIAL POLICY, NATIONAL TECHNOLOGICAL SYSTEM AND INTERNATIONAL COMPETITIVENESS

In addition to protection, domestic competition policy and other measures already discussed above, another important component of industrial policy in the exemplar East Asian countries has been a national strategy for technological development. The World Bank reports invariably stress the importance of primary and secondary education for achieving economic growth. They do not pay sufficient attention, however, to tertiary education and to the technological infrastructure both human and physical which late industrializers require to catch-up with the advanced countries. Yet, it is precisely in these areas that the East Asian countries have excelled, which in turn has played a major role in enhancing their international competitiveness and their outstanding export success (Singh, 1989, 1994b).

A national system of technological advancement was first advocated by Friedrich List in the first half of the 19th century to enable Germany to catch-up with Great Britain. Although "catch-up" was much easier then than it is for today's developing countries, many of List's insights remain valid.[12] Following the end of WWII, the Japanese adopted a national technological system which spans the government, the firms, the universities, and indeed, the society as a whole. Freeman (1989) identifies the following to be the principal elements of this national technoeconomic strategy:

1　The ability to design and redesign entire production processes, whether in shipbuilding, machine tools or any other industry.
2　The capacity at national, government level to pursue an integration strategy which brings together the best available resources from universities, government, research institutions, private or public industry to solve the most important design and development problems.
3　The development of an educational and training system which goes beyond the German level in two respects. First, in the absolute numbers of young people acquiring higher levels of education, especially in science and engineering. Second, in the scale and quality of industrial training which is carried out at enterprise level.
4　The policy of eschewing, as noted earlier, foreign investment as a principal means of technology transfer.
5　The emergence of a far more flexible and decentralized management system, permitting

both greater horizontal integration of design, development and production and more rapid response to change.

6 Close cooperation between the central government and Keiretsu (large conglomerate groupings in Japanese industries) in identifying future technological trajectories, and taking joint initiatives, to adopt these to enhance the country's prospective competitiveness.

It is notable that many Asian countries including Korea, Taiwan and China, have been consciously following the Japanese model and building their own national technological systems in the light of their resources and requirements. It is also striking that several of these countries now have a higher annual output of graduate engineers per 100, 000 of population than Japan. These countries are thus trying to outdo Japan in this respect, just as Japan outstripped the United States. Freeman (1989) calls attention to the fact that the third country in the world to introduce and export 256K memory chips after Japan and the United States was not an advanced industrial country but South Korea. It took that country less than 30 years, starting from a position of barely any industry at all, to become a significant player in the world electronics industry.

None of the above is to underestimate the formidable problems which the late industrializers face just to keep in step with the fast pace of technological change in the world economy, let alone to catch up. Lall (1994) and others have pointed to the formidable technological and other barriers to entry[13] in the world markets which less developed country firms face. To meet these technological challenges, developing countries require a continuing build-up of national technological capability through an integrated system in the ways outlined above. It is an incremental and long-term process requiring concerted national effort in which the government necessarily plays a leading direct as well as a crucial coordinating role. Without such effort, countries such as Korea or Taiwan would not have been able to hold their share of world manufacturing exports, let alone greatly increase them as they have so successfully done over the last two decades or more.

The World Bank emphasis on early education would not appear to be an adequate means of enhancing the international industrial competitiveness of semi-industrial countries. To compete in the world industrial economy, it is also essential to have higher educational institutions, scientists, technologists and engineers. It is useful in this context to go back to the earlier discussion of changing factor proportions and its implications for comparative advantage and structural changes in the economy. The changing factor proportions (in the sense of human capital and skill formation) over time in the East Asian countries, was clearly not simply an outcome of "natural market forces" as per capita income rose. Rather these developments were very much guided by the visible hand of the government in terms of its national priorities.

CONCLUSION

As detailed in the previous pages, there has been considerable progress in the debate between heterodox and World Bank economists concerning the outstandingly successful development experience of East Asian economies such as Japan or Korea. There is now general agreement that governments in these countries intervened heavily in all spheres of the economy in order to achieve rapid economic growth and fast industrialization. It is also common ground that during the course of their development these countries did not have free and flexible internal or external product and capital markets. Although these countries were export oriented, they eschewed close integration with the international economy in terms of imports, foreign direct investment or capital flows. The governments of these countries also controlled and guided the competitive process in the domestic product and capital markets through a highly effective combination of interfirm cooperation and oligopolistic competition.

There are, of course, still important areas of disagreement – particularly in relation to the industrial policy ineffectiveness doctrine of the World Bank economists. Nevertheless, on the whole, there is now much less disagreement on the analytical and empirical issues than on policy. A main reason for the policy differences is the belief of Bank economists that other countries do not have the institutional capacity to implement the optimum degree of competition and openness which the exemplar East Asian countries achieved. How valid is this view?

The important point to note here is that the Japanese model was itself imitated by the Koreans and by the Taiwanese. When Korea decided to embark on the Japanese model in the 1960s, as World Bank economists themselves admit, that country did not have the necessary institutional capacity. The Korean bureaucracy at the time was incompetent and corrupt, as indeed was the case with the Kuomintang bureaucracy when it arrived in Taiwan from mainland China. Yet these countries were able to create the right kind of bureaucracy and the other necessary institutions required for implementing the Japanese model. If these institutions can be created by Korea and Taiwan, and later on by Malaysia or Indonesia, it may also be possible to establish them in many other countries. In the end therefore, this analysis raises the following question: if in view of the ubiquitous coordination failures in the less-developed economies, state-directed industrialization on the Japanese or Korean pattern is the first best policy for achieving rapid economic growth, should the World Bank not concern itself more with the institutional imitation and innovation of the kind outlined above, than with prescribing market-friendliness or close integration with the world economy (which these countries did not practice)?

NOTES

* This chapter has been adapted from, Singh, A. (1994) "Openness and the Market Friendly Approach to Development: Learning the Right Lessons from Development Experience," in *World Development*, Vol. 22, No. 12, pp. 1811–1823 (Elsevier Science Ltd).

1 The World Bank's annual *World Development Reports* are useful sources for the analysis of these issues. For reasons given in [the second section], however, the two most important documents in this context are World Bank (1991, 1993). The latter are seminal works which provide a comprehensive account of Bank economists' thinking on these and other development problems and their conclusions on public policy. These are therefore the specific documents this paper draws upon in all references made to the Bank's analyses.

2 See the commentaries in this journal by Amsden (1994) or World Bank (1993).

3 There is an enormous literature on the subject. For a lucid analysis of the relevant issues under discussion here, see Nelson (1981).

4 The classic references here are Verdoorn (1949) and Kaldor (1966). For a review, see McCombie (1987). The TFP growth table in the 1991 Report shows that in general, the larger the decline in the growth of output (in 1973–87 compared with the earlier period), the greater the reduction in TFP growth, much as would be predicted by Verdoorn's Law. Moreover, the South Asia region is the only one to record an increase in TFP growth in the second period; it is also the only one with a substantial trend increase in GDP growth in that period.

5 During 1950–73, when the OECD economy grew at an unprecedented rate of almost 5% per annum – twice its historic trend rate of growth – has rightly been termed the Golden Age of capitalism. Glyn *et al.* (1990) provide a detailed analysis of why the Golden Age rose in the first place and why it fell following the 1973 oil shock. See also Maddison (1982); Bruno and Sachs (1985); Kindleberger (1992). To avoid misunderstanding, it must be emphasized that we are

not considering here the question of short-term demand management, but rather that of the forces which affect the long-term rate of growth of demand.

6 See for example Lucas (1973).

7 See further Johnson, Tyson and Zysman (1989). There have been important changes in the 1970s and the 1980s in the nature and conduct of MITI's industrial policies, compared with the 1950s and the 1960s. In general, MITI does not now have the same kind of coercive policy instruments it did in the high-growth period. It therefore has to use more indirect instruments as well as moral persuasion to a far larger degree.

8 Thus the Miracle Study: "We define industrial policies, as distinct from trade policies, as government efforts to alter industrial structure to promote productivity-based growth" (World Bank, 1993, p. 304).

9 The question of the time horizon over which the costs and benefits of industrial policy interventions are assessed is of crucial importance. Amsden and Singh (1994) point out that for 30 years there were few foreign cars to be seen on Korean roads and few Korean cars to be seen on foreign roads. In other words, the Korean government provided protection to the car industry for long periods of time because of the difficulties involved in the learning and the assimilation of foreign technology in developing countries.

10 See for example Krugman (1987) and Rodrik (1992).

11 On this point, see the interesting review by Lucas (1990) or Helpman and Krugman (1989).

12 See further Freeman (1989).

13 The Miracle Study itself confirms these points. See Box 3.3 on Samsung industries on p. 130.

REFERENCES

Amsden, A. (Ed.), "The World Bank's East Asian Miracle: Economic Growth and Public Policy," Special Section, *World Development*, Vol. 22, No. 4 (1994).

Amsden, A., *Asia's Next Giant* (New York, Oxford University Press, 1989).

Amsden, A. H., and Singh, A., "The optimal degree of competition and dynamic efficiency in Japan and Korea." *European Economic Review*, Vol. 38, No. 3/4 (April, 1994), pp. 941–951.

Aoki, M., "Toward an economic model of the Japanese firm," *Journal of Economic Literature*, Vol. 28, No. 1 (1990), pp. 1–27.

Boltho, A., "Was Japan's industrial policy successful?" *Cambridge Journal of Economics*, Vol. 9, No. 2 (June, 1985a), pp. 187–201.

Boltho, A., "Japan's industrial policy," in Z. A. Silberston, and A. M. Schaefer (Eds.), *Industrial Policy and International Trade* (Philadelphia, PA: University of Pennsylvania Press, 1985b).

Bruno, M., and J. Sachs, *Economics of Worldwide Stagflation* (Cambridge, MA: Harvard University Press, 1985).

Caves, R., and M. Uekusa, *Industrial Organisation in Japan*, (Washington, DC: The Brookings Institution, 1976).

CEPG (Cambridge Economic Policy Group), *Economic Policy Review*, No. 5 (1979).

Chakravarty, S., and A. Singh, *The Desirable Forms of Economic Openness in the South*, Mimeo (Helsinki, WIDER, 1988).

Chang, H. J., "Explaining 'flexible rigidities' in East Asia," in T. Killick (Ed.), *The Flexible Economy* (London: Routledge, forthcoming).

Cho, Dong-Sung, *The General Trading Company: Concept and Strategy* (Lexington, MA: Lexington Books, 1987).

Dore, R., *Flexible Rigidities: Industrial Policy and Structural Adjustment in the Japanese Economy 1970–80* (London: The Athlone Press, 1986).

Dore, R., "Latecomers' Problems," *The European Journal of Development Research*, Vol. 1, No. 1 (1989).

Felix, D., "Industrial development in East Asia: What are the lessons for Latin America?," *UNCTAD Discussion Paper*, No. 84, (May, 1994).

Freeman, C., "New technology and catching up," *The European Journal of Development Research*, Vol. 1, No. 1 (1989), pp. 85–99.

Freeman, C., *Technology Policy and Economic Performance: Lessons from Japan* (London: Frances Pinter, 1987).

Glyn, A., A. Hughes, A. Lipietz, and A. Singh, "The rise and fall of the Golden Age," in S. Marglin and J. Schor (Eds.), *The Golden Age of Capitalism* (Oxford: Clarendon Press, 1990), pp. 39–125.

Helpman, E., and P. Krugman, *Trade Policy and Market Structure* (Cambridge, MA: The MIT Press, 1989).

Johnson, C., L. Tyson, and J. Zysman, *Politics and Productivity* (New York: Harper Business, 1989).

Kaldor, N., *Causes of the Slow Rate of Economic Growth in the United Kingdom*, Inaugural Lecture (Cambridge: Cambridge University Press, 1966).

Kim, Mahn-Je, *Korea's Successful Economic Development and the World Bank*, Mimeo (1992).

Kindleberger, C., "Why did the Golden Age last so long?," in F. Cairncross, and A. Cairncross (Eds.), *The Legacy of the Golden Age* (London and New York: Routledge, 1992), pp. 15–44.

Krugman, P., "Is free trade passé?," *Journal of Economic Perspectives*, Vol. 1, No. 2 (1987), pp. 131–144.

Lall, S., "Review of World Bank, 1993," *World Development*, Vol. 22, No. 4 (1994).

Lucas, R. E. Jr., "Review of trade policy and market structure by E. Helpman and P. Krugman," *Journal of Political Economy*, Vol. 98, No. 3 (1990).

Lucas, R. E., Jr., "Some international evidence on output-inflation trade-offs," *American Economic Review* (June 1973).

Maddison, A., *The Phases of Capitalist Development* (Oxford: Oxford University Press, 1982).

Magaziner, I., and T. Hout, *Japanese Industrial Policy* (London: Policy Studies Institute, 1980).

McCombie, J. S. L., "Verdoorn's Law," in J. Eatwell, M. Millgate and P. Newman (Eds.), *The New Palgrave Dictionary of Economic Thought*, (London: Macmillan, 1987), pp. 804–806.

Nelson, R., "Research on productivity growth and productivity differences: Dead ends and new departures," *Journal of Economic Literature*, Vol. 19, No. 3 (1981).

OECD, *The Industrial Policy of Japan* (Paris: OECD, 1972).

Okimoto, D. I., *Between the MITI and the Market* (Stanford, CA: Stanford University Press, 1989).

Rodrik, D., "The limits of trade policy reform in developing countries," *Journal of Economic Perspectives*, Vol. 6, No. 1 (1992).

Sachs, J., "Trade and exchange rate policies in growth-oriented adjustment programs," in V. Corbo, M. Khan and K. Goldstein (Eds.), *Growth-Oriented Structural Adjustment* (Washington DC: IMF & World Bank, 1987).

Shinohara, M., *Industrial Growth, Trade and Dynamic Patterns in the Japanese Economy* (Tokyo: University of Tokyo Press, 1982).

Singh, A., "Du plan au marché: la réforme maîtrisée en Chine," *Revue Tiers-Monde*, Vol. 35, No. 139, 1994.

Singh, A., "State Intervention and 'market-friendly' approach to development: A critical analysis of the World Bank theses" in A. Dutt, K. Kim and A. Singh (Eds.), *The States, Markets and Development* (London: Edward Elgar, 1994a).

Singh, A., "Global economic changes, skills and international competitiveness," *International Labor Review*, Vol. 133, No. 2 (1994b), pp. 167–183.

Singh, A., "The 'Market-Friendly Approach to Development' vs. 'Industrial Policy'," University of Duisburg, *INEF-Report*, Heft 4 (1993).

Singh, A., "Third World competition and de-industrialization in advanced countries," *Cambridge Journal of Economics*, Vol. 13, No. 1 (1989), pp. 103–120.

Singh, A., "North Sea oil and the reconstruction of UK industry" in F. Blackaby (Ed.), *De-Industrialisation* (London: Heinemann Educational Books, 1979), pp. 202–224.

Tsuru, S., *Japan's Capitalism: Creative Defeat and Beyond* (Cambridge: Cambridge University Press, 1993).

UN, *Transnational Corporations from Developing Countries* (New York: United Nations, 1993).

Verdoorn, P., "Fattori che regolano lo sviluppo della produttivitá del lavaro," *L'Industria* (1949).

Wade, R., *Governing the Market* (Princeton, NJ: Princeton University Press, 1990).

World Bank, *The Challenge of Development: World Development Report* (New York: Oxford University Press, 1991).

World Bank, *The East Asian Miracle* (New York: Oxford University Press, 1993).

Yamamura, K., "Caveat emptor: The industrial policy of Japan," in P. Krugman (Ed.), *Strategic Trade Policy and the New International Economics* (Cambridge, MA: The MIT Press, 1988).

INDEX

Note: page numbers in **bold** type denote **Figures**. Page numbers in *italic* type denote *Tables*